MW00388535

BUILDING A REPUBLICAN NATION IN VIETNAM, 1920–1963

*A Study of the Weatherhead East Asian Institute
and the US-Vietnam Research Center*

BUILDING A REPUBLICAN NATION IN VIETNAM, 1920–1963

EDITED BY NU-ANH TRAN
AND TUONG VU

University of Hawai'i Press

HONOLULU

First printing, 2023

Library of Congress Cataloging-in-Publication Data

Names: Tran, Nu-Anh, editor. | Vu, Tuong, editor.
Title: Building a republican nation in Vietnam, 1920–1963 / edited by
    Nu-Anh Tran and Tuong Vu.
Other titles: Studies of the Weatherhead East Asian Institute, Columbia
    University.
Description: Honolulu : University of Hawai'i Press, [2022] | Series:
    Studies of the Weatherhead East Asian Institute, Columbia University |
    Papers from a conference on Republican Vietnam, held at the University
    of Oregon, October 14–15, 2019. | Includes bibliographical references
    and index.
Identifiers: LCCN 2022038388 | ISBN 9780824892111 (hardback) | ISBN
    9780824893835 (pdf) | ISBN 9780824893842 (epub) | ISBN 9780824893859
    (kindle edition)
Subjects: LCSH: Republicanism—Vietnam (Republic)—Congresses. | Vietnam
    (Republic)—History—20th century—Congresses. | Vietnam
    (Republic)—Politics and government—20th century—Congresses. | LCGFT:
    Conference papers and proceedings.
Classification: LCC DS556.8 .B86 2022 | DDC 959.7/03—dc23/eng/20220817
LC record available at https://lccn.loc.gov/2022038388

Cover art: "The great rally at Lam Sơn Square, Saigon, August 31, 1963." Thanh Mỹ,
cover photo, *Sáng dội miền Nam* 51 (September 1963). Courtesy of Tuong Vu.

Cover design: Aaron Lee

University of Hawai'i Press books are printed on acid-free paper and meet the guidelines
for permanence and durability of the Council on Library Resources.

Contents

CHAPTER TEN

When State Propaganda Becomes Social Knowledge
Y Thien Nguyen
202

Acknowledgments

This volume is a product of a conference on Republican Vietnam held at the University of Oregon on October 14–15, 2019. Participants in the conference came from all over the United States as well as Germany, Australia, the United Kingdom, and Vietnam. We are deeply indebted to the enthusiasm of all participants, who helped make that event a truly stimulating and memorable gathering.

At the University of Oregon, the leadership and staff of the Global Studies Institute, in particular Holly Lakey and Cindy Nelson together with Dennis Galvan and Lori O'Hollaren, deserve great thanks for providing critical institutional, financial, and logistical support. We also acknowledge the Department of Political Science, the Program of Asian Studies, and the University of Oregon Libraries for their additional assistance.

Our most generous and inspiring supporters include Mr. and Mrs. Nguyễn Đức Cường, Mr. Hoàng Đức Nhã, the late Phạm Kim Ngọc, Dr. Trần Quang Minh, Mr. and Mrs. Nguyễn Lương Quang, Professor Nguyễn Mạnh Hùng, and Mr. and Mrs. Nguyễn Tường Thiết. We appreciate their advice, encouragement, and generosity tremendously and wish to dedicate this volume to them and the Vietnamese of their generation.

We are also grateful to other community leaders, writers, artists, and activists who participated in or supported the event in numerous ways, including Nancy Bui, Linda Ho Peche, Bùi Văn Phú, Nguyễn Đình Thắng, Ngô Văn, Hà Thúc Tiến, Bùi Đình Đại, Võ Thành Nhân, and Kính Hoà. We thank journalists and reporters from *Người Việt,* Voice of America, the BBC Vietnamese language program, and the Saigon Broadcasting Television Network for making our conference known to those not able to attend.

Keith Taylor, Olga Dror, Christopher Goscha, Peter Zinoman, Mark Sidel, Lien-Hang Nguyen, Edward Miller, and Sean Fear offered valuable advice during and after the conference. At the US-Vietnam Research Center, Alex-Thai Vo, Nguyễn Lương Hải Khôi, and Nguyễn Thị Thủy deserve special thanks for putting tremendous energy into planning the event, hosting guests, and interviewing participating scholars.

We also wish to thank many presenters at our conference whose works, we hope, have appeared or are to appear soon in other publications. These include Christoph Giebel, Mark Sidel, Edward Miller, Nathalie Huynh Chau Nguyen, Olga Dror, Phạm Thị Hồng Hà, Adrienne Minh-Chau Le, Wynn Gadkar-Wilcox, Alvin Bui, Jason Gibbs, Nguyễn Đức Cường, Hoàng Đức Nhã, Trinh Luu, Sean Fear, Tuan Hoang, Vinh Pham, David Prentice, George Veith, Phạm Vũ Lan Anh, Trương Thùy Dung, Nguyễn Thị Từ Huy, and Hao Jun Tam.

Great thanks must go to Trinh Luu whose dedication and experience helped greatly in the preparation for the volume. Nu-Anh Tran wishes to acknowledge the benefits of a fellowship from the University of Connecticut Humanities Institute while she began this project and drafted her portion of the introduction. We also thank Peter Lavelle for his bibliographic assistance.

At Columbia University's Weatherhead East Asian Institute, Lien-Hang Nguyen has offered generous advice and support that were instrumental for the publication of the manuscript. Diana Witt created a superb index and graciously agreed to work with us on short notice. Finally, we truly appreciate Masako Ikeda, our editor at the University of Hawai'i Press, for her great enthusiasm in the project and her patient and helpful guidance as we moved along.

Abbreviations

ANOM	Archives Nationale d'Outre-Mer
ARV	Association for the Restoration of Vietnam (Việt Nam Phục Quốc Hội)
ARVN	Army of the Republic of Vietnam
BCCGT	Ministry of Public Works and Transportation Collection (Phông Bộ Công Chánh và Giao Thông)
BYT	Ministry of Health Collection (Phông Bộ Y Tế)
CĐCN	*Con đường chính nghĩa*
CDF	Central Decimal Files
CDTC	Communist Denunciation Campaign (Chiến Dịch Tố Cộng)
CIP	Commodity Import Program
DABI	Directions des Archives et des Bibliothèques
DRV	Democratic Republic of Vietnam
FRUS	*Foreign Relations of the United States*
GCMR	General Commission for Migrants and Refugees (Phủ Tổng Ủy Di Cư và Tỵ Nạn)
HCI	Haut Commissariat de France pour l'Indochine
HĐQNCM	Revolutionary Military Council Collection (Phông Hội Đồng Quân Nhân Cách Mạng)
NARA	National Archives and Records Administration
NLF	National Liberation Front
NRF	National Resistance Front (Mặt Trận Quốc Gia Kháng Chiến)
NRM	National Revolutionary Movement (Phong Trào Cách Mạng Quốc Gia)

NUFLV	National United Front for the Liberation of Vietnam (Mặt Trận Quốc Gia Thống Nhất Giải Phóng Việt Nam)
NVKQG	Service of the National Archive Collection (Phông Nha Văn Khố Quốc Gia, sometimes called the Phông Nha Văn Khố và Thư Viện Quốc Gia)
PB	Archives Privée Papiers Boudet
PSP	Political Study Program (Chương Trình Học Tập Chính Trị)
PThTVNCH	Office of the Prime Minister Collection (Phông Phủ Thủ Tướng Việt Nam Cộng Hòa)
PTTĐICH	Office of the President Collection, First Republic (Phông Phủ Tổng Thống Đệ Nhất Cộng Hòa)
PTTĐIICH	Office of the President Collection, Second Republic (Phông Phủ Tổng Thống Đệ Nhị Cộng Hòa)
PTUDCTN	General Commission for Migrants and Refugees Collection (Phông Phủ Tổng Ủy Di Cư và Tỵ Nạn)
RG	Record Group
ROK	Republic of Korea
RVN	Republic of Vietnam
SDP	Social Democratic Party (Việt Nam Dân Chủ Xã Hội Đảng)
SVN	State of Vietnam
TĐBCPNP	Government Delegate of Southern Vietnam Collection (Phông Tòa Đại Biểu Chính Phủ Nam Phần)
TNQTVN	General Department of Customs of Vietnam Collection (Phông Tổng Nha Quan Thuế Việt Nam)
TQT	General Department of Customs Collection (Phông Tổng Quan Thuế)
TTLTQG1	National Archives Center 1 (Trung Tâm Lưu Trữ Quốc Gia 1)
TTLTQG2	National Archives Center 2 (Trung Tâm Lưu Trữ Quốc Gia 2)
TVQGNV	National Library of Southern Vietnam Collection (Phông Thư Viện Quốc Gia Nam Việt)
UNESCO	United Nations Education, Scientific, and Cultural Organization
US	United States
USAMGIK	United States Army Military Government in Korea
USD	United States dollars
VNSL	A Brief Outline of Vietnamese History (Việt Nam sử lược)
VVA	Vietnam Virtual Archive, Texas Tech University

BUILDING A REPUBLICAN NATION
IN VIETNAM, 1920–1963

Rethinking Vietnamese Republicanism

Nu-Anh Tran and Tuong Vu

Nearly a century ago, in July 1922, some of the most knowledgeable and influential Vietnamese activists and intellectuals gathered at a dinner in the Montpartnasse Hotel in Paris.[1] They included Phạm Quỳnh, Nguyễn Văn Vĩnh, Cao Văn Sến, Phan Châu Trinh, and Nguyễn Ái Quốc. The first two traveled from French Indochina; the rest were living in France at the time. The event that brought them together was the Colonial Exhibition organized by the French government in Marseilles and held from April to November 1922. It was not the first time some of them had met, nor were the guests at the dinner representative of all political and social movements among Vietnamese under French rule. Nevertheless, it was perhaps the only occasion at which all five were present and were specifically asked to present their political positions. The idea for the dinner came from Lê Thanh Cảnh and Trần Đức, both of whom belonged to the Indochinese delegation at the Exhibition.

According to Cảnh, who had been Nguyễn Ái Quốc's classmate at the Quốc Học School in Huế in 1907–1908, who was a journalist at the time, and who recounted the event about fifty years later, a debate took place among the five and included several tense moments. Whereas the prominent editor and scholar Phạm Quỳnh looked to England and Japan and supported a constitutional monarchy for a future independent Vietnam, the journalist and translator Nguyễn Văn Vĩnh advocated the abolition of the Annamese monarchy altogether to turn Annam and Tonkin (central and northern Vietnam today) from protectorates into French colonies. Vĩnh believed that direct rule under France as experienced in Cochinchina (southern Vietnam today) would bring much more rapid social and cultural changes that could eventually lead to a strong and modern Vietnamese nation.

Also an admirer of French civilization, the engineer Cao Văn Sến supported the Constitutionalist Party, led by a group of Vietnamese elites in Cochinchina, but was critical of French colonial policy. Like Vĩnh and in opposition to Quỳnh, the revolutionary Phan Châu Trinh was bitterly antimonarchical, yet the tension was mainly between him and Nguyễn Ái Quốc, the young revolutionary upstart who had once been his protégé but by that time had become a communist. Quốc advocated a violent strategy to overthrow French rule in Indochina rather than one premised on broad reforms to modernize Vietnamese society and culture first. At one point, Quốc reportedly became agitated and raised his voice at Trinh, accusing the latter of sounding just like the French governor of Indochina.

In hindsight, the meeting underscored the diverse and often opposing visions and ideas among Vietnamese activists and intellectuals at the time. Beyond the different attitudes toward the monarchy, the main contention was between republican and communist activists. The former included Trinh, Sến, and perhaps Vĩnh who believed in republican ideas of democracy and constitutionalism. The latter, represented solely by Quốc, placed their faith in Marxist-Leninist ideology and strategy and dismissed republican ideas as a mere fig leaf for class domination under capitalism. What vision would best serve their country was an open question, but the debate among these leading patriots would in time break out into a savage civil war that shaped the fate of Vietnam for the rest of the twentieth century. Phạm Quỳnh would be executed by communist forces in Huế after Nguyễn Ái Quốc (now Hồ Chí Minh)'s Indochinese Communist Party seized power in August 1945 at the end of World War II. Although for a long time most historians of modern Vietnam have been preoccupied with Hồ Chí Minh and the communist movement, this book hopes to advance a new trend by refocusing scholarly attention on Vietnamese republicanism as a major political tendency and tradition throughout modern Vietnamese history. Based on fresh archival sources, we seek to offer a more historically grounded interpretation of how modern Vietnam emerged and became what it is today. In the process, we revisit many long-standing debates on the causes of the Vietnam War and on the origins of the Republic of Vietnam (RVN) founded by Ngô Đình Diệm.

As a political ideology, republicanism provides a philosophical basis for a representative government that governs based on the consent of the governed. A republic stands in direct opposition to a monarchy, under which government is the personal property of rulers. Emerging in Western Europe in the eighteenth century, republicanism also challenged church authority in state affairs. Republican thinkers have also, to varying degrees, emphasized the political rights of individuals, the rule of law, and the separation of powers among government branches.

Republican ideas spread to French Indochina at the turn of the century and infused Vietnamese thinking with new concepts about the modern nation-state and the ideal forms of politics. By the 1920s, republican ideas had been adopted by many Vietnamese elites, including both revolutionaries such as Phan Châu Trinh and reformers such as Bùi Quang Chiêu. These ideas influenced the young men and women who advocated for Vietnam's self-rule, including those who chose communism, which superimposed the idea of class struggle on top of republican thinking.

Although French authorities suppressed Vietnamese demands for independence from both republicans and communists, republican activists were partly tolerated by the colonial government and were far more popular than communists in the competition between the two groups for leadership of the nationalist movement. When the communists took power in 1945, they had to appropriate many republican ideas to win the support of the colonial intelligentsia. By the time Ngô Đình Diệm established the Republic of Vietnam in 1955, major political groups and individuals who helped create that state were united in their rejection of communism. Many were ardent adherents to republican ideas and struggled to see them realized in an extremely difficult postcolonial context.

As the Cold War between the two ideological camps emerged in the mid-1950s, Vietnam became embroiled in a civil war in which republicans in South Vietnam sought support from the United States and communists in the North looked for alliance with the Soviet Union and China. By the 1960s, many activist-scholars in the antiwar movement in the United States believed that North Vietnam's communist government was the true heir to Vietnam's patriotic traditions and the legitimate government of all Vietnamese. The South Vietnamese republican government to them was a mere creation of the United States to stop the spread of communism into Southeast Asia. Over time, this partisan argument became the orthodox interpretation of modern Vietnamese history, denying the local roots of republican politics in Vietnam that had existed before the import of communism into Indochina. Influenced by propaganda from the northern communist state, the orthodox view teleologically set Vietnam on the communist path as a natural and inevitable development.

In the last decade, new scholarship has begun to reassess the significance of republicanism in Vietnamese history. The growing interest in Republican Vietnam owes much to a younger generation of scholars who view communism merely as one of many political tendencies that found traction in modern Vietnam and does not have any more inherent legitimacy than the rest. Republicans, monarchists, and anticommunists are treated as agents of history who had a hand in shaping twentieth-century Vietnam, even if they were eventually defeated by the communists.

This book presents cutting-edge research on the ideological and institutional foundations of the RVN during its First Republic (1955–1963), traceable to the colonial period. The First Republic was the first opportunity for Vietnamese republicans to realize their ideals, and we will learn many aspects of their effort. Building on the new scholarship, we argue that the Vietnam War began as a civil war and that the Republic of Vietnam grew out of authentic Vietnamese aspirations. This argument focuses on history but has implications for our understanding of contemporary politics in Vietnam and in the Vietnamese diaspora. Despite the defeat of the RVN in 1975, those aspirations have lived on in the diaspora and are reappearing in Vietnam today, after three decades of market reform, as more and more citizens demand democratic reforms and respect for the rule of law.

In this introduction, we first examine the historiography of the First Republic to provide a sense of how historians have grappled with the challenges of understanding modern Vietnamese history, and where we are at this point in terms of our knowledge about the First Republic. We then explore French colonial and Vietnamese republicanism in Indochina and under the First Republic. Both displayed internal tensions between ideals and practices. Third, we offer a comparison of the RVN and the Republic of Korea. Both republics faced similar constraints and underwent comparable developments, yet republican institutions were much more robust in South Korea than in South Vietnam. The comparison finds the cause in the RVN's relative independence from the United States.

HISTORIOGRAPHY OF THE FIRST REPUBLIC

A fundamental question has driven much of the historiography on the First Republic: what is the best framework for studying Ngô Đình Diệm's tenure? Whereas some described the RVN as belonging to global patterns of decolonization, others located the Saigon-based state in specific strands of Vietnamese or American history. But much of this research reflected inadequate training or partisan commitments. The Anglophone scholarship on Diệm's rule can be divided into four overlapping waves: the first by mostly nonspecialists in the late 1950s and 1960s, a second by Vietnam scholars from the mid-1960s to the 2000s, the third by American diplomatic historians after the mid-1980s, and the current wave beginning in the early twenty-first century by scholars from multiple fields.

The earliest Westerners to write about the RVN were journalists, diplomats, aid workers, and researchers who visited Vietnam during Diệm's rule. They came to witness or contribute to the American project of building up "Free Vietnam" but had no Vietnamese-language skills. These nonspecialists interpreted the regime through the framework of modernization theory, which posited that all societies followed the same unilinear process of development from tradition to modernity. Theorists considered Latin America, Asia, and Africa to be traditional and associated modernity with democratization, industrialization, secularization, and other characteristics attributed to the mid-century United

States.[2] Adopting this criterion, the early writers argued that the First Republic was a traditional state that had yet to make the leap into modernity.

Indeed, the allegedly traditional character of Diệm's rule was a virtual consensus. Many writers portrayed the leader as a mandarin, that is, a Confucian scholar-official who served in Vietnam's precolonial administration. Admirers praised him as the embodiment of a noble though undemocratic tradition of politics, and detractors complained that his autocratic tendencies reflected Vietnam's imperial heritage.[3] Some attributed the authoritarianism of the First Republic to the legacy of French colonialism; others suggested that Diệm's rule combined traditional Confucianism and Catholicism with modern, Western-style authoritarianism.[4] The most serious effort to make sense of the RVN's politics is the now forgotten work of John Donnell, one of the few early researchers to learn Vietnamese. Donnell found that several competing doctrines animated the political life of the First Republic, and the resulting clash accounted for the seeming contradictions between the democratic rhetoric and authoritarian practices of the RVN.[5]

The escalation of the Vietnam War in the mid-1960s inaugurated a new wave of research, this time by political scientists with language competency. These pioneers founded the Anglophone field of Vietnam studies and profoundly shaped academic understanding of Vietnam for decades to come. The most urgent concern of this second wave was to explain the strength of the communist belligerents, and the political scientists largely preferred to study the Democratic Republic of Vietnam (DRV, or North Vietnam) and the National Liberation Front (NLF), relegating the RVN to a little more than a foil to the communists. Equally significant was how the Vietnam scholars framed their analysis. Placing the conflict within the longer span of Vietnamese history, they agreed with earlier writers that the RVN was an authoritarian regime born of Western colonialism and elite traditionalism. The Vietnam scholars, though, insisted that the communist belligerents grew out of indigenous patriotism and revolutionary nationalism. Taken together, the researchers delineated two parallel trajectories in Vietnamese history: an illiberal tradition represented by the RVN and an emancipatory one embodied by the DRV and NLF. The argument implied that the communists were the only morally legitimate side in the conflict, a claim that reflected the researchers' partisan, antiwar stance.

The first work to introduce the framework of the parallel trajectories was *The United States in Vietnam* (1967), a popular book by political scientists George Kahin and John Lewis that became the "bible" of the American antiwar movement. The volume was transitional in that the coauthors had no Vietnamese-language training similar to that of the early experts, but Kahin and Lewis anticipated later research by Vietnam scholars. Kahin and Lewis argued that the RVN's predecessor, the State of Vietnam, failed to inspire nationalist support in the early 1950s, and the First Republic carried on this legacy as an unpopular, oppressive state. In contrast, the communists achieved legitimacy during the First Indochina War, came to represent "patriotic nationalism and courageous opposition to French rule," and eventually organized the NLF in response to Diệm's misrule.[6]

Vietnam scholars elaborated on this framework. Focusing specifically on the revolution in the southern countryside, Jeffrey Race and David Elliott traced the communist movement from the Việt Minh of the 1940s to the NLF of the 1960s. Their research also pointed to a parallel continuity: the same landlord interests that controlled the rural administration during the late colonial period dominated the First Republic.[7] Other researchers extended the temporal scope of the communist trajectory. David Marr's scholarship in the 1970s and 1980s charted a direct lineage from the anticolonial resistance of the late nineteenth century to the revolutionary nationalist and communist movements of the 1920s. According to Marr, the anticolonialists and the communists drew on an ancient Vietnamese identity based on historical resistance to northern domination.[8] William Duiker stretched the narrative forward from the 1930s to the victory of the DRV at the end of the Vietnam War and argued that the communists triumphed because they successfully presented themselves as more nationalist than their Vietnamese rivals.[9] William Turley synthesized much of the Vietnam scholarship when he claimed that the communist revolution drew on the precolonial tradition of opposition to foreign rule but that the RVN inherited its corrupt leadership and social fragmentation from French colonialism.[10] The best-selling *Fire in the Lake* (1972), by the journalist Frances Fitzgerald, who knew no Vietnamese, popularized an even cruder, more simplistic version of this narrative.[11] Read against the backdrop of the Vietnam War, the dominant research in Vietnam studies casts the communists as belonging to the *only* right side of history.

Vietnam scholars were certainly correct to point to the continuities between the State of the Vietnam and the RVN and between late colonial communism and the later DRV and NLF, but writers selectively highlighted certain developments while ignoring others. Many politicians and parties in the RVN also traced their origins to the revolutionary nationalism of the 1920s and 1930s, yet researchers were hesitant to locate the origins of the Saigon-based government in the revolutionary politics of this earlier era.[12] Scholars also ignored more liberal trends embodied by the South Vietnamese republic. The problem was as much ideological as methodological. Researchers belonging to the second wave typically relied on communist Vietnamese sources rather than documents produced by the RVN, the very type of sources necessary for understanding the Southern regime's connections to the past. By retrospect, it seems judicious to acknowledge that all Vietnamese belligerents inherited aspects of the revolutionary past, but researchers compressed complex developments into two opposing teleologies of national emancipation and elite authoritarianism.

As the passage of time transformed the Vietnam War into a historical event, American diplomatic historians came to study the RVN within the framework of American foreign policy. This third wave of researchers argued that the Southern state was an instrument of US imperialism. The more extreme version of the argument insisted that the United States created the RVN outright. Historians claimed that Washington selected Diệm for the premiership, suggested that the Central Intelligence Agency masterminded the mass migration of Northerners to the South, and described the RVN as little more than an army installed by the Americans.[13] The more moderate version of the argument stressed that it was US policy to establish a viable noncommunist government. Scholars emphasized the role of Eisenhower's administration in the formation of the RVN, found that American assistance was critical to the survival of Diệm's government, and credited foreign aid for winning over the support of the urban middle class for the Saigon-based state.[14] For diplomatic historians, the First Republic was best understood as an extension of US intervention rather than an authentically Vietnamese entity. The key claims of the second and third waves of scholarship reached a popular audience through the journalist Stanley Karnow's *Vietnam: A History* (1983, revised 1997).[15]

Within American diplomatic history, a relatively uninfluential body of research known as the revisionist school countered that Diệm was a traditional, nationalist autocrat who rightly understood that local political conditions necessitated strongman rule.[16] Yet the revisionist research suffered from the same shortcomings as the more orthodox American diplomatic history. Both made bold claims about the character of the RVN and the origins of the regime without consulting Vietnamese-language sources. At the most fundamental level, researchers of the second and third waves assumed that only one Vietnamese nation could be legitimately represented by either the communists or the RVN. Scholars apparently could not conceive of a pluralistic Vietnam in which multiple groups might plausibly claim political legitimacy.

These many weaknesses left the scholarship vulnerable to vigorous challenges. Often described as the "new Vietnam War scholarship," the new research has shifted decisively away from the communist-centric and American-centric focus, uses Vietnamese-language sources produced by the RVN and its former citizens, and avoids partisan assumptions about moral legitimacy. The current wave began in the early 2000s, when a young generation of American diplomatic historians took advantage of the normalization of relations between the US and Vietnam to explore previously inaccessible Vietnamese archives. Armed with requisite language training, these historians analyzed the First Republic as a distinct political entity within the framework of the Vietnamese-American alliance or international relations more generally. The researchers highlighted the contributions of Vietnamese political actors and linked the RVN to the Vietnamese nationalist movement. Philip Catton and Edward Miller rejected the characterization of Diệm as a traditional mandarin and contended that the founder of the Republic was a conservative, nationalist modernizer who harbored visions of nation-building distinct from American designs.[17] Geoffrey Stewart went further to argue that Diệm's program of nation-building was outright revolutionary and likened him to other Third World nationalists.[18] Jessica Chapman showed that the domestic conflict between Diệm and the southern sects had serious ramifications for international relations and traced the sects to the frontier political culture of southern Vietnam.[19] But even as these historians undermined the truisms of the second and third waves, the framework of international history discouraged a deeper exploration of Vietnamese ideas and actions. Researchers often gave fuller explanations of American policies than Vietnamese programs and sometimes treated Diệm and his officials as the sole representative of the RVN.

Freshly minted Vietnam scholars rushed to address the lacunae created by the young diplomatic historians and the previous waves of scholarship. Many Vietnam specialists devoted more serious attention to the culture and ideas of the First Republic. Tuan Hoang contended that Northern migrants in the RVN developed a coherent critique of Vietnamese communism based on their experience of the August Revolution and the First Indochina War, Nguyễn Tuấn Cường found that Diệm's promotion of Confucianism was part of a larger Confucian revival across contemporary East Asia, and Mitchell Tan highlighted the importance of ideology in Saigon's relations with anticommunist Asian allies.[20] By placing the RVN in the context of inter-Asian relations, the work of the second two scholars freed the First Republic from the conceptual straitjacket of Vietnamese-American diplomacy. Other researchers stressed the political diversity of the RVN beyond Diệm's political faction. Conventional wisdom long held that Vietnamese Catholics and Northern migrants constituted the political base of the South Vietnamese republic, but Van Nguyen-Marshall, Phi Van Nguyen, and Jason Picard demonstrated that these groups were internally diverse and pursued agendas that were sometimes at odds with Diệm's government.[21] Additionally, Stan Tan's research on the central highlands and David Bigg's work on the Mekong Delta and greater Huế region moved beyond Saigon to study state formation, war, and the environment on the political and geographical margins of the First Republic.[22] Despite these contributions, however, Vietnam scholars have yet to propose a framework to replace the outdated claim that the RVN grew out of traditional mandarinism and foreign colonialism.

VIETNAMESE REPUBLICANISM
AND THE FIRST REPUBLIC

We propose republicanism as an alternative historical framework for understanding the RVN. Republicanism was a global trend that originated in the French revolution. Adherents championed representative government, the universal rights of man, civil liberties, and the primacy of the nation while opposing monarchism, aristocratic privilege, and church authority.[23] French imperialism spread these ideas to Vietnam, and two distinct varieties of republicanism developed in dialogue with each other: French colonial republicanism and Vietnamese republicanism. Significantly, both forms advocated liberal ideals but failed to live up to those principles, and the history of republicanism in Vietnam was never completely authoritarian nor outright emancipatory. Indeed, we emphasize these internal tensions to call attention to the ambivalent character of the RVN and the longer history to which the regime belonged.

French officials claimed that colonialism would introduce the values of republicanism to the rest of the empire and lift the colonized to the same level of civilization as the French. When the natives were sufficiently enlightened, France would restore their sovereignty.[24] But colonial policy in Vietnam gave the lie to republican ideals.[25] French republicans may have disavowed royalism at home, but they maintained the Vietnamese monarchy, stripped the king of any authority, and turned him into an instrument of colonial rule. The French also failed to establish genuinely representative institutions in the colonies. Southern Vietnam received a seat in the French legislature, and the colonial state formed elected assemblies in each region of Vietnam. The majority of the native population, however, did not have the right to vote. The authorities restricted the franchise to French settlers and Vietnamese elites who fulfilled the stringent requirements for French naturalization and interfered in legislative and colonial elections.[26]

Many Vietnamese nevertheless embraced republicanism and pursued various strategies to advance democratic ideals. Reformers such as Bùi Quang Chiêu, Phạm Quỳnh, and Trần Trọng Kim actively cooperated with the colonial government in hopes of implementing moderate changes within the existing system.[27] Dissidents such as Phan Châu Trinh adopted a more adversarial stance. They railed against French colonialism for preserving the monarchy and abusing the peasantry and demanded that the government fulfill its civilizing mission.[28] The colonial state brooked criticism from neither quarter, and the authorities ignored the demands of the reformers and jailed the dissidents.

By the 1920s, such high-handedness combined with the French refusal to implement reforms drove yet other Vietnamese down the path to revolution. The revolutionaries aimed to overthrow the colonial state and form a republic themselves. The most famous example was the Vietnamese Nationalist Party (Việt

Nam Quốc Dân Đảng), established in 1927. Party leaders embraced Western concepts such as universal suffrage, the freedom of press, and human and citizens' rights.[29] The party also drew on the Chinese republicanism of Sun Yat-sen, who stressed the collective liberty of the nation and envisioned a strong, centralized democratic state that enjoyed greater power than its Western counterparts.[30] Many other revolutionary nationalist parties adopted republican principles as well. Yet Vietnamese republicans could be as hypocritical as their French colonial counterparts. Bùi Quang Chiêu and his associates did not advocate universal suffrage because they wanted to limit the franchise to elites like themselves,[31] and revolutionary nationalists sometimes violated democratic ideals for political gain, as will be seen.

The only major group to reject republicanism were the Vietnamese communists. Hồ Chí Minh and many of his comrades began their journey as republicans before discovering proletarian revolution.[32] The relationship between republicanism and communism grew antagonistic in the 1920s, and anticommunism (or, more properly, anti-Stalinism) became a defining element of republican thought by the next decade. French colonial republicans denounced the Russian Revolution and Stalinist totalitarianism, and Vietnamese politics polarized between the communists, on the one hand, and reformers and revolutionary nationalists, on the other. The latter still favored republican principles and complained that the communists were factional and controlled by a foreign body. The communists countered that nationalism was parochial and republicanism too reformist.[33]

Republicanism remained influential even with the rise of fascism during World War II. In 1940, the colonial state came under the authority of Vichy France and dismantled even the most moderate of republican institutions in Vietnam. The new governor-general replaced the ostensibly representative bodies with appointed ones and practically suspended applications for naturalization by Vietnamese natives.[34] The year also marked the start of the Japanese Occupation. The Japanese paid lip service to liberating Vietnam from Western colonialism, held up fascist Japan as an alternative model of political modernity, and championed imperial rule and Asian racial superiority. In reality, the Japanese allowed the French to continue administering the colony and offered protection to only select Vietnamese nationalists, namely, the followers of Cường Để, an anticolonial Vietnamese prince based in Japan. Significantly, these activists espoused aspects of republicanism despite their alliance with Japanese fascists, organizing a new revolutionary party that envisioned the restoration of both the prince and popular elections.[35] Vietnam's Asian overlords declined to follow the party's program, however. In March 1945, the Japanese overthrew the French in a lightning coup and established a Vietnamese government known as the Empire of Vietnam under the nominal reign of Emperor Bảo

Đại, the reigning Vietnamese monarch. Bảo Đại's government, which was led by the scholar Trần Trọng Kim, declared Vietnam independent from France, implemented the nationalization of education and civil service, released political prisoners (including many communist leaders), and liberalized the press and many political activities (within limits granted by the Japanese).[36]

The contest between communism and republicanism intensified after World War II. Just days following Tokyo's surrender, the communists beat out the revolutionary nationalists to seize power from the Empire of Vietnam, and Hồ Chí Minh triumphantly declared the independence of the Democratic Republic of Vietnam. Yet the acolytes of Marx understood that republican institutions conferred a mantle of legitimacy. Presenting themselves as republicans, Hồ Chí Minh and his associates organized popular elections based on universal suffrage to select Vietnam's first national assembly. Under pressure from the Guomindang Chinese occupation authorities, the communists offered the revolutionary nationalist parties a bloc of unelected seats in the assembly and several cabinet portfolios, which were accepted without scruples about democratic procedures. The DRV's foray into democratic politics ended within a year, and the long-simmering tensions between the communists and other Vietnamese activists escalated into a civil war.[37]

Meanwhile, the French sought to recolonize Vietnam, and the First Indochina War broke out between France and the DRV in December 1946. The colonial war intertwined with the Vietnamese civil war and gradually brought together Vietnamese and French colonial republicans. Both groups resolved to challenge the DRV by forming an alternative Vietnamese state, though the strategic convergence concealed divergent objectives. The French hoped to restore colonial rule and promised to give Vietnam limited autonomy and a local parliament within a federal Indochinese state. Vietnamese republicans, however, envisioned a fully independent democratic republic or a constitutional monarchy.[38] Under the leadership of Bảo Đại, the former head of the defunct Empire of Vietnam, these varied efforts eventually gave rise to the State of Vietnam (SVN), a nominally independent government formed in 1949 that was part of the Indochinese Federation and that deferred to France in military, diplomatic, and economic affairs. As the chief of state, Bảo Đại immediately appealed to republican sensibilities when he promised to hold national elections on the country's political system as soon as conditions allowed.[39] But not until 1953 did the SVN institute a three-stage process of democratization, starting with municipal and provincial elections.[40] The slow pace of reforms irritated many Vietnamese republicans, who agitated for a complete break with France and full-fledged representative democracy.[41] The First Indochina War ended in 1954 with the Geneva Accords signed by France and the DRV. The accords mandated a ceasefire between all belligerents and temporarily partitioned Vietnam. The French and the SVN withdrew troops and personnel to the South, and the DRV regrouped its forces to the North. The SVN, whose interests were ignored by the French and the DRV, protested the agreement to no avail and would later refuse to implement a (non-binding) clause on reunification elections.

Bảo Đại appointed Ngô Đình Diệm the prime minister of the State of Vietnam just weeks before the ceasefire. Diệm was a devout Catholic who had experimented with a wide range of political strategies. He had served as a reformist mandarin in Bảo Đại's royal court in the 1930s and later joined the pro-Japanese party that supported Cường Để during World War II. Diệm later sided with Bảo Đại during the First Indochina War but ultimately rejected the SVN as too dependent on France. Diệm subsequently turned to revolutionary nationalism and emerged as the figurehead of an underground, largely Catholic movement in the early 1950s. His brother Ngô Đình Nhu organized the movement on Diệm's behalf and was a vocal proponent of multiparty democracy.

Diệm's rule continued the contradictory history of republicanism in Vietnam. Similar to the French colonial state, his government drew inspiration from democratic ideals while honoring them in the breach. Perhaps no event exemplified the discrepancy as starkly the plebiscite to overthrow Bảo Đại in October 1955. Reflecting the long-standing republican opposition to monarchism, Diệm billed the election as a choice between democracy and royal rule. Government propaganda praised Diệm's character and the virtues of democracy but castigated Bảo Đại as a morally corrupt king and stressed the defects of monarchism. The wording of the referendum linked the removal of Bảo Đại to the installation of Diệm as chief of state with the mandate to establish a democracy. Yet the government flagrantly interfered in the elections. The authorities blocked any counter-campaigning by Bảo Đại, instructed newspapers to smear the former emperor, and manipulated the vote count to deliver an overwhelming victory to Diệm. After winning, the premier changed the name of the government to the Republic of Vietnam and appointed himself its first president. Diệm also refused to engage in consultations with the DRV about the reunification elections, and the partition of Vietnam became permanent.

The president's violations of democratic norms dismayed other republican nationalists, and they too followed in the footsteps of earlier republicans. Similar to the reformers of old, some chose to engage in the legal, democratic process. They ran for public office and gently admonished the government to liberalize. Others resembled colonial-era dissidents and aggressively polemicized against the president. These critics invoked principles such as representative government and civil liberties to demand immediate change. The response of the president was as harsh as that of the colonial state. Diệm disqualified opposition candidates during elections, arrested his critics, and shuttered newspapers that dared to defy him. The repression pushed some former revolutionary parties back into underground activism, and they once again conspired to overthrow the government. In that way, the First Republic carried on the cycle of reformism, dissidence, repression, and revolution. Placed within the longer history of republicanism, the RVN proved an earnest though deeply flawed experiment in Vietnamese democracy.

Republicanism was not the only ideological trend to shape the First Republic. Diệm certainly believed in representative institutions and popular sovereignty, but he considered liberal democracy to be inadequate for ensuring human freedom. The first president of the RVN subscribed to Emmanuel Mounier's philosophy of personalism. Personalists defined freedom as the positive right to contribute to the common good of the community and understood democracy to be the political means that ensured all members of a community the right to develop their potential for goodness. Therefore, the republican form of government was only a temporary phase in the quest for an ever-better political system that would enable individuals to become more virtuous.[42] Accordingly, the president and his associates described the RVN as a personalist democracy rather than a liberal democracy to stress that the First Republic was an unfinished innovation on the old republican project.

THE FIRST REPUBLIC IN COMPARATIVE PERSPECTIVE

The great paradox that South Vietnam's First Republic was heir to a decades-old local republican tradition yet at the same time a deeply flawed republican experiment can be better understood in a comparative perspective. In this section, we attempt a comparison between the RVN's First Republic to South Korea's First Republic during their first decade after colonial rule. It is now untenable to claim that Ngô Đình Diệm's Republic was a US creation, and the comparison suggests the implications of this fact for its evolution as well as a possible explanation for the paradox.[43]

The comparison between the RVN's First Republic to the First Republic of the Republic of Korea (ROK, or South Korea) is apt because the two cases shared not only the historical era defined by Cold War and decolonization, but also their authoritarian politics and pattern of evolution. The RVN's First Republic emerged a decade after World War II in the depths of a raging Cold War and the war between France and Hồ Chí Minh's forces. It existed for nine years before it collapsed in a military coup that took place in the midst of widespread popular protests, rising military threat from communist North Vietnam, and tension with its chief foreign ally, the United States. In contrast, South Korea's First Republic was established in 1948 at the onset of the Cold War and survived an all-out attempt at takeover by North Korea between 1950 and 1953. Korea's First Republic ended in 1960 in its twelfth year with the resignation of its founding president, Rhee Syngman, under the pressure of massive popular protests but without military involvement or foreign meddling. Within a year, however, the military under General Park Chung Hee took power in a bloodless coup (still no US meddling).

Both republics thus experienced war or intense threats of war as well as authoritarian rule. Both were close US allies and depended greatly on American support. Both lasted for about a decade and ended up with military regimes (South Korea with a lag of less than a year). Of course, differences between the two were numerous. This section highlights in particular that both state-led nationalism and republican institutions were weaker in the RVN than in the ROK. This difference was the result of many factors, including the personal backgrounds of the two leaders and the historical conditions when they assumed office.

On proclaiming the Vietnamese republic in 1955, President Ngô Đình Diệm presented himself as a republican and a nationalist. His father, Ngô Đình Khả, was a high-ranking mandarin in the royal court in Huế who collaborated with French colonial rulers even as he harbored reformist ambitions. In 1907, Khả refused to join others at the court to request the abdication of Emperor Thành Thái at the order of French officials. For this act, he lost his position but gained fame as a patriot.

A graduate at the top of his class at the School of Administration, Ngô Đình Diệm advanced in the colonial bureaucracy from a junior official to provincial chief of Bình Thuận. Among the accomplishments in his bureaucratic career was his suppression of a plot to organize an uprising possibly initiated by the communists. At thirty-two, Ngô Đình Diệm was invited to join the cabinet of a new emperor, Bảo Đại, as minister of the interior but resigned after only two months, criticizing the French for their unwillingness to grant the Huế Court any autonomy and to allow the creation of an assembly of representatives elected by Vietnamese. This courageous act cemented Diệm's reputation as a determined nationalist and republican.

For the next decade through the end of World War II, Diệm continued to expand his networks among nationalist circles just as an older brother, Ngô Đình Thục, gained national stature as the third Vietnamese bishop. Diệm's nationalist credentials helped him escape execution in late 1945 when he was arrested by Hồ Chí Minh's government. They set him up as a candidate for prime minister first under the Japanese in early 1945 and later under Bảo Đại in the early 1950s. They helped him attract the attention of American leaders in the early 1950s. They helped his younger brother, Ngô Đình Nhu, build an organization in Vietnam that supported him when Diệm was finally appointed as Bảo Đại's prime minister in 1954.

Ngô Đình Diệm did not monopolize Vietnamese nationalism and faced the most serious challenge from Vietnamese communists who in the mid-1940s also presented themselves as nationalists. Although Diệm's nationalist reputation was unquestionable, he was vulnerable in many ways. First, he was Catholic, a member of a minority religion that many Vietnamese viewed with suspicion as a tool of French colonialism to dominate Vietnam. As will be seen, this aspect was a key difference between Diệm and his South Korean counterpart, President Rhee of the First Republic of Korea. Hồ Chí Minh could pretend to dissolve the Indochinese Communist Party to persuade people that he represented the Vietnamese nation and not any political party. Diệm could not have done that with the Catholic Church, however, nor did he want to.

Second, Ngô Đình Diệm was too closely associated with the Vietnamese monarchy. His father resisted the French but served the Nguyễn monarch Thành Thái loyally. He himself had been an official of the Huế court as a young man until 1932. He resigned but twenty years later was appointed as prime minister by the same (now former) monarch. The referendum to abolish the monarchy to be replaced with a republic was first proposed by Diệm's rivals and only later did he embrace it. The Nguyễn dynasty, except for a couple of independent-minded kings, had been and was blamed by a generation of activists since the early 1900s for having lost the country to the French. They were, in the eyes of many Vietnamese, considered puppets of France. This was another important difference between Diệm and Rhee; the latter was imprisoned for many years by a Korean monarch for his support for reform before the Japanese formally took over Korea as a colony.

Third, Ngô Đình Diệm's First Republic built on the state apparatus that served French colonial rule, including the post–World War II period in French-controlled zones. Diệm's military was led by French-trained officers and before 1954 fought under French command. This was perhaps a great liability in the competition for legitimacy with the communists, but Rhee's military and police in South Korea's First Republic had a similar problem. At the same time, the state apparatus of the ROK expanded greatly and contributed to the defense of South Korea during the Korean War, which perhaps alleviated the stigma of past collaboration with the Japanese.

In contrast with those of Ngô Đình Diệm, Rhee Syngman's nationalist credentials stood on far firmer grounds not because he loved his country more than Diệm but because of many historical circumstances beyond either man's control. Born in 1875 (twenty-six years before Diệm) to a family with distant royal lineage traced back to King Taejo, founder of the Choson dynasty in the fourteenth century, Rhee grew up poor but enjoyed a solid education in the classics.[44] Yet his repeated failures in the national civil service examination led him to seek a Western-style education at a school operated by an American-run mission in 1895.

Under the influence of his teachers, including many American missionaries and S'o Chae P'il (also known as Philip Jaisohn), a prominent Korean nationalist who had been trained in the US as a medical doctor, Rhee became a modern reformer. He joined the Independence Club established by S'o in 1896 and founded journals to advocate reforms.[45] Appointed to King Kojong's Privy Council, Rhee later supported a failed plot to force the king to abdicate in favor of his son, who embraced pro-Japan reformist tendencies. For this act, Rhee was imprisoned for nearly five years, from 1899 to 1904. In prison, he converted to Christianity and wrote a book analyzing Korean history and politics.

By the time of his release, Japan had taken Russia to war over Korea. Rhee's American connections helped persuade King Kojong to send him on an official mission in late 1904 to request help from the US. Although Rhee was able to meet with Theodore Roosevelt, the American president ignored his pleading and traded US recognition for Japan's dominance of Korea in return for Japanese reciprocal recognition of American interests in the Philippines. After his failed mission, Rhee stayed on in the US, completing his bachelor's from George Washington University, his master's from Harvard, and his doctorate from Princeton. From then until late 1945, when he returned to liberated Korea, he spent his time between Hawai'i and the mainland US to galvanize overseas Koreans for support, traveling to Shanghai to (briefly) lead the Provisional Government of Korea established in 1920 by Korean activists in exile, and to Geneva in 1933 to lobby foreign countries for Korean independence. Because of this long sojourn abroad, Rhee was therefore far more established than Diệm in nationalist circles and gained vastly more international exposure and experience. Despite his numerous controversies, Rhee towered over his rivals in the exiled Korean anticolonial movement.

Being a Christian did not impinge on Rhee's nationalist credentials, as Diệm's had done, and may actually have helped him. Korea was colonized by Japan, and the Protestant Church created by American missionaries was not associated with colonialism as the Catholic Church was in Vietnam. American missionaries sheltered many Korean activists from Japanese police, and rising American power attracted the imagination of anticolonial Koreans the same way that the Soviet Union inspired Vietnamese communists. The majority of earlier leaders of Korea's nationalist movement were in fact Christians, from S'o Chae P'il to Sun Chu Kil. The latter played a leading role in the March 1 movement that erupted across Korea demanding Korean independence. Fewer than 1 percent of Koreans were Christians, but sixteen of thirty-three signers of the declaration on March 1 were.[46]

We have seen that Rhee was not closely associated with the Korean monarchy, and his association was from before Korea became a Japanese colony in 1910. By 1945, that association must have become ancient history for most Koreans. What Rhee shared with Diệm was that he also relied on the Japanese-trained police, who were much hated by Koreans. Overall, however, on his return to Korea as a nationalist, Rhee had far fewer vulnerabilities than Diệm. The challenge to state-led nationalism in the RVN thus came not only from Hồ Chí Minh and the communists but also from Ngô Đình Diệm's background and the birth of the Bảo Đại government under the French.

Yet Diệm's weaknesses in nationalist credentials relative to Rhee's were compensated by the historical context when he became Bảo Đại's prime minister in 1954. Let us first examine the South Korean context in late 1945 when it was under the full control of the US Army Military Government in Korea (USAMGIK) led by General Hodge. Although Rhee was respected on his return, his strong anticommunist views stood out and he was not in favor of General Hodge. Until 1947, the United States still respected its agreement with the Soviet Union to place the entire Korean Peninsula under a United Nations trusteeship in preparation of eventual unification and self-rule. Although he suppressed the communists, General Hodge sought to promote the collaboration of South Korean leaders on the right and the noncommunist left. Rhee not only opposed the trusteeship plan but also rejected working with North Korean leader Kim Il-sung to unify Korea. He even went to the United States to lobby for a separate South Korea. As the Cold War brewed in Europe, US policy in South Korea shifted and Rhee won approval for his idea of organizing a separate government for South Korea.[47]

Under the direct supervision of the USAMGIK and the United Nations, the elections for a National Assembly took place in May 1948. Rhee's party won a plurality of 26 percent and independents accounted for 40 percent. The newly elected National Assembly proceeded to draft a constitution according to which the president would be elected by this body but not by the popular vote. Even though his party did not control the majority of the National Assembly, Rhee easily won with 180 of 196 votes, making him the first president of the South Korean republic. Rhee thus took power under US tutelage, and the First Republic of the ROK was in every sense a creation of the USAMGIK legitimized by popular elections. During his presidency, Rhee would seek to reduce the power of the National Assembly, crack down on opposition, and harass and perhaps even assassinate his rivals, but he was never able to dispense with or disempower elections in South Korea.

The circumstances between 1945 and 1948, when Rhee came to power, contrasted starkly with those Diệm faced in 1954 and 1955. Although the US had been providing assistance to the French in their war against Hồ Chí Minh's forces, the French remained in full control of noncommunist areas, including Emperor Bảo Đại's National Army. Appointed by Bảo Đại, Diệm faced vigorous challenges: the forces controlled by various religious sects in southern Vietnam, the Bình Xuyên group that controlled much of Saigon, and even National Army commander General Nguyễn Văn Hinh. American officials were ambiguous about Ngô Đình Diệm and only supported him after he defeated his challengers.

Once Diệm emerged as the clear winner, the US swiftly offered him full support. Washington gained some leverage over Diệm's government but was not in a position to shape the fundamental character of the regime as it had in South Korea in 1948.

Staunch American support helped Diệm remove Bảo Đại in a referendum in 1955, paving the way for him to become the first president of the RVN. Diệm was also able to sideline the various political groups that had earlier supported him against Bảo Đại, establishing a constitution and a National Assembly that gave him personal control over Vietnamese politics afterward. Rhee fought hard during the Korean War against the ROK National Assembly to amend the constitution so that he could be popularly elected. From the start, however, the RVN National Assembly never had any real power. Overall, South Koreans were to enjoy greater political freedom than South Vietnamese.[48]

Relative to their counterparts in the ROK under Rhee Syngman, republican institutions in the RVN's First Republic were impotent, explained in part by the historical circumstances of their birth. Although the US had full control over the creation of the ROK state, it had to rely on Diệm for the same task in South Vietnam after he survived the early challenges. Full American control of the ROK process enabled the creation and later maintenance of republican institutions. The Cold War also had become a more pressing concern for the US in 1954, when Diệm ascended to office, than it had been in 1947–1948, when Rhee took power. This heightened concern might have elevated Diệm's bargaining position relative to the US and resulted in his having full freedom to shape republican institutions in the RVN to perpetuate his power.

Until recently, orthodox scholarship on the Vietnam War disparaged the RVN as a creation of the US, suggesting a lack of indigenous roots and domestic legitimacy. If the RVN is viewed as an heir to the republican tradition that had developed its roots on Vietnamese soil since the 1900s (as discussed earlier), this stigma is plainly wrong. Yet, in comparison with the ROK, the RVN might have acquired more robust republican institutions had it indeed been a US creation. The ROK was far more a US creation. Republican institutions in the ROK created under direct US control enjoyed real representative powers, outlived Rhee Syngman and military rule, and would become the foundation of South Korea's vibrant democracy today. The association of being a US creation with a lack of legitimacy is therefore spurious. Like Rhee, Diệm rose to power thanks to his own efforts under chaotic conditions. Like Rhee, Diệm was known to have strong autocratic tendencies. The emasculated republican institutions in the RVN under the First Republic were not just because of those tendencies but also because of the historical context.

Weak American control over the RVN's First Republic at birth relative to the ROK's First Republic also explains the different ways the two republics ended. In the face of popular protests again him in the summer of 1963, Ngô Đình Diệm's government was repressive while refusing to reform as the Kennedy administration demanded. In response, the US supported the military coup against him. This coup led to a series of others that destabilized and rendered the RVN unable to cope with the communist onslaught, ultimately forcing the US to intervene militarily. In South Korea, by contrast, facing similar popular protests in early 1960, Rhee resigned, making way for a civilian government led by the opposition party and a lively civil society. Washington did not intervene, and no military coup took place until a year later. The US also played no role in that coup, led by General Park Chung Hee in 1961, but did quickly intervene to stabilize the situation. The regime transition in South Korea was entirely a Korean affair that took place with almost no American knowledge or meddling even though the South Korean military was more or less under US command. This fact suggests stronger American control of the situation in South Korea than in South Vietnam.

THE CHAPTERS AHEAD

This book has ten chapters. In the first, Peter Zinoman reviews the historiography of modern Vietnam and the general historiography and popular discourse about the Republic of Vietnam. Despite its novelty as a theme, its moment has finally arrived, though much remains to be done to change popular understanding of the RVN and Vietnamese republicanism generally. By way of example, Zinoman analyzes Viet Thanh Nguyen's *The Sympathizer,* a novel that recently won a Pulitzer Prize, to show how it is pervaded by an excessively negative view of the RVN, similar to much US-centric scholarship on the RVN.

Next are three chapters that examine various strands and aspects of republican thought from the 1900s to the 1940s. In chapter 2, Nguyễn Lương Hải Khôi focuses on Trần Trọng Kim's *A Brief History of Vietnam* (*Việt Nam sử lược,* 1920), the first modern textbook of Vietnamese history and used widely during the colonial period and in the Republic of Vietnam. This chapter examines *Việt Nam sử lược* in the intellectual context of Vietnamese social evolutionism in the early twentieth century and analyzes its core elements to call attention to the contributions of early republicans to the construction of modern Vietnamese nationalism.

By the 1930s, a young generation of Vietnamese republicans educated in modern Franco-Vietnamese schools came of age and were represented by the Self-Reliant Literary Group (Tự Lực Văn Đoàn). In chapter 3, Martina Thucnhi Nguyen examines the journals *Mores* (*Phong hoá*) and *These Days* (*Ngày nay*) published by this group, paying particular attention to the group's demands for institutional reform, colonial and legal reform, and rejection of monarchy. Nguyen argues that the Self-Reliant Literary Group sought to realize a postcolonial vision of a democratic and autonomous Vietnam founded on republican ideals.

As the global Cold War intensified the rivalry between Vietnamese republicans and communists, republican thought and movements took on a robust anticommunist character. Yen Vu in chapter 4 examines the political vision of Trần Văn Tùng, a francophone literary figure and active member of the expatriate Vietnamese community who sought an anticommunist nation-building project for Vietnam. His idea of a "new nationalism" for a new Vietnam was grounded in a rhetoric of republicanism and developing a new generation of youth. Examining this particular strand of nationalism grants more agency to the Vietnamese regarding their nation-building efforts, which enables scholars to understand important alternatives to the Diệm or Communism binary that has enveloped Western narratives of the Vietnam War.

If chapters 2 to 4 examine the transformation of republican ideas in the first half of the twentieth century, chapters 5 and 6 focus on the different concepts of democracy and the struggle among various groups and individuals to achieve democracy in the First Republic. The First Republic was Vietnamese republicans' first opportunity to exercise power as an independent nation. How did they cope with the challenges of building a postcolonial nation in a divided country? Was the republican vision realized?

In chapter 5, Nu-Anh Tran examines the debate between Ngô Đình Diệm's faction and his rivals in the summer and fall of 1955. Virtually all anticommunists favored democracy, but they defined democracy in starkly different ways, disagreed on the degree of democracy that was suitable given the communist threat, and debated the range of parties and individuals that had a legitimate place in politics. Diệm and his followers were the most illiberal elements in the debate, and their victory over other anticommunists placed the RVN on the path to authoritarianism.

Chapter 6, by Duy Lap Nguyen, examines the theory of personalism that informed the Strategic Hamlet Program during the First Republic. The theory, Nguyen argues, was not a conservative ideology but a form of Marxist humanism, espousing the ideal of the withering away of the state. The aim of the program was not only to overcome the insurgency but also to carry out a social revolution to establish a decentralized political system. This goal, however, would put the leaders of the republican government directly at odds with the interests of the Southern urban elite and played a crucial role in the failure of the First Republic.

The last four chapters of the volume examine nation- and state-building efforts under the First Republic. In chapter 7, Jason Picard seeks to explain the rise of regional animosity in South Vietnam due in part to the migration of more than 860,000 Northerners to the South over 1954 and 1955. Scholarship has conventionally portrayed Southern hostility toward migrants as the consequence of two factors, religion and favoritism. However, a closer look at the archives reveals a host of other factors, including economics, cultural distinctions, and history.

Chapter 8 by Cindy Nguyen examines the decolonization and development of the National Library of South Vietnam (Thư Viện Quốc Gia) from 1948 to 1958. Despite the chaos of the postcolonial transition and the lack of resources, the National Library was a site where the nationalist vision of the South Vietnamese republic was realized. In particular, the government and library administrators conceived of the National Library as the protector of "national heritage" by assembling and preserving Vietnamese literature, reference works, and contemporary periodicals. Administrators envisioned the National Library as a modern, public service of popular education for Saigon urbanites and students to connect with global news and literature.

In chapter 9, Hoàng Phong Tuấn and Nguyễn Thị Minh analyze the perspectives of writers and managing editors in the three prominent magazines in the First Republic from 1955 to 1960. Their analysis focuses on the identity and historical imagination of the new literature these writers and artists took part in creating. According to the authors, the new society was a free society, and the new literature was developed on the basis of creative freedom in literature and arts. The chapter also shows that, despite facing doubts and questions later, these writers and artists still insisted on the identity that was imagined and constructed from this early stage.

The final chapter, chapter 10, by Y Thien Nguyen, focuses on the process of anticommunist subject formation during the First Republic using the unstudied Political Study Program (Chương Trình Học Tập Chính Trị) to explore the development and transformation of South Vietnamese anticommunism. In the context of the South Vietnamese narrative on the Geneva Accords (an anticommunist narrative taught through the PSP that persisted throughout the era), the chapter examines the ways in which South Vietnamese anticommunism as a discourse has endured. Nguyen argues that the persistence of South Vietnamese anticommunism came about through a ritualization of anticommunist beliefs and practices and a persistent and modular deployment of anticommunist narratives.

Together, the chapters force scholars of modern Vietnam to take seriously the significance of republican ideas and the efforts by various republican groups to live up to them. In his chapter, Zinoman heralds the arrival of the "republican moment" in the study of Vietnamese history. We welcome readers of this book to share with us our excitement at this critical moment.

A NOTE ON TERMINOLOGY

Some readers may be confused by the different ways of dividing Vietnam. Most Vietnamese think of their country as being divided into three cultural and geographic regions, and the French colonial government formally divided the country into three administrative units. The volume refers to this tripartite division in the lower case: northern, central, and southern Vietnam, or the north, the central region, and the south. The Geneva Accords of 1954 divided Vietnam at the seventeenth parallel, and the volume refers to the areas above and below the parallel in upper case: North and South Vietnam, respectively. The Republic of Vietnam, the South Vietnamese republic, and Republican Vietnam refer to the government based in Saigon rather than the entire area below the seventeenth parallel.

NOTES

1. Lê Thanh Cảnh, "Thử đi tìm một lập trường tranh đấu cho dân tộc Việt nam," in *Phan Châu Trinh toàn tập*, ed. Chương Thâu et al., vol. 3 (Đà Nẵng: Nhà Xuất Bản, 2005), 125–131. This article first appeared in the fifth number of the irregular periodical of the Hội Ái Hữu Cựu Học Sinh Quốc Học, published some time in the early 1970s in the RVN. The piece is also available at Pham Ton's blog, https://phamquynh.wordpress.com/2012/05/31/roi-mai-tranh-truong-quoc-hoc/ (accessed May 5, 2021).

2. Nils Gilman, *Mandarins of the Future: Modernization Theory in Cold War America* (Baltimore, MD: Johns Hopkins University Press, 2003).

3. Denis Warner, *The Last Confucian* (New York: Macmillan, 1963); and Anthony Bouscaren, *The Last of the Mandarins: Diem of Vietnam* (Pittsburgh, PA: Duquesne University Press, 1965).

4. For the connection between Diệm's politics and French colonialism, see Robert Scigliano, *South Vietnam: Nation under Stress* (Boston, MA: Houghton Mifflin, 1963), 36–100. For claims that Diệm combined traditional and modern influences, see Bernard Fall, *The Two Viet-Nams: A Political and Military Analysis,* 2nd rev. ed. (New York: Frederick A. Praeger, 1967), 236–237; and Joseph Buttinger, *Vietnam: A Dragon Embattled,* vol. 2, *Vietnam at War* (New York: Frederick A. Praeger, 1967), 935.

5. John Donnell, "Politics in South Vietnam: Doctrines of Authority in Conflict" (Phd diss., University of California, Berkeley, 1964). See also John Donnell, "National Renovation Campaigns in Vietnam," *Pacific Affairs* 32, no. 1 (March 1959): 73–88; and John Donnell, "Personalism in Vietnam," in *Problems of Freedom,* ed. Wesley Fishel (New York: Free Press of Glencoe, 1961), 29–67.

6. George Kahin and John Lewis, *The United States in Vietnam* (New York: Dial Press, 1967), 29.

7. Jeffrey Race, *War Comes to Long An: Revolutionary Conflict in a Vietnamese Province* (Berkeley: University of California Press, 1972); and David Elliott, *The Vietnamese War: Revolution and Social Change in the Mekong Delta, 1930–1975,* concise ed. (Armonk, NY: M. E. Sharpe, 2007).

8. David Marr, *Vietnamese Anticolonialism, 1885–1925* (Berkeley: University of California Press, 1971); and David Marr, *Vietnamese Tradition on Trial, 1920–1945* (Berkeley: University of California Press, 1980). See also Huỳnh Kim Khánh, *Vietnamese Communism, 1925–1945* (Ithaca, NY: Cornell University Press, 1982).

9. William Duiker, *The Communist Road to Power in Vietnam,* 2nd ed. (Boulder, CO: Westview, 1996). See also Carlyle Thayer, *War by Other Means: National Liberation and Revolution in Viet-Nam, 1954–60* (Sydney, AU: Allen and Unwin, 1989), xx.

10. William Turley, *The Second Indochina War: A Short Political and Military History, 1954–1975* (Boulder, CO: Westview Press, 1986).

11. Frances Fitzgerald, *Fire in the Lake: The Vietnamese and the Americans in Vietnam* (New York: Vintage Books, 1972).

12. Van Nguyen-Marshall makes a similar point. See Van Nguyen-Marshall, review of *Vietnam's Lost Revolution*, by Geoffrey Stewart, *H-Diplo Roundtable Review* 19, no. 45 (July 23, 2018): 14–15.

13. Gabriel Kolko, *Anatomy of a War: Vietnam, the United States, and the Modern Historical Experience* (New York: Pantheon Books, 1985), 546; and Marilyn Young, *The Vietnam Wars, 1945–1990* (New York: Harper Perennial, 1991), 45, 54. For later iterations of the same arguments, see Seth Jacobs, *America's Miracle Man in Vietnam: Ngo Dinh Diem, Religion, Race, and the US Intervention in Southeast Asia, 1950–1957* (Durham, NC: Duke University Press, 2005); and James Carter, *Inventing Vietnam* (Cambridge: Cambridge University Press, 2008).

14. David Anderson, *Trapped by Success: The Eisenhower Administration and Vietnam, 1953–61* (New York City: Columbia University Press, 1991); John Prados, *Vietnam: History of an Unwinnable War* (Lawrence: University Press of Kansas, 2009); George Kahin, *Intervention: How America Became Involved in Vietnam* (New York: Anchor Books, 1987), 84–88; and George Herring, *America's Longest War: The United States and Vietnam, 1950–1975*, 5th ed. (New York: McGraw-Hill, 2014).

15. Stanley Karnow, *Vietnam: A History* (New York: Penguin Books, 1997).

16. Mark Moyar, *Triumph Forsaken: The Vietnam War, 1954–1965* (Cambridge: Cambridge University Press, 2006). See also Geoffrey Shaw, *The Lost Mandate of Heaven: The American Betrayal of Ngo Dinh Diem, President of Vietnam* (San Francisco, CA: Ignatius Press, 2015).

17. Philip Catton, *Diem's Final Failure: Prelude to America's War in Vietnam* (Lawrence: University Press of Kansas, 2002); and Edward Miller, *Misalliance: Ngo Dinh Diem, the United States, and the Fate of South Vietnam* (Cambridge, MA: Harvard University Press, 2013). For another work that employed a similar framework but without using Vietnamese-language sources, see Ronald Frankum Jr., *Vietnam's Year of the Rat* (Jefferson, NC: McFarland, 2014).

18. Geoffrey Stewart, *Vietnam's Lost Revolution: Ngô Đình Diệm's Failure to Build an Independent Nation, 1955–1963* (Cambridge: Cambridge University Press, 2017).

19. Jessica Chapman, *Cauldron of Resistance: Ngo Dinh Diem, the United States, and 1950s Southern Vietnam* (Ithaca, NY: Cornell University Press, 2013).

20. Tuan Hoang, "The Early South Vietnamese Critique of Communism," in *Dynamics of the Cold War in Asia*, ed. Tuong Vu and Wasana Wongsurawat (New York: Palgrave Macmillan, 2009), 17–32; Nguyễn Tuấn Cường, "The Promotion of Confucianism in South Vietnam (1955–1975) and the Role of Nguyễn Đăng Thục as a New Confucian Scholar," *Journal of Vietnamese Studies* 10, no. 4 (Fall 2015): 30–81; and Mitchell Tan, "Spiritual Fraternities: The Transnational Networks of Ngô Đình Diệm's Personalist Revolution and the Republic of Vietnam, 1955–1963," *Journal of Vietnamese Studies* 14, no. 2 (Spring 2019): 1–67.

21. Van Nguyen-Marshall, "Tools of Empire? Vietnamese Catholics in South Vietnam," *Journal of the Canadian Historical Association* 20, no. 2 (2009): 138–159; Jason Picard, "'Renegades': The Story of South Vietnam's First National Opposition Newspaper, 1955–1958," *Journal of Vietnamese Studies* 10, no. 4 (Fall 2015): 1–29; Jason Picard, "Fertile Lands Await: The Promise and Pitfalls of Directed Resettlement, 1954–1958," *Journal of Vietnamese Studies* 11, no. 3–4 (Summer-Fall 2016): 58–102; and Phi Van Nguyen, "Fighting the First Indochina War Again?: Catholic Refugees in South Vietnam, 1954–59," *Sojourn* 31, no. 1 (March 2016): 207–246. See also Peter Hansen, "Bắc Di Cư: Catholic Refugees from the North of Vietnam and Their Role in the Southern Republic, 1954–1959," *Journal of Vietnamese Studies* 4, no. 3 (fall 2009): 173–211; and Peter Hansen, "The Virgin Heads South: Northern Catholic Refugees and their Clergy in South Vietnam, 1954–1964," in *Casting Faiths: Imperialism and the Transformation of Religion in East and Southeast Asia*, ed. Thomas Dubois (New York: Palgrave, 2009), 129–151.

22. Stan Tan, "'Swiddens, Resettlements, Sedentarizations, and Villages': State Formation Among the Central Highlanders of Vietnam under the First Republic, 1955–1961," *Journal of Vietnamese Studies* 1, no. 1–2 (February/August 2006): 210–252; Stan Tan, "The Struggle to Control Land Grabbing: State Formation on the Central Highlands Frontier under the First Republic of

Vietnam (1954–1963)," in *On the Borders of State Power in the Greater Mekong Region*, ed. Martin Gainsborough (London: Routledge, 2008), 35–50; David Biggs, *Quagmire: Nation-Building and Nature in the Mekong Delta* (Seattle: University of Washington Press, 2010); and David Biggs, *Footprints of War* (Seattle: University of Washington Press, 2018).

23. Peter Zinoman, *Vietnamese Colonial Republican: The Political Vision of Vũ Trọng Phụng* (Berkeley: University of California Press, 2014), 4–6.

24. Philippe Peycam, *Birth of Vietnamese Political Journalism: Saigon, 1916–1930* (New York: Columbia University Press, 2012), 35–37, 40–41.

25. Zinoman, *Vietnamese Colonial Republican*, 7–8.

26. Peycam, *Birth of Vietnamese Political Journalism*, 43–44, 53–55, 87–89; and Milton Osborne, *The French Presence in Cochinchina and Cambodia: Rule and Response, 1859–1905* (Ithaca, NY: Cornell University Press, 1969), 119–130.

27. Christopher Goscha, *Vietnam: A New History* (New York: Basic Books, 2016), 124–127; and Peycam, *Birth of Vietnamese Political Journalism*, 64–65.

28. Goscha, *Vietnam: A New History*, 102–105.

29. Hue-Tam Ho Tai, *Radicalism and the Origins of the Vietnamese Revolution* (Cambridge, MA: Harvard University Press, 1992), 183–185; and Goscha, *Vietnam: A New History*, 130–136.

30. Marie Claire Bergère, *Sun Yat-sen*, trans. Janet Lloyd (Stanford, CA: Stanford University Press, 1998), 373–376; and Sidney Chang and Leonard Gordon, *All under Heaven: Sun Yat-sen and His Revolutionary Thought* (Stanford, CA: Hoover Institution Press, 1991), 110.

31. Tai, *Radicalism*, 42–43; Goscha, *Vietnam: A New History*, 127.

32. Goscha, *Vietnam: A New History*, 137–144; Brett Reilly, "The Origins of the Vietnamese Civil War and the State of Vietnam" (PhD diss., University of Wisconsin, Madison, 2018), 18–23.

33. Zinoman, *Vietnamese Colonial Republican*, 85–130; Reilly, "Origins," 9–59.

34. Eric Jennings, *Vichy in the Tropics: Pétain's National Revolution in Madagascar, Guadeloupe, and Indochina, 1940–1944* (Stanford, CA: Stanford University Press, 2001), 177–187.

35. Reilly, "Origins," 139–141.

36. Goscha, *Vietnam: A New History*, 191. See also Vũ Ngự Chiêu, "The Other Side of the 1945 Vietnamese Revolution: The Empire of Viet-Nam (March-August 1945)," *Journal of Asian Studies* 45, no. 2 (February 1986): 293–328.

37. Goscha, *Vietnam: A New History*, 233–235.

38. Goscha, *Vietnam: A New History*, 200–202, 212–221, 237–248; Reilly, "Origins," 63–65, 84–106, 194–197.

39. Reilly, "Origins," 241–242.

40. Brett Reilly, "The Sovereign States of Vietnam, 1945–1955," *Journal of Vietnamese Studies* 11, no. 3–4 (Summer-Fall 2016): 103–139, reference to 122–123.

41. Phong Thủy, "Ý nghĩa và giá trị cuộc Đại Hội Đoàn Kết ngày 6–9-53," *Xã hội* 8 (September 15, 1953): 2, 35; "Vấn đề độc lập Việt Nam: Quyết nghị," *Thần chung* 1403 (October 17–18, 1953): 1.

42. Dries Deweer, "The Political Theory of Personalism," *International Journal of Philosophy and Theology* 74, no. 2 (2013): 108–126.

43. For an effective and concise rebuttal of this orthodox argument, see Edward Miller, "War Stories: The Taylor-Buzzanco Debate and How We Think about the Vietnam War," *Journal of Vietnamese Studies* 1, no. 1–2 (February/August 2006): 465–466.

44. Young Ick Lew, *The Making of the First Korean President: Syngman Rhee's Quest for Independence 1875–1948* (Honolulu: University of Hawai'i Press, 2014), esp. 1–17.

45. On the Independence Club, see Michael Robinson, *Cultural Nationalism in Colonial Korea, 1920–1925* (Seattle: University of Washington Press, 1988), 24–28.

46. In Soo Kim, *Protestants and the Formation of Modern Korean Nationalism, 1885–1920* (New York: Peter Lang, 1996), 168. See also Kenneth Wells, *New God, New Nation: Protestants and Self-Reconstruction Nationalism in Korea, 1896–1937* (Honolulu: University of Hawai'i Press, 1990); Yi Mahn-yol, "The Birth of the National Spirit of the Christians in the Late Choson Period," trans.

Ch'oe Un-a, in *Korea and Christianity,* ed. Chai-Shin Yu (Seoul: Korean Scholar Press, 1996), 39–72.

47. On the politics involving the elections and creation of the Republic of Korea in the south, see Richard Allen, *Korea's Syngman Rhee: An Unauthorized Portrait* (Rutland, VT: Charles E. Tuttle Company, 1960), 87–100.

48. Pak Chi-Young, *Political Opposition in Korea, 1945–1960* (Seoul: Seoul National University Press, 1980); Ki-shik Hahn, "Underlying Factors in Political Party Organization and Elections," in *Korean Politics in Transition,* ed. Edward Reynolds Wright (Seattle: University of Washington Press, 1975), 85–104; Charles Kim, *Youth for Nation: Culture and Protest in Cold War South Korea* (Honolulu: University of Hawai'i Press, 2017), 109–136; Robert Scigliano, *South Vietnam;* Fall, *The Two Viet-Nams;* Nu-Anh Tran, *Disunion: Anticommunist Nationalism and the Making of the Republic of Vietnam* (Honolulu: University of Hawai'i Press, 2022).

CHAPTER ONE

A Republican Moment in the Study of Modern Vietnam

Peter Zinoman

In two senses, the study of modern Vietnamese history today is in something of a republican moment. It is in the sense that, for the first time, a small but critical mass of scholars is highlighting the significance for Vietnamese political history of a local republican tradition that has roots in both the French colonial encounter and the transnational intellectual networks traversing East, South, and Southeast Asia. Derived originally from an eighteenth-century ideological impulse that animated the revolutions of 1789 and 1848 and infused the political culture of France's Third Republic (1870–1940), republicanism celebrated liberty, equality, and fraternity and promoted democracy, science, education, and the rule of law. In its earliest incarnation, republicanism's most prominent opponents were the twin despotisms of monarchy and organized religion. Later versions of republicanism, especially those prominent in Asia, targeted Western imperialism as an additional archenemy.

Given its partial French pedigree, it is not surprising that early accounts of republicanism in Vietnam focused on European residents in Indochina including moderately progressive attorneys, newspapermen, and officials.[1] More recent studies have explored Vietnamese republicanism in the *quốc ngữ* press of the colonial era and in the ideological leanings of local activists and intellectuals. In this way, what Oliver Wolters might have called the "localization" of the tradition is a defining preoccupation of this republican moment.[2]

A republican moment in the scholarship, in a different sense, may also be discerned in a recent upsurge of interest in the relatively short-lived postcolonial nation-state known as the Republic of Vietnam (RVN). Established as a rival to the communist Democratic Republic of Vietnam (DRV) after the 1954 Geneva Accords, the RVN survived south of the seventeenth parallel for two decades until April 1975. Led by an elite that had been exposed to republican political culture during the late colonial era, the RVN establishment grappled with this tradition even if it did not always respect or honor it. Although depictions of the RVN rightly emphasize its authoritarianism, militarism, and ill-fated relationship with the US, an enduring republican impulse south of the seventeenth parallel may be observed as well. It is there in the machinery of democratic government including elections and legislative politics as well as in critical aspects of civil society such as a private press, independent labor unions, autonomous religious institutions, and student activism. None of these manifestations of republican culture survived in the DRV, and republican norms there were rarely invoked in public after the suppression of the so-called Nhân Văn–Giai Phẩm movement of the late 1950s. In the South, on the other hand, republicanism was present in many incarnations including as a standard against which domestic critics within the RVN appraised their government.

Scholars are now exploring both the Republic of Vietnam and the broader Vietnamese republican political tradition, but the same cannot be said for journalists and popular writers. Indeed, one of the most striking features in the broader discourse on modern Vietnamese history is the stark disconnect between academic and non-academic interpretations of many topics, including this two-headed republican theme.

THE REPUBLICAN TRADITION

The novelty of this theme deserves note before any exploration of its rise and the divergent approach toward it adopted in scholarship and popular discourse. The terms "republic" and "republicanism" do not appear in the indexes of the three most important English-language works of colonial-era Vietnamese intellectual history—Alexander Woodside's *Community and Revolution in Vietnam* (1976), David G. Marr's *Vietnamese Tradition on Trial, 1920–45* (1980), and Hue-Tam Ho Tai's *Radicalism and the Origins of the Vietnamese Revolution* (1992).[3] Nor do they appear as items in the index of standard academic political histories of the late colonial era, such as William Duiker's *The Rise of Nationalism in Vietnam, 1900–1941* (1976) or Huỳnh Kim Khánh's *Vietnamese Communism, 1925–1945* (1980).[4] During the same era, the most important French historians of Vietnam—Bernard Fall, Georges Boudarel, and Pierre Brocheux among them—exhibited a similarly tepid interest in Vietnamese republicanism.[5]

Among the first scholars to look at republicanism in Indochina were historians of the French empire such as J. P. Daughton and Martin Thomas who started to address it in the early 2000s.[6] Cognizant of debates over the link between French republicanism and French imperialism, these scholars explored republican impulses animating the imperial project in French Indochina especially in their interaction with republicanism's traditional enemies: the political right and the Catholic Church.[7] During this era, French scholars worked in a similar vein, analyzing the republican project of reformist colonial officials such as Jean-Marie de Lanessan, Paul Beau, Albert Sarraut, and Alexandre Varenne.[8] The agenda of this new work went against the grain of an older scholarship that treated the ideology of French imperialism in a cruder and more undifferentiated fashion. The older scholarship emphasized overlap between the interests and perspectives of French missionaries and secular French officials; the new scholarship highlighted dissension between the two groups and traced these conflicts to ideological differences that had long divided republicans and their enemies in the Metropole. Although much of this work explored republican impulses expressed by members of colonial Indochina's French political establishment, important studies of local chapters of the Freemasons and the civil rights group, the League of the Rights of Man (Ligue des Droit de l'Homme), by Jacques Dalloz and Daniel Hémery cast an interesting light on manifestations of the republican tradition in mixed-race spaces.[9]

The earliest efforts to explore republican ideas in more exclusively Vietnamese intellectual life in Indochina focused on the patriotic Confucian scholar Phan Châu Trinh and, to a lesser extent, Phan Bội Châu. "Phan Châu Trinh started a reformist movement whose more radical aim was a democratic republic," wrote Joseph Buttinger in 1967.[10] Buttinger adds that Phan Bội Châu abandoned his vision of new monarchy in favor of republicanism too. "Although still dedicated to revolutionary action in 1912, [Phan Bội] Châu had to give in to the now dominant republican trend in the national resistance movement."[11] Despite the provocative implication of this claim—that a republican trend dominated the Vietnamese national movement in the early twentieth century—Buttinger never pursues it. Nor does he examine in any detail the republican content of either scholar's writings.

In 2009, forty-two years later, Vĩnh Sính published the first serious study on this topic in a volume titled *Phan Châu Trinh and his Political Writings*.[12] It located Phan Châu Trinh's republicanism in his strong support for "popular rights (*dân quyền*), democracy (*dân chủ*), and self-rule (*tự trị*)" and in his equally full-throated hostility to monarchy and autocracy. This hostility looms large in Phan Châu Trinh's 1922 "Letter to Emperor Khải Định," which Vĩnh Sính translates in its entirety.

In France at that time, distinguished philosophers such as J. J. Rousseau, Montesquieu, Voltaire and others, one after another rose up to expound their views of popular rights. Within a few decades, the influence of their ideas was felt throughout Europe. . . . Eventually their ideas triumphed and the head of the French King, Louis XVI, was set on top of the guillotine. . . . From that time on, (After the Revolution) France adopted a republican system, with a parliament with legislative power and a governing cabinet responsible to the parliament. At present, the fact that the autocratic monarchy is vanishing in the world, and that mankind thus can enjoy liberty is all thanks to the sanguinary struggle of the French people. Why doesn't Your Majesty make arrangements with the minister of colonial affairs to take a tour of the Palais Bourbon, where you may obtain some notion of the spirit of Liberty, Equality and Fraternity of the people of a Republic? If you will compare it with the gloomy thousand-year tyranny in our country, you will see that the sacred and inviolable ideals of popular rights are like the sun at noon, shining all over the world and leaving no room for autocratic monarchy to survive, let alone a barbaric tyranny.[13]

In a series of important earlier studies, Vĩnh Sính wrote about the transfer of republican concepts to Vietnamese intellectuals from Phan Châu Trinh's generation via Chinese and Japanese reformist writings.[14]

Despite the unmistakable republican language Vĩnh Sính cited, earlier interpretations of Phan Châu Trinh highlighted other influences on his political thought. Both Woodside and Marr emphasized his Confucian orientation and touted his significance as a nationalist more than as a radical republican.[15] They also dwelled on his pacifism and his reformism, familiar preoccupations of Vietnamese communist scholarship.[16] Where Phan Châu Trinh's republican instincts were most apparent, according to this earlier scholarship, was in his contempt for the Vietnamese monarchy and his call for its abolition. To be fair, Marr also mentioned Phan Châu Trinh's rhetorical commitment to "the high ideals of the French Revolution" but never used the term "republican" to describe him.[17]

The Vĩnh Sính volume from 2009 was followed by three books that both used the term and dwelled on the significance of the republican tradition in colonial Vietnam. The first, by Philippe Peycam, started as a doctoral dissertation at the School of Oriental and African Studies supervised by the late great Ralph Smith.[18] A history of southern Vietnamese newspapers during the 1920s, it was published in 2012 as *The Birth of Vietnamese Political Journalism: Saigon, 1916–1930*.[19] In a chapter titled "French Republicanism and the Emergence of Saigon's Public Sphere," the book argues for the great impact of republicanism on Vietnamese political culture during the era.

Colonial France had introduced republicanism into southern Vietnam under the pretext that its model of universalism would create a modern society in a backward colony. The colonial state did not anticipate a growing number of "natives"—mainly from the newly established urban bourgeoise—who would embrace Western modernity and the French republican message for the purposes of creating a modern local political culture on their own terms.[20]

Along with several other central claims, Peycam's book demonstrates the wide range of southern Vietnamese intellectuals whose political agenda might be characterized, in some form or another, as republican.

Just two years later, in 2014, I released a monograph on the Hanoi writer Vũ Trọng Phụng titled *Vietnamese Colonial Republican: The Political Vision of Vũ Trọng Phụng*.[21] In it, I argue that Vietnam's greatest modern writer expressed a strong republican vision even if his preferred forms of expression—fiction and first-person reportage—discouraged him from releasing a manifesto on the topic. What I call a "late republican vision" in Vũ Trọng Phụng's writing may be discerned in his opposition to unbridled capitalism, in his disapproval of communist despotism, in his sympathy for the underdog, and in his strong advocacy for science, education, freedom of expression, the rule of law, and the welfare state. The label also fits because his literary heroes—Victor Hugo and Émile Zola—were giants of literary republicanism. Although I do not develop the point systematically, I point out that many elements of Vũ Trọng Phụng's republican sensibility were shared by friends and colleagues—writers such as Phan Khôi, Lan Khai, and Ngô Tất Tố—who also wrote for Tân Dân Publishing House. Like these celebrated and popular figures, Vũ Trọng Phụng was an influencer and perhaps even a barometer whose writing tracked changes in certain sectors of public opinion. I also argue that the posthumous late-1950s promotion of Vũ Trọng Phụng by members of the Nhân Văn–Giai Phẩm group might reveal the persistence of this tradition among a subsection of postcolonial DRV intellectuals. In 2021, Martina Thucnhi Nguyen published an important book that drew attention to a "significant overlap" between Vũ Trọng Phụng's republican vision and the project of the hugely influential Self-Strength Literary Group.[22]

The third recent volume to foreground the role of republicanism in modern Vietnamese history is Christopher Goscha's *The Penguin History of Modern Vietnam,* published in 2017.[23] The theme is introduced in early chapters that link the late nineteenth-century imperial conquest to the rise to power in France of fervently republican politicians such as Jules Ferry. These chapters also locate a republican impulse in the efforts of ambitious colonial officials such as Paul Doumer and Albert Sarraut to strengthen and centralize the colonial state and to reform (in a moderately progressive direction) colonial policy and practice. Following Vĩnh Sính, Goscha takes pains to identify parallel Asian sources of Vietnamese republicanism, including the writing of Chinese and Japanese reformists around the turn of the century and the model provided by the Indian National Congress in the 1920s.[24]

The localization of the republican tradition is the subject of chapter 5, titled "The Failure of Colonial Republicanism Vietnam," in which Goscha highlights Phan Châu Trinh's support for republican ideals such as "the rights of man" and "representative government."[25] Pursuing the theme, Goscha refers to Phan Châu Trinh's 1907 open letter to Paul Beau as a Vietnamese "J'Accuse"—invoking Émile Zola's famous declaration on the Dreyfus Affair, a quintessential expression of early twentieth-century republican values. Goscha makes the provocative point that Hồ Chí Minh's famous "Claims of the Vietnamese People" ("Revendications du peuple annamite")—sent to the American secretary of state at the Paris peace talks of 1919—focused on republican reforms, not communism or independence. After World War I, a local republicanism was energized, reaching its peak with the program of Governor-General Sarraut that included enhanced support for education, democracy, state centralization, judicial reform, anticorruption, and the vernacular-language press. Sarraut's reforms found support among reform-minded Vietnamese, who Goscha argues "bet on colonial republicanism"—Nguyễn Văn Vĩnh, Bùi Quang Chiêu, Nguyễn Phú Khai, and Huỳnh Thúc Kháng. Moving into the 1920s, Goscha describes a strain of republican reformism focused on achieving political representation for a new bourgeois class led by Dương Văn Giáo, Nguyễn Phan Long, and Bùi Quang Chiêu. The appearance of "the most prominent (Vietnamese) republican"—the brilliant journalist and political activist Nguyễn An Ninh—reflected the growth of a new strain of youth-oriented radical republicanism also associated with Nguyễn Thái Học and the militant Việt Nam Quốc Dân Đảng. Goscha sees France's mistreatment of the constitutionalists as foolish repression of a moderate republicanism that, if left alone, could have evolved in the noncommunist direction that India's Congress Party did. But France's heavy-handed overreaction left bourgeois republicanism in a "stillborn state," inadvertently providing a boost to the local Stalinists.

It is striking how large republicanism looms in Goscha's understanding of the political dynamics of the colonial era relative to previous general histories of the country.[26] Because Goscha's authoritative text will likely remain the standard historical survey for the foreseeable future, his engagement with republicanism may encourage further interest in the topic. The belatedness of this development, however, raises an obvious question: Why has Vietnamese republicanism only become an object of study in the last decade?

Three reasons are worth considering. One is that few colonial-era Vietnamese self-identified as followers of *chủ nghĩa cộng hòa,* the most common term for *républicanisme* according to Đào Duy Anh's respected 1931 dictionary. Perhaps because of its earlier association with imperial expansion, the term was never embraced by Vietnamese activists in the same spirit as communist, socialist, anarchist, Stalinist, Trotskyist, constitutionalist, or nationalist (all terms by which people referred to themselves during the era). Proponents of the significance of colonial republicanism (such as myself) must therefore acknowledge questions raised about this thesis by the relative obscurity of the term during the era.

A second reason for the neglect of republicanism is the impact of the Vietnam War on the scholarship. During the conflict, left-leaning antiwar proponents of what became the orthodox school disparaged the shallow ideologies of noncommunist political alternatives. Relative to Hồ Chí Minh's movement with its Marxist clarity, the political ideology of both his colonial-era rivals and successive postcolonial RVN regimes was hopelessly murky and reactionary. When a noncommunist political orientation was apparent, as true of constitutionalism during the interwar era or the personalism of the late 1950s and early 1960s, orthodox scholars tended to belittle them as inauthentic, incoherent, and ineffectual. The DRV had an ideology, according to orthodox scholars, but the RVN did not unless a slavishly pro-American anticommunism qualifies as such. For orthodox scholars, the superficiality of ideology in the RVN damaged its political legitimacy especially relative to its communist rival to the north. To the extent that orthodox scholars characterized RVN regimes ideologically, they relied on negative labels such as authoritarianism, militarism, or even fascism. In this context, a political orientation such as republicanism featured too many positive connotations to be useful to the budding orthodox school that crafted its historical arguments with an eye toward their potential utility in the rhetorical conflict over the war.

This idea leads to a third reason for the recent rise of interest in the topic: a generational shift among scholars toward a postwar perspective on national history. It is probably no coincidence that the three scholars who have pushed the republican theme the hardest—Peycam, Goscha, and myself—are all in our fifties and were children when the Vietnam War came to an end. As a result, the only Vietnam that we know personally is the authoritarian and repressive Socialist Republic. Rather than knocking the ideas of noncommunist nationalists, we are—like many local intellectuals and democracy advocates—more invested in puncturing the myths of communist historiography and exploring political "roads not taken" during what is often presented as the inevitable rise to dominance of Hồ Chí Minh's communists.

Although a local republican tradition has started to loom large in academic histories of modern Vietnam, it has yet to make a dent in more popular discourse about the country's past. Perhaps the best example is the hugely influential documentary by Ken Burns and Lynn Novick, *The Vietnam War,* which totally ignores the tradition in its treatment of the colonial origins of the conflict. Instead, as I explain in greater detail elsewhere, Burns and Novick advance the thoroughly misleading thesis that Hồ Chí Minh's Communist Party was the only serious anticolonial force in the country prior to World War II.[27] This argument allows the filmmakers to highlight a loaded contrast between the durable and authentic nationalist-communist tradition embodied by the DRV and the thin pseudo-nationalism of the RVN, a spurious political tradition hastily improvised by American cold warriors and their local clients. But, like Hồ Chí Minh, Ngô Đình Diệm and his successors were also the legatees of older local political traditions such as colonial republicanism and anticommunist nationalism. This insight is overlooked in the Burns-Novick documentary, which treats the RVN as an American puppet devoid of local roots or history before the Cold War. By failing to acknowledge the colonial-era history of republican nationalism, the documentary gives the false impression that the RVN was less rooted in the Vietnamese historical experience than the communist DRV and therefore was less of a legitimate political force.

THE REPUBLIC OF VIETNAM

In contrast to the scholarship on Vietnamese republicanism, which appeared only in the past decade, writing on the southern Republic of Vietnam has been around for several generations. What is relatively new, however, is a recent break in the discourse on the RVN, from a harshly negative assessment that first emerged during the 1960s to a more complex and evenhanded view that dates from the 1990s and early 2000s. During the war, the most influential renderings of the RVN were disparaging depictions by antiwar journalists and academics such as Frances Fitzgerald, David Halberstam, and George Kahin.[28] The RVN inspired similar vitriol among the first generation of postwar historians, whether liberals George Herring and Neil Sheehan or radicals Marilyn Young and Gabriel Kolko.[29] For both liberals and radicals, the Republic of Vietnam was a puppet of the United States created to stem the spread of communism in Asia. The RVN political leadership was nepotistic and authoritarian, the elite was venal and corrupt, and the military was cowardly and incompetent. The RVN also paid a price for its ideological incoherence. The American presence dampened nationalist sentiment and damaged popular support for the state's anticommunism, which was viewed as an inauthentic foreign import. The culture and society of the RVN also received rough treatment in portrayals that emphasized the growth of prostitution, crime, drug abuse, and social inequality in the cities and clumsy security initiatives and flawed nation-building programs in the countryside.

The problem with these negative representations of the RVN is not that they are wholly untrue. It is instead that they tell only part of the story. They ignore the country's competitive political culture, its freewheeling civil society, its interesting intellectual and cultural life, and the anti-totalitarian idealism of many of its supporters. They also disregard the relationship between many of the most illiberal features of the RVN and the ruthless, externally supported guerilla movement arrayed violently against it. It is difficult to protect civil liberties when fighting a brutal insurgency.

What then explains the sharply negative depiction of the RVN that crystallized during this period? Several things.

One was a deep disapproval on the part of many scholars and journalists of the American intervention, and a related tendency to romanticize America's enemy and disparage its ally. For observers whose main objective was to hasten an American withdrawal, this tendency made practical sense. A second factor is that the RVN was largely open to foreign researchers during the era. These outside observers were able to view up close the many ugly aspects of a poor postcolonial society mobilized for civil war. Because the DRV at the time was almost completely off-limits to foreigners (outside the diplomatic corps, fellow travelers, and Chinese workers and advisers), it avoided a similar level of scrutiny. Finally, portrayals of the RVN produced after the war were undoubtedly shaped by the defeat and, ultimately, disappearance of the country as an independent geopolitical entity. Preoccupied with these two massive blots on the RVN's historical record, it is not surprising that scholars during the immediate postwar era fixated on the roots of these dramatic failures.

The past several decades have witnessed the emergence of a revisionist scholarship on the RVN. An early example is Neil Jamieson's 1993 study *Understanding Vietnam,* which featured an idiosyncratic and sympathetic ethnography of South Vietnamese culture and society during the war.[30] A turning point in the scholarship came with Philip Catton's *Diem's Final Failure,* published in 2002, which kicked off an important collective effort to revise the reputation of Ngô Đình Diệm and the government he led between 1954 and 1963.[31] Although not uncritical of its subject, Catton's book emphasized the ideological autonomy of the Ngô Đình Diệm regime and its deeply troubled relationship with the United States. For Catton, Ngô Đình Diệm was nobody's puppet. Catton argued for the coherence of Ngô Đình Diệm's political project, the roots of which he located in a domestic anticommunist, nationalist tradition and a progressive social Catholicism. Numerous scholars followed in Catton's footsteps in pursuit of new perspectives on the Ngô Đình Diệm decade.[32] Interesting revisionist approaches to the RVN under Ngô Đình Diệm's successors have also been published.[33] Less dismissive accounts of the Southern Vietnamese army include those by Robert Brigham, Nathalie Huynh Chau Nguyen, and Andrew Wiest.[34] In addition, a growing number of scholars have studied the rich literature, music, and intellectual life of the RVN.[35]

THE RVN IN *THE SYMPATHIZER*

Although revisionist interpretations of the RVN are ascendant in the scholarly literature, the same cannot be said for accounts of the war intended for broad public consumption. This is the same dynamic we saw with the discourse on republicanism—rising in the scholarship but absent in popular accounts. A good example is Viet Thanh Nguyen's novel *The Sympathizer,* first published by Grove Press in 2015.[36] It is safe to assume that many more people will read the novel than all the writing of all the new scholars of the Republic of Vietnam combined. A *New York Times* best-seller, the novel has won eight literary awards to date, including the 2016 Pulitzer Prize for Fiction. Based on the success of the novel, Viet Thanh Nguyen won a MacArthur Foundation Fellowship and a Guggenheim Award in 2017. Acclaim for the novel has granted him a large public platform that includes regular space on the op-ed pages of the *New York Times* and *Time Magazine.* Although he addresses many topics in his role as a public intellectual, the Vietnam War and its legacy and representation remain persistent areas of interest. They sit at the center of his nonfiction *Nothing Ever Dies: Vietnam and the Memory of War,* published by Harvard University Press in 2016.[37] They are also central themes of *The Sympathizer,* which opens in Saigon right before its fall to communist forces and follows a cast of largely Vietnamese characters involved in the war and its contentious aftermath.

So, how does *The Sympathizer* portray the Republic of Vietnam?

The question is tricky for two reasons. First, everything presented in the novel is filtered through the voice and consciousness of its anonymous narrator, a Franco-Vietnamese, double-agent loyal to the communists, who infiltrates South Vietnamese society and later the Vietnamese diasporic community in California. It could be argued, therefore, that everything in the book should be read as the view of its main character, not its author. Second, the narrative of the novel is revealed to be part of an elaborate confession that the narrator must produce while incarcerated by communist security forces. Thus it could be argued that the narrator's treatment of the RVN reflects what he believes his communist interrogators want to hear. On the other hand, it also feels significant that the narrator of *The Sympathizer* is relatively vague as a specific character and that he expounds in the text on a dizzying range of erudite concerns that more recall a college professor than a spy. (Would a spy muse this much on the "politics of representation"?) Moreover, although the revelation that the entire narrative is a forced confession may muddy the message the novel delivers, my sense is that it (however implausible) will not diminish the strong general impression about the nature of the RVN. Because the narrator's account is the only one offered at any length, it endows the novel with a general point-of-view that shapes public understanding.[38]

In general, the depiction of the RVN in *The Sympathizer* tracks closely with the views of the orthodox school. "Our politicians managed the shabby comic operetta of our country," the narrator opines, "an off-key travesty starring plump divas in white suits and mustachioed prima donnas in custom tailored military uniforms."[39] The highest-ranking RVN official in the novel, the General, is depicted as slavishly devoted to France and the United States: "a man who had faith in [both] the *mission civilisatrice and* the American Way" (emphasis added).[40] Further underlying his "compradore" character, the General's opposition to communism is borrowed from abroad. It was "at Fort Benning in '58, where Green Berets inoculated him permanently against communism."[41] The narrator sees the real-life President Ngô Đình Diệm in a similar vein, as a creature of foreign interests, referring to him as "an American puppet" who thought he was president.[42] A devotion to foreigners defines ordinary citizens as well: "The atmosphere was strangely quiet in Saigon," the narrator explains, describing the city on the eve of its fall:

> Most of the Saigonese citizenry behaving like people in a scuppered marriage, willing to cling gamely to each other and drown so long as nobody declared the adulterous truth. The truth in this case was that at least a million people were working or had worked for the Americans in one capacity or another from shining their shoes to running the army designed by the Americans in their own image to performing fellatio on them for the price, in Peoria or Poughkeepsie, of a hamburger.[43]

After its fidelity to outsiders, the most prominent feature of the RVN in the novel is its corruption. "Our society had been a kleptocracy of the highest order," the narrator explains, "the government doing its best to steal from the Americans, the average man doing his best to steal from the government, the worst of us doing our best to steal from each other."[44] The Army of the Republic of Vietnam (ARVN) is depicted as equally corrupt and venal, qualities that come to the fore when the narrator offers a handful of junior officers precious plane tickets out of the doomed city:

> I summoned the five chosen officers for a very private meeting, one by one. We leave tonight? asked the very nervous colonel, his eyes big and wet. Yes. My parents? The parents of my wife? asked the major, a crapulent devotee of the Chinese restaurants in Cholon. No. Brothers, sisters, nieces and nephews? No. Housekeepers and nannies? No. Suitcases, wardrobes, collections of china? No. The captain, who hobbled a bit because of venereal disease, threatened to commit suicide unless I found more seats. I offered him my revolver and he skulked off. In contrast, the young lieutenants were grateful. Having earned their precious positions via parental connections, they bore themselves with the herky-jerky nervousness of marionettes.[45]

The absence of even a shred of empathy in this portrayal is remarkable. As their entire world crumbles around them, ARVN officers portrayed as either teary-eyed, infected with venereal disease, or gluttonous, obsess over the fate of their china collections and their servants.

Worse than its corruption is ARVN's strangely violent posture toward its own people. Describing the fall of central Vietnam, the narrator says, "We could not believe that Da Nang and Nha Trang had fallen, or that our troops had shot civilians in the back as they all fought madly to escape on boats and barges."[46] Later he describes South Vietnamese boat refugees being "robbed and raped by their own soldiers."[47] He also bemoans the RVN military's penchant for domestic political violence: "Our air force had bombed the presidential palace, our army had shot and stabbed to death our first president and his brother, and our bickering generals had fomented more coups d'etat than I could count."[48]

The novel's depiction of women and gender relations follows orthodox tropes as well. As in many Hollywood Vietnam movies, the only female characters in the Saigon chapters are the corrupt wives of corrupt officials and prostitutes. A glimpse of "a covey of call girls, vacuum-packed into micro-miniskirts and fishnet stockings" named Mimi, Phi Phi, and Ti Ti prompts an extended digression on this familiar topic. "Most were poor, illiterate country girls," the narrator explains, "with no means of making a living except to live as ticks on the fur of the nineteen-year old American GI."[49] Although this depiction is familiar to audiences of *Full Metal Jacket,* it is not supported in recent scholarship on the history of Vietnamese sex work by social scientists.[50] The brilliant oral histories carried out by Mai Lan Gustaffson, in particular, portray sex workers as far more sophisticated and ambivalent historical agents than the broad (and frankly, tired) stereotypes found in *The Sympathizer.*

Also, as in many Hollywood movies, the novel features graphic sexual violence that includes two gang rapes, one committed against a female communist agent by RVN policemen and another committed by communist guerillas on a young southern woman. Differences in the portrayal of these episodes reveal the novel's orthodox take on the relative capacity for depravity of each side in the civil war. The rape perpetrated by the communists occurs as part of an *Apocalypse Now*–style movie that occupies a big middle section of the narrative. Hence it is not a real rape. It is a simulated rape, devised by "the Auteur" as a piece of heavy-handed anticommunist propaganda. The narrator describes the scene briefly and figuratively as a writhing "human octopus."[51] On the other hand, the rape perpetrated by the RVN policemen really happens and is genuinely shocking both in the detail in which it is portrayed and in the depth of its moral depravity. Supervised by American advisers, three RVN policemen take turns having violent forced intercourse with a female communist agent. The novel details each assault including a final, especially horrific one in which the perpetrator penetrates the agent with a shaken-up long-necked bottle of soda.

It is striking how much of *The Sympathizer*'s portrait of war-era Saigon resembles orthodox American accounts. Corrupt, bickering, incompetent, puppets of foreign influence, the RVN elite receives rough treatment in the novel.

The Sympathizer thematizes few of the important insights from the new scholarship concerning the complexity of South Vietnamese politics and the richness of Saigon's cultural and intellectual life. It pays less attention to the communist side but its few communist characters, the Watchman and the female prisoner, are cast in a rare heroic light. It offers no heroes on the Southern side. Nor do many characters transcend the stereotypes (brassy prostitutes, cowardly generals, and corrupt officials) found in orthodox English-language representations.

What is striking is the overlap between Burns and Novick and Viet Thanh Nguyen in their stubborn fidelity to a dated, politically driven vision of the war and the RVN. What is unfortunate is the huge reach of their influence relative to the scholarship.

So, what is to be done here? Alas, I do not have a good answer.

Again, the basic problem is that advances in the scholarship are not trickling down into the broader public discourse. The Vietnam War is not the only historical issue marked by this kind of interpretive bifurcation; it may, however, be an extreme example. One thing worth noting is that the evolution over time of the scholarship on republicanism and the Republic of Vietnam should make us guardedly optimistic. It shows that change is possible even though it may come slowly and fitfully, in a kind of one-step forward and two-steps backward rhythm.

In the scholarly discourse, a changed view of republicanism and the RVN came into focus because of the efforts of two kinds of scholars—those who put their heads down and produced revisionist research and those who attacked, sometimes quite forcefully, the old paradigm through reviews and historiographical polemics. New scholarly insights about republicanism and the Republic of Vietnam can be infused into the public discourse, I think, in the same way, through a combination of public-facing research and creative advocacy. Fortunately, we already have interesting examples of both tactics. As forms of popularizing research, we have Alex Thai Vo's innovative web-based oral histories and Olga Dror's translation of southern Vietnamese fiction.[52] Examples of advocacy are weaker, as evidenced by the relatively muted response to the political distortions of both the Burns film and *The Sympathizer*. But scholars such as Keith Taylor, Alec Holcombe, and Haydon Cherry have already provided excellent examples of aggressive reviewing and critical historiographical analysis.[53] By building on this existing tradition, I am hopeful that those carrying out cutting edge scholarship can influence broader perceptions of these critical historical questions.

NOTES

1. See, for example, Walter Langlois, *André Malraux: The Indochina Adventure* (New York: Frederick A. Praeger, 1966).

2. O. W. Wolters, *History, Culture and Region in Southeast Asian Perspectives,* rev. ed. (Ithaca, NY: Cornell University Southeast Asia Program, 1999).

3. Alexander Woodside, *Community and Revolution in Modern Vietnam* (Boston, MA: Houghton Mifflin, 1976); David Marr, *Vietnamese Tradition on Trial: 1920–1945* (Berkeley: University of California Press, 1980); and Hue-Tam Ho Tai, *Radicalism and the Origins of the Vietnamese Revolution* (Cambridge, MA: Harvard University Press, 1992).

4. William Duiker, *The Rise of Nationalism in Vietnam, 1900–1941* (Ithaca, NY: Cornell University Press, 1976); and Huỳnh Kim Khánh, *Vietnamese Communism, 1925–1945* (Ithaca, NY: Cornell University Press, 1982).

5. Bernard Fall, *The Two Viet-Nams: A Political and Military Analysis,* 2nd rev. ed. (New York: Frederick A. Praeger, 1967); Georges Boudarel and Nguyễn Văn Ký, *Hanoi: City of the Rising Dragon* (Lanham, MD: Rowman & Littlefield, 2002); and Pierre Brocheux, *The Mekong Delta: Ecology, Economy and Revolution, 1860–1960* (Madison: University of Wisconsin Center for Southeast Asian Studies, 1995).

6. J. P. Daughton, *An Empire Divided: Religion, Republicanism, and the Making of French Colonialism, 1880–1914* (Oxford: Oxford University Press, 2006); and Martin Thomas, "Albert Sarraut, French Colonial Development and the Communist Threat," *Journal of Modern History* 77, no. 4 (2005): 917–955.

7. Alice Conklin, *A Mission to Civilize: The Republican Idea of Empire in France and West Africa, 1895–1930* (Stanford, CA: Stanford University Press, 1997); and Gary Wilder, *The French Imperial Nation-State: Negritude and Colonial Humanism Between the Two World Wars* (Chicago: University of Chicago Press, 2005).

8. Gilles de Gantès, "Protectorate, Association, Reformism: The Roots of the Popular Front's Republican Policy in Indochina," in *French Colonial Empire and the Popular Front: Hope and Disillusion,* ed. Tony Chafur and Amanda Sackur (New York: St. Martin's Press, 1999), 109–131; Daniel Hémery, "En Indochine francaise, reformisme colonial et *nationalisme* vietnamien au XXe siècle: La sarrautisme at ses avatars," *Études indochinoises* 3, no. 25 (1993): 109–135; and Agathe Larcher-Goscha, "La légitimation française en Indochina: Mythes et réalités de la 'collaboration franco-vietnamienne' et du réformisme colonial, 1905–1945" (PhD diss., Université de Paris VII, 2000).

9. Jacques Dalloz, "Les vietnamiens dans la franc-maçonnerie colonial," *Revue française d'histoire d'outre-mer* 85, no. 320 (1998): 103–118; and Daniel Hémery, "L'Indochine, les droits humains, 1899–1954: Entre colonisateurs et colonisés, la Ligue des droits de l'homme," *Revue francaise d'histoire d'Outre-mers* 88, no. 330–331 (January 2001): 223–239.

10. Joseph Buttinger, *Vietnam: A Dragon Embattled,* vol. 1, *From Colonialism to the Vietminh* (New York: Frederick A. Praeger, 1967), 151.

11. Buttinger, *Vietnam: A Dragon Embattled,* 151.

12. Vĩnh Sính, ed. and trans., *Phan Châu Trinh and His Political Writings* (Ithaca, NY: Cornell University Southeast Asia Program, 2009).

13. Vĩnh Sính, *Phan Châu Trinh,* 99.

14. Vĩnh Sính, "Chinese Characters as the Medium for Transmitting the Vocabulary of Modernization from Japan to Vietnam in the early Twentieth Century," *Asian Pacific Quarterly* (October 1993): 1–16; and Vĩnh Sính, "Phan Bội Châu and Fukuzawa Yukichi: Perceptions of National Independence," in *Phan Bội Châu and the Đông-Du Movement,* ed. Vĩnh Sính, Lạc Việt Series no. 8 (Yale Center for International and Area Studies, Council on Southeast Asia Studies, 1988), 101–149.

15. For Marr's most extensive treatment of Phan Châu Trinh's political vision, see David Marr, *Vietnamese Anticolonialism, 1885–1925* (Berkeley: University of California Press, 1971), 156–184; and Alexander Woodside, *Community and Revolution in Modern Vietnam* (Boston, MA: Houghton Mifflin, 1976), 36–43.

16. Tôn Quang Phiệt, *Phan Bội Châu và Phan Chu Trinh* (Hanoi: Nhà Xuất Bản Ban Nghiên Cứu Văn Sử Địa, 1956).

17. Marr, *Vietnamese Anticolonialism*, 162.

18. Philippe Peycam, "Intellectuals and Political Commitment in Vietnam: The Emergence of a Public Sphere in Colonial Vietnam, 1916–1928" (PhD diss., School of Oriental and African Studies, 1999).

19. Philippe Peycam, *The Birth of Vietnamese Political Journalism: Saigon, 1916–1930* (New York: Columbia University Press, 2012).

20. Peycam, *Birth of Vietnamese Political Journalism*, 67.

21. Peter Zinoman, *Vietnamese Colonial Republican: The Political Vision of Vũ Trọng Phụng* (Berkeley: University of California Press, 2014).

22. Martina Thucnhi Nguyen, *On Our Own Strength: The Self-Reliant Literary Group and Cosmopolitan Nationalism in Late Colonial Vietnam* (Honolulu: University of Hawai'i Press, 2021), 12.

23. Christopher Goscha, *The Penguin History of Modern Vietnam* (London: Penguin Books, 2017).

24. Here he relies heavily on Agathe Larcher-Goscha's illuminating "Bùi Quang Chiêu in Calcutta (1928): The Broken Mirror of Vietnamese and Indian Nationalism," *Journal of Vietnamese Studies* 9, no. 4 (Fall 2014): 67–114.

25. Goscha, *Penguin History*, 127–156.

26. Gosha provides a more expansive version of this argument in an earlier article. See Christopher Goscha, "Aux origines du républicanisme vietnamien: Circulations mondiales et connexions colonials," *Vingtième siècle* 131 (July-September 2016): 17–35.

27. Peter Zinoman, "The Vietnam War and the History of the Vietnam War," review of *The Vietnam War*, directed by Ken Burns and Lynn Novick, *H-Diplo Roundtable Review* 21, no. 3 (September 13, 2019): 21–31.

28. Frances Fitzgerald, *Fire in the Lake: The Vietnamese and the Americans in Vietnam* (New York: Vintage Books, 1972); David Halberstam, *The Making of a Quagmire* (New York: Random House, 1965); and George Kahin and John Lewis, *The United States in Vietnam* (New York: Dial Press, 1967).

29. George Herring, *America's Longest War: The United States and Vietnam, 1950–1975* (New York: Wiley, 1979); Gabriel Kolko, *Anatomy of a War: Vietnam, the United States and the Modern Historical Experience* (New York: Pantheon, 1985); Neil Sheehan, *A Bright Shining Lie: John Paul Vann and America in Vietnam* (New York: Random House, 1988); and Marilyn Young, *The Vietnam Wars, 1945–1990* (New York: Harper Perennial, 1991).

30. Neil Jamieson, *Understanding Vietnam* (Berkeley: University of California Press, 1993).

31. Philip Catton, *Diem's Final Failure: Prelude to America's War in Vietnam* (Lawrence: University Press of Kansas, 2003).

32. Jessica Chapman, *Cauldron of Resistance: Ngo Dinh Diem, the United States, and 1950s Southern Vietnam* (Ithaca, NY: Cornell University Press, 2013); Olga Dror, *Making Two Vietnams: War and Youth Identities, 1965–1975* (Cambridge: Cambridge University Press, 2018); Jessica Elkind, *Aid under Fire: Nation Building and the Vietnam War* (Lexington: University of Kentucky Press, 2016); Tuan Hoang "Ideology in Urban South Vietnam, 1950–1975" (PhD diss., University of Notre Dame, 2013); Kevin Li, "Partisan to Sovereign: The Making of the Bình Xuyên in Southern Vietnam, 1945–1948," *Journal of Vietnamese Studies* 11 no. 3–4 (summer-fall 2016): 140–187; Edward Miller, *Misalliance: Ngo Dinh Diem, the United States, and the Fate of South Vietnam* (Cambridge, MA: Harvard University Press, 2013); Jason Picard, "Fragmented Loyalties: The Great Migration's Impact on South Vietnam, 1954–1963" (PhD diss., University of California, Berkeley, 2014); Geoffrey Stewart, *Vietnam's Lost Revolution: Ngo Dinh Diem's Failure to Build an Independent Nation, 1955–1963* (Cambridge: Cambridge University Press, 2017); Stan Tan, "'Swiddens, Resettlements, Sedentarizations, and Villages': State Formation among the Central

Highlanders of Vietnam under the First Republic, 1955–1961," *Journal of Vietnamese Studies* 1, no. 1–2 (February/August 2006): 210–252; Mitchell Tan, "Spiritual Fraternities: The Transnational Networks of Ngô Đình Diệm's Personalist Revolution and the Republic, 1955–1963," *Journal of Vietnamese Studies* 14, no. 2 (Spring 2019): 1–67; and Nu-Anh Tran, "South Vietnamese Identity, American Intervention, and the Newspaper *Chính Luận* [Political Discussion], 1965–1969," *Journal of Vietnamese Studies* 1, no. 1–2 (February/August 2006): 169–209.

33. Sean Fear, "The Ambitious Legacy of Ngô Đình Diệm in South Vietnam's Second Republic, 1967–1975," *Journal of Vietnamese Studies* 11, no. 1 (Winter 2016): 1–75; Van Nguyen-Marshall, "Student Activism in Time of War: Youth in the Republic of Vietnam, 1960s-1970s," *Journal of Vietnamese Studies* 10, no. 2 (Spring 2015): 43–81; Lien-Hang Nguyen, "Cold War Contradictions: Towards an International History of the Second Indochina War, 1969–1973," in *Making Sense of the Vietnam War: Local, National and Transnational Perspectives,* ed. Mark Philip Bradley and Marilyn B. Young (Oxford: Oxford University Press, 2008), 219–250; Keith Taylor, ed., *Voices from the Second Republic, 1967–1975* (Ithaca, NY: Cornell University Southeast Asia Program, 2014); and George Veith, *Black April: The Fall of South Vietnam, 1973–1975* (New York: Encounter Books, 2013).

34. Robert Brigham, *ARVN: Life and Death in the South Vietnamese Army* (Lawrence: University Press of Kansas; 2006); Nathalie Huynh Chau Nguyen, *South Vietnamese Soldiers: Memories of the Vietnam War and After* (Santa Barbara, CA: Praeger, 2016); and Andrew Wiest, *Vietnam's Forgotten Army: Heroism and Betrayal in the ARVN* (New York: New York University Press, 2008).

35. Jason Gibbs, "Songs of Sympathy in Time of War: Commercial Music in the Republic of Vietnam" in *Republican Vietnam, 1963–1975: War, Society, Diaspora,* ed. Trinh Luu and Tuong Vu (Honolulu: University of Hawai'i Press, forthcoming); Nguyễn-Võ Thu Hương, "Life after Material Death in South Vietnamese and Diasporic Works of Fiction," *Journal of Vietnamese Studies* 3, no. 1 (Winter 2008): 1–35; Trinh Luu, "Vietism: Human Rights, Carl Jung, and the New Vietnamese" in *Republican Vietnam, 1963-1975: War, Society, Diaspora,* ed. Trinh Luu and Tuong Vu (Honolulu: University of Hawai'i Press, forthcoming); and John Shafer, *Võ Phiến and the Sadness of Exile* (Dekalb: Northern Illinois University Center for Southeast Asian Studies, 2006).

36. Viet Thanh Nguyen, *The Sympathizer* (New York: Grove Press, 2015).

37. Viet Thanh Nguyen, *Nothing Ever Dies: Vietnam and the Memory of War* (Cambridge, MA: Harvard University Press, 2016).

38. I thank Hao Jun Tam for sharing with me his thoughts on this matter.

39. Viet Thanh Nguyen, *The Sympathizer,* 23.

40. Nguyen, *The Sympathizer,* 3.

41. Nguyen, *The Sympathizer,* 11.

42. Nguyen, *The Sympathizer,* 44.

43. Nguyen, *The Sympathizer,* 7.

44. Nguyen, *The Sympathizer,* 85.

45. Nguyen, *The Sympathizer,* 12.

46. Nguyen, *The Sympathizer,* 3.

47. Nguyen, *The Sympathizer,* 3.

48. Nguyen, *The Sympathizer,* 24.

49. Nguyen, *The Sympathizer,* 36.

50. Kimberly Kay Hoang, *Dealing in Desire: Asian Ascendancy, Western Decline, and the Hidden Currencies of Global Sex Work* (Berkeley: University of California Press, 2015); and Mai Lan Gustafsson, "'Freedom. Money. Fun. Love': The Warlore of Vietnamese Bargirls," *Oral History Review* 38, no. 2 (2011): 308–330.

51. Nguyen, *The Sympathizer,* 275.

52. Nhã Ca, *Mourning Headband for Hue,* trans. Olga Dror (Bloomington: University of Indiana Press, 2014).

53. Keith Taylor, "Robert Buzzanco's 'Fear and (Self) Loathing in Lubbock,'" *Journal of Vietnamese Studies* 1, no. 1–2 (February/August 2006): 436–452; Alec Holcombe, "The Role of the Communist Party in the Vietnamese Revolution: A Review of David Marr's *Vietnam: State, War and Revolution, 1945–1946*," *Journal of Vietnamese Studies* 11, no. 3–4 (Summer-Fall 2016): 298–364; and Haydon Cherry, review of *Nothing Ever Dies: Vietnam and the Memory of War*, by Viet Thanh Nguyen, *Journal of Southeast Asian Studies* 49, no. 1 (February 2018): 177–179.

CHAPTER TWO

Early Republicans' Concept of the Nation

Trần Trọng Kim and Việt Nam sử lược

Nguyễn Lương Hải Khôi

In the early twentieth century, as republican ideas spread to French Indochina through the writings of Japanese and Chinese intellectuals, a modern understanding of history was born in Vietnam. This chapter analyzes Trần Trọng Kim's best-known work, *A Brief History of Vietnam* (*Việt Nam sử lược,* or *VNSL*), published in 1930, to explore the perceptions of Vietnamese republicans in the early twentieth century. For much of the remaining century, this work was profoundly influential for generations of Vietnamese yet it has never been the subject of serious study. Mindful of space constraints, this chapter focuses only on the core elements of the early republican nationalist view of Vietnamese history as conveyed in the book. This view was fundamentally different from the perceptions of history both by historians of the royal court in previous eras and by communist historians from the 1950s onward.

Trần Trọng Kim (1883–1953) was the first modern Vietnamese historian, the first scholar to study the history of Vietnamese thought, and the first author of many Vietnamese textbooks, of which *VNSL* was one. Most related research has focused on Kim's role as the prime minister of the Empire of Vietnam in 1945 and has overlooked his important role as a scholar and that he was chosen to be prime minister primarily because of his scholarly reputation.

Born in 1883 to a gentry family in Hà Tĩnh, Kim studied the Chinese classics as a child and went to study in France from 1906 to 1911.[1] He served in the colonial school system and occupied a series of important positions until his retirement in 1942: inspector of Franco-Vietnamese primary schools (1921), director of the board for writing primary textbooks (1924), and director of elementary schools for boys in Hanoi (1933). In addition, he was a member of the Tonkinese Chamber of the People's Representatives (Chambre de Représentants du Peuple,

Viện Dân Biểu Bắc Kỳ) and served in leadership roles in many civic associations. He was deputy head of the Literature Department of the Association for Intellectual and Moral Advancement (Hội Khai Trí Tiến Đức) and director of the Division of Buddhist Studies in the Tonkinese Buddhist Revival Association (Hội Chấn Hưng Phật Giáo Bắc Kỳ). Kim wrote more than twenty books that can generally be grouped in three types: history, philosophy, and philological textbooks.[2]

Việt Nam sử lược was the first modern study of Vietnamese history written in the romanized Vietnamese script (*quốc ngữ*) during a socially and spiritually transformative period of the country. The work sought to build a foundation for Vietnamese to understand the history of Vietnam in the first half of the twentieth century. It was not written in the chronicle style of kings and dynasties, as premodern historians had done. Instead, it explained the causal relationship of historical phenomena focusing on three aspects: culture, society, and politics.[3] Influenced by social evolutionary theory in fashion at the time, *VNSL* not only reinterpreted Vietnamese history entirely but also promoted modern nationalist ideas centered on the concept of a national soul.

Although neglected by foreign scholars, *VNSL* enjoyed great influence on Vietnamese intellectuals and students before 1954 and in the Republic of Vietnam (RVN) from 1954 to 1975. Literary critic Thiếu Sơn commented in 1931 that *VNSL* "is not only a valuable textbook of history [for students] but also a book for all those who want to know the history of our nation."[4] Another literary critic, Vũ Ngọc Phan, affirmed in 1942 that Trần Trọng Kim was the first modern historian who wrote in the Vietnamese script on both the political history of Vietnam and the history of Vietnamese thought. Although the book's subtitle was "A brief history," Phan wrote, "it covers a great deal of issues in the past eras of our country's history and deserves being considered as a valuable book."[5] In 1943, literary scholar and activist Nguyễn Văn Tố remarked in an interview that "Kim's history book has been the most valuable one. The author searched historical documents directly in ancient Chinese texts, and he arranged the materials and divided the eras appropriately. . . . He paid attention to the history of the nation rather than that of kings."[6]

In the RVN after 1954, the scholar Phạm Thế Ngũ praised Trần Trọng Kim as a leading scholar of the first half of the twentieth century, calling *VNSL* "irreplaceable" because at that time it was still the only complete survey of Vietnamese history.[7] In North Vietnam, however, *VNSL* was banned as soon as the communists took over. The first attack on the book was in 1955, by communist historian Trần Huy Liệu.[8] Liệu affirmed that until that time, *VNSL* had been the only complete survey of Vietnamese history and thus even more dangerous for the communist revolution. In a review of the development of the "historical science" published in 1980 by Văn Tạo, director of the Institute of History in Hanoi, the book was accused of holding "feudal and colonial views."[9] In 1989 in another publication, Văn Tạo went further to charge Trần Trọng Kim of being a "counterrevolutionary."[10] Given such criticism, *VNSL* was not reprinted in communist Vietnam until the 1990s, and even then the censors removed many passages determined as contradicting the communist narrative of history.

This chapter is divided into two parts. The first discusses the intellectual context of the book in the first two decades of the twentieth century, when republican and nationalist ideas spread to Vietnam from Japan and China. The second analyzes how Trần Trọng Kim used the concept of a national soul to narrate and interpret two thousand years of Vietnamese history.

VIỆT NAM SỬ LƯỢC, EVOLUTIONARY HISTORY, AND THE NATIONAL SOUL

The evolutionary theory of history proclaims that the history of human society has evolved from simple to complex forms. This theory is attributed to Herbert Spencer, whose concepts of military and industrial societies inspired Fukuzawa Yukichi in Japan.[11] Fukuzawa further divided human history into three stages—the "barbarous," "semi-civilized," and "civilized"—and argued that Meiji Japan needed to advance from the military society of the Bakufu era to an industrial society.[12] In China, the theory gained many followers, among the best known of whom was Liang Qichao, a thinker during the late nineteenth and early twentieth century who in turn had a great influence on intellectuals in colonized Vietnam.[13]

The soul of the nation was a crucial idea in Japan and China and gained a following in Vietnam as well. For most Japanese thinkers in the Meiji era, Japan had to combine Western technology and spirit with the soul of Japan to catch up with the West and reach the latter's level of civilization (Jp. *wakon yōsai,* Viet. *hòa hồn dương tài*). They largely associated the soul of Japan (*wakon*) with the country's traditional values. However, as Norio Ota notes, "Fukuzawa Yukichi is somewhat different. . . . his approach was unique among the so-called *wakon yōsai* group. He envisioned the transformation of Japan into a civil and democratic society."[14] Fukuzawa believed that Japan had to build an entirely new spirit, including the spirit of science, democracy, individual freedom, and civil society. For him, Japan could not learn new Western technology without creating such a spirit. Following Fukuzawa, Liang Qichao introduced the idea of building a "new people" (Ch. *xinmin,* Viet. *tân dân*) to prevent China from perishing. According to Liang, to build a new people, China had to first build a national soul. Phan Bội Châu read Liang's *The Soul of China* (*Zhongguo hun*) in Vietnam before launching the Eastern Travel Movement (Đông Du, 1905–1909).[15] He and other Vietnamese thinkers applied the concepts of the soul of Japan and the soul of China to their own country and developed new Vietnamese terms to describe

Vietnam's national soul (Viet. *quốc hồn*), the soul of the nation (Viet. *hồn nước*), and the soul of Vietnam (Viet. *Việt Nam hồn*).

Influenced by Liang's ideas, the Tonkin Free School (Đông Kinh Nghĩa Thục, 1907–1908) in Hanoi published a textbook in classical Chinese titled *The Civilization of New Learning* (Ch. *Wenming xinxue ce*, Viet. *Văn minh tân học sách*, 1906). The book argued that human society evolved from low to high through the barbarous (*dã man*), semi-civilized (*bán khai*), and civilized (*văn minh*) stages. The Vietnamese version of evolutionary history also considered the history of relations between nations as a competition for survival. This viewpoint became the basis for analyzing the modern era, when Vietnam was colonized. In the view of evolutionary history, Vietnam was defeated in the nineteenth century by France because it failed to choose between the French and Chinese civilizations. This notion was very clear in many other publications at the time.[16]

The meaning of the term "national soul" remained vague when it first appeared in Vietnam in the textbook of the Tonkin Free School. Phan Châu Trinh clarified the concept in "Song to Awaken the National Soul" ("Tinh quốc hồn ca"), a long poem written in *quốc ngữ* (vernacular Vietnamese) and taught at the school. Trinh explained that Vietnamese lost their country because their national soul was weak and cowardly, causing this soul to "look for decadent paths to follow" (*tìm những đường hủ bại mà đi*).[17] Therefore, to save the country, it was necessary to awaken the national soul and make it follow the right path. Trinh described the soul of Vietnam based on three elements: education, character, and the spirit of solidarity born from a shared understanding and belief in the nation. In terms of education, whereas Westerners preferred to study for a career and master a technology, Vietnamese only learned to memorize Chinese "vain literature" (*ngũ ngôn, bát cổ, lờ mờ nghĩa đen*). This was why the Vietnamese character was dominated by cowardice, arrogance, and sloppiness (*nhân tâm kiếp đọa, phong tục kiêu ngoa, cẩu thả*).

Trinh also compared the Vietnamese national character with those of the West and the US to clarify how the Vietnamese character caused the country to fail when it encountered the modern era. According to Trinh, whereas Westerners and Americans had "no regrets in assuming social obligations" and fighting for their countries, Vietnamese accepted living as slaves to others, looked only for personal gain, and disparaged those who devoted themselves to social obligations. Whereas Westerners invested money and intellect to compete with each other to develop sophisticated machinery and advanced technology, Vietnamese only "competed against each other to hold lavish banquets, spend money, and buy and sell titles of nobility" (*đua ăn tiệc lớn, đua xài bạc muôn, đấu những chuyện bán buôn quyền tước*). Western political officials were mostly talented individuals who respected the people (*lấy dân làm nền*) and never bothered to flatter their superiors because they were elected by the population.[18] In contrast,

Vietnamese officials gained political power though money and flattery, not by popular elections, so they never took care of the people and used their positions to benefit only themselves.[19]

In terms of national solidarity, whereas Westerners and Americans shared a feeling for their country and could unite to improve it based on a spirit of national solidarity against outsiders, Vietnamese people only cared about their personal interests and even killed each other for individual benefit, so their community quickly fell apart like "a sand dune . . . destroyed by a hurricane."[20] Finally, Trinh called on Vietnamese people to try to learn "all civilized things" in order to evolve. They would glorify their ancestors and race when they did so.[21]

On one hand, the contrast clearly expressed the idea of social evolutionism that considered the West to be "civilized" and Vietnam to be still at the "barbarian" level. On the other hand, the contrast also conveyed many republican values that promoted education, science, commerce, democracy, and the rule of law. About ten years later, Phan Châu Trinh's ideas about the national soul were further developed by Nguyễn Bá Trác and Phạm Quỳnh, the two editors-in-chief of *Southern Wind (Nam phong)*.[22] In 1917, Trác wrote a Chinese-language article titled "The Theory of Nationalism" (Ch. "Minzu zhuyi lun," Viet. "Dân tộc chủ nghĩa luận"), emphasizing that the national soul was the fundamental element on which nationalism could be built. To him, the national soul was a "metaphysical masterpiece, located in the spiritual realm, similar to a soul in a body." Its functions are to "envelop the nation's intellectual background and its sentiments and help the nation to perceive itself as a nation, to be able to revive itself, to achieve self-determination, and to cultivate and nurture its power."[23] In an essay in *quốc ngữ* titled "The Evolution of the United States" ("Sự tiến hóa của nước Mỹ") and published in 1918, Phạm Quỳnh defined the concept of the national soul as "a common belief making the people in that country know that they belong to a large, durable, and permanent entity that still lives after they have passed away. The national soul symbolizes the reputation of the glorious works that their predecessors performed, that their generation is doing, and that the future generations will continue." For Quỳnh, the national soul also encompassed the characteristics and spirit of the nation. Quỳnh argued that the American national soul embodied freedom, self-reliance, self-control, adventure, creativity, and rationalism. That national soul did not exist by default but instead had to be built through philosophy, literature, political thought, religious spirit, philosophy of education, and civil society.[24]

VNSL fully reflected the intellectual trend of the time. Besides the concept of the national soul, the book also introduced numerous Western concepts that had not appeared in Chinese and Vietnamese texts until the late nineteenth century, such as evolution (*tiến hóa*), politics (*chính trị*), polity (*chính thể*), history (*lịch sử*), ethnic nation (*quốc gia dân tộc*), national language (*quốc ngữ*), the people (*nhân dân*), ideology (*tư tưởng*), patriotism (*lòng yêu nước*), competition (*cạnh tranh*), civilization (*văn minh*), technology (*kỹ thuật*), and education (*giáo dục*).

Trần Trọng Kim claimed that the purpose of writing *VNSL* was to "help the youth today to know something about our country's history, so as not to shame our national soul." For him, the understanding of history (answering the question "where do we come from?") and politics (answering the question "what do we do now as a community?") were only two sides of the same coin: if the Vietnamese people understood their national history, they would have a strong national soul, including nationalism and patriotism. Until his time, though, the historical record was merely a history of dynasties and kings, not a history of the nation. Consequently, the national spirit had been weak if it had even existed. It was the state of "shame for our national soul." Therefore, building an understanding of national history was to build the national soul.

The meaning of national soul for Trinh, Trác, and Kim was much broader than the concept of nationalism. The national soul expressed a spiritual form of the collective understanding of a nation that had its own history, language, culture, and ideology. Additionally, it was also a national identity, built by education, literature, art, religion, ideology, and social forces, and was the spiritual foundation on which a nation was born and existed. For Kim, writing a book of Vietnamese history using the national language was to realize the purpose of building that national soul. He used the concept of the national soul to draw an evolutionary map of the Vietnamese spirit.

Unlike others before him, Kim deployed evolutionary theory and the concept of national soul to systematically study Vietnamese history. The concept of the nation connected the past and the present in *VNSL*: perceptions about history dictated perceptions about the nation, which produced perceptions about the present. He viewed a historian's tasks as "finding the original causes" (*tìm tòi cái căn nguyên*) and to clearly understand the "evolutionary level of a nation" (*trình độ tiến hóa của một dân tộc*). People could look at their history to understand how previous generations "had to work hard to capture a position under the sun." The notion of "capturing a position under the sun" reflected the ideas of social Darwinianism.[25] Nations must compete with each other to evolve; whoever won would survive, whoever lost would perish.

Trần Trọng Kim divided Vietnamese history into five epochs based not on the dynasties that had ruled Vietnam but on the evolutionary level and the ability of the country to respond to the external challenges: ancient times (barbarous period), the period under "Northern rule" (learning Chinese civilization), the era of autonomy (building Vietnam's national soul), the period of north-south division (civil war and expansion of southern territory), and the early modern era (failure to choose the modern French model over the outdated Chinese one). He considered Vietnam in the early period of Chinese domination to be an "uncivilized land" (*vùng đất chưa khai*) relative to China as a "civilized country."[26] For the French colonial period, he acknowledged the modernizing activities of the colonial government such as "civilizing the people [and] developing education."[27]

In the same way that his periodization differentiated between evolutionary levels, Kim's interpretation of history was based on three central questions. First, how did Vietnam evolve from semi-civilization in the ancient period to the civilized period? Second, in the past, had Vietnam been able to overcome challenges posed by higher civilizations? If so, what factors helped the Vietnamese to do so? Third, would the Vietnamese become a nation of creativity? To answer these questions, the key concepts in *VNSL* were race, assimilation, creativity, culture, evolution, education, and the national soul.

Viewing history from an evolutionary perspective, Kim asked why Vietnamese civilization as well as Chinese civilization had been "frozen" for centuries without creating Western-style evolution. Based on the stagnation of education and society in Vietnam during the "feudal" period, Kim was skeptical of the Vietnamese capacity for creativity and innovation: Vietnam learned Confucianism from China but could not create "a spirit of our own people."

> Customs and politics are made through education and religion. Our people studied the education and religion of China so that we could follow everything. But after all, all our things are inferior to those of China, and we have not by ourselves discovered and created anything that can be considered as excellent or as defining the spirit of our own race. Why?[28]

Kim then invoked geography, education, and national characteristics to explain why Vietnam was not creative in ideology and scholarship.[29] The country's geography and territory locked its people in the Red River Delta. As a result, the Vietnamese "have rarely left the territory" and "have not seen the good and bad things of other people," so they could not evolve. This geographical trap pushed the country into an ideological trap in which

> from thought to real world action, we imitated everything from China. Anyone who imitated China was good, [and] those who could not copy were bad. . . . [we] refused to compare what was better and what was worse, [and] did not attempt to invent new and good things. [We] only decided that [Chinese] people were better than us, so it was enough for us to imitate them.[30]

Despite recognizing that in history Vietnam did not evolve through creativity, nationalists such as Trần Trọng Kim nevertheless looked for and tried to promote symbols that could represent the creativity of the Vietnamese nation. To do so, Kim chose Nguyễn Du's *The Tale of Kiều* (*Truyện Kiều, Truyện Thúy Kiều*):

The Tale of Thúy Kiều is an excellent literary work that is able to capture all the feelings and social situations [and] describe every scene in human life. Moreover, every part of this work is elegant. The poetic language is also beautiful. Speaking in today's language, *The Tale of Thúy Kiều* is really the great literary work of our nation.[31]

Remarkably, Kim was the first historian to write about *The Tale of Kiều* in a historical study. He chose this work because it was written in the demotic Vietnamese script (*chữ nôm*) rather than classical Chinese; for him, it was the text that reached the highest linguistic level. His judgment spurred a movement to promote and revise the longstanding elite view of *The Tale of Kiều*. In the 1920s, following Kim's argument in *VNSL,* other members of the Association for Intellectual and Moral Advancement—such as Phạm Quỳnh, Bùi Kỷ, and Nguyễn Văn Vĩnh—began promoting Nguyễn Du as a symbol of national creativity and the national soul.[32]

Their efforts provoked immediate rebuke by those intellectuals trained in the Chinese classics, who pointed to the low appreciation of *The Tale of Kiều* by intellectuals of earlier periods. For example, Ngô Đức Kế (1878–1929), a Confucian intellectual who passed the metropolitan exams in 1901 under the Nguyễn dynasty, argued that *The Tale of Kiều* was popular among the common people but was nothing more than an entertaining story, far too low to represent the national soul. In the debate about *The Tale of Kiều* initiated by Phan Khôi in 1930, another traditional intellectual, Huỳnh Thúc Kháng, derided the work as a pornographic book (*dâm thư*) and dismissed its protagonist Thúy Kiều as a prostitute.

Despite the criticism, the notion that *The Tale of Kiều* is a representation of Vietnam's national soul triumphed over critics throughout the country by the middle of the twentieth century. Ironically, in 1955, Trần Huy Liệu criticized Trần Trọng Kim's *VNSL* as "traitor to the nation" on the grounds that Kim had criticized the Vietnamese people for not being creative. To prove that Kim was wrong, Liệu cited the names of some "great writers" in history, such as Nguyễn Du, who had created "great literary works" for the nation.[33] Liệu did not forget to remind readers that the communist party represented that creative ability in the new era, but conveniently ignored that it was Kim who had first elevated Nguyễn Du's *The Tale of Kiều* to the level of elite culture to represent the nation's creativity.

THE NATIONAL SOUL AND VIETNAMESE HISTORY

Trần Trọng Kim explained the rise and decline of Vietnam over time based on the strength or weakness of the national soul. For example, its strength from eleventh to fourteenth century explained Vietnam's ability to win back its autonomy from China in the fifteenth:

> The Lý and Trần dynasties had the merit of creating a strong national soul. That was the reason why, at the end of the Trần dynasty when the Hồ dynasty misguided the country and the Chinese invaded and attempted to annex our nation, our people knew how to unite to restore the homeland.[34]

However, his biggest concern was the current shortcomings of the Vietnamese national soul in regard to protecting the homeland, which contrasted with the positive characteristics of more advanced countries.

Kim especially emphasized the negative traits of the Vietnamese when he examined the two times when the country had lost its sovereignty. The first was when it was annexed by China's Ming dynasty in the fifteenth century. The second was his era, when it was colonized by the French. In both cases, he criticized the Vietnamese character for lacking independence and self-reliance. In particular, the Vietnamese lost their country due to their political naivety, their blind faith in Chinese kindness, and their ideological dependence on China. He criticized the choice of the majority of intellectuals in the early fifteenth century who "competed against each other" to serve the Ming invaders, "doing cruel things toward Vietnamese that were crueler than the Chinese did."[35] Because of a weak national soul, people were oblivious to their "obligations to the nation." He defined the "obligations of the people to the nation" (cái nghĩa của dân với nước) as the duty to "put public interest above private benefit [and] national rights above the rights of the family" and to live for the nation as an entity that transcended the family and individual.[36]

Vietnamese historiography before the late nineteenth century had never asserted that China was a threat to the survival of Vietnam.[37] Incidents of Chinese invasions were remembered but premodern Vietnamese elites considered China an exemplary model of civilization, as mentioned. VNSL was the first book to systematically portray the Chinese as a historical threat to national survival, an idea which has since become part of the new identity of the Vietnamese nation in the modern era.

In Kim's view, one of the weaknesses of Vietnam's national soul in the past was that its people were deceived by the appearance of Chinese kindness and forgot China's wicked essence:

> Even if the Chinese people were generous to come and help us [when we asked], it was not glorious to depend on others. But in fact, those bad guys have always been waiting for opportunities to entrap us, like naïve children, in order to strangle us. Yet why do we still not know our foolishness?[38]

In the 1900s, Phan Bội Châu, Phan Châu Trinh, and others in the Tonkin Free School had criticized Vietnam for failing to preserve its independence by modernizing its politics, education, and economy. In *VNSL,* Kim not only lamented such stagnation but also directly and clearly rejected the Chinese model and condemned Vietnamese who wanted to depend on China.

Affirming that China had been a weak country in the nineteenth century, unable to save itself, Kim criticized Vietnamese for continuing to hold to their faith in China:

> Our imperial court at that time thought that France intentionally annexed us and China could defend us, so they sent Phạm Thận Duật to Tianjin to ask for help. It was only because we Vietnamese did not have a self-reliant mentality. We just asked other people for help, not knowing that the Chinese could not even protect their own country, how could they help us? However, not only did China not save us, but it also wanted to take the opportunity to invade our country.[39]

Blind faith in China made Vietnamese elites also blind to the fact that "from the beginning of the nineteenth century onwards, the life and scholarship around the world have improved so much and the competition among countries has become much more intense than before."[40] This put Vietnam "in great danger," and it failed when facing French colonization. To Kim, the ultimate cause of this was a weak national soul based on ethnic characteristics and on outdated and weak education, culture, and ideology, all of which were shaped by political, social, and economic structures.

Communist historians writing in the 1950s and after agreed with Trần Trọng Kim in his conclusion that Vietnam had failed to respond correctly to the historical challenge and that this failure had caused the country to fall victim to colonialism, but offered very different diagnoses of the problem. Two leading scholars, Trần Huy Liệu and Trần Văn Giàu, blamed two specific groups for the country's failure: the "cowardly" Nguyễn dynasty and the *Việt gian,* or "insidious and treacherous Vietnamese."[41] A third group, who received more sympathy, included patriotic intellectuals, but they were not capable nor equipped with a true path—a golden weapon that only the communists had. The communist historical model accepted only binaries: patriotism and "national betrayal" (*bán nước,* or selling out the country), bravery and cowardice, and the Vietnamese people and the *Việt gian.* These concepts were interconnected in this particular manner: the patriotic Vietnamese people bravely fought the French even as the cowardly Nguyễn dynasty and other collaborators "sold" the nation to French colonial capitalists. This model ignored the presence of the Qing army and the series of battles between Qing China and France to gain control over Vietnam in the 1880s. It distorted historical reality by labeling as "patriotic" the scholarly (*văn thân*) class that did not yet have nationalist sentiments. It also reduced history to only military events between Vietnam and France and neglected social and cultural history.[42]

In contrast, to understand why Vietnam was colonized in the nineteenth century, Trần Trọng Kim surveyed political, social, and cultural forces to explain the choices the country had made. Kim noted "honest people" like Trương Đăng Quế, Vũ Trọng Bình, Phan Thanh Giản, Nguyễn Tri Phương, and Hoàng Diệu who surrounded the king, but that "they were all old people, who did not understand the modern world." Beyond that, "our forces at that time were so vile. They could not keep up anymore even if we had wanted to reform, so everything was broken." Kim went on to analyze the cultural and educational context:

> Imperial mandarins were those who worked for the Dynasty to help the King to take care of the country. Yet those who had held political responsibility in our country cared only about literature and were skilled only in writing literature. When discussing national affairs, they only quoted Chinese stories thousands of years ago, such as Emperor Yao . . . and the Zhou dynasty to set an example for the present time. [With those quotations] they could proclaim themselves to be more civilized than other people and to treat others as barbarians. Ugh! Most of our imperial mandarins at that time were that kind of people. Although a few had been out of the country, seen the spectacle of the world, and come back to talk about it, the elderly people at home dismissed it as "foolish talk" that was harmful to [traditional] rule![43]

In other words, although the most ethical mandarins—such as Phan Thanh Giản, Nguyễn Tri Phương, and Hoàng Diệu—wanted wholeheartedly to help Emperor Tự Đức, they were helpless. The education they had received, the culture of the imperial mandarinate in which they were immersed, and the system they worked for did not enable them to deal with the new challenges.

Trần Trọng Kim also presented a careful analysis of Emperor Tự Đức. In his view, Tự Đức was not a completely conservative monarch who would absolutely refuse to reform the way communist historians have depicted him. In fact, he "often asked about the strategy of 'enriching the country, strengthening the army'" (Viet. *phú quốc cường binh,* Jp. *fukoku kyōhei*). Tự Đức frequently urged the imperial mandarins to consider the proposals for economic, educational, and political reforms. He also consulted Nguyễn Đức Hậu, Nguyễn Trường Tộ, Nguyễn Điều, Đinh Văn Điền, Nguyễn Hiệp, Lê Đĩnh, and Phan Liêm on plans to avoid the "serious threat of losing the country." In return, Tự Đức only received conservative responses from the majority of the mandarins, who claimed that those proposals "were just foolish talk and nobody would listen to them," or "all of the [mandarins] argued that foreign trade was not convenient [for operation]" and "for other issues, suggested the Emperor to ask the provinces for their opinions first." Kim concluded that "the king was not unwilling to change but the mandarins only wished to maintain the old customs for their own convenience."

Kim went on to point out that the underlying reason for such conservatism lay in the educational system, where the purpose of study was to "get a good recommendation for a higher social position." Those who passed the exams were "overconfident that they were talented . . . and did not pay attention to practical science and learning." In the end, "the majority just wanted to pass the exams to become officials," which did not help the country in a practical sense.[44] Beyond that, he analyzed, the curriculum was outdated.

> How much effort did learners have to make to memorize the Chinese *Four Books* and *Five Classics* and the annotations of previous Confucian scholars in those books? . . . They only focused on how to master all the literary skills that the exams required: [namely,] annotating Confucius' books and writing [poems] and essays in the classical style. The [exam system] used pompous literature [*hư văn*] to evaluate practical skills. It used pompous beauty to measure social, economic, and political capacities.[45]

In such a system, "anyone who was good at annotating Confucius's books thought of himself as better than other people; anyone who was good at poetry and poetic prose thought that he was also good at national management. They were foolish, silly, and ignorant in real life but presumptuous and arrogant." To Kim, "that was the level of court intellectuals in our country. During a very dark time in our national life, our soul was still sunken in the daydreams of our outdated worldview."

This understanding of Trần Trọng Kim about the cultural foundation of Vietnamese feudal elites in the nineteenth century reflected his concept of a national soul in the context of an evolutionary view of history; he explained the success and failure of a nation based on its adaptability to historical changes. The sole experience Vietnamese literati had was traditional Chinese culture, which prevented them from adapting to the new challenges from Western civilization.

In 1955, Trần Huy Liệu attacked Trần Trọng Kim for not analyzing social factors to explain historical events.[46] Yet Liệu ignored Kim's in-depth analysis of the social classes as well as their educational and cultural backgrounds that determined Vietnam's fate over time, especially in the nineteenth century. For the nineteenth century in particular, Kim went further to survey the economic base that trapped the Vietnamese elites in that cultural foundation.

To explain the socioeconomic basis of the mental failure of elites in the nineteenth century, Kim analyzed the status of the "four categories" of Vietnamese people in traditional Confucian society: scholars, peasants, artisans and craftsmen, and merchants (*sĩ nông công thương*). He pointed out that the class of artisans and craftsmen

> employed only small-scale technologies and crafts such as the spinning wheel, fabric weaving, silk weaving, making fishnets, and salt and fish sauce production . . . ,

not being able to use advanced technologies to expand their wealth like in other countries ... The workers were often uneducated, and their year-round work as hired laborers earned barely enough to feed themselves.

The trading class was "very poor," he lamented.

The traders of other countries travelled to trade around the world. They exported and imported. They ran huge businesses that were worth millions and hundreds of millions. Our traders traveled to nowhere in their whole life, just staying inside the country and trading in petty goods. As a result, many great benefits [from trade] in our country accrued to outsiders.

Kim concluded, "Technology was like that and trading was like that—how could our country be rich? Therefore, among the four classes only peasants and scholar-officials were important."[47] In the final analysis, though, as he argued, peasants were too poor and the scholar-officials opposed Westernization and modernization. Thus no social forces in Vietnam at that time supported economic and political reform.

In summary, in Trần Trọng Kim's interpretation, the nineteenth century was not simply a time that Vietnam was invaded by the French, the selfish and cowardly Nguyễn kings surrendered, and the heroic people fought the invaders. On the contrary, it was a chaotic century, a time that Vietnam had to overcome the traditional system to build a new national soul and to catch up with modern values that promised opportunity and progress. Unfortunately, the social forces in Vietnam at that time, from the elite mandarins of the Huế court to the local scholar gentry, from artisans and craftsmen to peasant farmers, were unable— save for a few individuals such as Nguyễn Trường Tộ—to realize the new contexts. They could not because they were handicapped in knowledge and vision and, most important, because they did not hold a true national soul.

Despite Vietnam's failure in the face of the French conquest, *VNSL* drew hope for the future from Vietnam's historical destruction of the kingdom of Champa. In premodern times, Vietnamese elites had considered the wars with Champa as a way to impose the tributary model on other smaller countries. In *VNSL*, Trần Trọng Kim used the Vietnamese destruction of Champa as evidence for the evolution of his nation. Vietnam, on the one hand, had struggled to survive when confronted by Chinese domination and, on the other, conquered a weaker nation.

In the first chapter, which provided an overview of Vietnamese history, Kim was in fact proud of the ability of the Vietnamese race to survive and conquer in the past:

Day by day, our Vietnamese race has grown more and more and more. In the north, there is strong and prosperous China. In the west, there are many forests and mountains that are difficult to cross. We have followed the coastline to advance southward, defeating Lâm Ấp [Ch. Linyi, another name for Champa], destroying Champa, occupying the land of Chân Lạp [Ch. Chenla, Cambodia], and creating the realm of Vietnam today.[48]

Kim invoked the case of Champa to answer the question whether "Vietnam was capable of competing with another civilization in the past." In *VNSL,* Kim mentioned Champa about 140 times, fully narrating the conflicts and cooperation between Đại Việt and Champa from the era of Chinese rule until the annexation of Champa. When discussing the Vietnamese conquest of Champa, he wept for the Cham people who "lost their country" and were forced to "assimilate" into Vietnamese culture, which resulted in "only a few thousand people" now left. The fate of Champa contrasted sharply with that of Vietnam:

Since the Vietnamese people established the country up to now over a few thousand years, we have been invaded and ruled by China many times. We have suffered but we still restored our autonomy and retained the special character of our race. This is enough to show that our spiritual force was not too mean and cheap.

Thus, although he lamented the fate of Champa, it was also a way of thinking about Vietnam during his own time, similar to how Phan Bội Châu cried for Ryukyu (Okinawa) in *A New Booklet on the Ryukyus Written in Blood and Tears* (Ch. *Liuqiu xuelei xinshu,* Viet. *Lưu Cầu huyết lệ tân thư*).[49] For Kim, Vietnam's success in its conquest of Champa apparently proved that it could learn to evolve and adapt in the modern era.

CONCLUSION

In the English-language scholarship since the late 1960s, Vietnam is commonly considered a united nation with a distinct identity formed over centuries of resistance against foreign invasions.[50] Influenced by the context of Cold War politics, scholars have regarded the Vietnamese communist party as the sole political force inheriting that national tradition of fighting against foreign aggression, whereas Vietnamese republicans and republicanism are not considered a serious subject of study.[51]

In Vietnam, communist historians have for decades spun a similar, self-serving narrative to justify their rule. For that reason, the evolving perceptions of the Vietnamese nation during the colonial period before communist rule were not considered an important issue and were either ignored in the historical narrative or referred to as the proof that only the communist party could lead Vietnam to victory in the struggle with foreign countries.

More recently, many foreign scholars have taken a serious look at Vietnamese republicanism.[52] However, little research has been undertaken on the republicans' perception of history and its relationship with republican nationalism. This chapter analyzes the new interpretation of Vietnamese history in Trần Trọng Kim's *Việt Nam sử lược* that reflected the modern ideas of republican nationalism that circulated among Vietnamese intellectuals at the beginning of the twentieth century. Those ideas originated from the West but arrived in Vietnam from Japan and China and were embedded in the theory of social evolution. The concept of the national soul that ran through *VNSL*'s narrative of two thousand years of Vietnam's recorded history conveyed Kim's robust belief in the historical existence and future prospects of his nation. At the same time, in Kim's view, the strength of the national soul in the modern era was predicated on a republican outlook that promoted science, education, democracy, commerce, and civic consciousness.

Although he was denounced by the communist regime and his works were banned inside Vietnam until recently, Trần Trọng Kim would be proud to witness the rise of anti-Chinese nationalist sentiments in Vietnam today given that he was the first historian to present China as not only a source of cultural borrowing but also a threat to Vietnam's survival. Whether China has actually been a threat to Vietnam or not, Trần Trọng Kim would chide the Vietnamese authorities today for suppressing those popular sentiments as well as for their failure to reform Vietnamese education and promote democracy.

NOTES

1. The biographical information about Trần Trọng Kim is drawn from Lê Thanh, *Phỏng vấn các nhà văn* (Hanoi: Đời Mới, 1943), 9–13. Like other classically trained scholars, Kim had a literary name, Lệ Thần, which meant "statesman of the previous dynasty." According to Vũ Ngọc Khánh, Kim's father Trần Bá Huân joined the Aid the King Movement (Cần Vương, 1885–1897), and his younger sister Trần Thị Liên joined the communist party in 1930 and died in 1964. See Vũ Ngọc Khánh, "Bàn thêm về Trần Trọng Kim," Văn Hóa Nghệ An, November 26, 2009, accessed April 5, 2011, http://vanhoanghean.com.vn/dat-va-nguoi-xu-nghe/nguoi-xu-nghe/1485-ban-them-v-trn-trng -kim.html (site discontinued).

2. Notable works by Trần Trọng Kim include *Nho giáo* (Hanoi: Trung Bắc Tân Văn, 1930); *Phật lục* (Hanoi: Lê Thăng, 1940); *Phật giáo* (Saigon: Tân Việt, 1940); *Phật giáo thuở xưa và Phật giáo ngày nay* (Saigon: Tân Việt, 1953); and *Quốc văn giáo khoa thư*, 3 vols. (Hanoi: Nha Học Chính Đông Pháp, 1926). See also Bùi Kỷ and Trần Trọng Kim, *Truyện Kiều chú giải* (Hanoi: Vinh Hưng Long, 1925); Trần Trọng Kim, Phạm Duy Khiêm, and Bùi Kỷ, *Văn phạm Việt Nam* (Hanoi: Lê Thăng, 1941).

3. Vũ Ngọc Phan, *Nhà văn hiện đại*, vol. 2 (Saigon: Đại Nam, 1959), 209–215.

4. Thiếu Sơn, "Lối văn phê bình nhơn vật, IV. Ông Trần Trọng Kim," *Phụ nữ Tân văn* 97 (August 27, 1931), 13; reprinted in Thiếu Sơn, *Phê bình và cảo luận* (Hanoi: Nam Ký, 1933), 34–35. Also reprinted in Thanh Lãng, *Mười ba năm tranh luận văn học,* vol. 2 (Hanoi: Văn Học, 1995), 252.

5. Vũ Ngọc Phan, *Nhà văn hiện đại*, 2:209.

6. Lê Thanh, "Cuộc phỏng vấn các nhà văn," 43.

7. Phạm Thế Ngũ, *Việt Nam văn học sử giản ước tân biên,* vol. 3 (Saigon: Quốc Học Tùng Thư, 1965), 301–302.

8. Trần Huy Liệu, "Bóc trần quan điểm thực dân và phong kiến trong 'Việt Nam sử lược' của Trần Trọng Kim," *Văn sử địa* 6 (March-April 1955): 20–37. *VNSL* appeared to remain in use even in areas under the control of the Việt Minh between 1947 and 1954. Writing in 1955, Liệu was angry that people continued to use the volume to study Vietnamese history and that it had not been replaced.

9. Văn Tạo, "Khoa học lịch sử Việt Nam trong mấy chục năm qua," in *Sử học Việt Nam trên đường phát triển,* ed. Ủy Ban Khoa Học Xã Hội Việt Nam, Viện Sử Học (Hanoi: Khoa Học Xã Hội, 1981), 9–35, esp. 22–23.

10. Văn Tạo, "30 năm tạp chí Nghiên cứu Lịch sử và sự cống hiến của nhà sử học Trần Huy Liệu," *Nghiên cứu lịch sử* 3–4 (1989): 1–5, esp. 3.

11. Herbert Spencer, "Progress: Its Law and Causes," *Westminster Review* 67 (April 1857): 445–485, esp. 445–447, 451, 454–456, 464–465. On Fukuzawa Yukichi, see Richard Rubinger, "Education: From One Room to One System," in *Japan in Transition: From Tokugawa to Meiji,* ed. Marius Jansen and Gilbert Rozman (Princeton, NJ: Princeton University Press, 1986), 210.

12. Fukuzawa Yukichi, *Bunmeiron no gairyaku* (An outline of a theory of civilization) (Tokyo: Iwanami shoten, 1931), 24–25.

13. Fung Po-Wa, "Ryo Keicho to Nihon: Fukuzawa Yukichi no keimō shisō to no kanren o chūshin ni" (Liang Qichao and Japan: On the connection with the enlightenment thinking of Fukuzawa Yukichi), *Hikaku bungaku bunka ronshū, Tokyo daigaku hikaku bungaku bunka kenkyūkai* (Departmental Bulletin Paper, Society of Comparative Literature and Culture University of Tokyo) 14 (September 1997): 49–62; Tân Nam Tử [Nguyễn Văn Vĩnh], "Duy tân," *Đăng cổ tùng báo* 812 (August 8, 1907): 306.

14. Norio Ota, "*Wakon-Yosai* and Globalization," in *Japan in the Age of Globalization,* ed. Carin Holroyd and Ken Coates (London: Routledge, 2012), 148–157, especially 152.

15. Shiraishi Masaya, *Betonamu minzoku undō to Nihon, Ajia: Fan Boi Chū no kakumei shisō to taigai ninshiki* (The Vietnamese national movement, Japan, and Asia: The revolutionary thought of Phan Bội Châu and his perceptions of the outside world) (Tokyo: Gannando shoten, 1993), 131–135.

16. The idea that Vietnam lost its sovereignty in the nineteenth century because it failed to choose between Chinese and Western civilization is widely discussed in the literature: Phan Bội Châu, *Yuenan wangguo shi* (Viet. *Việt Nam vong quốc sử,* Eng. History of the loss of Vietnam); Phan Bội Châu, *Yuenan guoshi kao* (Viet. *Việt Nam quốc sử khảo,* Eng. An outline of the history of Vietnam); Hoàng Cao Khải, *Yue shi jing* (Viet. *Việt sử kính,* Eng. The mirror of Vietnamese history); and Hoàng Cao Khải, *Yue shi yao* (Viet. *Việt sử yếu,* Eng. An outline of Vietnamese history, 1914). For Vietnamese translations of these works, see Phan Bội Châu, *Việt Nam vong quốc sử,* in *Phan Bội Châu—tác phẩm chọn lọc,* ed. Trần Hải Yến (Hanoi: Nhà Xuất Bản Giáo Dục, 2009), 115–134; Phan Bội Châu, *Việt Nam quốc sử khảo,* trans. Chương Thâu (Hanoi: Giáo Dục Publisher, 1962); Hoàng Cao Khải, *Gương sử Nam* [*Yue shi jing*] (Hanoi: Defour et Ng.-Văn-Vĩnh, 1910); Hoàng Cao Khải. *Việt sử yếu,* trans. Lê Xuân Giáo (Saigon: Phủ Quốc Vụ Khanh Đặc Trách Văn Hóa, 1971).

17. Phan Châu Trinh, *Phan Châu Trinh toàn tập,* vol. 2. (Đà Nẵng: Nhà Xuất Bản Đà Nẵng, 2005), 344.

18. Phan Châu Trinh, *Phan Châu Trinh toàn tập,* 2:356.

19. Phan Châu Trinh, *Phan Châu Trinh toàn tập,* 2:357.

20. Phan Châu Trinh, *Phan Châu Trinh toàn tập,* 2:349.

21. Phan Châu Trinh, *Phan Châu Trinh toàn tập,* 2:351.

22. Nguyễn Bá Trác participated in Phan Bội Châu's Đông Du Movement, traveled to Japan and then China, returned to Vietnam in 1914, and began working with Phạm Quỳnh three years later as the editor of the Chinese-language section of *Nam phong.* The communists executed both Trác and Quỳnh immediately after seizing power in August 1945.

23. Nguyễn Bá Trác, "Minzu zhuyi lun" (Viet. Dân tộc chủ nghĩa luận, Eng. Theory of nationalism), *Nam phong* 1 (July 1917): 6.

24. Phạm Quỳnh, "Sự tiến hóa của nước Mỹ," *Nam phong* 14 (August 1918): 59–67.

25. Trần Trọng Kim, *Việt Nam sử lược (VNSL)*, vol. 1 (Hanoi: Trung Bắc Tân Văn, 1920), 1.

26. *VNSL*, 1:55–56.

27. Trần Trọng Kim, *Việt Nam sử lược*, vol. 2 (Hanoi: Trung Bắc Tân Văn, 1920), 300–301.

28. *VNSL*, 1:61.

29. Trần Trọng Kim was the first Vietnamese thinker who wrote philosophically on Confucianism. Alexander Woodside has commented that Kim did not rely on his own Vietnamese tradition of Confucianism to develop new thoughts, unlike other Asian thinkers working in the same neo-Confucian context of the early twentieth century, such as Hattori Unokichi in Japan. Kim's book on Confucianism was more than eight hundred pages long, but the section about Vietnamese Confucianism accounted for only fifteen pages because there was little to write on the topic. See Woodside, *Community and Revolution in Modern Vietnam* (Boston, MA: Houghton Mifflin Company, 1976), 107.

30. *VNSL*, 1:61–62.

31. *VNSL*, 2:155.

32. Trần Trọng Kim, along with the scholar Bùi Kỷ, published *The Annotated Tale of Kiều (Truyện Kiều chú giải)* in *quốc ngữ* in 1925. This work is the most cited book in the literary criticism on the *Tale of Kiều* in Vietnam. According to some scholars, Kim modernized the *Tale of Kiều* when he transliterated it from the demotic script (*chữ nôm*) into *quốc ngữ*, making the text "more beautiful" and "more modern" than the original. Kim's efforts inspired the next generation of scholars, including Hoàng Xuân Hãn who tried to restore the original text of the *Tale of Kiều* (and who served as the minister of education in the Trần Trọng Kim's cabinet in 1945). See Hoàng Xuân Hãn, Đào Thái Tôn, and Nguyễn Tài Cẩn, *Nghiên cứu văn bản "Truyện Kiều" theo phương pháp Hoàng Xuân Hãn* (Hanoi: Đại Học Quốc Gia Hà Nội, 2016).

33. Trần Huy Liệu, "Bóc trần quan điểm thực dân và phong kiến trong 'Việt Nam sử lược' của Trần Trọng Kim," 30. In the same paragraph, Liệu misspelled the name of Đoàn Thị Điểm, an important eighteenth-century poet, as "Nguyễn Thị Điểm," which showed his poor knowledge of Vietnamese premodern literature.

34. *VNSL*, 1:iv.

35. *VNSL*, 1:179.

36. *VNSL*, 1:168.

37. The *Unification Records of the Imperial Lê* (Viet. *Hoàng Lê nhất thống chí*), a novel first published during the Nguyễn dynasty and written in the style of a classic Chinese novel, contained the "Call of the Quang Trung Emperor" that portrayed China as a threat to the existence of Vietnam, but this statement appears to have been added later to the versions that were published around the turn of the century. See Ngô Gia Văn Phái, *Hoàng Lê nhất thống chí*, trans. Nguyễn Đức Vân and Kiều Thu Hoạch (Hanoi: Văn Học, 2004), 355–356; Phạm Tú Châu, *Hoàng Lê nhất thống chí: văn bản tác giả và nhân vật* (Hanoi: Khoa Học Xã Hội, 1997), 14.

38. *VNSL*, 1:169.

39. *VNSL*, 2:261.

40. *VNSL*, 2:212.

41. The epithet *Việt gian* (the insidious and treacherous Vietnamese) is a concept that appeared after 1945, borrowed and modified by the Việt Minh from the Chinese epithet *Hanjian* (Viet. *Hán gian*, the insidious and treacherous Chinese) to depict other Vietnamese, including those who cooperated with the French, as traitors and counterrevolutionaries.

42. Trần Huy Liệu et al., eds., *Tài liệu tham khảo lịch sử cách mạng cận đại Việt-Nam*, 12 vols. (Hanoi: Văn Sử Địa, 1957); Trần Huy Liệu, *Lịch sử tám mươi năm chống Pháp* (Hanoi: Văn Sử Địa, 1957).

43. *VNSL*, 2:212.

44. *VNSL*, 2:216–217.

45. *VNSL*, 2:217.

46. Trần Huy Liệu, "Bóc trần quan điểm thực dân và phong kiến trong 'Việt Nam sử lược' của Trần Trọng Kim," 29.

47. *VNSL*, 2:217–219.

48. A similar sentiment can be found in Phan Bội Châu, *Việt Nam quốc sử khảo*, 132–133.

49. In communist historiography, the Vietnamese invasions of Champa and Cambodia have been ignored because they would contradict the historical construction of a Vietnamese people who always love peace and have been a victim of foreign invaders. Champa's history has been largely erased from Vietnamese history for half a century. When *VNSL* was republished in Vietnam in 1999, sections 6 ("Taking the Land of Champa") and 7 ("The Opening of Southern Vietnam and Relations with Chân Lạp") of chapter 6, volume 2, were censored.

50. Woodside, *Community and Revolution in Modern Vietnam*; William Duiker, *The Rise of Nationalism in Vietnam 1900–1941* (Ithaca, NY: Cornell University Press, 1976); David Marr, *Vietnamese Tradition on Trial, 1920–1945* (Berkeley: University of California Press, 1981); and Huỳnh Kim Khánh, *Vietnamese Communism 1925–1945* (Ithaca, NY: Cornell University Press, 1982).

51. For a detailed analysis of scholarly debates on Vietnamese nationalism, see Tuong Vu, "Vietnamese Political Studies and Debates on Vietnamese Nationalism," *Journal of Vietnamese Studies* 2, no. 2 (2007): 175–230.

52. Vĩnh Sính, *Phan Châu Trinh and His Political Writings* (Ithaca, NY: Cornell University Press, 2009); Peter Zinoman, *Vietnamese Colonial Republican: The Political Vision of Vũ Trọng Phụng* (Berkeley: University of California Press, 2013); and Christopher Goscha, *Vietnam: A New History* (New York: Basic Books, 2016). For a review of historiography on the topic, see chapter 1 in this volume.

CHAPTER THREE

The Self-Reliant Literary Group and Colonial Republicanism in the 1930s

Martina Thucnhi Nguyen

Republican ideas spread to Indochina around the turn of the century through Japanese and Chinese intellectuals and scholars such as Fukuzawa Yukichi and Liang Qichao.[1] These ideas were reflected in the writings of Phan Châu Trinh, Nguyễn Bá Trác, and Trần Trọng Kim. The attitudes among younger Vietnamese who came of age in the late colonial decade of the 1930s, though, were also shaped by direct experience with French colonialism after the Great War, as World War I was called at the time. On the one hand, these young Vietnamese were exposed to the liberal values of the Enlightenment and the connected political ideology of republicanism through the modern Franco-Vietnamese education system. In its Westernized curriculum, an entire generation of students had grown up studying not classical Chinese but instead vernacular Vietnamese and French along with science, French history, and literature. On the other hand, these same Vietnamese experienced firsthand how the French colonial government would often violate these proclaimed republican principles in their unequal policies and unfair treatment of the colonized. This chapter focuses on how the stark contrast between French republican ideals and the realities of colonial rule shaped the republican vision of the Self-Reliant Literary Group (Tự Lực Văn Đoàn), arguably the most important Vietnamese intellectuals of this interwar generation. Founded in 1932 by the writer and journalist Nguyễn Tường Tam, best known by his nom de plume Nhất Linh, the group profoundly influenced the development of modern Vietnamese literature, journalism, publishing, and art for decades to come. Its members established two of the highest circulating and most influential journals in all of Indochina—*Mores* (*Phong hóa*), Vietnam's first satirical newspaper and its successor publication *These Days* (*Ngày nay*). Using innovative literary contributions and the widely read journals, the Self-Reliant Literary Group members launched a far-reaching program of social reform that modernized and improved the lives of everyday Vietnamese.

This chapter argues that the Self-Reliant Literary Group sought to realize a postcolonial vision of Vietnam as a democratic republic and founded on republican ideals. In this future Vietnamese state, political sovereignty was to be held by the people and expressed through their elected representatives. The nationalist political vision was a response to the hypocrisy of France's imperial project in Vietnam, in particular its ineffectual representative bodies, its strict press censorship, and its attempts to preserve the monarchy. Yet the members of the Self-Reliant Literary Group did not advocate the overthrow of colonialism to achieve this vision (at least not at this point), and in fact rejected the idea of a violent revolution. Instead, the group demanded that the French live up to the ideals they so forcefully proclaimed and to grant the people of Tonkin a number of political and legal rights and reforms. The group's aversion to anticolonial struggle underscored the belief that Vietnam was not yet ready for autonomy and that the country needed first to build the foundations for democratic statehood before even considering decolonization, lest it fall into tyranny.

Republicanism, especially as borne out in France, has been a multifaceted and elastic political ideal. Although the tenets of republicanism fluctuated over the nineteenth and twentieth centuries, a core set of five values defined it: popular sovereignty, rationality, universality, patriotism, and belief in political structures.[2] These values often clashed with the realities of statehood and the urgencies of political survival, and French republicans often had to work through internal inconsistencies by managing conflicting goals. This was especially the case with the issue of colonialism. Although colonialism was inconsistent with the republican project, survival of the republic itself superseded any moral objections on the part of political leaders. Additionally, the idea of France's civilizing mission further justified and rationalized the colonial project by giving economic exploitation a benevolent veneer.[3] Indigenous elites across the French empire wrestled with republican ideals vis-à-vis the realities of their colonial condition.[4] In his study of the writer Vũ Trọng Phụng, Peter Zinoman describes the variant of republicanism that developed among Vietnamese in colonial Indochina as encompassing anticapitalism, a commitment to freedom of speech and the rule of law, and a taste for literary realism. Over the course of the nineteenth century, the tradition further developed a vehement opposition to communism and faith in social science, both of which became entrenched in the Third Republic.[5]

A number of the colonial republican principles that Vũ Trọng Phụng espoused are evident in the intellectual, cultural, and social activities of the Self-Reliant Literary Group: its coverage of the Tonkinese Chamber of the People's Representatives illustrates its commitment to popular sovereignty and faith in political structures; its campaigns against superstition and championing of science highlight the group's belief in a rational, secular political order; its patriotism is manifest in its insistence on writing in the romanized Vietnamese script (*quốc ngữ*) and its push to create a modern Vietnamese national literature; and, finally, its desire to improve the conditions of women and peasants emphasizes its belief in the universality of democratic ideals. However, the group's politics also diverged from that of Vũ Trọng Phụng in significant ways. Perhaps because of its members' leftist leanings, anticommunism did not feature as prominently in the group's writings, and the group exhibited unshakable optimism toward the transformative potential of politics, particularly mass activism. Most important, the group's cosmopolitan nationalism advanced a vision of a postcolonial Vietnam and a prescriptive blueprint to achieve it. Thus, although the group and Vũ Trọng Phụng may have had similar political values, only the group promoted a nationalist agenda by participating in formal political activity.

Among members of the Self-Reliant Literary Group, Hoàng Đạo contributed most prolifically to formulating its political ideology. Sometimes using the pseudonym Tứ Ly or Tứ Linh, Hoàng Đạo penned editorial commentaries on local and national news, theoretical essays on various ideologies, and analytical articles on aspects of colonial policy. He had a penchant for serialized educational articles on politics; for example, one in 1939 dealt with various forms of governance, and another from 1940 explained the basics of "citizen's education" *(công dân giáo dục)*. After Hoàng Đạo, Khái Hưng also played an important role in articulating the group's political outlook, despite his reputation as the most "romantic" novelist of the group. His column "The Story of the Week" ("Câu Truyện Hàng Tuần") in *These Days* commented on politics at all levels, from municipal elections to European parliaments.[6] Other members, such as Thạch Lam and Thế Lữ, occasionally wrote on politics but never enough to discern their individual political sympathies. Although Nhất Linh became the most politically active member of the group in the post-1945 period, he contributed little to the political conversations of the 1930s. During the group's most openly political period, from 1936 to 1940, Nhất Linh was mostly preoccupied with the League of Light, a philanthropic organization he founded to combat unsanitary housing conditions in urban and rural areas. Because Hoàng Đạo wrote most of the political essays and commentary, his ideas represented those of the group.

This chapter outlines the major tenets of the Self-Reliant Literary Group's political project in three sections, paying particular attention to the group's demands for institutional, colonial, and legal reform, and its rejection of monarchy. The main primary sources are the two newspapers of the group, *Mores* (1932–1935) and *These Days* (1935–1940). The contents of the two publications showed a gradual shift of the writers' attitudes from mildly to sharply critical of the colonial regime. In the early years of *Mores,* the group's understated political commentary focused on two aims: first, to use the press to build an informed readership and future citizenry, and, second, to point out the deficiencies of the French colonial project in Vietnam. In *These Days,* the group's appeals for political reform became more strident, requesting legal and institutional changes outright. An examination of these writings reveals that not only were group members ardent believers in republican values, but that they also saw those values as the foundation for a future autonomous Vietnamese state. However, the group did not advocate violent anticolonial struggle to establish this postcolonial vision. Although it became more vocal in its criticism of colonialism, it never openly called for the overthrow of the French. Its political writings suggest instead that members did not believe that Vietnam was ready for autonomy and favored more gradualist pathways toward statehood.

THE TONKIN CHAMBER OF REPRESENTATIVES AND INSTITUTIONAL REFORM

The earliest and most sustained discussion on politics in the group's journals surrounded the Tonkinese Chamber of the People's Representatives (Chambre de Représentants du Peuple, or Viện Dân Biểu Bắc Kỳ), the protectorate's indigenous elected consultative assembly. Despite the democratic implications of its name, the chamber held little influence and no power, both having been eroded by the colonial state since it was established in 1886.[7] The chamber met once a year in the autumn for eight days to discuss budgetary matters and elect officers. Coinciding with this meeting, the Self-Reliant Literary Group published an annual special issue (or sometimes a series) dedicated to its proceedings. After its special Lunar New Year issue, coverage of the chamber remained the longest-running yearly feature in the group's journals, spanning *Mores* and *These Days* from 1932 until 1938. The issue enticed its readers with both straightforward news and scintillating insider tittle-tattle: "Reports, interviews, and analysis of the chamber and its members. How the representatives work. Scheming and plotting by various members. The secret negotiations in the battle for chamber president."[8] The group intended its coverage to expose the impotence of the chamber and its members, thus highlighting the disingenuousness of the French imperial policy of association in Vietnam.

The first year journalists were allowed to attend the annual sessions of the chamber was 1932, and the reporters at *Mores* took full advantage of the new access. Every special issue included humorous reportage of the chamber's minutes, describing the dynamics of the meetings in painstaking detail. The coverage provided information about each representative, including the clique to which he belonged and who his rivals were, as well as caricatured images of the representatives' appearance. Quite often, the paper would also include cartoons that identified all the representatives serving in the chamber, as in figure 3.1.

HỘI ĐỒNG.....

1. Ông nghị Bùi, 2. Ông Phạm-huy-Lục, 3. Ông Trần-trọng-Kim, 4. Ông Lại-văn-Trung, 5. Ông Vũ-đỗ-Thin, 6. Ông Hoàng-hữu-Huy (chủ-nhiệm báo Đông-Pháp), 7. Ông Nguyễn-công-Tiểu (chủ-nhiệm Khoa-học tạp-chí), 8. Ông Bùi-xuân-Học (chủ-nhiệm Ngọ-báo), 9. Ông Nguyễn-văn-Tam (chủ-nhiệm báo Essor commercial), 10. Ông Nguyễn-văn-Vĩnh, 11. Ông Nguyễn-Lễ, 12. Ông Nguyễn-huy-Hợi, 13. Ông Vũ-văn-An, 14. Ông Nguyễn-thừa-Đạt, 15. Ông Là-qui-Trạch, 16. Ông Lê-văn-Phúc, 17. Ông Ngô-liên-Cảnh, 18. Ông Nguyễn-hữu-Hoan, 19. Ông Ngô-trọng-Trí, 20. Ông Vũ-văn-Đinh, 21. Ông Nguyễn-hữu-Cư.

Figure 3.1.   Cartoon from *Mores* 68 (October 13, 1933): 1.

Readers of *Mores* would have immediately recognized Lý Toét sitting among the representatives. By far the most ubiquitous cartoon character in the group's newspapers, this country bumpkin was the most recognized cultural icon of the 1930s. His appearance hinted not only at the presence of the traditional mandarinate in the proceedings, but also at *Mores*' low opinion of the chamber. More important, however, this cartoon provided readers a way to put faces to names, creating a visual language which *Mores* could easily employ in the future. For example, readers could later easily recognize Nguyễn Huy Hợi's freckles (#12), the bags under Lê Văn Phúc's eyes (#16), and Ngô Trọng Trí's egg-shaped head (#19) in *Mores*' subsequent caricatures and cartoons. The immediacy of knowing what these officials looked like made the chamber's political proceedings seem less removed, inviting readers to know exactly was happening in their representative body. Each special issue promised an in-depth look into the internal workings of the chamber, so that readers "*know* how the representatives are working and *observe* the actions of the chamber."[9]

By inviting readers to pay attention to the chamber, the paper aimed to expose the institution's fundamental ineffectiveness and corruption. The writers at *Mores* could scarcely contain their scorn for what they perceived as the pomposity, laziness, and incompetence of the representatives. *Mores* often singled out and shamed representatives by name, calling them to task. *Mores* mocked Lê Văn Phúc for his subservient politeness, demanding him to "have a backbone when you're in the chamber!" The paper similarly lambasted conservative mandarin Lai Văn Trung for remaining quiet and not contributing to discussions, commenting that he was "following the example of his most venerated Confucius." In another instance, *Mores* castigated two representatives from Phú Thọ who gave conflicting facts about the head tax in their provinces: "You don't even know the policies of your own province! How could you discuss other important issues with any mastery? You'd better go and learn the taxation policies of your area." As the group boldly said, "The representatives will answer to us."[10] The special issues suggest that the group had wanted the chamber to be a viable, functional representative body and that its intention was to inculcate the habits and practices of engaged citizenship in its readers.

In its coverage, *Mores* also revealed the chamber's sad internal state of affairs. Because the colonial government prohibited political parties, the Chamber of Representatives lacked the political and ideological fault lines of European parliaments. Instead, members coalesced into clientelist cliques centered around rival bosses. When representative Nguyễn Công Tiễu lamented the lack of organized groups in the chamber, Tứ Ly sarcastically corrected him that the chamber did in fact have them: those that wear medallions and those that do not; those that wear Western clothing and those in traditional tunics; as well as the young, the old, and the middle-aged. Not only that, Tứ Ly continued, the chamber even modeled itself on representative bodies in Europe: "We have leftist groups: people who sit in the chairs on the left. We also have rightist groups: people who sit in the chairs on the right. And centrist groups: those who walk down the central aisle."[11] Underlying Tứ Ly's humor was the critique that by banning political parties, the colonial state allowed the Vietnamese to ape Western democratic practices without any real substance. In European parliaments, the tradition of sitting on the left and right signified important and profound ideological differences, representing diametrically conflicting worldviews and bitter disputes over the role of society, economy, and the state. The group intimated that the Tonkinese chamber lacked this sense of ideological and political difference that would not only set opposing groups apart but also encouraged cohesion from within them. Without these clear differences, members of the chamber were prone to petty factionalism and opportunism.

Yet despite the detailed descriptions and strident criticism, *Mores* offered no solutions for the dismal state of affairs in the Tonkinese chamber. It was not until *These Days* that the Self-Reliant Literary Group changed its tone, announcing that "The Chamber of Representatives must change." It was no longer useful to focus on the corrupt behavior of individual representatives, they argued, as this was merely a symptom of larger systemic problems, of "decay at the roots."[12] Instead, Tứ Ly called for two major political reforms: to expand the powers and prerogatives of the chamber and to extend voting privileges to more Vietnamese. He argued that as a mere consultative institution, the chamber held no substantive power. The chamber's annual meeting was a mere formality; the government had no legal obligation whatsoever to act on its recommendations. Tứ Ly wrote that "such powers are too narrow and not worthy of the exalted name 'Chamber of the People's Representatives' that Governor-General Varenne graciously gave it in 1926. Rather, we should have kept the old name 'Consultative Chamber' to save us the shame and to match more closely with reality." He called for the expansion of the chamber's powers: "It must have the capacity to make decisions, at least similar to the Colonial Council [Hội Đồng Quản Hạt] in Cochinchina."[13] Tứ Ly believed that a chamber with greater legislative power would instill in its members a greater sense of responsibility, which in turn would encourage talented and driven people to run for public office, replacing the disreputable representatives and thereby invigorating the chamber with a new sense of purpose.

Tứ Ly likewise advocated the expansion of indigenous suffrage. He argued that the people do not support the chamber because they do not directly elect their representatives. "A quarter of the chamber is appointed by the government," Tứ Ly wrote, "and the remaining three-quarters do not represent all citizens, only a few. The overwhelming majority of the people do not have the right to vote." For the chamber to be authoritative, it must stand for the interests of a large electorate. Therefore, Tứ Ly argued, "We must change the eligibility to vote. For the chamber's voice to have impact it must have the widespread support of the people. For this to happen, we must expand suffrage by allowing the freedom to form political parties, to assemble, and to freely speak."[14] For Tứ Ly, the right to vote cannot be separated from a thriving political culture and civil society in which people are free to debate ideas, meet in public, and form associations. *These Days* would continue to make these demands through the years, forming the foundation of the group's republican ideology and cosmopolitan nationalism.

Not only did the Self-Reliant Literary Group use its journals to make political demands and publicize its own political opinions, it also wanted to report what the average person thought of the chamber. In 1938, *These Days* introduced what was perhaps one of the first instances of public opinion polling in Vietnam. In its annual special issue, *These Days* published the opinions of twenty-one Vietnamese titled "Surrounding the Chamber" ("Chung quanh Nghị Viện"). Thế Lữ realized the novelty of this kind of journalism, remarking, "In our country, interviews like this have never been done by any newspaper. Reporters are also not accustomed to conducting such interviews, and the subjects are not used to being interviewed."[15] The paper intended its polling sample to be a representative cross section of Tonkinese society that featured men and women from different classes, professions, and geographical areas. In the introduction, *These Days* promised readers that "the answers here are word for word, candid, and sincere. This is the honest public opinion [*dư luận*] of all classes towards the Chamber of Representatives." Interviewees included a Buddhist monk, a rickshaw driver, a songstress (*cô đầu*), a bookstore owner, a roaming peddler, and a Confucian village elder. Subjects were asked a series of questions about the chamber; their answers revealed that most Vietnamese were apathetic, suspicious, or ignorant about the colonial representative body. Two-thirds of those polled did not realize that the chamber was going into session; well over half answered that the chamber did not benefit them or were completely ignorant. Despite their unfavorable opinions, many interviewees preferred it to the mandarinate: one-third of respondents chose representatives over mandarins as opposed to one-seventh; the rest answered ambiguously. Although only a small sample, the interviews published in *These Days* hinted at the extent of the chamber's lack of influence in the everyday lives of Vietnamese.

For the Self-Reliant Literary Group, the vox populi and the expression of public opinion were closely tied to its republican pluralist values. On the surface, the group wanted to hold the Chamber of Representatives accountable for its inefficacy. The group was most likely aware of the power of public opinion in Western democracies to influence political developments; it communicates to a country's leaders about what the public is actually thinking and allows them to tailor their policies accordingly. The group perhaps hoped that widespread knowledge of the low opinion people had of the chamber would shame the representatives into reform. However, the poll's attempt to give voice to a cross-section of Tonkinese society marks a departure in the relationship between newspapers and readers. Before the group, many vernacular newspapers assumed a didactic role, conceptualizing the reading public as impressionable, empty vessels ready to receive education or entertainment. Newspaper content was distilled through a top-down network of gatekeepers including writers, editorial boards, and owners. In contrast, the poll attempted to convey not just unfiltered public opinion but also specifically the views of the most disenfranchised sectors of society. This suggests that the group wanted their readers to know what their fellow Vietnamese thought, in the hopes of invoking shared sympathies that held promise of a political community. Moreover, as avid readers of metropolitan newspapers, the group members were undoubtedly aware of the crucial democratic role the press played in representing political issues and ideas to the reading public, of turning a passive audience into active political participants. In this regard, the group was contemporaneous with developments in global polling practices. *These Days*' 1938 poll appeared only a few years after the 1935 founding of the world's most famous professional polling bureau—the American Institute of Public Opinion, the precursor of the Gallup Organization. Branches of this organization soon followed in Britain (1937) and France (1938).[16] The group adopted and localized the practice of public opinion polling from Western countries to foster democratic sensibilities and encourage the development of civil society in Vietnam.

As its coverage in both *Mores* and *These Days* illustrates, the Self-Reliant Literary Group believed that the Tonkinese Chamber of Representatives was in need of urgent reform. The group realized that correcting the behavior of corrupt politicians alone would not resolve the chamber's problems, which required more ambitious changes in the political system and civic culture. The group therefore mobilized its newspapers to agitate for these changes. On one hand, it demanded political concessions from the colonial government, including the expansion of suffrage, free speech, and the right of free assembly. At the same time, it encouraged the Vietnamese people to hold the colonial state accountable and demand their rights. The group expressed optimism that over time, these efforts would yield a new political culture:

> We should not be discouraged. Collective intelligence [*dân chí*] is improving by the day. Those in the chamber who only know how to fall asleep, or pontificate idly, or exploit their position for their personal gain, will gradually disappear. The powers of the chamber will expand. Who knows, maybe the chamber will have a bright future? It would depend on when this new culture permeates all people.[17]

This "new culture" amounted to nothing short of building a civil society on a foundation of republican values. The group's sustained campaign to reform the chamber underscores its belief in political institutions and processes of representative government. Its members' calls for the expansion of suffrage illustrate their commitment to popular sovereignty and equality for colonized peoples. However, underneath the group's calls for a new political culture lay the critique that Vietnamese were not ready for the responsibilities of democracy, having not yet cultivated the requisite knowledge, skills, and disposition for citizenship. As the group hinted in their writing, the prospect of self-governance was perhaps a long way off.

VIETNAMESE SELF-DETERMINATION AND LEGAL REFORM

Given the group's belief in democracy and representative institutions, what did it think about colonialism, that blatant infringement on national sovereignty and republican values? In a series of articles in the autumn of 1937, Hoàng Đạo made the group's strongest case for Vietnamese self-determination. He started by asking a pointed question: "Is it ethical to take colonies?" His answer was a resounding "no." He argued that even those who support the practice "cannot hide the fact that from the beginning, colonialism is the brutalization of the weak by the strong, a selfish undertaking for the profit of one side." Hoàng Đạo echoed the argument made by J. A. Hobson and later reworked by Lenin that imperialism was the inevitable result of capitalist expansion and its insatiable need for new markets.[18] He recalled how France had vowed that it "will never wage war for the purpose of conquest and will never use violence to destroy the freedom of any other people."[19] For the sake of economic profit, however, France had ignored its ideals and joined the scramble for colonies.

Hoàng Đạo completely rejected the principle of assimilation, in which the colony would become an integrated yet remote part of France, its people refashioned (as best as possible) into Frenchmen. Hoàng Đạo wrote that the Vietnamese were a people "with a past that could be called glorious, who have reached a high level of civilization, with a cooperative spirit and unified in character and language. For us, the policy of assimilation would be a mistake." He insisted that the Vietnamese did not want to be Frenchmen. Instead, they wanted "to enjoy the freedoms of democracy and gradually observe and take responsibility for the affairs of their country. When the people of Annam have the right, in freedom, to choose those who will govern them, their wishes will largely be fulfilled."[20] Here, Hoàng Đạo stated in no uncertain terms his nationalist vision: that Vietnam should not be a part of France, that it should be democratic and have the right to self-determination and national sovereignty. However, Hoàng Đạo did not mention how or when this will happen, or whether it would be violently and swiftly or gradually, which suggests that he did not believe the time was right to realize this vision.

In his other writings, however, Hoàng Đạo hinted at a possible scenario for gradual decolonization. As morally wrong as imperial conquest might be, Hoàng Đạo admitted that "colonies are already a reality." He argued that therefore the colonizers "must find a way to benefit the colonized, even at their own expense. Only then could they erase the memories of past violence and have enough reason to stay in another people's land."[21] For Hoàng Đạo, the only conscionable way to deal with existing colonies was to gradually phase them out.[22] He advocated international mediation in colonial matters, citing the League of Nations' mandate system. Hoàng Đạo explained that in the wake of World War I, "colonialism is not as before, but is instead guiding the way for the colonized to become autonomous, and when ready they will enjoy the right of self-determination."[23] Hoàng Đạo's argument implied that he did not trust France to willingly give up its overseas colonies, but did trust the international community to mediate the transition to autonomy. Although he never stated it outright, it seems likely that Hoàng Đạo envisioned Vietnam following just such a program of international trusteeship.

For Hoàng Đạo, the most important condition of freedom for colonized peoples was legislative power: "If the power to create laws rests in the hands of the colonized, they can self-govern and put themselves on equal footing with the mother country." Hoàng Đạo pointed out that British colonies enjoyed such freedoms but that France still followed the Napoleonic practice of "rule by edict or decree." The president of the republic could issue edicts and change colonial policy at will, which Hoàng Đạo likened to the powers of an absolute monarchy. Further compounding Indochina's legal problems was that edicts were often poorly enforced in the colonies. It was common for governor-generals and residents to delay or block the implementation of metropolitan decrees. For Hoàng Đạo, the flexibility and quick response built into the edict system was not necessarily an asset in legislative matters: "a law needs to be clear and adequate. For this to happen it must be carefully discussed and debated, then enforced. Once in place, to change the law should be difficult; any reason to actually change a law must be a legitimate one."[24] He advocated a more deliberate and procedural lawmaking process in colonial matters, and, more important, the expansion of legislative powers for the Vietnamese.

Hoàng Đạo's views on the edict system were born out of experience with colonial press laws limiting freedom of speech. The group encountered the injustice of the colonial legal system firsthand in 1936, when censors suspended *Mores* for three months without explanation. Through the years, *These Days* demanded freedom of speech, even publicly defending rival newspapers that the group felt received unfair treatment. On a number of occasions, *These Days* supported the communist paper *Le Travail* against the colonial government. When authorities arrested its editor Trịnh Văn Phú and writer Nguyễn Văn Tiến for "disturbing the peace and creating a disturbance of a political nature," Hoàng Đạo defended the pair by pointing out the injustice of that particular law. *These Days* even went so far as to convene a meeting at its headquarters with other newspapers to discuss ways to help the *Le Travail* writers win their eventual release.[25]

Hoàng Đạo took even greater umbrage from the fact that the press laws were arbitrary even within Indochina. In Cochinchina, *quốc ngữ* newspapers did not have to seek government permission, whereas in Tonkin they were subjected to a lengthy and difficult process to obtain a permit. The difference, as Hoàng Đạo pointed out, lay in the fact that Cochinchina enjoyed full status as a French colony. Hoàng Đạo explained that "the French press laws have a clause that states that 'these laws apply to all overseas colonies.'" As protectorates, Tonkin and Annam were subject to different regimes. To this Hoàng Đạo exclaimed, "What a confused jumble. But in Indochina, everything is complex, especially the law.

We must fix this confusion. Southerners or Northerners, we are all Annamese, we should live under the same legal system as well."[26] Rather than enjoy a procedural system characterized by consistency and transparency, Vietnamese were forced to deal with arbitrary and perpetually changing governance.

For Hoàng Đạo, the "confused jumble" of the press laws was but a symptom of a larger legal problem created not just by the edict system, but also by Tonkin's indeterminate status as a protectorate. He lamented that "a protectorate is not a separate nation, nor can it become part of the mother country . . . [its people] cannot become citizens of France, nor can they enjoy the rights reserved specifically for the colonies."[27] The Self-Reliant Literary Group argued on a number of occasions (especially regarding the Chamber of Representatives and press laws) that Tonkin should enjoy the same rights, legal system, privileges, and status as Cochinchina, and that the only way to build civil society among the Vietnamese was with uniform implementation and equal representation across all of Indochina. In other words, the group suggested that they would rather have Tonkin become a full-fledged French colony than remain in the ambiguous ad hoc status of protectorate. Tonkin, Tứ Ly argued, was ready for legal reforms:

> Some have said that the collective intelligence in the North has not yet reached those standards. . . . That is an unfounded statement. The Colonial Council in Cochinchina has had the power to make decisions since 1880—would anyone dare to say that the collective intelligence of the South at that time was any higher than the North today?[28]

From the group's point of view, the only way for Tonkin to enjoy greater political rights and privileges was, paradoxically, to be further enchained—by going from arbitrary rule by edict as a protectorate to the legal privileges and procedures enjoyed by a full colony. Hoàng Đạo demanded that France develop "a law that clearly states the rights of colonial citizens, a foundation. A constitution for the citizens of the colonies." Legislative powers should be delegated to each colony, "so that the laws made would meet the unique needs of that colony and the people can participate in the affairs of their country."[29] This constitution would "affirm that Annam will enjoy democratic rights and freedoms, and enjoy a representative body elected by universal suffrage."[30] At first glance, it may seem like Hoàng Đạo was indulging in a political pipe dream, that somehow France would go against its own self-interest and develop republican institutions in Vietnam. But in light of his nationalist vision of a self-determining and democratic Vietnam and his expressed interest in the League of Nations' mandate system, Hoàng Đạo's demand suggests a gradual process of implementing home rule that would ultimately end in autonomy.

REJECTION OF MONARCHY

Given the group's desire to see Vietnam as a democratic republic, it is under-standable that its members did not hold the most conservative political institu-tions, the mandarinate and the monarchy, in very high regard. Their low opinions of the monarchy and various figures within the Huế court—most notably Phạm Quỳnh—had always simmered beneath the surface of their satire, but in 1939 the group openly proclaimed them. In August of that year, the Francophone newspa-per *The Indochinese Will* (*Volonté Indochinoise)* leaked rumors that the French colonial government had finally decided to formally honor the Patenôtre Treaty of 1884 and return Tonkin to the monarchy. Under the terms of the treaty, France would control Cochinchina as a colony, and the emperor would retain adminis-trative power over the protectorates of Tonkin and Annam. Over the ensuing decades, however, French officials mostly ignored these terms and gradually eroded imperial authority. Finally, in a coup d'état, the Convention of November 6, 1925, divested the emperor of what little remaining power he held and trans-ferred it to the French residents-superior. This relegated the emperor to a mere figurehead for trivial formalities and rituals.[31]

Over the years, supporters of the monarchy continued to call for the restora-tion of imperial power as outlined by the treaty. In 1930, the most vocal of these supporters, Phạm Quỳnh, advanced his ideas in a famous article in *Southern Wind* titled "Towards a Constitution" ("Vers une constitution"). He demanded that France formally honor the terms of the 1884 treaty, return executive power to the emperor, and give Vietnam greater national autonomy. In Phạm Quỳnh's view, these demands were best met by establishing a constitutional monarchy. He believed that the most advantageous way to accommodate both Vietnamese political aspirations and French interests was not to overthrow the traditional institutions of the monarchy and mandarinate but to modernize and transform them. The cause of corruption and decay of these institutions, he argued, lay in their complete lack of authority, which could be reformed by restructuring the power-sharing relationship between Paris and Huế. He advocated that France set up a true protectorate according to the terms of the treaty, in which the colonial government would play a limited advisory role and the emperor would hold administrative and executive powers. The resident-superior of Annam and a rep-resentative in Hanoi would represent French interests; a council of ministers would advise and assist the emperor in matters of state. The Vietnamese people would be given limited democratic representation through the Chamber of Representatives, which would be given wider legislative powers.[32]

For these reforms, Phạm Quỳnh found an ally in Pierre Pasquier, governor-general of Indochina from 1928 to 1934. Pasquier believed that a rejuvenated monarchy could help advance French aims in Indochina. In 1932, the two worked together to bring the nineteen-year-old Emperor Bảo Đại back from his studies in France as part of a larger plan to reform the Vietnamese imperial court. It all started promisingly enough. The Convention of 1925 was abolished, and a royal decree issued outlining a reform program to be executed in the areas of education, the mandarinate, justice, and the Chamber of Representatives. Much to the surprise of colonial officials, the young emperor showed some initiative in this plan to revive the monarchy. Shortly after his return, Bảo Đại banned the kowtow, dismissed the old Council of Ministers, and toppled the Catholic mandarin Nguyễn Hữu Bài as prime minister to take over the position himself. He named a new council, appointing younger and more progressive figures, including Phạm Quỳnh as minister of national education, Ngô Đình Diệm as minister of the interior, and Bùi Bằng Đoàn as minister of justice. Unfortunately, it soon became clear that despite French promises for greater autonomy, the colonial government had no intention of relinquishing any real authority. In a move that would win him much respect as a man of integrity and conviction, Ngô Đình Diệm resigned in protest after less than three months in office. Phạm Quỳnh stayed on, wiping out whatever little remained of his patriotic credentials and cementing the criticism of him from intellectual circles as a French stooge.[33]

Despite the setbacks, Phạm Quỳnh doggedly agitated for a "return to 1884" throughout the 1930s.[34] In 1939, he traveled to Paris to persuade the French Ministry of Colonies (now headed by the radical Georges Mandel) to adopt this plan. Back in Vietnam, rumors began circulating in the press that Paris intended to return Tonkin to imperial control. These rumors set off a series of strong objections among the Tonkinese elite, including the Self-Reliant Literary Group. In his analysis of the situation, Hoàng Đạo argued that pro-monarchist factions had misread the treaty. He cited the monarchist newspaper *The Strong South* (*Nam Cường*), which maintained that a return to the 1884 treaty would facilitate democratic reforms, such as establishing a constitution, representative bodies, and a system of checks and balances. Although pleased that a monarchist journal would even entertain the thought of a limited monarchy, Hoàng Đạo pointed out that *The Strong South* conflated the imperial court with democratic institutions:

> *The Strong South* is jumping ahead of itself. Who knows if it is unintentional or wishful thinking? To return domestic control to the court according to the 1884 Treaty is one thing, but to expand the power of the Chamber and extend citizen's rights to the people of Annam is something completely different, let's not mistake that. This error is one with grave consequences.

Hoàng Đạo pointed out that even if executive control were returned to the emperor, it remained a royal prerogative to establish a representative chamber and extend civil rights. The imperial court could very well revert to absolutism or, as Hoàng Đạo put it, "move heaven or earth if it pleased them," and France would lose its oversight privileges to check the monarchy.[35]

Hoàng Đạo not only refuted the monarchist argument for the 1884 treaty, he completely rejected the idea of a constitutional monarchy—which had its most ardent supporter and theoretician in Phạm Quỳnh. Hoàng Đạo remarked that "To take the freedom and rights of an entire people and place it at the whim of a few is a dictatorship, nothing else!" He believed that monarchy and democracy were fundamentally at odds:

> A constitutional monarchy [*chính thể quân chủ lập hiến*], as many have argued, does not make sense at all; neither the divine right of kings nor democracy is followed completely. If one follows the divine right of kings, the king's power is derived from God; the desires of his subjects, the people, cannot limit it. The king can allow them to enjoy a few rights, a few freedoms, but the king always maintains the right to revoke them. If he cannot, then there is no way that his power is god-given. According to democracy, the issue of succession cannot be reconciled with its most fundamental ideal, that of the rule of the people. Even if a king is elected by the people, then only he represents the people; his children and descendants ascending the throne have nothing to do with the people. Reconciling the power of the king with the rule of the people does not coincide with reason.[36]

In later writings, Hoàng Đạo denied the divine right of kings to the Vietnamese monarchy when he described it as a "manmade bond, loose and without any strength."[37] Hoàng Đạo did not trust the monarchy to establish representative institutions and expand citizens' rights. After all, the establishment of constitutional monarchies in Europe resulted only from long-fought processes of chipping away at absolutist power.

Rather than reverting to the old Patenôtre Treaty, a number of Self-Reliant Literary Group members suggested signing a new pact with France. As Khái Hưng wrote, "We are ready to sign another treaty with France, one in which our rights would matter." In his column, Hoàng Đạo added that the monarchists

> have forgotten that even if we abrogate the 1884 Treaty, we could always sign a new one. Yes, why don't we sign a new treaty between Vietnam and France, one that matches the current level of Vietnamese development and progress? Why don't we convene representatives to negotiate with the French government towards a genuine constitution that that protects freedom of democracy and unalienable human rights for the Vietnamese people? Why can't we do that?[38]

Members of the Self-Reliant Literary Group were suspicious of monarchy in all its forms, even a potentially benevolent one. For them, it was far more preferable to build a civil society on transparent political procedures than on the whims of a few powerful individuals. The Self-Reliant Literary Group made the case for a secular liberal democracy founded on popular representation—in other words, a democratic republic.

In the wake of the objections by northern intellectuals such as the Self-Reliant Literary Group, the minister of colonies finally put the rumors to rest by declaring them false. As archival documents indicate, the French had no intention of giving away their administrative authority over Tonkin, especially given growing Japanese influence in the region.[39] The brouhaha over the 1884 treaty lasted a little over three weeks. Nevertheless, this short episode illustrates the group's antimonarchical sentiments and their disdain for supporters of the imperial court. The group's writings reveal that it believed the monarchy to be a hopelessly obsolete institution not worth reforming, rejected the idea of a constitutional monarchy, and reiterated its support for a secular, liberal democracy based on the rule of law.

Writing in July 1939 to commemorate the anniversary of the French Revolution, the group subtly criticized the wide gulf between the exalted ideals of French republicanism and the inherently unequal realities of French colonial rule in Indochina. *These Days* prominently featured a Vietnamese translation of the Declaration of the Rights of Man and Citizen as well as a detailed analysis of the document. In the same issue, the paper printed a series of cartoons satirizing life in colonial Vietnam. Drawn by Tô Ngọc Vân and titled "Games and Diversions: the 14 of July in France and Indochina," these cartoons portrayed the relationship between France and its Indochinese colony as a series of fairground contests and events (see figure 3.2). One of the cartoons, "Blindman's Bluff," featured a blindfolded Lý Toét and Xã Xệ chasing two goats labeled "Freedom" and "Equality." A caption below another explained, "Newsreel on screen: An image of Georges Mandel sharing a piece of the 'sweet cake of Rights.' In a flash, the 'cake' has disappeared. The Vietnamese craned their necks in anticipation, their mouths watering." When read together, the meaning of the Declaration and cartoon becomes clear: France had betrayed its republican ideals through colonial conquest.

CONCLUSION

From *Mores'* and *These Days'* coverage of politics, it becomes apparent that the members of Self-Reliant Literary Group believed in French republican ideals but not the way France was undermining them in her colonies. The group's calls to expand suffrage and widen the chamber's powers underscore its belief in popular sovereignty and trust in political structures. Its demands for greater Vietnamese autonomy and equality under the law echo the Enlightenment values of

Figure 3.2. Cartoon by Tô Ngọc Vân, from *These Days* 170 (July 15, 1939): 14.

universality and patriotism. Its complete rejection of monarchy emphasizes its conviction that democracy and transparent political procedures are preferable to the arbitrary rule of a vested few. Fervent colonial supporters of republican values, the group also campaigned against rule by edict, criticized harsh press laws, and called for a colonial constitution—in short, it demanded that the colonial government live up to the ideals it so openly proclaimed. In response to this colonial condition, the group's brand of cosmopolitan nationalism would seek to realize its colonial republican ideals through moderate left politics, firmly grounded in self-reliance.[40] Vietnamese could borrow the tools and materials from outside, but they had to take ownership and build their nation themselves from the ground up. The group's political project aimed at building an engaged, informed readership (and eventually electorate) committed to the collective good of a future Vietnamese republic.

The Self-Reliant Literary Group's social and cultural reform project cannot be separated from its politics—they were one and the same. The building of civil society in Vietnam lay below *Mores*'s humor and satire in the same way that the group's attack on familial oppression constituted the destruction of an entire feudal economic order. The group's insistence on writing only in *quốc ngữ* had clear patriotic implications, and its publishing enterprises aimed at creating informed proto-citizens. Along with these cultural and social reforms, the group also had a substantive and far-reaching political vision for Vietnam—one in which its citizens enjoyed democratic freedoms, transparent political procedures, representative institutions, and the rule of law. The Self-Reliant Literary Group's championing of republican values and its later embrace of center-left politics envisioned no less than a complete restructuring of Vietnamese society—a revolution in its own right.

NOTES

This essay reworks chapter 4 of my book *On Our Own Strength: The Self-Reliant Literary Group and Cosmopolitanism in Late Colonial Vietnam* (Honolulu: University of Hawai'i Press, 2021).

1. See Nguyễn Lương Hải Khôi's chapter 2 in this volume.

2. Sudhir Hazareesingh, *Political Traditions in Modern France* (Oxford: Oxford University Press, 1994), 68.

3. Alice Conklin, *A Mission to Civilize: The Republican Idea of Empire in France and West Africa, 1895–1930* (Stanford, CA: Stanford University Press, 1997); Elizabeth Heath, *Wine, Sugar, and the Making of Modern France: Global Economic Crisis and the Racialization of French Citizenship, 1870–1910* (Cambridge: Cambridge University Press, 2014); and Martin Thomas. *The French Empire Between the Wars: Imperialism, Politics and Society* (Manchester, UK: Manchester University Press, 2005).

4. Gary Wilder, *The French Imperial Nation-State: Negritude and Colonial Humanism Between the Two World Wars* (Chicago: University of Chicago Press, 2005).

5. Peter Zinoman, *Vietnamese Colonial Republican: The Political Vision of Vũ Trọng Phụng* (Berkeley: University of California Press, 2014), 5–6.

6. For "citizens' education," see both *Ngày nay* 99 (February 27, 1938) 3; and *Ngày nay* 194 (December 30, 1939): 15. Khái Hưng's column ran from February 1938 through September 1939. Save for this column, Khái Hưng's writing rarely ever mentioned politics.

7. While serving as governor-general in the 1920s, Alexandre Varenne expanded the chamber's powers, changing its name to the Chamber of the People's Representatives. After Varenne's departure, the colonial government quickly limited the chamber's new powers. See "Lịch Sử," insert in *Ngày nay* 128 (September 18, 1938): 5; and Trương Bửu Lâm, *Colonialism Experienced: Vietnamese Writings on Colonialism, 1900–1931* (Ann Arbor: University of Michigan, 2000), 13–14.

8. Advertisement in *Ngày nay* 127 (September 11, 1938): 11.

9. Advertisement in *Ngày nay* 127 (emphasis added).

10. For Lê Văn Phúc, see "Từ nhỏ đến nhớn," *Phong hóa* 22 (November 18, 1932): 4. For Lai Văn Trung and the representatives from Phú Thọ, see Tứ Ly, "Từ cao đến thấp," *Phong hóa* 69 (October 20, 1933): 5. For the group's bold statement, see advertisement in *Ngày nay* 127.

11. Tứ Ly, "Đảng Phái," *Phong hóa* 121 (October 26, 1934): 5.

12. Tứ Ly, "Viện dân biểu cần phải thay đổi," *Ngày nay* 85 (November 14, 1937): 952.

13. The Cochinchinese Colonial Council enjoyed far greater powers than the Tonkinese chamber. It was allowed to set the personal property tax rate, vote on the colonial budget and public works, and take action in the name of Cochinchina unless otherwise performed by the governor-general. See Jean LeClerc, *De l'évolution et du développement des institutions annamites et cambodgiennes sous l'influence française* (Rennes: Edoneur et Ruesch, 1923), 120, cited in Allan Goodman, *Politics in War: The Bases of Political Community in South Vietnam* (Cambridge, MA: Harvard University Press, 1973), 15.

14. Tứ Ly, "Viện dân biểu cần phải thay đổi."

15. Thế Lữ and Trọng Lang, "Chúng tôi đi phỏng vấn" *Ngày nay* 127 (September 11, 1938): 15.

16. Nick Moon, *Opinion Polls: History, Theory and Practice* (Manchester, UK: Manchester University Press, 1999), 14; and Susan Herbst, "Surveying and Influencing the Public: Polling in Politics and Industry," in *The Cambridge History of Science,* vol. 7, *The Modern Social Sciences,* ed. Ted Porter and Dorothy Ross (Cambridge: Cambridge University Press, 2003), 585.

17. Tứ Linh, "Các ông nghị," *Phong hóa* 22 (November 18, 1932): 1.

18. Hoàng Đạo, "Lấy thuộc địa có chính đáng không?" *Ngày nay* 77 (September 19, 1937): 759–760.

19. Hoàng Đạo, "Quyền sống của mọi nước," *Ngày nay* 162 (May 20, 1939): 10.

20. Hoàng Đạo, "Thuộc địa Pháp—Chính sách," *Ngày nay* 80 (October 10, 1937): 831–832.

21. Hoàng Đạo, "Thuộc địa Pháp."

22. Hoàng Đạo, "Cộng tác đề huề," *Ngày nay* 78 (September 6, 1937): 783.

23. Hoàng Đạo, "Quyền sống của mọi nước."

24. Hoàng Đạo, "Thuộc địa Pháp—Chế độ chỉ dụ," *Ngày nay* 81 (October 17, 1937): 855.

25. See Hoàng Đạo, "Từng tuần lễ một," *Ngày nay* 38 (December 13, 1936): 540; Hoàng Đạo, "Từng tuần lễ một," *Ngày nay* 44 (January 24, 1937): 682; and Hoàng Đạo, "Từng tuần lễ một," *Ngày nay* 59 (May 16, 1937): 328. As a participant in the committee, *These Days* played a role in the release of these two political prisoners. When they were later rearrested, *These Days* convened a meeting at its headquarters to discuss how to help them. See "Báo giới bắc kỳ can thiệp lần thứ hai vào việc hai bạn Phú, Tiến, bị bắt giam," *Ngày nay* 122 (August 7, 1938): 4.

26. Hoàng Đạo, "Tự do ngôn luận: Mở báo quốc ngữ không phải xin phép nhưng chỉ ở thuộc địa," *Ngày nay* 34 (November 15, 1936): 442.

27. Hoàng Đạo, "Các hạng thuộc địa," *Ngày nay* 79 (October 2, 1937): 807.

28. Tứ Ly, "Viện dân biểu phải thay đổi."

29. Hoàng Đạo, "Thuộc địa Pháp—Chế độ chỉ dụ," *Ngày nay* 81 (October 17, 1937): 855.

30. Hoàng Đạo, "Người và việc," *Ngày nay* 176 (August 26, 1939): 4.

31. William Duiker, *The Rise of Nationalism in Vietnam, 1900–1941* (Ithaca, NY: Cornell University Press, 1976), 170–171.

32. Duiker, *Rise of Nationalism in Vietnam,* 172–173. Even in 1930, Phạm Quỳnh's idea was met with criticism, most vocally and famously by Nguyễn Văn Vĩnh. The debate between Phạm Quỳnh's idea of constitutionalism (*lập hiến*) and Nguyễn Văn Vĩnh's supervised rule (*trực trị*) defined the political and intellectual discourse of their generation. The younger generation, which included the Self-Reliant Literary Group, rejected both ideas and formulated their own for an independent Vietnam.

33. Duiker, *Rise of Nationalism in Vietnam,* 172–173; and Arthur Dommen, *The Indochinese Experience of the French and the Americans: Nationalism and Communism in Cambodia, Laos, and Vietnam* (Bloomington: Indiana University Press, 2001), 45–47.

34. Neil Jamieson, *Understanding Vietnam* (Berkeley: University of California Press, 1993), 89.

35. Hoàng Đạo, "Trở lại hòa ước 1884: Tiến bộ hay thoái bộ?" *Ngày nay* 175 (August 19, 1939): 11, 14.

36. Hoàng Đạo, "Chính thể quân chủ và cộng hòa," *Ngày nay* 103 (March 27, 1938): 3–4.

37. Hoàng Đạo, "Công dân giáo dục: Nước Nam," *Ngày nay* 165 (June 10, 1939): 10.

38. Hoàng Đạo, "Trở lại hòa ước 1884."

39. Duiker, *Rise of Nationalism in Vietnam,* 176.

40. For the center-left views and politics practiced by the group, see Martina Thucnhi Nguyen, "Political Ideology and Postcolonial Vision," chapter 4 in *On Our Own Strength,* 120–153.

CHAPTER FOUR

Trần Văn Tùng's Vision of a New Nationalism for a New Vietnam

Yen Vu

"What is a nationalist? It is simply a conscious and lucid man, open to all new ideas, who, rejecting all individualism and anarchy, advocates the Nation as the first form of a human society."

—Trần Văn Tùng

In a letter to the editor in the *New York Times* in 1953, Vietnamese essayist and historian Trần Văn Tùng publicized his position on liberty and independence for Vietnam. These were the founding tenets for his understanding of nationalism, one that would be distinct from the communist movement. In his letter, he acknowledged the American global anticommunist strategy but also its idealism and pointed out that foreign aid, though perhaps well-intended from both the French and Americans, "[has] not clarified the Vietnamese situation, which appears more unstable than ever."[1] This is because any foreign aid cannot grant Vietnam the most powerful weapons of all: independence and liberty. In other words, independence was something to be developed from within, not granted by another power. This letter would be the first of several addressed to the American public over the course of a decade in which Trần Văn Tùng would declare his political ideas, introduce the existence of the Democratic Party of Vietnam, and establish early on a difference between the independence of the anticolonial Vietnamese revolution and the independence he sought as a nationalist.[2]

Trần Văn Tùng is not a figure we hear about often in a political context. He is instead better known for his literary works of francophone literature, notably for the titles *Rêves d'un campagnard annamite* (1940) and *Bach Yên, ou, fille au coeur fidèle* (1946), both of which have also been recognized by the French public, if not by the French Academy then by journals such as *Lettres françaises* and scholars such as Paul Claudel. Any existing scholarship on Tùng's writings have predominantly treated his work within the limits of colonial or Franco-Vietnamese relations. These sparse works either categorize him as the obedient Vietnamese student or scholar or see little connection between Tùng's poetics and politics, leaving little room for the depth of plans he intended for Vietnam.[3] His literary corpus therefore has yet to be examined using the political lens through which they were written or his diplomatic activity explored with the same conviction that afflicted the writer regarding the internationalization of the Vietnamese nationalist cause.

On the one hand, studies of the Francophone figures such as Trần Văn Tùng remain in the context of French and Francophone literature, which therefore do not place him within the larger context of Vietnamese culture and the changing politics of the twentieth century. Conversely, scholars of Vietnam do not include these writers within studies of Vietnamese nationalism. This chapter thus contributes to both the fields of Vietnam and French studies and draws connections that are important for better understanding not only these intellectual figures but also the Vietnamese historical and political contexts that surrounded them. In proposing to examine the works of this writer turned diplomat, I turn in particular to his idea of nationalism, expressed in his later works, and its ambivalent relationship with the legacy of republican ideals.

In the context of Francophone Vietnamese intellectuals, Tùng was an engaged intellectual who could be likened to Nguyễn Mạnh Tường, whose formation in law and literature greatly influenced his participation in politics in North Vietnam. The latter, educated in France, applied his Western education to make social criticisms under the Vietnamese communist party, and is most known for his contribution in the journal *Giai phẩm* in 1956. That is, although he initially supported the party's efforts to rebuild society after colonial independence, their increasing infringement on individual and intellectual freedom made him, along with many other writers and intellectuals, critical of the direction the party was headed. Despite the different contexts in which they operated, their political stance could be traced back to a similar liberal, humanist standpoint, in which freedom, and especially intellectual freedom, was the foundation of a functional society and should thus be protected. Ironically, both intellectuals would find their pursuit of such freedom interrupted; Nguyễn Mạnh Tường excommunicated for expressing his candid critique of the Land Reform campaign in 1956, and Trần Văn Tùng relegated to political "noise" from abroad.

Among the categories of noncommunist, nationalist revolutionary movements in South Vietnam, which included the Đại Việt parties, the Catholic and Cần Lao Party of the Ngô family, the southern political and religious parties, and the republican and democratic parties, it is precisely this last category that has received the least attention in scholarship.[4] As a proponent of the Democratic Party of Vietnam, Tùng sought an anticommunist, anticolonialist, and anti-Diệm alternative. His ideas for a free, sovereign nation, though perhaps only made public to the American readership beginning in 1953, had already been set in motion, reflected upon, honed, and developed at least a decade earlier with the publication of his novel *Bach Yên*. It was not until the Elysée Accords of 1949, signed by former Emperor Bảo Đại and French President Vincent Auriol promising Vietnam independence, that Tùng began to write explicitly on this topic. Tùng subsequently released four consecutive essays on Vietnam published exclusively with Editions de La Belle Page in Paris from 1950 to 1953. The first three of these are most similar in kind and address nationalism directly; the last is a collection of Vietnamese legends that ground Vietnamese identity and nationalism in folklore. These essays most likely speak to an educated elite whom Tùng believed to be both responsible and capable of reconstructing a new nation. After these essays were published, Tùng started actively communicating with the American and French public about Vietnam, its people and its politics, particularly during the last years of the Diệm administration. These essays thus mark his transition into politics, but with the authority and respect of a "poet in touch with his native country," as one prefacer claims, rather than an ambitious politician.[5]

Focusing on the political perspectives that inform Tùng's writings, I examine in particular his vision for a new nationalism as it unraveled after the 1949 Elysée Accords, its local and international appeal, and its program for a free and democratic Vietnam. This includes a critical examination of the republican legacies in Tùng's idea of new nationalism as well as a discussion of the Democratic Party of Vietnam that emerged overseas, to be distinguished from the party founded in 1944 that later merged with the Việt Minh. As a consequence, we can appreciate a more complex understanding not only of Trần Văn Tùng, but also of Vietnamese nationalism, not to be conflated with communism nor aggregated in the general category of anticolonialism.

DISAGGREGATING IDEAS OF VIETNAMESE NATIONALISM

Much of the discussion on Vietnamese nationalism, despite overlap with Vietnamese narratives, has been dominated by external or academic views. For example, the vicissitudes of how scholars understand nationalism reflect both American involvement in Vietnam and the ways in which the field has changed in the last fifty years. We might understand nationalism during the final decades of colonial rule in Vietnam in terms of binary oppositions between those in favor of independence and those for further collaboration, or even between communist and anticommunist movements. After 1945, nationalist parties such as the Việt Nam Quốc Dân Đảng were quickly extinguished as a collective entity and the idea of nationalism soon became conflated, both in scholarship and by political actors, with the anticolonial and anti-imperial position offered by communism, the reconstruction of the nation after independence monopolized by communist strategies. Such was the understanding of many Americans, swayed by the antiwar movement, who saw Hồ Chí Minh and his party first as nationalists and only then as communists fighting for a self-determined government.

There has arguably always been a distinction, albeit blurred or sometimes intangible, between how the Vietnamese themselves understood ideas of nationalism and how scholarship or the external world represented those ideas. Only more recently has scholarship—sources permitting—granted purchase to this distinction, giving voice and agency to the diverse ideas of those living in Vietnam throughout that conflicted nation-building era between 1945 to 1975.[6] Within this volume, for example, both Duy Lap Nguyen and Nu-Anh Tran contribute ways in which politicians in the Republic of Vietnam interpreted and applied ideas of democracy. Nu-Anh Tran focuses on the 1955 elections to address the debate over democracy and the extent to which it can exist in the period of constitutional transition and political debate. Nguyen's analysis follows Ngô Đình Diệm's election victory and traces his Strategic Hamlet Program back to the Emmanuel Mounier's definition of personalism, to eradicate capitalism and liberal ideals of democracy. These perspectives allow us to move beyond the conflated triumph of nationalist and communist agendas and to pay more attention to the question that many other Vietnamese were asking themselves: what was that reconstructed Vietnamese nation for which they fought supposed to be?

Disaggregating ideas of Vietnamese nationalism is complex; it requires not only the distinction between communist and nationalist struggles but also the acknowledgment of differences between the various nationalist movements. It prompts seemingly obvious questions: Did being "nationalist" mean patriotic? Did it automatically include advocacy for independence? Was nationalism committed to the ethnic identities of people, or was it state-centered?[7] Was it an end goal or part of the process of becoming a nation? Different political groups had different answers to these questions, and such plurality, or "contested nationalism," has been one proposed way to understand the complexity of Vietnam's trajectory as both a single and partitioned nation.[8] During the thirty years of continual shift in Vietnam's geopolitical boundaries and statuses, the negotiation of Vietnamese nationalism also reflected those changes. Vũ Văn Thái, the director general of foreign aid and budget under the Diệm administration and subsequently Vietnamese ambassador to the United States in 1965, captures in one essay that unfixed quality of nationalism by writing, "Independence alone is an empty proposition. It has to be accompanied by a concept of nationhood which would both fulfill the rising expectations of the people, and at the same time preserve the essentials of the Vietnamese way of life."[9] As we see for Thái, it is unclear what that concept would be. Writing on Vietnamese nationalism in 1966 for the journal *Vietnamese Perspectives,* he claims that the Vietnamese nation was getting closer than ever to fruition. Even despite being critical of the Diệm administration, for example, he still acknowledges the optimism and pride of the people in seeing a constitution for an independent Vietnam proclaimed in October 1956 for the first time. In noting such progress, Thái allows us to make two important observations. First, nationalism is both an ideal to be achieved as well as something that required conscious reflection and work. Second, the commitment to responding to the people's expectations underlines the representative and democratic quality of that process.

Although no clear relationship between Thái and Tùng as individuals has been established to date, their writing to foreign audiences reflects similar conceptions of nationalism. This allows us to make some inferences about how educated intellectuals, particularly those abroad, might understand the fate of their country. Like Thái's, Tùng's understanding of nationalism also drew on a process that required constant reflection while being committed to an end goal, what he calls "the law of perpetual becoming."[10] However ambiguous it may be, that goal would entail both the preservation of a Vietnamese identity and a response to the people's needs. He never explicitly defines nationalism, but we find in his essay *Le Vietnam au combat* (1951) that Vietnamese nationalism is quickly associated with a discussion of basic rights: "They [the Vietnamese people] claim the right to rule themselves, according to their own aspirations . . . Do you not find this to be in our most basic right? The right to exist, to live?"[11] Vietnamese nationalism is also inseparable from a love for one's country that leads one to surpass oneself, defeat enemies, to harbor a "tenacious will to live and to be."[12] In relating the will to live and survive together as a kind of raison d'être, Tùng's view of nationalism is also unmistakably philosophical. What then makes Tùng's nationalism "new" and how does he imagine it applied to the reconstruction of Vietnam, as early as 1950?

The way Tùng uses *nouveau* in his essay series first indicates renewal: a new rapport between Asia and France, a new school of nationalists, a youth emerging from a new generation, or even a resurrected nation, renewal in these senses as part of a natural cycle of development.[13] His "new" nationalism was also meant to be distinct from communism, "new" used to deliberately separate his cause from that other struggle for independence that has occupied the meaning of nationalism until that point in both scholarship and the Vietnamese political struggle. Tùng's "new" is therefore not by any means "original." In fact, the echo of republican ideals in his writing has already been evoked by many Vietnamese intellectuals and literati before him since the turn of the twentieth century. But Tùng is not as interested in novelty as he is in calling for change, both in terms of the political situation in Vietnam and in how nationalism is understood. In drawing on ideals such as representation, diversity in opinions, and liberty in expression when speaking about nationalism, he is in effect reminding his Vietnamese, French, and American audiences of the foundational elements that created a nation as they each know it, whether an American nation, a French one, or a modern Vietnam imagined by early nationalists like Phan Châu Trinh, Phan Bội Châu, and the younger Hồ Chí Minh.[14]

Where Tùng's nationalism overlaps with republicanism is in the democratic ideals and humanist philosophies that underlie his advocacy for freedom and the need to respond to basic rights of the people. He rejects corruption and inherited systems and rules and instead emphasizes liberty, especially as the young generation embraces it. Although he does not explicitly address social critiques of capitalism and inequality, it is precisely in the abstract quality of the individual that he negotiates this relationship with republicanism. Within the larger context, particularly in what Peter Zinoman calls the "republican moment of scholarship," Tùng's perspective contributes to the breadth of alternative possibilities for a republican South Vietnam and eventually a noncommunist Vietnamese nation.

Now, having made a direct connection to republican ideals in Tùng's, and even Thái's, understanding of Vietnamese nationalism, it is also necessary to address the delicate balance between the particular and universal tropes of identity and freedom. Where particularity ends and universalism begins in the application of republicanism is a distinction fraught with tension and ambiguity. In the civilizing mission that underlay French colonization, for example, the effort to assimilate native populations into European cultures was premised on a belief of universalizing modernity and civilization. But this, as reforms soon indicated, violated the very liberties promised in the ideology behind republicanism. Put differently, Tùng's emphasis on a Vietnamese identity in his idea of nationalism, despite being deeply influenced by values such as liberty and the basic human right to existence, also simultaneously thwarts the abstract universality of the Enlightenment ideology from which many of these republican ideals derive. In fact, rather than being a mere application of Enlightenment values, Tùng's divulgence on nationalism is a direct challenge to its republican legacy, because it ultimately reveals what Terry Eagleton calls the "impossible irony" of nationalism.[15] Pitching the Vietnamese cause as an international problem appeals to this universal ethos for liberty, but this is not Tùng's end goal. For Tùng, Vietnam is to participate in the free world with its own identity. As Eagleton writes, "the *telos* of the entire process [of achieving this freedom] is not, as the Enlightenment believed, universal truth, right and identity, but concrete particularity," that concrete particularity being distinct Vietnameseness.[16] In light of the interaction between freedom and identity in his development of nationalism, Eagleton explains the inherent irony in the politics of difference: in order to exercise the abstract universal right to be free, one is autonomous only in living out one's particular difference. Such is the "dialectical twist" in the Enlightenment ideal of freedom.

Although Tùng's nationalism is structurally grounded on a European model, it is not without qualifications. The effort to explain what Vietnam is and to trace its history, as the opening in *Le Vietnam et sa civilization* (1952) tries to do with the question "Qu'est-ce que le Viet-Nam?," prioritizes this ethnic identity and centers Tùng's patriotism in these essays. He writes in January 1950 in the first essay of the series, "My writings, words and actions, from now on, will be dictated by the unique love for 'Dai Viet.'"[17] It is this love for his country that gets him attention from many French readers, impressed by the way Tùng is able to represent Vietnam. For Tùng, then, what is most important is to strike a harmony between being a Vietnamese nation and being a nation in the world.

NATIONALISM AND REPUBLICANISM IN TRẦN VĂN TÙNG'S LITERARY WRITINGS

Born in 1915 in Cần Thơ, Trần Văn Tùng grew up in a rural setting with access to a traditional education, because although his father was a farmer, his mother came from a mandarin's family. As recorded in his memoir *Souvenirs d'un campagnard annamite* (1939), later published as *Rêves d'un campagnard* (1940, 1946), he admired the scholarship and respected position of a mandarin in the village. After being introduced to French culture at a young age, however, he left his rural family life to study in Hanoi. Such autobiographical elements are also incorporated into his novel *Bach Yên,* where the main character, Van, is tormented by the conflicts between the urban and rural setting, his family and his studies, his native Vietnamese culture and his adoration for French culture. Despite being educated first in the romanized Vietnamese script (*quốc ngữ*), Tùng's writing career began predominantly in French and was informed thoroughly by French thought. This is reflected in his first two works, *L'Ecole de France* (1938) and *Aventures intellectuelles* (1939), the second of which won the Prix de la Langue Française for its extension of French thought outside France. Both works bring together a collection of excerpts from important French writers, especially known from the nineteenth and twentieth century, such as Stephane Mallarmé, Paul Valéry, and André Gide.

It was not until 1946 that Tùng's political stances would become clear in his first and only novel, *Bach Yên ou fille au coeur fidèle*. The title is already suggestive of the female figure as a mouthpiece for patriotism and nationalism. This story of an ill-destined romance between two young lovers from different social milieux is a commentary on the way society views the new generation and, by extension, their potential to initiate change in society. At the very center of the novel is a call to action to Vietnamese youth, a monologue in the protagonist's voice, that claims the democratic ideals important to Tùng. More specifically, in eschewing tradition and the existing political structures, he instead highlights the importance of civic participation of youth to establish and maintain a common good, that is, a new Vietnam that would benefit all. Bach Yên, the desired modernized Vietnamese woman, becomes the confidante for the liberal thoughts of Van, the protagonist:

> I cannot accept that our generation is ridiculed, scorned, and surveilled by these old traditionalists. Why does the torch of life remain eternally in the hands of young people? It's our turn to speak out! To us, life! To us, hope, joy, happiness! To us, victory! We need another sky, another earth, a new society![18]

The novel also offers a social commentary on the role of women in society, supporting their access to education and greater freedom to make their own decisions. Considering Bach Yên's literary role as an object of desire that only assists the protagonist's expression of thoughts, however, Tùng's position on gender equality remains largely underdeveloped.

Despite being an initial supporter of the Bảo Đại administration, insofar as it meant Vietnam could be independent, Tùng soon had several changes of heart. Seeing that Bảo Đại was incapable of leading Vietnam, he switched allegiances to Ngô Đình Diệm between 1952 and 1954, then to exiled politician Trần Văn Hữu as potential successor to Diệm after detecting corruption in the Diệm administration. Eventually, he would simply advocate for his own Democratic Party of Vietnam as the most viable option for South Vietnamese leadership. His anticommunist sentiments came from both principle and personal tragedy, because all twelve of his brothers and sisters were either assassinated or imprisoned during the communist takeover of central Vietnam. He continued his career as a diplomatic representative on behalf of Vietnam and in 1950, was sent by then President Trần Văn Hữu as a representative to the Eleventh Conference of the Institute of Peace Relations at Lucknow. From there he started to develop and share ideas of this new nationalism, recorded in his writings but also in the international press. Tùng was also an adviser to the Assembly of the French Union before assuming the role of secretary general of the Democratic Party of Vietnam.

As a writer, Tùng was able to wield support and publicity for his later political writings. From the beginning of his career, nearly all of his works include a paratextual element such as a preface or foreword from a prominent French figure, including Georges Lecomte, who was the president of the Académie Française in 1946, and René Cassin, a prominent human rights politician. Tùng was especially aware of the efficacy of casting his ideas for Vietnam far and wide. What is more is that he made this expansive communication clearly known, the paratextual matter in texts as evidence of this intention. In one copy of *Le Viet-Nam face à son destin,* a note written by Tùng tells us about his avid communication with editors. It is addressed to the director of *Carrefour,* a weekly paper in Paris, asking him to mention it in his paper. He therefore tried to speak to multiple audiences, the American public being only one of them. The idea was not only to bring more attention to Vietnam or to rally international intervention against the rise of communism but to also make the Vietnamese cause an international one, the application of liberty during a nation's transitional moment as a global, relatable, human concern.

In examining this interaction between nation and world, particular and universal, it is important to consider the close connection between literature and politics for writers such as Tùng emerging after the 1930s. The preoccupation with French writers and French thought is a distinct quality of these Vietnamese writers of French expression. In the same way that the writer Phạm Văn Ký contemplated on sincerity through André Gide and the Symbolist poets and in the same way that Cung Giũ Nguyên drew on ideas of freedom from Enlightenment thinkers, Tùng's preoccupation with liberty led him to linguistic, philosophical, and political reflections on Vietnam as a modern nation. Because this cohort of writers was the first to be educated in Franco-indigenous schools and to have a choice in which language they could use to express themselves, the faculty of liberty is particularly meaningful. A faculty at the disposition of each individual, it represented a larger ability to choose and construct one's fate independent of traditional or familial expectations. For centuries, the Vietnamese individual was occluded by the collective, liberty compromised for the respect of traditions, order, and status. As one of Tùng's peers, Cung Giũ Nguyên, wrote in a 1954 essay, "Volontés d'existence," this shift to valorizing the individual was not only modern, it was also necessary to widen Vietnamese perspectives and thresholds. Nguyên's essay, published in a collection with the same title, elaborates on the Vietnamese trajectory in understanding one's existence, within the context of earlier institutions and limitations toward an individual, internal, and philosophical experience of freedom. This quest for freedom begins by shifting the priority from worshiping a fixed past to imagining a future to construct. And to Nguyên, this conversion was only possible through contact with an Other that challenged the way these beliefs shaped the emerging generation's understanding of the present: "The encounter with the West hastened the emergence of the individual, walled between these inadequate conceptions of social reality and human reality."[19] This might imply that colonialism was inevitable, or even justifiable, but it is more insightful to think about this encounter with the West as a process that prompted a conscious effort toward comprehension. Language becomes crucial, as does an openness to difference, otherwise the individual and his culture remain resistant to possible change.[20]

The relationship that these writers have with the French language and literary scene therefore is extremely delicate: seeking to understand and be understood is integral to one's will to exist and persist.[21] Tùng also directed a journal for the Democratic Party of Vietnam whose title was similar to that of Nguyên's essay, *La volonté du Vietnam,* as a vessel for communication. The journal included French- and English-language essays on the importance of a Vietnamese and French cooperation as well as items of general interest on Vietnamese culture and history. As was true for Nguyên, the implication for Tùng of this human will, or *volonté,* and the capacity to choose to do or not do something has a larger political significance. Determining that Vietnam has a *volonté* implies its sovereignty and independence, even in the context of an overarching French Union. Choice in expression seeks to fulfill a human desire for comprehension, extrapolating a minor sense of liberty to a sense of liberty that an entire country seeks. In this way, liberty is both an individual and a human concern. The cult of the individual is not independent of one's place in the world; respect for oneself is interchangeable with the respect one earns from others.[22] Only when something as particular as a Vietnamese identity and the freedom to exercise what that means is abstracted to a human experience can others truly comprehend the Vietnamese cause.

With the advantage of his French connections, Tùng was able to frame the quest for liberty as a human concern in a way that related the Vietnamese cause to other arguments for human rights more generally. His rapport with René Cassin was particularly useful in this regard because the French lawyer was a key figure in establishing the United Nations' Universal Declaration of Human Rights (Droits de l'homme). Cassin's preface to *Le Viet-Nam face à son destin* (1950) came two years after his work drafting the declaration in 1948. Having worked on Jewish emancipation in the wake of World War II, Cassin saw a similar cause in the Vietnamese situation and thus found another case to internationalize human rights. He writes in the preface of Tùng's text,

> Do we not know from our own experience how much the learning or relearning of liberty is difficult, what pitfalls, what temptations must blow away or repulse the most modest citizens as the highest ranking leaders, if they want the new or renewed State to not be a simple façade behind which an oligarchy rules for its sole gain, but on the contrary a milieu of progress, appropriate to the fulfillment of individuals and of liberties?[23]

Although Cassin is most likely speaking from his experience and observation of World War II events as well as his own investment in Jewish emancipation, his statement is also relevant for predicting the reality of the Vietnamese government. Tùng is framed here not so much as an ideal francophone writer or colonial pupil for others to follow in example but as an ally with a similar "human call for responsibility."[24] What one finds in Tùng's text, according to Cassin, is not a "geographical manual or a political methodology" but multiple sources of patriotism that the author calls 'a Vietnamese nationalism.'" Most strikingly, the reader finds a close connection to France through "a national doctrine founded on principles of equality, justice and fraternity."[25] Furthermore, this nationalism that was as universal in this sense as it was specific to Vietnam, "attached by all its natural fibers to the native land," changes the way that Tùng's advocacy for nationalism could be understood. It therefore spoke not only to the Vietnamese but also to other people of similar predicament, and the choice to include Cassin certainly opened Tùng to a larger readership even beyond literary intellectuals. In offering Tùng the legitimacy for his strand of nationalism, one imbued with humanistic ideas, this preface functions symbiotically, also giving Cassin a case to promote his agenda for human rights.

LEGACIES OF REPRESENTATION AND RESPONSIBILITY

Indeed, the role of the individual in the construction of country as a republican ideal is not new, especially to the Vietnamese: Phan Châu Trinh was one of the first Vietnamese to incorporate it into his reforms. Having formulated his antimonarchist position from the writings of East Asian reformists Liang Qichao, Kang Youwei, and Nakae Chomin, as well as their interpretation of France's republicanism, Trinh saw the necessity of modernizing the country with the aid of the Third Republic. His essay "A New Vietnam Following the Franco-Vietnamese Alliance" addressed the self-strengthening of his people to form a national identity. Despite the evils of colonialism, he saw assimilation as a necessary step in eliminating the monarchy and its ties to a feudal system that no longer worked for the Vietnamese people.[26] Trinh was not alone to believe in the potential of republicanism in Vietnam; many of his peers in Paris, including Phan Văn Trường, Phan Bội Châu, and Hồ Chí Minh, tried to hold French Governor-General Sarraut and his administration accountable to their promises of civil liberties and representative politics. Such measures for representation could even be identified in the much antagonized Phạm Quỳnh and his efforts to push the limits for the freedom of expression and press and indigenous representation in the colonial assembly. Although many would not consider Phạm Quỳnh a republican for his support of the monarchy, these values were nevertheless important to his campaign and agenda for advancing Vietnamese culture. It followed a logic similar to Trinh's thinking: only when the Vietnamese were seen as capable of making decisions for their country and were allowed an opportunity to do so could they prove that they were modernizing.

Following this legacy of a "New Vietnam" in which careful consideration of the circumstances were necessary before abolishing all foreign contact, Tùng's appeals to the existing relationships with both the United States and France was an attempt to gain an advantage from those sources of aid. At the same time, Vietnam's nation-building project had to begin from the inside, the Vietnamese needed to educate themselves about the nation, to learn to love and defend their country.[27] Likewise, Tùng believed in the individual's contribution to the country, meant to be carried out through love for country and the responsibility to serve it.[28] With Tùng's cohort a generation later, beneficiaries of the schools and systems implemented by earlier reforms, the reiteration of republican values core to the construction of a nation becomes especially pertinent in the face of competing movements for independence.

What also marked this generation was their conviction that the emergence and development of Vietnamese youth was synonymous with that of the nation. In many ways, then, Tùng's emphasis on youth intersected with mainstream narratives, particularly that of the communist party. But for Tùng, as it had been for Trinh, this relationship between youth and nation was directly tied to education and colonial reform. With more access to new forms of expression, liberation of the individual from traditional and familial constraints would lend itself to the symbolic liberation of the country. Vietnamese youth therefore became the object of many of his essays on nationalism. In 1950, he called for the need to

> rely on the emerging generations, and its rich assemblage of intelligence, force, ardor, and will. More than any other country, Vietnam needs a healthy, courageous and audacious youth to raise its prestige and fulfill its historical mission. It is this youth who will carry the immortal torch of the country.[29]

Again in 1952, he dedicated his last chapter, "La pensée guide l'action," to *la nouvelle jeunesse du Viet-Nam.* The same message resonates:

> What life do you want to live, a life of vice, of debauchery? . . . A life that is easy and monotonous? . . . May your life, oh valiant brother, be one in search for an order, in pursuit of an ideal, the production of a work, the accomplishment of a mission![30]

Contrary to the myth that any movement outside the revolution was subject to idleness and indulgence, young nationalists were charged with the reconstruction of their country. Tùng politicized the social category of youth by attaching them to political and social change but not violent revolution. Like his law of perpetual becoming, "a young and modern nation does not know to be something rigid, immobile . . . it is something that lives, quivers, changes, transforms, grows, renews, embellishes itself, improves itself constantly."[31] What distinguishes this youth from others is the encouragement for discovery and curiosity, for although their responsibility is clear, they are also sincere about their efforts to reconcile their confusion with their expected national duty. This kind of negotiation is the only way that a nation can evade the risk of extinction or disappearance, for a nation needs to continuously return to this fountain of youth and evolution. As a member of this new generation educated in French himself, Tùng in his trajectory from scholar to diplomat illustrates how much these literary and philosophical possibilities influenced his political ideas.

WORKING WITH AMERICAN MODELS OF DEMOCRACY

Despite the broad gestures toward representation, Tùng's essays and general program were still addressed to an intellectual elite. In other words, this was a major flaw in Tùng's idea of representation, because although education became more widespread, it was still not accessible to all Vietnamese. This elite bore the task of a "pedagogical mission," to "shape the youth, educate the people, bring them toward progress," and it is to this elite that the "highest functions of the state must be granted."[32] In May 1955, this elite took the official form of the Democratic Party of Vietnam.

Founded by Nguyễn Thái Bình, a Vietnamese dissident residing in Paris, with Trần Văn Tùng as the secretary general, the Democratic Party of Vietnam positioned itself as a viable third solution, an alternative to the binary choice between Diệm or a communist government. A brief summary of the party is laid out in Nguyễn Thái Bình's 1962 publication *Vietnam: The Problem and the Solution.* For the American public, Bình's presentation of the Democratic Party would be particularly familiar, citing the age-old democracy trifecta of a government "of the people, by the people, and for the people." This quote, known to most from its mention in Abraham Lincoln's Gettysburg Address in 1863, is also a direct reference to the Declaration of Independence, even though the official document itself does not contain these words verbatim. What is most striking about these words in Bình's introduction of his party is its centennial anniversary near the time of Bình's publication, as well as the circumstances for the speech, dedicated to the fallen American Civil War soldiers at Gettysburg, Pennsylvania. Bình's direct reference to a familiar symbol of democracy in relation to a party consisting of nationalists and patriots realigns nationalism with democracy, the voice of the people being a crucial component to the successful expression of nationalism.

Although Bình never uses the term "civil war" explicitly, both he and Trần Văn Tùng are clear about the current war being an internal one, only to be resolved between the Vietnamese themselves. The threat was not only foreign ideology but also the loss of democracy more generally under Diệm's government. In fact, to Bình and Tùng, the main reason for the success of the communist-led National Liberation Front in the South was not because the people of the South supported communism but instead because the organization presented its ideology as the only alternative to a corrupt and totalitarian society.[33] In other words, the current Diệm administration, which Bình and Tùng believed to be motivated by familial, private, and foreign interests rather than by those of the people, only exacerbated the tendency of the people to turn to communism for relief.

As an exile and expatriate in France, Tùng was able to write with more freedom about Vietnam even though he was not directly in touch with the everyday happenings or political constituents in the country. He was openly critical of the Ngô Đình Diệm administration and was even reported in September 1963 to urge for a united anti-Diệm stand among the exile community in Paris.[34] Like many Vietnamese, however, he had initially trusted in Diệm to take on an effective fight against communism. In 1952, when Tùng came to the United States for the Far East Conference in New York City, he visited Diệm at the Maryknoll Seminary in Ossining, New York, to advise him to return to Vietnam to fight the communist cause. Some would later criticize Tùng for having made this trip in the first place. Within a few years, however, Tùng became disillusioned by Diệm's oppressive policies. In fact, Diệm's ban of opposition parties in Vietnam violated what Tùng valued to be an important democratic quality: the freedom to express differing, even revolutionary ideas. Many Vietnamese dissidents were put in prison or sought refuge abroad; they organized themselves in Paris and circulated nationalist, anti-Diệm publications among themselves.[35]

Bình and Tùng's anti-Diệm, anticommunist, antifeudal, and antineutralist positions were broadcast in various news articles and publications, but also reiterated in letters addressed to the John F. Kennedy administration between 1961 and 1963. In July 1961, Bình wrote to presidential adviser Walt Rostow regarding the corruption of the Diệm administration, saying, "Diệm is anti-communist only because he is anti-anything that opposes him." He asked the United States to send an investigation committee to track down where American funds were being funneled because the Vietnamese people were surely not seeing any of them.[36] He sent the exact same letter to Arthur Schlesinger, the special assistant to the president, dated the same day and likely to National Security Adviser McGeorge Bundy as well.[37] Bình continued to write to Rostow despite little evidence that Rostow ever returned his letters. In October that year, Bình sent him a letter outlining a clear alternative to Diệm's government, proposing a provisional government made up of "younger field-grade officers of the South

Vietnamese Army" and a subsequent transition to a civilian government afterward. His plan also suggested continued American aid, but to gradually shift that aid toward economic and cultural development.[38] Bình sent a copy of *The Problem and the Solution* to White House Press Secretary Pierre Salinger in December that year and to Kennedy's appointments secretary Kenneth O'Donnell in February the following year.[39] Correspondences between Bình and the American personnel seem to have tapered off by the end of 1962.

Like Bình, Tùng also actively wrote to the Kennedy administration and even tried to seek meetings with them during his visit to Washington in March 1962. A week before his trip, on March 7, he enclosed in his letter to Salinger a copy of the speech he planned to give during the visit.[40] The speech made a point of "linking American and Vietnamese destinies," which aligned the Vietnamese cause to the American principles of freedom and democracy. "But surely," Tùng wrote, "there must be a limit beyond which a great nation cannot go without denying its own greatness and betraying its principles, those principles and ideals from which it has drawn its strength and its glory." Also important was Tùng's commentary on Vietnamese morale, for without a proper government and a reason to save a nationalist Vietnam, "the Vietnamese people were disheartened and discouraged." These letters may have swayed some Americans to consider taking them seriously because in one memorandum from Michael Forrestal to Ambassador Averell Harriman in February 1963, Forrestal suggested the possibility of expanding contacts between US personnel in Saigon and noncommunist elements of the Vietnamese opposition. It is unclear from this note which noncommunist elements he meant, though if he was referring to the Parisian dissidents, actions on such measures were never taken. When Tùng wrote to Schlesinger in October 1963, Schlesinger forwarded both his letters to Forrestal. In response a week later, on October 24, Forrestal curiously advised Schlesinger that "at this stage," it would be best to "keep our traffic pretty bland."[41]

With the help of Bundy and Schlesinger, Bình and Tùng's letters were circulated within the administration, though the Vietnamese men only ever received tepid responses to acknowledge their reception. A few considerations may explain this reaction. As Sean Wilentz suggests, President Kennedy's Cold War realism did not make room for Vietnamese perspectives such as the Democratic Party of Vietnam, which like Schlesinger seemed to support a middle ground alternative between an anticommunist and anti-authoritarian government.[42] This meant that despite how "unsavory" a regime was deemed, US foreign policy would back whichever one it perceived to be most stable and viable to beat back communism. That these Vietnamese nationalists hailed from Paris rather than from Saigon was also a major point of contention for the Americans, in that they seemed too far removed to be able to make convincing commentary on South Vietnam's state of affairs.[43] Furthermore, it is also likely that American politicians considered these "disaffected intellectuals" with caution, especially in the early correspondences of 1961 and 1962, to prevent stirring any suspicion or ambiguity regarding American intentions in Vietnam.[44]

Such developments did not hinder Tùng from continuing to advocate for his party's mission, and the elimination of Diệm and Nhu in 1963 only further prompted them to concretize their plan for rebuilding Vietnam as a democratic nation. In January the following year, a few months after Diệm's death, Tùng published with the Democratic Party of Vietnam a report titled the "Fundamental Conditions for Victory in Vietnam." Arguably one of the more concrete political documents Tùng had written, the report consolidates the various ideas that Bình and Tùng had communicated to the American public over the previous few years outlining what Tùng called a Nationalist Program for Unity and Progress that touched on economic and agrarian reform, reorganization of the military, and reforms to foreign policy. He outlined a revision of the "political physiognomy" that would consist of a president, three vice presidents for each region, and a National Congress that would balance executive power. Military reform would purge the army of corrupt elements and place civilian control in the hands of intellectual elites. Most notably, he saw the importance of building social infrastructure, including hospitals, schools, housing developments, modern universities, railways, as early twentieth-century intellectual Phan Châu Trinh had always envisioned. Although the details to realizing these reforms were not yet outlined, Tùng's guiding principle was to "restore to each Vietnamese citizen his fundamental rights as a free man in an independent society and to assure protection of these rights under due process of law."[45]

Returning to the roots of his cause for nationalism, the ineffective containment of communism was ultimately a problem of democracy. Tùng believed that corruption and false promises led to waning popular support and bad faith and prejudice toward foreign aid. This not only puts the Vietnamese people in a bad light to the rest of the world, it prevents the general protection of their rights and dignity. It repeats his earlier proclamation about the individual: he who respects will be respected in return. Restoring Vietnamese dignity was therefore a major stake in winning the war against communism.

After this last 1964 publication, news regarding Tùng or his Democratic Party of Vietnam is strikingly sparse. During this period of active public and political intervention, however, what we can learn through an examination of Tùng's nationalism—its foundation on liberty, youth, and democracy—is the extent to which the Vietnamese were committed to their nation-building project, even despite the American disregard for their plans. In a speech to the American press in Paris, Tùng expressed his frustration in this regard by asking, "Does America really have a conscience . . . ? Where is the conscience of the Free World? Is it dead or is it only sleeping?"[46] What would the outcome have been, we might wonder, had the Democratic Party been given a chance to realize its program? Having predicted the "steady deterioration of social, economic and political conditions" and "stressed the need for a new government made up of dedicated Nationalist leaders," they were met with "stolid resistance" while the United States adopted an extreme "sink or swim" mentality. In this sense, was the American administration the biggest obstacle to a Vietnamese nationalist victory?

In the last decade, nationalism as an ideology has taken a particularly malignant turn in response to the erasure of borders and the increasing flow of people and ideas. "New nationalism" in this sense is used as a basis for anti-immigration, nativist positions that privilege homogeneity in the guise of a collective welfare. But new nationalism has not always implied such a separatist perspective. In an earlier, rather famous evocation of this idea, American President Theodore Roosevelt seemed to harp on the opposite message. His speech in Osawatomie, Kansas, in 1910 called for a collective mindset that would protect human welfare and property rights. When Barack Obama evoked the idea again a century later in 2011, he reiterated its strong reminder of America's democratic foundations, in which each individual is entitled to work and earn the fruit of that labor. The capacity to partake in the economy in this way is fundamental to the liberties that the Declaration of Independence guaranteed.

It is curious then that in his idea of a nation, Tùng had already evoked similar ideas in the first installment of his essay series:

> The working class will reassume an important role in society! To each, his work! To each man's work, his compensation! All Vietnamese who work will be nourished, clothed and decently sheltered. Education and civic rights will be available to everyone . . . Our first concern is to make of every citizen a man, and to give him all the changes of becoming a free man, taking into account his faculties and potential.[47]

The commitment to recognizing the working class and the restoration of a meritocratic system where work is repaid by an appropriate compensation is imperative in a democratic nation. Whether Tùng was inspired by American or French democratic ideals seems less important than that they were closely aligned, and continued to be, even in the midst of the Vietnamese dilemma. Perhaps then, Tùng's early ideas of nationalism in the 1950s anticipated the later desire for its redefinition in light of societal transformations under the communist regime as well as Diệm's administration. It is as Vũ Văn Thái aptly writes in 1966:

> If all the turbulent developments of the present can be channeled into a concept which would maintain harmony between the basic values of Vietnamese identity and the need for representative government and a just society, then the evidence will have been provided that the alternative to communism in the emerging nations does exist.[48]

98   Chapter 4

NOTES

Epigraph. Trần Văn Tùng, *Le Viet-Nam face à son destin* (Paris: Editions de la Belle Page, 1950), 19.

1. Trần Văn Tùng, letter to the editor, *New York Times,* October 24, 1953.

2. Tùng also wrote to the *New York Times* in August and September 1955 and November 1961 and appeared in the *Buffalo Evening News* in September 1962. Additionally, the *Washington Post* reported on his visit to Washington in March 1962.

3. See Henry Hazlett, "L'Annam vu par Trần Văn Tùng" (masters' thesis, University of Washington, 1950), 72; and Karl Britto, *Disorientation: France, Vietnam, and the Ambivalence of Interculturality* (Hong Kong: Hong Kong University Press, 2004), 28.

4. François Guillemot, "Penser le nationalisme révolutionnaire au Viêt Nam: identités politiques et itinéraires singuliers à la recherche d'une hypothétique," *Moussons: recherches en sciences humaines sur l'Asie du Sud-Est* 13–14 (2009): 147–184, especially 154.

5. Trần Văn Tùng, *Le Viet-Nam face à son destin,* ix.

6. See in particular Tuong Vu, "Triumphs or Tragedies: A New Perspective on the Vietnamese Revolution," *Journal of Southeast Asian Studies* 45, no. 2 (2014): 236–257; Nu-Anh Tran, "Contested Identities: Nationalism in the Republic of Vietnam (1954–1963)" (PhD diss., University of California, Berkeley, 2013); and Guillemot's "Penser le nationalisme."

7. Consider the borderless approach to nationalism in Benedict Anderson's concept of imagined communities, Ernest Gellner's argument for identical ethnic and political boundaries, and Nu-Anh Tran's argument that the state consolidates the legitimacy around nationalism. See Benedict Anderson, *Imagined Communities: Reflections on the Origin and Spread of Nationalism* (London: Verso, 1991); Ernest Gellner, *Nations and Nationalism: New Perspectives on the Past* (Ithaca, NY: Cornell University Press, 1983); and Tran, "Contested Identities."

8. Tran, "Contested Identities," 14.

9. Vũ Văn Thái, "Vietnamese Nationalism under Challenge," *Vietnam Perspectives* 2, no. 2 (1966): 3–12, especially 3.

10. Trần Văn Tùng, *Le Viet-Nam face à son destin,* 9.

11. Trần Văn Tùng, *Le Viet-Nam au combat: nationalisme contre communisme* (Paris: Editions de la Belle Page, 1951), 14.

12. Trần Văn Tùng, *Le Viet-Nam au combat,* 30.

13. Trần Văn Tùng, *Le Viet-Nam face à son destin,* 9, 19, 32; Trần Văn Tùng, *Le Viet-Nam au combat,* 16–17.

14. Christopher Goscha, "Aux origines du républicanisme vietnamien: circulations mondiales et connexions colonials," *Vingtième siècle* 131 (2016): 17–35, especially 33.

15. Terry Eagleton, "Nationalism: Irony and Commitment," in *Nationalism, Colonialism and Literature* (Minneapolis: University of Minnesota Press, 1990), 23.

16. Eagleton, "Nationalism: Irony and Commitment," 30.

17. Trần Văn Tùng, *Le Viet-Nam face à son destin,* xxvi.

18. Trần Văn Tùng, *Bach Yên ou fille au coeur fidèle* (Paris: J. Susse, 1946), 116.

19. Cung Giũ Nguyên, *Volontés d'existence* (Saigon: France-Asie, 1954), 7.

20. Cung Giũ Nguyên, *Volontés d'existence,* 40.

21. Paratextual material, including prefaces and introductions to many Vietnamese Francophone works, can be read in a new political light in their effort to be widely read and understood. For example, see Cung Giũ Nguyên, "Liminaire," introduction to *Volontés d'existence;* Đào Đăng Vỹ, preface to *L'Annam qui nait* (Hue: Imprimerie du Mirador, 1938); and even Phạm Quỳnh's opening remarks in his Paris Conferences, *Quelques conférences à Paris* (Hanoi: Imprimerie de Le Van Phuc, 1923).

22. Cung Giũ Nguyên, *Volontés d'existence,* 73.

23. Trần Văn Tùng, *Le Viet-Nam face à son destin*, xii.
24. Trần Văn Tùng, *Le Viet-Nam face à son destin*, xiii.
25. Trần Văn Tùng, *Le Viet-Nam face à son destin*, xii.
26. Goscha, "Aux origines du républicanisme vietnamien," 33.
27. Vĩnh Sính, *Phan Châu Trinh and His Political Writings* (Ithaca, NY: Cornell University Press, 2009).
28. Trần Văn Tùng, *Le Viet-nam et sa civilisation* (Paris: Editions de la Belle Page, 1952), 109.
29. Trần Văn Tùng, *Le Viet-Nam face à son destin*, 51
30. Trần Văn Tùng, *Le Viet-nam et sa civilisation*, 97–98.
31. Trần Văn Tùng, *Le Viet-Nam face à son destin*, 8.
32. Trần Văn Tùng, *Le Viet-Nam face à son destin*, 26.
33. Nguyễn Thái Bình, *The Problem and a Solution* (Paris: Viet-Nam Democratic Party, 1962), 103; Trần Văn Tùng, *The Fundamental Conditions for Victory* (no publisher, 1964), 2.
34. Peter Grose, "Vietnamese Exile Leader in Paris urges Anti-Diệm Stand," *New York Times,* September 11, 1963.
35. Two such publications included the "confidential bulletin" *Sword of Free Vietnam* and the "White Paper on Ngô Đình Diệm's regime," a collection released in 1961 by the Free Democratic Party of Vietnam Overseas Organization that included previously published articles and opinion pieces critical of Diệm. Copies of these publications were also sent to the Kennedy administration. See various copies of the publications in White House Central Subject Files, Box 75, John F. Kennedy Presidential Library (Kennedy Library).
36. Nguyễn Thái Bình to Rostow, July 18, 1961, White House Central Subject Files, Box 75, Folder 1, Kennedy Library.
37. Nguyễn Thái Bình to Schlesinger, July 18, 1961, Arthur Schlesinger Private Papers, Box WH-19, Folder 10, Kennedy Library; Bundy to Battle, July 24, 1961, White House Central Subject Files, Box 71, Folder 1, Kennedy Library.
38. Nguyễn Thái Bình to Rostow, October 23, 1961, White House Central Subject Files, Box 75, Folder 1, Kennedy Library.
39. Nguyễn Thái Bình to Salinger, December 1961; Nguyễn Thái Bình to O'Donnell, February 20, 1962, both in White House Central Subject Files, Box 75, Folder 2, Kennedy Library.
40. Trần Văn Tùng to Salinger, White House Central Subject Files, Box 75, Folder 2, Kennedy Library.
41. Forrestal to Schlesinger, October 24, 1963, Arthur Schlesinger Private Papers, Box WH-19, Folder 10, Kennedy Library.
42. Sean Wilentz, foreword to *The Politics of Hope and The Bitter Heritage: American Liberalism in the 1960s,* by Arthur Schlesinger (Princeton, NJ: Princeton University Press, 2007), xxiv.
43. One letter to the editor expressed reservations regarding Tùng's announcement of his party in the *New York Times.* The letter writer considered it suspicious that Tùng "does not say who his colleagues are, what their number, nor explain the curious fact that it emanates from Paris and not Saigon." See Christopher Emmett, letter to the editor, *New York Times,* August 23, 1955.
44. Although Schlesinger described the Paris-based activists as "disaffected intellectuals" who still made a great deal of sense, American officials deemed it contrary to national interests to respond to the dissidents' letters. For Schlesinger's view of the Vietnamese dissidents, see Schlesinger to Bundy, November 15, 1961, Arthur Schlesinger Private Papers, Box WH-19, Folder 10. For reluctance to reply to their letters, see Stoessel (on behalf of Dungan) to Goodpastor, January 20, 1961, White House Central Subject Files, Box 75, Folder 1, Kennedy Library.
45. Trần Văn Tùng, *Fundamental Conditions for Victory,* 7.
46. For the speech, see Trần Văn Tùng to Schlesinger, October 15, 1963, Arthur Schlesinger Private Papers, Box WH-19, Folder 10, Kennedy Library.
47. Trần Văn Tùng, *Le Viet-Nam face à son destin,* 51.
48. Vũ Văn Thái, "Vietnamese Nationalism under Challenge," 12.

CHAPTER FIVE

How Democratic Should Vietnam Be?

The Constitutional Transition of 1955–1956 and the Debate on Democracy

Nu-Anh Tran

In the early days of 1956, the poet, scholar, and career civil servant Đoàn Thêm gathered with friends to discuss contemporary Vietnamese politics. Thêm served as the deputy chief of cabinet in Ngô Đình Diệm's administration but did not belong to any known political group. At the time, Diệm's anticommunist government in Saigon was in the middle of a constitutional transition, and Thêm listened carefully as his friends argued about the democratic institutions of the new republic, especially the future national assembly. One friend sided with Diệm, two championed the emerging political opposition, and Thêm and the others did not explicitly align with either side. The first friend insisted that the government should appoint the members of the assembly in order to minimize disagreement and block potential sabotage by Vietnamese communists and the French. The opposing pair countered that the government would use such appointments to sideline its anticommunist rivals. "So that means that you fear not only the [French] colonialists and the communists but also other groups and factions. Then how is that democratic?" the supporters of the opposition asked. The follower of Diệm replied that it was necessary to restrict freedom in order to protect it, but the others rebutted, "Why do you accept [the idea of] freedom but not allow others to enjoy it?" The first side affirmed that the assembly could debate freely as long as dissenting factions deferred to national leaders when disagreements arose. The other side retorted that such a situation lent itself to dictatorship and demanded institutional checks on Diệm's authority. Weighing the different arguments, a friend who had not taken a position told Thêm in a pessimistic tone, "We are standing before two opposing views: freedom and guidance."[1]

Đoàn Thêm's account, included in his memoir written years later, was a sort of Melian dialogue about the strengths and weaknesses of a democratic system. The discussion dramatized the disagreements between Diệm's faction and competing political groups during the constitutional transition of 1955–1956. Although the writer simplified the nuanced arguments of the different camps, the dialogue captured the contradictory character of Vietnamese republicanism during Diệm's rule. On the one hand, anticommunist politicians embraced the idea of a democratic republic because it offered an alternative to communist dictatorship and colonial authoritarianism. They believed that democracy ensured liberty, could restrain arbitrary rule, and promised to deliver legitimacy based on popular sovereignty. On the other hand, the heterogenity of multiparty politics and the vulnerability of the electoral process worried Vietnamese leaders. Many believed that the solution to this conundrum was to implement partial democracy, but politicians defined democracy in different ways and could not agree on the degree of democracy that was suitable for Vietnam. These differences divided Diệm's faction from other anticommunists and gave rise to the seemingly interminable factionalism that troubled his rule.

These contradictions came into high relief during the political debates that erupted in the second half of 1955. The juncture marked the early months of the constitutional transition and constituted a brief window during which a more democratic future seemed possible. At the start of the transition, the State of Vietnam (SVN) ruled largely through executive power. Former emperor Bảo Đại was the unelected chief of state with the authority to appoint the prime minister, and the latter selected cabinet ministers and other high-level officials. The government introduced elections in early 1953, though only at the local level. Ngô Đình Diệm assumed the premiership in July 1954 and repeatedly promised political reforms but was preoccupied with military threats to his government from other anticommunists, including the southern sects. It was not until Diệm defeated the Bình Xuyên gang in the Battle of Saigon in late April 1955 that he could turn his attention to systemic reforms. Some sectarian groups rallied to Diệm and, during the heat of battle, urged the premier to establish a republic based on popular sovereignty. Diệm's partisans wholeheartedly endorsed the effort as well. The call marked the start of the constitutional transition and unleashed a series of passionate political debates throughout the summer and fall.

The debates initially centered on the comparative virtues of different political systems and how to start the transition, then shifted to focus on the constitutional process and the legitimacy of political opposition. There were three distinct camps. Ngô Đình Diệm and his followers, whom I call the Diemists, were the most illiberal. They conceived of democracy in unusually abstract terms, wanted to monopolize power, and aimed to establish an authoritarian government dressed up in representative institutions. The political parties affiliated with the southern sects occupied a middling position, and a northern activist named Phan Quang Đán represented the most liberal camp. The second two camps eventually allied against the Diemists and insisted on a multiparty government, though no activist favored a full-fledged liberal democracy. Increasingly impatient, the Diemists peremptorily sidelined the emerging political opposition. In the end, Diệm's victory over his rivals was a triumph for authoritarianism as much as for himself and his partisans.

My study of political debates in the mid-1950s departs from the existing scholarship in arguing that the constitutional transition was a battle of ideas as much as a struggle for power. Most accounts of this period focus only on the political and military contest between Diệm and the sects, ignoring the ideas that drove either camp.[2] A few studies analyze the Diemist vision, but none have considered the sects' political aims.[3] By ignoring the political arguments of the different sides, researchers have missed what was at stake in the struggle. It was not just a question of which group would prevail but whose ideas would shape the government.

This chapter has affinities with several others in this volume. Akin to Martina Thucnhi Nguyen's chapter on the political vision of the Self-Reliant Literary Group in the 1930s, this chapter examines contested conceptions of a democratic republic in South Vietnam in the mid-1950s. Many leaders in Saigon believed in popular sovereignty and representative democracy just like the literary group, but they had survived revolutionary violence at the hands of the communist as well as a brutal war of decolonization, known in the West as the First Indochina War (1946–1954). The politicians were less confident that republicanism could deliver political stability and security than the literary group had been decades earlier. This chapter is also in step with Duy Lap Nguyen's research on Ngô Đình Diệm and the philosophy of personalism, though I focus on the political rather than the economic dimensions of personalism. I agree with Duy Lap Nguyen that Diệm's politics set him apart from other Vietnamese leaders, but I contend that the opposition did not necessarily favor a bourgeois democracy.

CAST OF CHARACTERS: THE DIEMISTS AND THE SECT PARTIES

The Diemist faction and their sectarian allies constituted the main interlocutors in the early phase of the debates. Diệm was the scion of a Catholic mandarin family whose ancestral home was near the old imperial city of Huế. He served a short stint in Bảo Đại's court in the 1930s and subsequently remained active in nationalist politics. When Bảo Đại and the French established the State of Vietnam in 1949, Diệm publicly declared that he would not join the government unless the French granted Vietnam political autonomy equal to dominion status within the British Commonwealth. The idealistic activist also called for a political and social revolution that would create a more prosperous, democratic, and free Vietnam.[4] Diệm went abroad the following year to escape attempts on his life by the communists and formed contacts with foreign leaders in the United States and Europe.

While Diệm was overseas, his brother Ngô Đình Nhu stayed in Vietnam and organized on Diệm's behalf. Nhu formed a small political group composed of Catholic socialist organizations, labor unions, and study groups in different parts of the country.[5] The defining characteristic of the group was support for Diệm as the future leader of Vietnam, and the coalition-like organization came to be known colloquially as the Ngô Đình Diệm faction (*phe Ngô Đình Diệm, nhóm Ngô Đình Diệm*). Diệm's relatives and other Catholics dominated the leadership of the faction, partly because the Ngô clan used social and familial connections as the basis for political organizing, but Vietnamese Catholics were never synonymous with the Diemists. The faction was distinct from the better known northern Catholic movement that originated in Bùi Chu and Phát Diệm dioceses, and several leading Diemists did not share the Ngô family's faith. The premier himself never joined the faction and preferred to act as a figurehead that inspired others to spontaneously organize.

Nhu was the main ideologue for his family and the Diemist faction. He was a disciple of the Catholic philosophy of personalism based on the writing of the French thinker Emmanuel Mounier. Nhu and other personalists argued that the ideal political system should be based on communities because communities fostered the development of the human person, that is, the individual embedded in a web of social relationships. In contrast, communism oppressed the individual, and capitalism led to the atomization of society.[6] In 1953, Nhu formed the Revolutionary Personalist Labor Party (Cần Lao Nhân Vị Cách Mạng Đảng, or Cần Lao), a semiclandestine party of elite cadres that would lead the Diemist faction. Some months after Diệm came to power, Nhu helped establish a mass party known as the National Revolutionary Movement, or NRM (Phong Trào Cách Mạng Quốc Gia) to act as a front for the Cần Lao. He served as Diệm's political adviser for the duration of the latter's rule.

Although the Diemist faction was one of many anticommunist nationalist groups, Nhu's activism increased its standing considerably. By the early 1950s, many nationalists had grown frustrated with the French reluctance to grant full independence to the SVN and Bảo Đại's failure to implement political reforms. The unrest opened up a political opportunity for the Ngô brothers, and Nhu helped organize a national conference of anticommunist nationalists in Saigon in 1953. The conference demanded a complete break with France and the establishment of democratic institutions in Vietnam. The event propelled the Ngô brothers to the forefront of nationalist politics and their rising prestige helped Diệm secure the appointment to the premiership from Bảo Đại.[7] France did not fully relinquish its remaining powers over the SVN until mid-1956.

The other main camp in the early debates was made up of the political parties that spearheaded the constitutional transition. These parties were associated with two sectarian groups, the Cao Đài and Hòa Hảo. The Cao Đài was a syncretic religion founded in 1926 and based in Tây Ninh province; the Hòa Hảo was a reformed Buddhist sect that emerged in 1939 in the Mekong Delta. The two religious groups formed their own armies at the end of World War II, fought against the French and the communists during the First Indochina War, and came to rule over large autonomous zones beyond the administrative reach of the central government of the SVN. By 1954, the once-unified military forces of both sects had splintered into multiple armed groups, each led by a different general. Three sect generals threw their support behind Diệm just before the Battle of Saigon. They agreed to relinquish their autonomous zones and integrate their soldiers into the national army. In return, the rallied sect groups expected to exercise influence through their affiliated political parties. The membership of these parties consisted primarily of sectarian soldiers and adepts, though some party leaders did not belong to either the Cao Đài or the Hòa Hảo faith.

The sect parties left behind scant sources and thus only a general sketch of their program and political leaders is possible. The largest sect group to rally to Diệm was the main Cao Đài army under the command of General Nguyễn Thành Phương. Phương was also the unofficial leader of the Association for the Restoration of Vietnam, or ARV (Việt Nam Phục Quốc Hội), the Cao Đài party formed in 1947.[8] The ARV advocated for land reform, democratic rights, and equality between social classes, and its leaders initially supported Bảo Đại's State of Vietnam.[9] By 1954, the party claimed to include six hundred thousand followers.[10] The foremost politician was Colonel Hồ Hán Sơn (real name, Hồ Mậu Đề), a young firebrand from north-central Vietnam and a rising star in the Cao Đài army.[11]

The most celebrated sectarian militant to side with Diệm was the rogue General Trình Minh Thế. Thế formed a breakaway Cao Đài army and founded his own party, the National Resistance Front, or NRF (Mặt Trận Quốc Gia Kháng Chiến), in 1951. The NRF championed democratization and the creation of a more egalitarian society but adamantly opposed Bảo Đại and monarchism.[12] General Thế's aide Nhị Lang (real name, Thái Lân) was the party's leading politician. Nhị Lang was a journalist from central Vietnam who had originally joined the illustrious Vietnamese Nationalist Party (Việt Nam Quốc Dân Đảng). He survived imprisonment at the hands of the communists and later switched affiliation to join General Thế in the maquis.[13]

The last rallied sect group was one of the smaller Hòa Hảo factions led by General Nguyễn Giác Ngộ, who affiliated with the recently revived Social

Democratic Party, or SDP (Việt Nam Dân Chủ Xã Hội Đảng). The founder of the Hòa Hảo faith had formed the SDP in 1947. The party was one of the most socially progressive of its time. The Mekong Delta had a highly stratified plantation society composed of wealthy landlords and indigent tenant farmers, and the party adapted the European vision of social democracy to address the specific needs of the southern peasantry. The SDP championed a multiparty democracy, a mixed economy with private and state-owned sectors, robust social services for the poor, and labor reform for peasants and workers.[14] Nguyễn Bảo Toàn, one of the founding members of the SDP, reorganized the party in early 1955 with himself as general secretary.[15] Toàn was a southern Catholic whose revolutionary career spanned Vietnam, China, and Europe, and his extensive contacts made him the most prominent sectarian politician.

The place of the sect parties in the political order remained uncertain despite their alliance with the Diemists. General Trình Minh Thế unexpectedly died fighting for Diệm during the Battle of Saigon. His reputation had lent the sect parties much of their prestige, and they saw their position slip precipitously afterward. When the premier formed a new cabinet on May 10, he felt secure enough in his position to exclude his sectarian allies from the government.

DIVERGENT CONCEPTIONS OF DEMOCRACY

The Diemists and the sect parties engaged in a vigorous debate that summer on how to define democracy and start the constitutional transition. The allies presented themselves as champions of democracy and argued that the government should become a constitutional republic with a representative assembly. Yet they actually advocated for what political scientists call a hybrid regime, that is, a mix of democratic and authoritarian features. Both camps liked to invoke popular sovereignty and called for the creation of representative institutions but favored severe limitations on civil liberties. Certain disagreements, though, were stark. The sect parties associated democracy with representative government, appeared to favor parliamentarism, and argued that the transition should start with the formation of an assembly and the disavowal of Bảo Đại. In contrast, the Diemists defined democracy more abstractly, preferred a presidential system, and insisted on beginning the transition with an election for the chief executive. These differences should be understood as one of degree rather than of kind given the many similarities between the allies, though the sect parties were more liberal.

The political views of the sect parties are somewhat elusive. The main source for understanding the parties are their newspapers, and the material is too thin to extract a coherent political theory. However, the sources do reveal that the sect parties associated democracy with representative government and insisted that the constitutional transition should begin with the formation of an assembly. *The*

Nation (Quốc gia), the newspaper of the NRF, argued that an elected assembly was democratic because it expressed the popular will: "To speak of a national assembly is to speak of a democratic structure that includes representatives of the people, representatives who are elected through a process that accords with the will of the people and who have the responsibility for undertaking national affairs on behalf of the entire people."[16] *The Nation* expected Diệm to start the transition with elections for an assembly and proposed indirect elections to filter out communist candidates.[17] The Social Democratic Party agreed that an assembly was important but worried that the preparation for an election could take months.[18] The party organ, *The Masses (Quần chúng)*, proposed that the government convene a provisional assembly with appointed members so that the people could immediately benefit from representative institutions. The journal asserted that even an unelected assembly was acceptable in present circumstances: "As an elected national assembly cannot be established swiftly under current conditions, then there should at least be a provisional national assembly to represent the form and principles of democracy."[19] The continual emphasis on a representative assembly suggests that the sect parties favored an empowered legislature and possibly even a parliamentary system in which the legislature enjoyed supremacy over the executive.

The other key feature of the sectarian plan was the removal of Bảo Đại. In particular, the Cao Đài parties expected Diệm to immediately disavow the chief of state. In early July, Nhị Lang of the NRF and Hồ Hán Sơn of the ARV held a press conference publicly demanding that Diệm clarify his position on Bảo Đại's status, but the premier declined to take any action in response.[20] Nguyễn Bảo Toàn of the SDP privately agreed with the Cao Đài parties, but the SDP instead adopted a moderate public stance and suggested leaving the question to the future assembly.[21]

Diệm and his advisers developed their plans for the constitutional transition without consulting the sect parties. The premier drew inspiration from Mounier's personalist philosophy and defined democracy as an ethical and humanistic impulse rather than a specific institutional form.[22] Mounier believed that the basis of democracy should be the person. He defined democracy as the political framework that could best ensure the freedom of persons to actualize their potential and fulfill their social obligations, and democratic leaders were spiritually superior individuals who tried to create such a framework.[23] Following Mounier, Diệm associated democracy with social and personal morality. "Democracy is a spiritual state, a way of living that respects the human person, both within ourselves and in others," the premier philosophized in the fall of 1955 when he established the republic.[24] Diệm did believe in representative government, but he considered any political form to be the temporary way toward the ultimate end. A report by the US embassy in Saigon confirmed that the Ngô family regarded basic features of democracy such as free elections and a free press to be tools. "As such, they are at times desirable and at other times unnecessary or even harmful," the report remarked drily.[25]

Some of Diệm's advisers unabashedly favored strongman rule rather than democracy. The premier's office circulated a position paper that summer most likely authored by Ngô Đình Nhu and his protégés in the cabinet, Information Minister Trần Chánh Thành and Nguyễn Hữu Châu. Châu was Nhu's brother-in-law and held the unwieldy title of minister of state at the prime minister's office. The paper contended that although the population clamored for democracy, Vietnam needed an undemocratic "strong state" (*chính quyền mạnh*) that could guide the country through present conditions. The authors insisted that only a strongman could simultaneously enjoy popular support and build a strong regime because Vietnamese people tended to rally around a leader rather than a party or a political theory. "In the East, in Vietnam, the populace has a practical way of thinking and will react to [a leader], will trust or disparage, will support or oppose [a leader], based on whether the individual is good or bad," the paper explained. The authors identified Diệm as the man of the moment: "Today, the masses no longer trust Mr. Bảo Đại and only see Mr. Ngô Đình Diệm as a worthy leader. There is no one else." The paper recommended that the government rally the population by "venerating" (*suy tôn*) Diệm. That is, the premier's advisers believed that devotion to Diệm could bind citizens together better than any political system—a proposition that implicitly justified a cult of personality.[26]

Diệm decided in late July or August that the country needed a presidential system with a powerful, popularly elected head of government similar to that in the United States. Unfortunately, few documents are available about his conception of presidentialism from this period, but sources suggest that he considered presidentialism to be more stable than a parliamentary government and more democratic than strongman rule. At the time, the primary models of democracy for Vietnamese anticommunists were French-style parliamentarism and American-style presidentialism, and Diệm's advisers nudged him toward the latter. The position paper rejected parliamentarism as too unstable. The authors likely had in mind the French Fourth Republic with its revolving door prime ministership and feared that such instability would trigger the collapse of the SVN. Instead, they favored a political system in which the executive was superior to the legislature. As the authors explained, "It is not yet possible to absolutely ensure that the prime minister's prestige will overwhelm the reputation of the national assembly." Until then, "power must be divided in such a way that the essential part remains in the hands of the government so that it can act with strength."[27] Edward Lansdale, a self-appointed adviser to Diệm and the head of an independent station of the Central Intelligence Agency in Saigon, also tried to persuade the premier of the virtues of the American political system and spent long hours explaining how the separation of powers functioned in the US.[28] The manifold arguments convinced Diệm to embrace presidentialism.

The Diemists believed that the transition to presidentialism should start with an election for the chief executive rather than an assembly. The position paper proposed that the government organize a plebiscite to depose Bảo Đại and grant Diệm "full powers" to draft a constitution. The authors stressed that the premier should be the sole candidate in the regime's first national election to strengthen his legitimacy and that the assembly should not form until after the constitution had been formalized.[29] The objective was to concentrate power in the presidency before a legislature was established. Other cabinet ministers embraced the proposal and agreed that the premier should seek a popular mandate as the first step of the transition. The premier appears to have consented to the plan by the end of August.[30]

Significantly, neither the sect parties nor the Diemists gave much consideration to civil liberties, and both camps willingly accepted restrictions on freedom in order to block communism. Although the rallied sect elements certainly believed in basic freedom, party organs defined civil liberties as the positive freedom to advocate for anticommunist nationalism rather than a negative freedom from external interference. In March 1955, the ARV's newspaper, *Vietnamese Politics* (*Việt chính*), published a letter from a reader that likely reflected the party's own position. The letter writer believed that freedom of speech only applied to certain ideas such as patriotism, democracy, and the "just nationalist cause" (*chính nghĩa quốc gia*), meaning anticommunist nationalism, but did not extend to promoting colonialism or communism.[31] In private, sect leaders brazenly accepted the violation of civil liberties. Nguyễn Bảo Toàn of the SDP even suggested that the government preemptively arrest all known communists and other subversives that might be elected to a national assembly.[32] The proposed measure, given the size of the communist party, would have constituted a massive violation of civil liberties.

Diệm and his followers espoused an even more restricted definition of liberty. The position paper dismissed freedom as a Western concept and considered only two types of liberty necessary for the Vietnamese people: freedom of expression to allow the population to show loyalty to the government, and freedom from the totalitarian system of surveillance and control allegedly practiced by communist regimes.[33] Diệm was similarly illiberal in conceptualizing freedom as the opportunity to fulfill one's obligations. When he promulgated the constitution in the fall of 1956, he admonished, "Every person must accept all aspects of his or her duty and must carry out that duty. That will create confidence and trust in society, which are the necessary conditions for democracy to develop and blossom."[34] In short, neither the sect parties nor the Diemists favored liberal democracy, but the latter camp was more authoritarian in advocating for the premier's personal leadership, the overconcentration of executive power, and severe limitations on civil liberties.

COMPETING ALLIES AND THE PLEBISCITE AGAINST BẢO ĐẠI

The balance of power between the Diemists and the sect parties tipped gradually in favor of the Diemists over the summer. The premier and his associates decided that the key to winning the debate was to overpower the sect parties politically; the Diemists poured their energy into expanding their faction. Both the National Revolutionary Movement and the Cần Lao party achieved explosive growth thanks to the Diemist control of the government. American embassy officials estimated that the twin parties boasted a combined membership of hundreds of thousands by the early months of 1956.[35] The NRM established a special wing for civil servants and all government employees were obligated to join. In July, the party launched its own newspaper, *National Revolution* (*Cách mạng quốc gia*), to serve as the unofficial mouthpiece of the regime. Fragmentary evidence suggests that the Cần Lao expanded as well, especially among military officers.[36] In contrast to the NRM and its focus on public activism, the Cần Lao specialized in secret surveillance and covert action. The secret party boasted its own intelligence service that collected information on other anticommunist political groups, infiltrated rival organizations, and secretly transmitted Ngô Đình Nhu's orders to state officials.[37]

Meanwhile, the sect parties found themselves at a disadvantage. Sect leaders did not control key positions in the government and could not coerce civil servants and military officers into joining the ARV, NRF, or SDP. More important, internal disagreements and military violence eroded the legitimacy of the sect parties. The rallied generals had broken with rival sectarian leaders to throw their lots in with Diệm, and those fissures divided the loyalty of Cao Đài and Hòa Hảo believers who otherwise might have supported the sect parties en masse. When Diệm sent the national army to attack dissident Hòa Hảo generals in the Mekong Delta in June and July, the fighting made political organizing impossible in much of the Hòa Hảo heartland. Financial problems plagued the parties as well. During the late years of the First Indochina War, the sect generals had received subsidies from the French to fight the communists and had channeled a portion of those funds into the sect parties. Diệm, however, reduced the payments as sectarian soldiers integrated into the national army, and the sect parties faced a shortfall in funds.[38] By mid-fall, the parties found themselves far weaker than their Diemist allies than ever before.

Superior strength enabled the premier to move forward with the Diemist plan for the constitutional transition. On October 23, 1955, and the government staged a referendum to depose Bảo Đại and make Diệm the new chief of state. The election was a show of Diemist strength rather than a reflection of the popular will, and the government actively interfered in the electoral process. Although the plebiscite contradicted sectarian plans for the transition, the sect parties welcomed the removal of Bảo Đại and fully participated in the campaign. Their cooperation revealed an underlying similarity between them and the Diemists. Both camps engaged in an unfair election despite their professed respect for democracy, and no evidence indicates that leaders on either side ever objected to the many irregularities.

The allies began working together on the referendum as early as September. The Diemists directed a massive petition drive to create the impression of popular demand for a plebiscite, and the sect parties dutifully produced a petition asking for a referendum to depose Bảo Đại and urging Diệm to become president.[39] The allies also formed a joint campaign committee and organized rallies and canvassed voters throughout early October.[40] Additionally, the sect parties urged their members and the public to overthrow Bảo Đại and support Diệm in building a democracy.[41]

The campaign reflected several tenets of Diemist politics, including the personalist conception of a democratic leader as a spiritually superior individual, the understanding of democracy as an ethical exercise, and the conviction that a leader could command loyalty better than an ideology. Government propaganda cast the plebiscite as a moral choice between the debauched, perfidious Bảo Đại and the upstanding, democratic Diệm. The purest distillation of the theme can be found in indoctrination materials targeting civils servants and soldiers. Study guides produced by the Ministry of Information informed government employees that the duty of every citizen was to vote for the worthiest leader. Bảo Đại was a lustful "nightclub emperor" who served foreign colonialism, whereas Diệm was "moral with a revolutionary spirit," and his government protected the people's interests, the study guide claimed.[42] Similarly, training materials for the military praised Diệm as the "nation's only savior" and argued that the entire population should "venerate" him as the new president.[43] The exhortation drew directly from the position paper written that summer. Even the ballot made clear that choosing Diệm meant choosing democracy. The government asked citizens to vote affirmative or negative on the following proposition: "I depose (remove) Mr. Bảo Đại and recognize (accept) Mr. Ngô Đình Diệm to be the chief of the State of Vietnam with the responsibility of organizing a democratic government." Accompanying the text was an unflattering picture of a stiff-lipped Bảo Đại in traditional garb and a photograph of a relaxed-looking Diệm in a modern suit mingling among supporters.[44] Taken together, the message was clear: voting was an ethical act based on the discernment of a leader's moral and political character.

The rigged plebiscite of October 23 was a landslide victory for the premier. The government pegged the turnout at almost 98 percent, and just over 98 percent of that number supported Diệm.[45] The vote count was obviously inflated, given that the tallied ballots exceeded the total number of voters in some localities.[46] Yet the premier and his followers hailed the victory as a mandate for his rule. On October 26, Diệm issued a provisional charter changing the name of the government to the Republic of Vietnam (RVN) and making himself the first president.[47] The new South Vietnamese republic was thus born of a flagrantly antidemocratic election.

"THEY HAVE GIVEN ME THE SOVEREIGNTY OF THE NATIONAL PEOPLE"

The plebiscite opened the way for a constitution and inspired a fresh round of debate on the constitutional process. The allies agreed on the desirability of a constitution and a constituent assembly but clashed over who would draft the document and how to select the assembly. These issues touched off a related controversy over the most suitable party system for Vietnam. As before, the Diemists advocated for Diệm's personal leadership and the supremacy of executive power, and the sect parties wanted the president to share power with a representative assembly. The debate took an unexpected turn under the influence of Phan Quang Đán, a recently returned nationalist activist and an ally of the sect parties. Đán argued that civil liberties and pluralism were essential for democracy and organized a political opposition to challenge the Diemists. The disagreement revealed that the anticommunists adopted a range of positions on the question of democracy and authoritarianism: the Diemists advocated for a highly authoritarian hybrid regime; the sect parties preferred a hybrid regime with a greater degree of liberty and pluralism; and Đán favored a robust democracy with only minor restrictions on freedom. In the end, Diệm and his followers forcibly suppressed his rivals to exercise full control over the constitutional process.

The SDP had argued that summer that an appointed constituent assembly chosen by the government and the various parties should draft the constitution. *The Masses* proposed that a special committee should determine the proportion of seats reserved for each party, and the parties should nominate deputies subject to the approval of the government. "In that fashion, we can avoid dictatorialness [in the relationship] between the government and the organizations over the selection of deputies," *The Masses* explained regarding the proposal.[48] The plan was likely the brainchild of Nguyễn Bảo Toàn and aligned with the sectarian preference for an empowered assembly. *The Masses* further contended that a constituent assembly was the only body that could legitimately draft the constitution. Referring to the envisioned assembly, the newspaper declared, "Everyone acknowledges that the fate of a country cannot be determined by an individual or a group of people. The fate of a nation must be determined by the entire nation, but how can the entire nation participate in national affairs if not through a national assembly, which gathers representatives of all classes of people[?]"[49] Unfortunately no records of any Cao Đài plans for a constituent assembly exist. The proposal for indirect elections did not specify that the assembly would have constituent powers.

In contrast, the Diemists anticipated that the president would lead the constitutional process with little participation from other groups; Diemist plans, however, would continue to evolve for several months. The provisional charter of October 26 specified that a commission would write the constitution and submit the draft to an assembly for approval, and elections for the assembly would take place before the end of the year.[50] The charter did not explain how the commission was to be constituted, but Diệm had every intention of packing the body with his supporters and thereby controlling the outcome. Moreover, the charter limited the power of the assembly to mere ratification, and rival parties would have little influence even if they won seats in the chamber. Diệm's plan did not adhere to democratic norms, but he and his partisans insisted that it was based on popular sovereignty. Indeed, the president seemed to think that the plebiscite had given him the right to dictate the constitutional process. Đoàn Thêm, Diệm's deputy chief of cabinet, recalled that the president often murmured to himself, "They have given me the sovereignty of the national people. *It's been placed in my hands because they trust me,* and it cannot be given to anyone else" (emphasis in the original).[51]

The debate on the constitutional process fueled a related disagreement on party systems. The sect parties championed a pluralistic, multiparty assembly. The SDP's *The Masses* claimed that the varied interests of the Vietnamese people led them to form many parties and that no single party could represent the entire population.[52] A genuinely representative assembly would therefore include diverse parties. "Only a national assembly, where the political parties meet," the newspaper contended, "can realize the cooperation of all political forces in the country because a national assembly is an institution that represents the supreme interests of the nation."[53]

The Diemist position was more complicated. The president and his inner circle thought that the government could not tolerate any internal opposition because of the communist threat; the Diemists favored a temporary phase of single-party rule followed by a transition to a two-party system.[54] "Our country has too many seeds of disorder. To my mind, there should only be one National Revolutionary Movement and one single political party, the Cần Lao," Diệm told a close confidante.[55] Along somewhat similar lines, American embassy officials found that Ngô Đình Nhu and Nguyễn Hữu Châu, whose title had changed to minister of state at the presidency, considered opposition to be meaningless because genuine patriots could not possibly disagree regarding the main tasks facing the government under present circumstances.[56] The underlying assumption was that Diemist policies constituted the only correct path for the country and that Diệm's faction alone was entitled to power.

Yet the Diemists did aim to form a two-party system of sorts. Diệm indicated to the Americans as early as mid-October that he preferred a government with two parties like that in the United States to a French-style multiparty system.[57] Following Diệm's lead, *National Revolution* rebutted the earlier argument by *The Masses* to warn against a multiparty system. The organ of the NRM admonished, "We do not want the future national assembly to turn into an arena with too many parties that are in opposition, that will tear each other apart, and that will exterminate each other."[58] The newspaper followed up with an editorial claiming that a two-party system was best for a country like Vietnam that was newly independent and threatened by communism.[59] The Diemists apparently envisioned a party system consisting of themselves and an extremely loyal opposition. American embassy officers found that the Ngô brothers believed a loyal opposition should concur with the government's main objectives and disagree only on how to achieve them, and oppositionists should never publicly criticize the regime.[60] Such toothless opposition amounted to single-party rule parading as a two-party system, but the Diemists believed that their version of a two-party system could reduce factionalism without obliterating differences.

"IF WE DO NOT HAVE FREEDOM, HOW ARE WE DIFFERENT FROM THE COMMUNISTS?"

Diemist control of the constitutional process distressed the sect parties, and they became receptive to the arguments of an alternative leader, Phan Quang Đán. Đán was a middle-aged doctor from north-central Vietnam who was more famous for his work in famine relief than for political activism.[61] He had joined the Vietnamese Nationalist Party during his college days, fled to southern China to escape Việt Minh violence, and broke with his party in 1948 to serve in the incipient administration that would become the State of Vietnam. The French granted the SVN too little independence to satisfy Đán, so the doctor went abroad to establish the Republican Party (Đảng Cộng Hòa) to advocate for full independence, democracy, and republicanism.[62] Đán's party distinguished itself from other anticommunists in stressing the importance of liberty. The party's ideology proceeded from the belief that freedom of thought was the source of human civilization and the basis for all other freedoms. The doctor favored strong legal protections for civil liberties, representative government at the local and national levels, broad participation in public affairs, and an independent judiciary.[63] Although Đán's party consisted only of two tiny branches in France and Thailand, he found ready allies among the sect parties when he returned to Vietnam in the early autumn.

Đán immediately moved the political debate in a more liberal direction. Whereas the sects advocated a hybrid regime with representative government and restricted civil liberties, he appeared to favor what is known as a militant democracy. A militant democracy is similar to a liberal democracy except that the former minimally restricts freedom to protect itself from extremist groups seeking to subvert democracy.[64] The concept was associated with the Federal Republic of Germany (West Germany) and other postwar democracies in Europe that sought to block the rise of communism and fascism through special legislation. Đán never used the term but, like other militant democrats, his vision combined pluralism and expansive civil liberties with specific, targeted restrictions.

The doctor argued that representative government would be meaningless without civil liberties and admonished Diệm for failing to ensure the freedom of Vietnamese citizens. "How can there be free elections in South Vietnam when essential democratic freedoms have not been promulgated, essential freedoms that allow Vietnamese nationalists to organize into legal political parties, to present their programs, and to defend their convictions?" Đán demanded in an updated version of his party's program issued in August 1955.[65] His complaint referred to a law that required political parties to receive legal recognition from the interior ministry before engaging in political activities. The law predated Diệm's tenure, and the president made full use of the provision to undermine rival parties. The Ministry of Interior ignored their applications for recognition, and most parties remained in a legal gray zone in which they were neither prohibited nor permitted to operate openly. Only the Diemist parties and the sect parties were considered legal.[66] Đán was especially concerned about freedom of speech and complained that the government controlled the press and censored all publications.[67] At the time, the Ministry of Information regularly issued instructions to newspapers on what to report, and the censorship office deleted phrases, lines, or entire articles before journals went to press.

Đán differed from many activists in that he worried more about the dangers of too little freedom than of too much. In an interview with the ARV's newspaper *Epoch* (*Thời đại*), he insisted that expanding liberty would strengthen support for anticommunist nationalism and implied that limiting freedom could hinder the cause. Greater liberty "will give the people a reason to oppose communism because if we do not have freedom, how are we different from the communists?" he asked rhetorically.[68] True to the principles of militant democracy, Đán believed that liberty should only be restricted in the case of specific, dangerous groups. The doctor conceded in an interview with *National Revolution,* "I also agree with virtually all of my nationalist comrades that there must be [measures to] prevent subversion from the communists, colonialists, and feudalists, but other than that, I think that the time has come to promulgate democratic freedoms so that the people of the nation can positively contribute to the project of nation-building in this new Vietnamese republic."[69] "Communists, colonialists, and feudalists" was an epithet used by the sect parties and the Diemists to refer to national enemies, namely, the communists, the remaining French presence, and Bảo Đại. Đán did not explain the degree to which he thought freedom should be curtailed, but his minimizing of the problem suggests that his position was far more liberal than the sect parties' narrow understanding of civil liberties.

The doctor agreed with the sect parties' embrace of pluralism and stressed that political diversity produced better decision-making. In a statement he sent to multiple newspapers in November, Đán explained that in a pluralistic political system, "the national people will hear the peal of many bells, will see many different aspects [of a problem], and will have the sufficient conditions to clear-sightedly determine how to resolve important national issues in a suitable manner."[70] He specifically championed the existence of a legal opposition. He told *Epoch* that democracies must have a legal, constructive opposition and considered the absence of one to be tantamount to communism or fascism.[71]

Unfortunately for Đán, Diệm had no intention of tolerating political opposition and used brute force to put an end to the debate. The president sent the police to harass the sect parties in early 1956, and many sect leaders fled abroad.[72] The police also briefly detained Phan Quang Đán.[73] Having silenced the opposition, the government proceeded to rig the elections for a constituent assembly. The result was a rubber stamp body that approved a constitution drafted by Diệm's closest associates and reflecting their politics. The president promulgated the document on October 26, 1956, the anniversary of the founding of the republic.

Although Đán and the sect parties failed to nudge the RVN in a more liberal direction, they left behind an enduring legacy of oppositional politics that served as the basis for later activism. Đán's advocacy for militant democracy launched his career as the foremost critic of Diệm's rule. The doctor became a regular writer for the first national opposition newspaper in 1957 and won an upset victory in the legislative elections of 1959, though the government blocked him from taking his seat in the assembly. The regime arrested him for his involvement in a failed coup the following year, and he counted his days in prison until Diệm's downfall in 1963. More broadly, the lively discussion between the Diemists and the opposition in 1955 set the terms of political discourse for the remainder of the RVN's existence. Leaders and activists continued to invoke democracy as the basis for political legitimacy while wrangling over civil liberties and multiparty politics. Their debate revolved around the unresolved questions that were at the heart of Vietnamese republicanism: what democracy meant and how democratic Vietnam should be.

NOTES

This essay is an abbreviated version of chapter 3 in my book *Disunion: Anticommunist Nationalism and the Making of the Republic of Vietnam* (Honolulu: University of Hawai'i Press, 2022).

1. Đoàn Thêm, *Những ngày chưa quên,* vol. 2 (Saigon: Phạm Quang Khai, 1969), 29, 30, 34.

2. Joseph Buttinger, *Vietnam: A Dragon Embattled,* vol. 2, *Vietnam at War* (New York: Frederick A. Praeger, 1967), 865–889; George Herring, *America's Longest War: The United States and Vietnam, 1950–1975,* 5th ed. (New York: McGraw-Hill, 2014), 63–68; Marilyn B. Young, *The Vietnam Wars, 1945–1990* (New York: Harper Perennial, 1991), 47–49; and John Prados, *Vietnam: History of an Unwinnable War* (Lawrence: University Press of Kansas, 2009), 42–54.

3. Jessica Chapman, *Cauldron of Resistance: Ngo Dinh Diem, the United States, and 1950s Southern Vietnam* (Ithaca, NY: Cornell University Press, 2013), 116–195; and Edward Miller, *Misalliance: Ngo Dinh Diem, the United States, and the Fate of South Vietnam* (Cambridge, MA: Harvard University Press, 2013), 124–148.

4. Ngô Đình Diệm, "Lời tuyên bố của chí sĩ Ngô Đình Diệm ngày 16 tháng 8 năm 1949," *Con đường chính nghĩa (CĐCN),* vol 1. (Saigon: Sở Báo Chí Thông Tin Phủ Thủ Tướng, 1955), 223–224.

5. Huỳnh Văn Lang, *Ký ức Huỳnh Văn Lang,* vol. 2, *Thời kỳ Việt Nam độc lập* (privately published, 2012), 213; and John Donnell, "Politics in South Vietnam: Doctrines of Authority in Conflict" (PhD diss., University of California, Berkeley, 1964), 93–97.

6. Philip Catton, *Diem's Final Failure: Prelude to America's War in Vietnam* (Lawrence: University Press of Kansas, 2002), 38–44.

7. Miller, *Misalliance,* 49–53.

8. A. M. Savani, *Notes sur le Caodaisme* (Saigon: self-published, 1954), 134–138; Robert Scigliano, *South Vietnam: Nation under Stress* (Boston, MA: Houghton Mifflin, 1963), 79.

9. Correspondence 49-S, Province Chief of Biên Hòa Province to Governor of Southern Vietnam, July 18, 1954, Folder 14606, National Archives Center 2 (Trung Tâm Lưu Trữ Quốc Gia 2 [TTLTQG2]), Ho Chi Minh City, Office of the Prime Minister Collection (Phông Phủ Thủ Tướng Việt Nam Cộng Hòa [PThTVNCH]); "Việt Nam Phục Quốc Hội nhóm đại hội toàn quốc," *Tiếng chuông,* February 8, 1955; and Savani, *Notes sur le Caodaisme,* 136–138.

10. Chapman, *Cauldron of Resistance,* 65.

11. For more on Hồ Hán Sơn's biography, see telegram 5119, Saigon to Secretary of State, May 7, 1955, National Archives and Records Administration (NARA), Record Group 59 (RG59), Central Decimal Files (CDF) 1955–1959, 751G.00/5-755; Nhị Lang, *Phong trào kháng chiến Trình Minh Thế* (Boulder, CO: Lion Press, 1985), 283–284; Cao Văn Luận, *Bên giòng lịch sử* (Saigon: Trí Dũng, 1972), 158.

12. "Manifesto of the Vietnamese Nationalist Resistants Front," despatch 32, Saigon to Department of State, July 22, 1954, NARA, RG59, CDF 1950–1954, 751G.00/7-2254.

13. Nguyễn Tường Thiết, "Chuyến tàu trong đêm," in *Nhất Linh, người nghệ sĩ, người chiến sĩ,* by Nhất Linh et. al. (Westminster, CA: Thế Kỷ, 2004), especially 319; Nhị Lang, *Phong trào kháng chiến Trình Minh Thế,* 63–64, 77–78; "Tiểu sử chí sĩ Nhị Lang (1923–2005)," Việt Nam Hải Ngoại Liên Minh Chống Cộng, accessed July 18, 2017, http://www.vnfa.com/vietlien (site discontinued).

14. Văn Lang, "Dân chủ," *Quần chúng,* November 20, 1946; Như Thúy, "Để hiểu thực trạng Miền Tây," part XVIII, *Quần chúng,* June 25–26, 1955; "Chương trình của Việt Nam Dân Chủ Xã Hội Đảng," in *Sấm giảng thi văn giáo lý toàn bộ,* by Huỳnh Phú Sổ (Saigon: Ban Phổ Thông Giáo Lý Trung Ương, 1966), 441–442. For more on the ideology of the Social Democratic Party, see Vương Kim [Phan Bá Cầm], *Lập trường Dân Xã Đảng* ([Saigon?]: Dân Xã Tùng Thư, 1971).

15. Nguyễn Long Thành Nam, *Phật Giáo Hòa Hảo trong dòng lịch sử dân tộc* (Santa Fe Springs, CA: Đuốc Từ Bi, 1991), 392–394, 411, 417, 581; Vương Kim, *Đức Huỳnh Giáo Chủ,* ch. 16, accessed May 6, 2020, https://www.hoahao.org/p74a3234/2/chuong-xvi-chanh-tri-viet-nam-dan-chu-xa-hoi-dang.

16. Quốc Gia, "Quốc hội dân cử," Dưới mắt chúng tôi column, *Quốc gia,* August 22, 1955.

17. Quốc Gia, "Hảy [sic] tiến gấp tới quốc hội dân cử," Dưới mắt chúng tôi column, *Quốc gia,* June 10, 1955; Quốc Gia, "Nên bầu cử quốc hội theo cách nào?" Dưới mắt chúng tôi column, *Quốc Gia,* June 14, 1955.

18. Quần Chúng, "Để tiến đến quốc hội dân cử," Ý kiến quần chúng column, *Quần chúng,* August 2, 1955.

19. Quần Chúng, "Cần phải có mặt của nhân dân!" Ý kiến quần chúng column, *Quần chúng,* August 3, 1955.

20. Telegram 6651, Saigon to Secretary of State, July 6, 1955, NARA, RG59, CDF 1955–1959, 751G.00/7-655.

21. Enclosure 2, despatch 13, Saigon to Department of State, July 13, 1955, NARA, RG59, CDF 1955–1959, 751G.00/7-1355; Quần Chúng, "Quốc hội lâm thời là một vấn đề khẩn yếu," Ý kiến quần chúng column, *Quần chúng,* August 10, 1955.

22. Miller, *Misalliance,* 137–140.

23. Emmanuel Mounier, *A Personalist Manifesto,* trans. St. John's Abbey (New York: Longmans, Green, 1938), 247–249; and Dries Deweer, "The Political Theory of Personalism," *International Journal of Philosophy and Theology* 74, no. 2 (2013): 108–126, especially 116–117.

24. Ngô Đình Diệm, "Bản tuyên cáo của Quốc Trưởng Việt Nam thành lập chế độ cộng hòa (26–10–55)," *CĐCN* 2:16–18, especially 17.

25. Despatch 44, Saigon to Department of State, August 8, 1956, NARA, RG59, CDF 1955–1959, 751G.00/8-856.

26. "Vấn đề chính thể, hiến pháp, quốc hội," undated, Folder 3908, TTLTQG2, PThTVNCH.

27. "Vấn đề chính thể, hiến pháp, quốc hội."

28. Edward Lansdale, *In the Midst of War* (New York: Fordham University Press, 1991), 328–330.

29. "Vấn đề chính thể, hiến pháp, quốc hội."

30. Lansdale later claimed that he suggested the idea of the plebiscite to Diệm in late September 1955, but contemporary documents clearly indicate that Diệm and his advisers had approved the plan earlier. See Lansdale, *In the Midst of War,* 331–333. For discussion of the plan by cabinet ministers and members of Diệm's circle, see telegram 6041, Saigon to Secretary of State, June 29, 1955, NARA, RG59, CDF 1955–1959, 751G.00/6-2955; telegram 244, Saigon to Secretary of State, July 16, 1955, NARA, RG59, CDF 1955–1959, 751G.00/7-1655; telegram 494, Saigon to Secretary of State, July 29, 1955, NARA, RG59, CDF 1955–1959, 751G.00/7-2955; and despatch 57, from Saigon to Department of State, August 26, 1955, 751G.13/8-2655, NARA, RG59, CDF 1955–1959.

31. Trần Thành Chí, "Cần phải xác định lại thái độ kiểm duyệt với văn nghệ và báo chí phản [sic] bội," *Việt chính,* May 27, 1955.

32. Enclosure 2, despatch 13, Saigon to Department of State, July 13, 1955, NARA, RG59, CDF 1955–1959, 751G.00/7-1355.

33. "Vấn đề chính thể, hiến pháp, quốc hội," undated, Folder 3908, TTLTQG2, PThTVNCH.

34. Ngô Đình Diệm, "Hiệu triệu quốc dân ngày lễ tuyên bố ban hành hiến pháp (26-10-1956)," *CĐCN* 3:11–14, especially 13. See also Miller, *Misalliance,* 139.

35. Despatch 246, Saigon to Department of State, February 6, 1956, NARA, RG59, CDF 1955–1959, 751G.00/2-656.

36. Phạm Văn Liễu, *Trả ta sông núi,* vol. 1 (Houston, TX: Văn Hóa, 2002), 340.

37. Nguyễn Thái, *Is South Vietnam Viable?* (Manila: Carmelo and Bauermann, 1962), 207–208; and Thomas Ahern Jr., *The CIA and the House of Ngo* (Washington, DC: Center for the Study of Intelligence, 2000), 117–118.

38. Intelligence dispatch 3475/DPG/QC/51P, "Hoạt động quốc gia: Mặt Trận Quốc Gia Kháng Chiến," September 29, 1955; intelligence dispatch 3592/DPG/CC/51P, "Hoạt động quốc gia: Việt Nam Phục Quốc Hội," October 12, 1955; intelligence dispatch 3664/DPG/QC/51P, "Hoạt động quốc gia: Việt Nam Phục Quốc Hội," October 20, 1955; intelligence dispatch 3690/DPG/QC/51P, "Hoạt

động quốc gia: Mặt Trận Quốc Gia Kháng Chiến," October 22, 1955, all in Folder 4349, TTLTQG2, Office of the President Collection, First Republic (Phông Phủ Tổng Thống Đệ Nhất Cộng Hòa [PTTĐICH]).

39. *Chánh nghĩa đã thắng* ([Saigon?]: no publisher, [1955?]), 45–49; petitions in Folder 18091, TTLTQG2, PTTĐICH.

40. "Phong trào nhân dân đòi truất phế Bảo Đại," *Tự do,* October 5, 1955; despatch 146, Saigon to Department of State, November 29, 1955, NARA, RG59, CDF 1955–1959, 751G.00/11-2955.

41. "Hiệu triệu của Mặt Trận Quốc Gia Kháng Chiến Việt Nam," *Quốc gia,* October 15, 1955; "Hiệu triệu của Đảng Dân Chủ Xã Hội Việt Nam," *Lửa sống,* October 20, 1955; intelligence dispatch 3663/DPG/QC/71/P, "Hoạt động quốc gia: Việt Nam Phục Quốc Hội," October 19, 1955, Folder 4349, TTLTQG2, PTTĐICH.

42. "Tài liệu học tập về cuộc trưng cầu dân ý ngày 23-10-1955," c. October 1955, Folder 639, TTLTQG2, PTTĐICH.

43. Official document 40/SD3DC/5 of the Third Field Division, Fourth Military Region, National Army, on the preparation for the plebiscite, October 15, 1955, Folder 21132, TTLTQG2, PTTĐICH.

44. For a facsimile of the ballot, see *Lửa sống,* October 15, 1955.

45. *Chánh nghĩa đã thắng,* 71.

46. Ahern, *CIA and the House of Ngo,* 93–94. For more on the electoral irregularities, see telegram 1846, Saigon to Secretary of State, October 25, 1955, NARA, RG59, CDF 1955–1959, 751G.00/10-2555; and despatch 146, Saigon to Department of State, November 29, 1955, NARA, RG59, CDF 1955–1959, 751G.00/11-2955.

47. "Hiến ước tạm thời của nước Việt Nam," *Tiếng chuông,* October 27, 1955.

48. Quần Chúng, "Cần phải lập ngay quốc hội," Ý kiến quần chúng column, *Quần chúng,* August 4, 1955.

49. Quần Chúng, "Nhiệm vụ của quốc hội lâm thời," Ý kiến quần chúng column, *Quần chúng,* August 5, 1955.

50. "Hiến ước tạm thời của nước Việt Nam."

51. Đoàn Thêm, *Những ngày chưa quên,* 63.

52. Quần Chúng, "Thế nhân dân," Ý kiến quần chúng column, *Quần chúng,* August 12, 1955.

53. Quần Chúng, "Quốc hội lâm thời là một vấn đề khẩn yếu."

54. Cao Văn Luận, *Bên giòng lịch sử,* 265.

55. Cao Văn Luận, *Bên giòng lịch sử,* 260.

56. Despatch 44, Saigon to Department of State, August 8, 1956, NARA, RG59, CDF 1955–1959, 751G.00/8-856.

57. Telegram 1672, Saigon to Secretary of State, October 14, 1955, NARA, RG59, CDF 1955–1959, 751G.00/10-1455.

58. Cách Mạng Quốc Gia, "Đảng phái trong nước Việt Nam dân chủ," Xây dựng column, *Cách mạng quốc gia,* November 2, 1955.

59. Telegram 2338, Saigon to Secretary of State, December 4, 1955, NARA, RG59, CDF 1955–1959, 751G.00W/12-455.

60. Telegram 2529, Saigon to Secretary of State, December 17, 1955, NARA, RG59, CDF 1955–1959, 751G.00/12-1755; despatch 44, Saigon to Department of State, August 8, 1956, NARA, RG59, CDF 1955–1959, 751G.00/8-856.

61. "Lịch trình tranh đấu của Đảng Cộng Hòa," July 20, 1955, Folder 130, TTLTQG2, Revolutionary Military Council Collection (Phông Hội Đồng Quân Nhân Cách Mạng [HĐQNCM]); Ray Fontaine, *The Dawn of Free Vietnam* (Brownsville, TX: Pan American Business Services, 1992), 21.

62. For more on Đán's biography and career before 1954, see "Lịch trình tranh đấu của Đảng Cộng Hòa"; Trường Thanh, "Chúng tôi phỏng vấn bác sĩ Phan Huy Đán," *Thời đại,* September 8, 1955; Thời Luận, "Để trả lời những sự vu khống về bác sĩ Phan Quang Đán," *Thời luận,* September

29–30, 1957; Scigliano, *South Vietnam,* 82–83; Fontaine, *Dawn of Free Vietnam,* 4–33; and Bảo Đại, *Le Dragon d'Annam* (Paris: Plon, 1980), 201.

63. Phan Quang Đán, *Volonté vietnamienne* ([Geneva?]: Thiêt Thuc, 1951), 9–11, 71–73.

64. Giovanni Capoccia, "Militant Democracy: The Institutional Bases of Demcoratic Self-Preservation," *Annual Review of Law and Social Science* 9 (November 2013): 207–226.

65. Phan Quang Đán, *Volonté vietnamienne,* 2nd ed. (Geneva: Imprimeries Populaires, 1955), ix.

66. Despatch 146, Saigon to Department of State, September 27, 1961, NARA, RG59, CDF 1960–1963, 751K.00/9-2761; Scigliano, *South Vietnam,* 80; P. J. Honey, "The Problem of Democracy in Vietnam," *World Today* 16, no. 2 (February 1960): 71–79, especially 73–74.

67. Phan Quang Đán, *Volonté vietnamienne* (1955), ix.

68. Trường Thanh, "Chúng tôi phỏng vấn bác sĩ Phan Huy Đán."

69. Lê Công, "Cuộc phỏng vấn bác sĩ Phan Quang Đán," *Cách mạng quốc gia,* November 23, 1955.

70. Phan Quang Đán, "Bác sĩ Phan Qu. Đán thanh minh về thái độ đối với chánh phủ," *Quốc gia,* November 21, 1955.

71. Trường Thanh, "Chúng tôi phỏng vấn bác sĩ Phan Huy Đán."

72. "Revolutionary Body's Headquarters Seized," *Times of India,* January 17, 1956; Nguyen Trung Truong, "Lịch trình và các sự hoạt động của Hội Đồng Nhân Dân Cách Mạng," May 8, 1956, Folder 4356, TTLTQG2, PTTĐICH.

73. Police interview of Phan Quang Đán, February 19, 1956, Folder 5969, TTLTQG2, PTTĐICH; telegram 3447, Saigon to Secretary of State, February 26, 1956, NARA, RG59, CDF 1955–1959, 751G.00W/2-2656.

CHAPTER SIX

Personalism, Liberal Capitalism, and the Strategic Hamlet Campaign

Duy Lap Nguyen

This chapter examines the Strategic Hamlet Campaign as an attempt by the First Republic of Vietnam (RVN; 1955–1963) to implement its official philosophy of personalism. In many earlier accounts of the conflict, this philosophy is dismissed as an ideological cover for the personal dictatorship of Ngô Đình Diệm and his family. In Gabriel Kolko's *Anatomy of a War,* personalism is described as a "corporatist and authoritarian" ideology "for the private use of power by Diem and . . . [his] cronies."[1] Created "to perform a comprador role for a foreign imperialism," the First Republic, purportedly lacking support from the Vietnamese masses, was compelled to resort to authoritarian measures such as the Strategic Hamlet Campaign to control its own population, forcing it into concentration camps.[2] These measures were defeated by the National Liberation Front, a revolutionary army whose "real power lay . . . in its . . . relationship to a decentralized mass movement and in the RVN's compounded weaknesses," including its dependence on a conventional army, sponsored by a foreign imperial power.[3]

This view of the First Republic has been challenged by newer accounts of the conflict. In his work on the Strategic Hamlet Campaign, Philip Catton characterizes the program as an attempt to carry out a social revolution similar to the one adopted by the National Liberation Front. The program was "an imitation of the 'Front' strategy employed by the Communists," an attempt to mobilize a decentralized mass movement against that of the insurgency in South Vietnam.[4] Defining the Ngôs, ideologically, as "conservative modernizers," Catton describes the Strategic Hamlet Campaign as "an anticommunist version of a people's war."[5]

More recent studies, however, seem to indicate that the similarities between the insurgency and the early RVN state extended beyond strategy. As Edward

Miller suggests, the political ideology of the First Republic may have been closer, in fact, to that of the communist party, whose method of revolutionary warfare was reproduced in the Strategic Hamlet Campaign. The program was informed by a "critique of liberal capitalism," developed by the French philosopher Emmanuel Mounier.[6] In this critique, liberal capitalism is characterized as a legacy of the "revolution of '89," which "was not a popular revolution but a bourgeois revolution."[7] For Mounier, the French Revolution established a supposedly free and enlightened regime that was founded, in fact, on the tyranny of capitalist production for profit and the bourgeois "illusion of popular sovereignty." Against the "falsely liberal regime of capitalist democracy," the personalists proposed a communitarian form of democracy, based on a communal organization of persons.[8]

"Following Mounier, Diem and Nhu," as Miller points out, "thought of personalism," not as a corporatist and authoritarian ideology, but "as a form of communitarianism."[9] For Nhu, the aim of the Strategic Hamlet Campaign was to establish a "'communitarian' spirit"[10] through the creation of a decentralized "guerilla infrastructure," used to "wage a real revolution" against the Stalinist revolution in the countryside.[11] To borrow the Vietnamese historian Nguyễn Xuân Hoài's recent description of the Ngôs' personalist party, the Strategic Hamlet Campaign was conceived as a "mass organization of communists aimed at attacking communists."[12] If the program was an anticommunist version of the people's war strategy, its aim, nevertheless, seems to have been closer to communism than to the economic and political liberalism prescribed by the American government.

This account of the communitarianism of the First Republic not only conflicts with the orthodox view of the latter as a reactionary puppet regime but also calls into question a fundamental assumption in many revisionist accounts of the conflict. The assumption is that the South Vietnamese republic, from beginning to end, was a nationalist government that aimed to establish a democratic alternative to communism based on the principle of popular sovereignty. This principle, however, was one that the founders of the early RVN explicitly repudiated. Repeating Mounier's critique of bourgeois democracy, Diệm rejected the principle of majority rule as the "supremacy of number,"[13] a form of government that, in Mounier's terms, constituted "a kind of oppression."[14] The communitarian ideal of democracy espoused by the First Republic was directly at odds with the liberal democratic reforms demanded by the Americans and the urban elite in the South. The latter's republicanism was opposed to what Diệm referred to as the precolonial "tradition of democracy and autonomy in the Village,"[15] an autonomy Nhu hoped to recover in a modernized form through the Strategic Hamlet Campaign.[16] During the war, this democratic tradition, as Francis Winters observed, was overlooked by the Americans, who tended to identify democracy with the electoral machinery of the parliamentary state:

To . . . Americans, fear of elections is the touchstone of political illegitimacy. In Vietnamese eyes, however, the indifference of Diem to such national elections may be less puzzling. For in the . . . history of Vietnam, no election beyond the village level had ever been held. Thus, the elevation of nationwide elections to the equivalent of the seal of legitimacy . . . seemed like another foreign intrusion.[17]

This essay argues that, despite its authoritarian character, the Strategic Hamlet Campaign was not simply an instrument of control the early RVN used to repress its own population. Rather, the program, informed by Mounier's personalism, which was in fact a form of French Marxist humanism, was intended as the primary vehicle for a full-scale political and social revolution.[18] Its goal, moreover, was not to create an alternative to communism based on capitalism and parliamentary government or bourgeois democracy. On the contrary, the Ngôs conceived of the Strategic Hamlet Campaign in explicitly Marxian terms, as a revolution that would supersede the parliamentary form of democracy, as the political superstructure of capitalism. Thus, as Nhu explained in an interview in September 1963, the program, by instituting free, secret elections of village councils in the South Vietnamese countryside, would preempt the role of the parliamentary state and its centralized form of electoral democracy: through "the strategic hamlets, a revolutionary movement starting from the base . . . it is inevitable that the whole superstructure will be profoundly modified, *with or without elections*" (emphasis added).[19] Although this social revolution was developed in part as a copy of the insurgency in the South, its ultimate aims, as I argue, were in certain respects more radical than those of the communist party.[20] The program was an attempt to create a decentralized system of autonomous communes that could bypass the central authority of the constitutional state, which the early RVN leaders regarded as a legacy of colonialism. The aim of this social revolution, therefore, was to establish a "democracy-at-the-base," at the level of the villages, which could create the conditions for a "withering away of the state."

This chapter ends on a speculative note with the following hypothesis: the failure of the Strategic Hamlet Campaign was not due to either its defeat by the communist insurgency or to popular backlash against the authoritarian methods used in its implementation. Instead, its collapse may have been the result of the conflict between the republicanism of the urban elite and the personalist ideal of democracy espoused by the leaders of the First Republic.

DEMOCRACY AND PERSONALISM
IN THE FIRST REPUBLIC

In a speech to the National Assembly in 1956, Ngô Đình Diệm underscored the "necessity of grounding [the] political life" of the newly founded republic on a "solid foundation" that would orient "action . . . towards great democratic progress." In the speech, the foundation that would guide the development of democracy in the South is identified as the philosophy of the "person" (*nhân vị*).[21]

As many have noted, however, the "personalist democracy" that emerged under the First Republic did not correspond to the image of a "democratic bastion of the Free World."[22] Having been established in a fraudulent referendum in 1955, the RVN in fact appeared to more closely resemble an authoritarian state. As the economist Milton Taylor explains, the regime "maintains a secret police . . . and detains some 40,000 political prisoners in concentration camps. Arrests are made arbitrarily, detention is indefinite, fair trial procedures are unknown, the safeguards of . . . juries and legal defense are virtually ignored, and almost all law is by edict."[23]

Because of this lack of democracy, the philosophy of the person proclaimed by the Ngôs, as Philip Catton points out, was widely dismissed by "domestic and foreign critics . . . either as a confusing curiosity or a thinly veiled cover for the Ngos' dictatorship."[24] For the regime's critics, therefore, who "found personalism vague and confusing," its official philosophy was merely an elaborate cover for authoritarian rule disguised as democracy, for "diemocracy."[25] Diệm's personalist republic was "theoretically a parliamentary democracy but actually a personal dictatorship."[26]

This gap between theory and practice is frequently cited to account for the collapse of the First Republic.[27] Because of its failure to implement its own ideal of democracy—by including, for example, oppositional parties and the protection of individual liberties—the regime was ultimately unable to win support from the people. Because of the lack of support, the RVN was compelled to employ authoritarian methods to preserve its illegitimate power.[28] The most disastrous of these methods, purportedly, was the draconian program of forced relocation through which the regime attempted to gain "control over the peasants by herding them into 'strategic hamlets.'"[29] Under the direction of Diệm's younger brother Ngô Đình Nhu, the Strategic Hamlet Campaign, which began in 1962, would stoke deep-seated resentment among the majority of the South Vietnamese population.[30] Instead of establishing a "stable, viable and democratic bastion of the free World," the policies implemented by Diệm and Nhu would destabilize the political situation, alienating the majority of its population, upon which the RVN depended for its survival.[31]

This assessment, however, would seem to be based on the assumption that the aim of the early South Vietnamese republic and its goal of "great democratic progress" was to establish a modern parliamentary government. Such a government, however, was a form of democracy that the Ngôs had expressly repudiated. "Our democracy," as an official RVN newspaper described it, "is not of the parliamentary type, but no doubt it is a democracy."[32] In another speech in

April 1956, Diệm contrasted the "personalistic tendency" of the RVN not only with the dictatorship of the communist party but also with the "political democracies" of Europe that were established in the eighteenth and nineteenth centuries based on "individualism and economic liberalism." In the twentieth century, as Diệm pointed out, the combination of capitalism and liberal democracy had lead "to the birth of fascism, which aims at a concentration of powers and a personal dictatorship."[33]

What this would seem to suggest is that the "great democratic progress" that Diệm evoked in the earlier speech cannot be understood as progress toward a modern representative government. On the contrary, the goal of the "personalist revolution" was to create what Ngô Đình Nhu referred to as a *real* democracy from the base . . . *against* formal and liberal democracy" (emphasis added).[34] In spite of his criticism of communism, moreover, Nhu would define this personalist form of democracy in explicitly Marxian terms, as a political structure corresponding to an anticapitalist organization of social production: "communitarian labor . . . and justice based on a social plan . . . rather than . . . submission to the capitalist order."[35] For Nhu, the realization of the ideal of the "person" presupposed the liberation of individuals from the alienation of capitalism, as the economic infrastructure of the freedoms afforded by bourgeois democracy. The "Vietnamese personalist and communitarian revolution conceives of human value as independent of money."[36]

PERSONALISM AND MARXISM

This communitarian and anticapitalist ideal of democracy was derived in part from Emmanuel Mounier's philosophy of personalism. Contrary to the conventional account of the latter, this philosophy was not a reactionary religious ideology. "We are a reactionary regime, you have been told," said Nhu sarcastically in an interview with *Le monde,* "are you aware of the fact that we take our inspiration from the thinkers of the Western Left, particularly the French? I don't want to name names [he laughed] or compromise anybody. . . . But you must realize that we base ourselves on personalism!"[37]

Despite its critique of Soviet communism (which was appropriated by Nhu), Mounier's political theology was "closer to Marxism" than liberal democracy in its anticapitalist orientation, as the philosopher Lucien Sève has pointed out. This "factor," according to Sève, connected intellectual "currents . . . like the existentialism of Sartre . . . and the personalism of Mounier," both of which "define themselves . . . with reference to Marxism."[38]

In Mounier's philosophy, the reference to Marxism is used specifically to distinguish the "person" from both the liberal subject of rights as well as the egoistic individual engaged in economic exchange on the market. For Mounier, the capitalist economy is based on what he described in Marxian terms as the "ideology and the prevailing structure of Western bourgeois society . . . Man in the abstract, unattached to any natural community, [is] the sovereign lord of a liberty unlimited and undirected."[39] Separated from the community and from communal production, this abstract subject exercises an individual liberty in pursuit of its private interest.

This freedom, however, engenders its opposite, in the form of the "capitalist tyranny" of production for profit.[40] In capitalism, the exercise of individual liberty results in a dehumanizing inversion of the means and ends of society.[41] Money as a means of exchange becomes the aim of production itself, subordinating individuals to the impersonal power of the market. On the other hand, capital develops the attributes of a subject or sovereign: "It is not money that is at the service of the economy and labor, it is the economy and labor that are at the service of money. . . . this sovereignty is the primacy of capital over labor."[42] Referencing the concept of commodity fetishism, Mounier describes humanity as subjected to the "mystifications into which man has been inveigled by social constructions derived from his material conditions."[43] Thus humanity is ruled by a sovereign economy that humanity itself has created: "It is not the economy that is at the service of man, but man who is at the service of economy."[44]

For Mounier, this depersonalized capitalist economy is ratified by the institution of parliamentary democracy, which represents the universal interest of abstract individuals in pursuit of their private ends. In recognizing only the right of egoistic individuals in the exchange of their private property, the modern representative state precludes the possibility of a community of persons, founded, in Nhu's words, on "communitarian labor . . . based on a social plan." The personalist critique of bourgeois democracy, then, is not that the state is simply a tool of the capitalist class. Rather, following Marx, Mounier argued that liberal democracy perpetuates the sovereignty of the capitalist economy itself in recognizing the freedom of abstract individuals, from which the depersonalized domination of the market arises.

Mounier rejected the "falsely liberal regime of capitalist democracy."[45] Instead, he argued that, "the liberal stage of democracy . . . will . . . be superseded. . . . Only on the foundation of a new social structure."[46] This new social structure, however, was not identified with the "massive Soviet state," and its centralized political and economic organization. Instead, the "tyranny" of the capitalist economy, along with the "oppression" of the "overly centralized apparatus" of the parliamentary and Soviet forms of the state, would be suppressed by the creation of "decentralized [political] communities" (communautés décentralisées) and a "decentralized economy," based on the principle of the person.[47] The new social structure, therefore, would constitute a "collective [form of] control, not statist, but decentralized."[48]

What this would appear to imply is that the official philosophy of the early RVN was not a theory of parliamentary democracy, which provided a thinly veiled cover for a personal dictatorship. It was instead a doctrine that espoused a Marxist humanist critique of liberal democracy as a political superstructure that perpetuates the alienation of persons and the domination of capital.

VIETNAMESE PERSONALISM

In Nhu's "Oriental personalism," Mounier's depiction of bourgeois society (as based on "Man in the abstract, unattached to any natural community") is appropriated as a critique of Western civilization itself: "Occidental countries had for their *structure* . . . Capitalism . . . for their *ideology* . . . Liberalism" (emphasis added).[49] In the Occidental ideology of liberalism, "man conceived as an individual, like in free capitalism, is an abstract man."[50] This abstract conception of man, as Madame Nhu suggested in a speech, was directly opposed to the principle of the person, which was to serve as the "clear and solid foundation" of the First Republic: "Our union will never be a disordered collection of individuals each following the sole aim of personal interest. Our union [draws] its strength from unity and discipline."[51]

Against the depersonalizing inversion in capitalism (whereby money, as a means of exchange, becomes the aim of production), Nhu, repeating Mounier's slogan, proclaimed that the "goal of production must be the satisfaction of needs."[52] Affirming the principle of communitarian personalism, Nhu declared that "production must serve the people," in contrast to the inhuman condition in capitalism, where "it is man," in Mounier's words, "who is in the service of the economy."[53]

For the Ngôs, moreover, the abolition of the Occidental structure of capitalism would coincide with the dissolution of liberalism. In accordance with Mounier's Marxist prescription, therefore, the political project of the early RVN was defined not as an attempt to establish a modern parliamentary state. Rather, the aim was to supersede the historical stage of capitalism and liberal democracy. Thus Diệm declared that "the time is gone when one had only to produce in order to sell, and only to sell in order to make profits," just as the "time is gone when democracy can be defined in terms of political and parliamentary liberties."[54]

For the Ngôs, then, as Phạm Văn Lưu has described, the 1955 referendum, which established a constitutional government, "adopting the institutions of parliamentary democracy from liberal states," was only a preliminary phase in a broader personalist revolution. In the next stage, the "superstructure" of the constitutional government (whose organization had been largely inherited from the colonial state) would be superseded in a "second revolution": "building a genuine democracy in the infrastructure. This was the Strategic Hamlet Program ... also known as the rural revolution."[55]

THE STRATEGIC HAMLET CAMPAIGN AND THE WITHERING AWAY OF THE STATE

As this description of the program implies, the Strategic Hamlet Campaign, contrary to the conventional view, was not simply a counterinsurgency strategy. Nor was it an authoritarian measure imposed by necessity in a state of emergency and in violation of the norms of democracy to save the institutions of the parliamentary government that had been adopted in 1955. Rather, the program was conceived as a tool for creating a "genuine democracy," a personalist democracy that would replace the parliamentary form of the state that served as the superstructure of capitalism. "To Nhu," then, "the Strategic Hamlet was never just a security measure against the VC [Viet Cong]; it was the vehicle for a full-scale political and social revolution that would put into practice the long-proclaimed ... ideals of the regime's own philosophy of 'personalism.'"[56] The personalist revolution, therefore, "found its concrete expression in the programme of Strategic Hamlets."[57]

In the program, the centralized structures of the national government, located in the cities, would be dissolved in the process of creating a decentralized infrastructure of communal production and local self-governance in the countryside. "Our primary task," as Nhu emphasized in an interministerial meeting on the Strategic Hamlets, "is to complete the political, economic ... and social revolution, advancing within each Strategic Hamlet and from the Strategic Hamlets to the Central Authority."[58]

For Nhu, this "democratization from the bottom up" (*dân chủ hóa ... từ dưới bùng lên*) would extend even to the office of the president, whose absolute authority would be used to initiate a revolutionary movement the aim of which was to dissolve the executive power itself.[59] The "Strategic Hamlet Programme by its internal logic ... cannot fail to limit the powers of Central agencies, and even the presidential powers. It is the whole government system which, proceeding by the democratic and revolutionary movement starting from the base, is being unavoidably altered little by little."[60]

This "democratic ... movement," which the Ngôs opposed to the "falsely liberal regime of capitalist democracy," would establish a "genuine democracy" without the state, a stateless form of communitarian communism. In this social revolution, therefore, the state assumes the paradoxical role of a centralized power seeking to create the conditions for its own dissolution. For Diệm, in fact, the outcome of the war would largely depend on whether the RVN could succeed in creating a decentralized system of semiautonomous rural communities, capable of superseding the authority of the central government. Echoing the communist slogan, "All power to the soviets," Diệm therefore declared that "real power lies in the villages and not in the cities. . . . The Central Government is nothing without the support of the people in the villages. This has long been understood by Asian and African Communists."[61] For the Ngôs, then, winning the war against insurgency would require the South Vietnamese republic to initiate a revolutionary movement that would serve, in the end, to abolish its own central authority: the "state," as Nhu explained, "must wither away. The sense of my life is to work so that I can become unnecessary."[62]

By late 1963, this process of decentralization, according to Nhu, had progressed to the point that the movement had begun to exceed his authority, making his executive function increasingly irrelevant. In accordance with the internal logic of the program, this function would be weakened by the growing autonomy of the villages, which imposed a decentralized form of control on the government, one that Nhu identified with democracy itself: "I do not control this Government. Rather is it the Strategic Hamlet movement which, little by little, has generated the procedures of control, that is democracy."[63] If the Strategic Hamlet Program was conceived as an anticommunist strategy, its aim, paradoxically, was a communist (or communitarian) one: the establishment of a form of democracy based on a withering away of the state. In Nhu's words, the "strategic hamlets are the basic institutions of direct democracy. When they developed and flourished . . . the state itself—as Marx said—will wither away."[64]

As Nhu reminded officials at a meeting on the Strategy Hamlet Campaign, the ideal of a stateless form of democracy distinguished the personalism of the RVN from the primitive Marxism espoused by the Vietnamese communist party.[65] For the latter, the creation of a decentralized system of semiautonomous communes (xã bộ) was regarded only as a temporary emergency measure, a means toward the ends of establishing a collective regime of labor (lao động) under the authority of a centralized socialist government. For this reason, according to Kolko, the "absolute necessity of decentralizing the war organization throughout the provinces" was continually in conflict with the "centralizing pretensions and . . . elitist organizational theory" of the Vietnamese communist party.[66]

For the party, therefore, as Nhu pointed out, the withering away of the state was a task to be undertaken only "after . . . the proletarian revolution, which means that people in the present must . . . sacrifice themselves for . . . the future."[67] In contrast, for the Ngôs, the ideal of a democracy-at-the-base, which would unravel the functions of the constitutional government, was the aim of the social revolution. "The Americans and the Vietcong imagine that the strategic hamlets are purely military institutions that will be liquidated as unnecessary once victory is achieved. The Americans and the Vietcong are both wrong."[68] The aim of the Strategic Hamlet Campaign was in fact exactly the opposite. The program was not simply an instrument of the state that would be "liquidated as unnecessary" after victory was achieved and the program had accomplished its purpose. The hamlets were not purely military organizations but instead "basic institutions of direct democracy" which, in a "final triumph of democracy," would allow the state itself to be liquidated and its executive power to be rendered irrelevant. Insofar as the establishment of a stateless democracy was the ultimate objective of the revolution itself, the possibility of a socialist future (which the party proposed to postpone until after the establishment of a dictatorship of the proletariat) was one that, for Nhu, was already present in the political form of the hamlet: "For us . . . people in the present possess the same value of those in the future. Therefore, we propose to savor whatever we attain in our struggle."[69]

This aspect of the Strategic Hamlet Campaign would appear to conform to Mounier's account of the *révolution personnaliste et communautaire* as a struggle for which there "are no necessary stages: the most Marxist revolutions have shown they know how to do without them."[70] Contrary to Frances Fitzgerald, therefore, Nhu (who supposedly "lacked the rigorous analysis of Marxism") had not "misinterpreted" Mounier's work "as a doctrine of the corporate state in which the alienated masses would find unity through . . . authoritarian social organizations."[71] Nhu's Strategic Hamlet Campaign was in fact an attempt to realize in practice the communitarian Marxism that Mounier opposed to the communism of "the massive Soviet state."[72]

But if this personalist revolution was the primary strategy of the First Republic against the communist party, then the war, in this early stage of the conflict, cannot simply be understood as a struggle between communism and democracy. Rather, given the communitarian character of the social revolution waged by the early RVN, the conflict perhaps could better be characterized as a contest between two versions of communism, Stalinist and Marxist humanist.[73]

THE SOUTH VIETNAMESE URBAN ELITE AND THE PERSONALIST THEORY OF UNDERDEVELOPMENT

Although the early RVN is often portrayed as the representative of the "feudal landlord class and comprador capital," the Ngôs, in fact, would come to conceive of their personalist revolution as a class struggle against the colonial-era elite.[74] As Nhu explained to US officials, in a class analysis of the condition of underdevelopment,

> Vietnam is a former colony, and a certain class of people were left behind after independence who remained attached to colonialism. This class has lost its privileges as the go between for the colonialists and the Vietnamese people. As former landowners, they are the victims of agrarian reform, and therefore discontent.[75]

During the colonial era, the development of capitalism in the South created a Westernized urban petite bourgeoisie, landlords who exploited a dispossessed peasantry and merchants whose "unscrupulous speculations" inflated the price of grain and imported commodities.[76] This "small but vocal bourgeoisie" made up the "bulk of the membership" of groups such as the Vietnamese Nationalist Party and the Constitutionalist Party, which supported Western-style democracy and the protection of civil liberties. Having few ties to the majority of the population in the countryside, these parties mainly "spoke for the interest of the affluent bourgeoisie in Saigon and the landlord class." Their "primary concerns were to promote the interests of indigenous merchants and to achieve equal pay for equal work for Vietnamese employees with their European counterparts."[77] Thus the demand for economic equality and majority rule was part of the politics of an elite urban minority who played a disproportionate role in the state, while monopolizing the profit created in the capitalist economy in the colony.

Despite the Ngôs' "profound hostility to the French-trained . . . Vietnamese elite," Diệm would fail during the early part of his presidency to eliminate this "middle class," refusing to enact a land reform policy that would have greatly diminished its power.[78] Although the policy conformed to the personalist principle that each individual should possess the material means for economic autonomy, Diệm had wished to distinguish his personalist program from that of the communist party.[79] Abhorring the violence and bloodshed produced by the disastrous land reform effort applied in North Vietnam, Diệm was determined to find an alternative to the strategy of class struggle.[80] Rather than imposing a radical redistribution of property, then, the early South Vietnamese republic would use population resettlement as a solution to the plight of the rural proletariat.[81]

As a result, however, the colonial-era elite, which had been swept away in the North by the communist party, would continue to "dominate . . . the urban economic and social scene" in the South, together with "what passed for a political opposition."[82] This class is one that the Ngôs would come to identify as one of the primary causes of underdevelopment. The urban elite overlapped with a group of "intermediary profit-takers" (working with foreign "banks, brokers, exporters [and] . . . rice merchants"), a comprador bourgeoisie whose "parasitic" activities "plague[d] . . . the Vietnamese economy."[83] Because of this go-between class, "Vietnamese commerce," according to an RVN study of South Vietnamese economy, "was reduced to the secondary role of a middleman working for foreign export-import firms. As for the industry, it was maintained at an embryonic stage."[84]

As the Ngôs would eventually recognize, this problem was only exacerbated by American aid. Instead of promoting economic development, aid instruments like the Commodity Import Program (CIP) reinforced the tendency among the

Vietnamese urban elite toward "unconstructive activities as usury [and] specula-tive trading in commodities."[85] During the First Republic, the program would help to create what Nguyễn Cao Kỳ would later describe as the economic oligar-chy of foreign importers: A "small minority of local capitalists, speculators and middle men have profited [from] the program, thus creating a new class of profi-teers who have contributed to an increase in social injustice and conflicts within Vietnamese society."[86]

Although the CIP helped engender support from the urban middle class in the South, the supply of foreign subsidized goods also competed with domestic production.[87] Thus the program, as one study concluded, "has not served to induce substantial economic development in Vietnam . . . because the cheap availability since 1954 of a large variety of Western-made products has tended to dampen the development of competing local manufactures."[88] For Diệm, the result was a gilded underdevelopment in which the abundance of consumer com-modities concealed the destruction of the country's industrial basis.[89] As one US official acknowledged, this problem was clearly understood by Nhu and "those Vietnamese who must cope with . . . American aid": "It is sad but true: the laws and regulations of the American aid program were simply not written for . . . effective implementation in underdeveloped countries."[90]

In the South, the process of underdevelopment had benefited the colonial-era elite, who acquired its capital "as the go between for the colonialists and the Vietnamese people." This wealth allowed the elite to establish its members in positions of power in the cities, where it became "especially prevalent among the Government bureaucracy." "As former landowners," and "victims of agrarian reform" (who had been spared from the class struggle, however, by the policy of population resettlement), this class demanded the inclusion of its oppositional parties within the RVN, calling for what the writer Minh Võ described as "democracy according to the notion of American democracy."[91]

These parties, however, as Nhu pointed out, were "not parties in any sense of the word. They are composed of a few score of disgruntled persons who have . . . no backing among the population."[92] By 1961, the urban elite, which was "iso-lated from the peasant mass," represented only 2 percent of the population.[93] Because it had "no appeal to the people," its demands for democracy, according to Nhu, were not really intended to win the support from the South Vietnamese masses. Instead, their goal was "to gain sympathy primarily from foreign sources—French, American or others."[94]

As Nhu argued, moreover, the support for these parties in the American media was largely the result of "the tendency of foreign correspondents to get their views from French and English speaking Vietnamese," Vietnamese who belonged to the educated elite.[95] Because of what Nhu referred to as "the effects of underdevelopment on public opinion," this tiny minority demanding majority rule was overrepresented in both the government bureaucracy and the international media.[96] As Joseph Mendenhall, a critic of Diệm and senior official at the American embassy, pointed out, the "educated class exerts a . . . predominant influence on international opinion because of the tendency of the foreign press to accept this class's judgment of the GVN [Government of Vietnam]."[97]

For the Ngôs, then, the opposition parties' demands for majority rule represented the interests of an overrepresented urban minority that had secured its position of power by profiting from the nation's underdevelopment. As Diệm said in an interview, "there is not a single one among them who is really democratic," even though their appeals to democracy "are very much appreciated by [a] . . . Western press which totally ignores the phenomenon of underdevelopment."[98]

But precisely because the urban elite had benefited from underdevelopment, its organizations were incapable of leading the country toward economic and political progress. Having risen through the ranks of "a highly centralized government," "a government in the French tradition," the political class, for example, embraced the "typical viewpoints of a French civil servant":

> We are also dealing with people who . . . are not really interested in looking downward toward helping their own people but in looking upward and carrying out an overall directive . . . conceived by people at the central level who have scarcely been out in the countryside and know their own people.[99]

The political class that operated this centralized structure was an obstacle to economic development, which required a more effective distribution of aid to the villages, where the majority of the population lived. "Ineffectiveness in administration at the national level, in carrying out the central functions of the government and in extending services to the countryside represent one of the GVN's main weaknesses."[100]

For the Ngôs, this fundamental weakness was also responsible for the lack of local initiative in the struggle against the insurgency.[101] Although the highly centralized government had created a class of officials that, in adopting the "viewpoints of a French civil servant," was detached from the Vietnamese masses, the hierarchical structure of the Army of the Republic of Vietnam encouraged a similar attitude among the military elite. Organized on "conventional lines to defeat a foreign invader and to occupy . . . a foreign country," this structure, which discouraged initiative at the bottom, "created a warlord outlook in the senior commanders" in regard to the population they were supposed to protect.[102]

As Robert Thompson notes, moreover, the US commitment to maintaining this ineffective and costly conventional army only increased the problems the CIP created: "To pay the recurrent expenditure on the armed forces, the South Vietnamese government was committed to accepting indefinite American aid on a large scale, including the import of subsidized consumer goods in order to generate local piastre funds to pay the army wage bill." Thus the American commitment to a conventional army, incapable of fighting an irregular war against the insurgency, and whose wages were tied directly to profits made by the class of importers, was also a primary cause of economic underdevelopment.[103]

From the Ngôs' perspective, therefore, the members of the urban elite were the agents of a centralized military and government bureaucracy that perpetuated economic dependence. Insofar as this structure blocked the development of an effective response to the communist "war of subversion," the growing political influence of the elite, buttressed by "sympathy primarily from foreign sources," threatened the survival of the RVN.

THE STRATEGIC HAMLET CAMPAIGN
AND THE URBAN ELITE

For the Ngôs, this growing influence of the elite implied that the war against the communist party could only be successfully prosecuted by a struggle against the capitalist class in the South. This class is implicitly named as part of the trio of enemies the Ngôs identified as the primary targets of the personalist revolution: "communism, underdevelopment and disunity."[104] If Diệm, according to Kolko, "never played the role of a wholly reliant comprador," it was perhaps because his social revolution was directly opposed to the comprador class that perpetuated underdevelopment. In the personalist program proposed in the manifesto of the Ngôs's Revolutionary Personalist Labor Party (Cần Lao Nhân Vị Cách Mạng Đảng), this "gang of capitalists" (bọn tư bản) is condemned for "building a career of wealth with the blood of laboring [cần lao] people."[105] If the Strategic Hamlet Program was "an anticommunist version of a 'people's war'" strategy," for Nhu, it was also, and more fundamentally, a struggle against capitalism: "I am really combating communism in order to put an end to materialistic capitalism."[106]

This statement would seem to suggest a reversal of the conciliatory attitude toward the Vietnamese middle class that Diệm had adopted in the early part of his presidency, a class that Nhu had repeatedly proposed to eliminate. "Nhu," as William Colby recalled in an interview, "constantly referred to the need to replace [it] through an authentic Vietnamese revolution."[107] In a speech in May 1962, the RVN minister of the interior, Bùi Văn Lương, appeared to confirm this shift in political strategy. The minister, as Catton explains,

> publicly admitted the government made a mistake after 1954 in preserving the
> position of the existing rural elite merely because it possessed administrative
> experience. The regime should have followed the example of its communist foe

in creating a new class of cadres, free of old feudal and colonial attitudes. The Strategic Hamlets would seek to remedy this oversight.[108]

One of the aims of the Strategic Hamlet Campaign, the task of creating a new class of cadres would not only entail a change in the personnel in charge of the various ministries in the central bureaucracy. For the Ngôs, it would also require the abolition of the organization of the parliamentary state as the political super-structure of capitalism, accompanied by the creation of a decentralized system of direct democracy and communitarian labor. "Our primary task," as Nhu emphasized at an interministerial meeting, "is to complete the political, eco-nomic . . . and social revolution, advancing within each Strategic Hamlet, and from the Strategic Hamlets to the Central Authority."[109] Thus, if the Strategic Hamlet Campaign was an anticommunist strategy, its ultimate aim was never-theless an apparently Marxian one: the withering away of the state. "That is right. I agree with Marx's final conclusion: the state must wither away—this is a condition for the final triumph of democracy."[110]

This Marxist (and personalist) ideal of democracy, as Nhu articulated it, was one to which Diệm, in spite of his reputation as a fervent anticommunist leader, would completely subscribe. Whereas US officials warned of the "danger that Nhu's attempted use of the strategic hamlet program for a 'revolutionary change of society'" could undermine democracy, Diệm passionately defended the pro-gram, not as a counterinsurgency strategy, but as a democratization from the bottom up.[111] As US Deputy Chief of Mission William Trueheart described it,

> What was remarkable was the stress he laid on his plans to democratize the coun-try from the bottom up and his very evident intent to impress on me his solidarity with the Nhus (I have never heard him refer to them so frequently). Diem spoke at length and with passion and considerable eloquence about the fundamental social and political revolution being carried out in Viet-Nam through the Strategic Hamlet Program. The theme was essentially that of Nhu, and Diem in fact spe-cifically acknowledged this.[112]

Thus, instead of implementing the program of democratic reform demanded by the Americans and the urban elite, the Ngôs attempted to carry out a social revolution "against formal or liberal democracy" in order to "democratize the country from the bottom up."

According to an American study, this social revolution would achieve con-siderable success in its goal of decentralizing the RVN government. From "an organizational standpoint the results were impressive. Virtually the entire bureaucracy from national level on down reoriented its activities to the hamlet program."[113] For Albert Fraleigh, one of the few American specialists who played a significant role in the program, the Strategic Hamlet Campaign had proved effective not only as a counterinsurgency measure but also as a way of addressing the issue of economic underdevelopment. The program had quickly "decentralized Vietnamese government . . . and brought rapid political, social and economic progress throughout the rural areas by early 1963." As a "real solution to the problems of underdevelopment," the Strategic Hamlet Campaign would also attempt to address its principal cause.[114] The program, as I mentioned, was aimed at more than overcoming the communist insurgency. It was also conceived as an instrument of class struggle against the urban elite as the cause of disunity and economic dependence. Nhu therefore "seized upon the Strategic Hamlets as a unique means of . . . bypassing and isolating the inhospitable urban political climate." Because the program "by its internal logic cannot fail to limit the powers of Central agencies," the establishment of a decentralized network of local self-government would proceed "even to the point of bypassing the Saigon-level ministry."[115] "Under the decentralization procedure funds are provided directly to the provinces, rather than through the ministries, for civil measures to establish [the] . . . hamlets and for a wide range of local development programs."[116] These measures in turn would create the conditions for a new leadership to emerge democratically in the villages, "from the bottom up," preempting the role of the political elite in Saigon. According to one US intelligence study,

> Inspired leadership is generally lacking in the central government. . . . In some provinces, however, this kind of leadership is being generated from the bottom up, by such efforts as the strategic hamlet program. Understanding that only through inspired leadership can the war be won, the President and other officials in Saigon appear not only willing but eager to see such leadership developed.[117]

Leading the local hamlet militias, this new class of cadre would reduce the need for the army, decentralizing the war against the insurgency while decreasing the RVN's dependence on American aid as well as the military elite it supported. Nhu "appreciated that if the programme was successful, it would be possible to build up on the peasant a base of political power which would more than counterbalance that of the army."[118]

This process of democratic decentralization, however, would require a temporary authoritarian concentration of power in the hands of the president and the political councilor, in what Nhu described as a dialectic of freedom and discipline, leading to a withering away of the state: "I am temporarily curtailing freedom to offer it in unlimited form. I am strengthening discipline to do away with its external bonds. I am centralizing the state in order to democratize and decentralize it."[119]

As Colby noted, this authoritarian attempt to decentralize the central authority, along with the "idea of a new popular elite coming out of the villages," would create a "contradiction" between the regime and the "elites in the cities."[120] The program to establish a democracy-at-the-base in the countryside was opposed to the interests of this group, who belonged to an urban comprador class that had previously served as a "go between for the colonialists and the Vietnamese people."[121] In that sense, the Strategic Hamlet Campaign was conceived as a kind of class struggle against an urban petite bourgeoisie that, as Colby explained, had "not [been] eliminated as they were in the North" by the communist party.[122]

From the perspective of this urban elite, however, the process of decentralization aimed at creating a democracy-at-the-base appeared to be exactly the opposite: an authoritarian concentration of power that, in bypassing the ministries and the military command, eliminated democratic protections on the executive branch.[123] This provided the pretext for the political class in Saigon to criticize the regime in the name of democracy and majority rule. "They . . . turned on Diệm," as Colby explained, "because . . . he had changed the old systems to their detriment . . . Then they got intoxicated . . . by the idea that if we just have more democracy everything will be all right."[124] Speaking on behalf of the urban elite, US officials condemned Ngô Đình Diệm for his undemocratic refusal to "delegate responsibilities to trusted and capable ministers" and "to appoint talented men to the cabinet."[125]

The increasingly vocal demands for liberal reform were not, however, the result of a popular backlash against the repression of government programs like the Strategic Hamlet Campaign. "The implementation of the program did stir some local grievances that may have found their way back to the cities," but the "urban political agitation that overthrew Diem was . . . wholly unconnected with the pacification effort per se."[126] The political opposition to Diệm in the cities was instead a consequence, paradoxically, of the increasing success of the program in creating a system of autonomous rural communities. Insofar as the Strategic Hamlet Campaign was based on the personalist principle of a democracy-at-the-base that would "limit the powers of Central agencies," its design was directly opposed to the democratic inclusion of "trusted and capable ministers" (ministers belonging to an urban elite who were generally lacking in inspired leadership). In demanding a liberal reform of the central government instead of a revolution against liberal democracy and a withering away of the state, the Americans and the urban elite, according to Diệm, were "in the name of liberty trying to crush the social revolution."[127]

DESTROYING DEMOCRACY IN THE NAME OF DEMOCRACY: A HYPOTHESIS

This personalist critique of underdevelopment suggests an account of the collapse of the First Republic that departs from the conventional explanation. This explanation holds that the Ngôs' authoritarian refusal to implement democratic reform deprived the regime of support from the people, support on which its survival depended. The argument, however, assumes that democracy must be identified with liberal democracy, with representative government inclusive of oppositional parties. Based on this assumption, the "Vietnamese Personalist and communitarian revolution" against capitalism and liberal democracy appears a contradiction in terms. As a consequence, the collapse of the First Republic (which was "theoretically a parliamentary democracy but actually a personal dictatorship") can be seen as a result of its failure to conform to its own ideal of democracy.[128]

This liberal ideal, however, was one that the Ngôs had expressly repudiated as the political platform of a Westernized urban elite, claiming to represent the majority of a population from which it was completely detached. Working as go-betweens for the international media and US imperialism, this educated minority perpetuated economic underdevelopment by asserting its particular interests as majority rule. From that perspective, though, the failure of the First Republic to achieve "great democratic progress" was not the result of an increasing disparity between the theory and practice of personalism. On the contrary, the philosophy of the Ngôs "found its concrete expression in the programme of Strategic Hamlets," in a social revolution against the urban elite, who opposed the regime "in the name of liberty" or liberal democracy. The development of democracy in the South was therefore marked not by a contradiction between theory and practice but by an increasingly irreconcilable difference between opposing ideals of democracy: bourgeois democracy and a communitarian personalist concept of direct democracy, which the Americans found difficult to distinguish from communism. Thus, according to Henry Cabot Lodge Jr., the personalist revolution was "the application of a straight Communist technique for the sake of . . . [the] cult of 'personalism.' This is apparently what is involved by what [Nhu] calls the 'revolution' (which he wants) as compared with what he calls the American 'reform' (which he disliked)."[129]

In the end, the failure of this revolution, as a US intelligence study affirms, was not the result of a superior strategy devised by the communist insurgency. Instead, the personalist revolution in the countryside, which was in the process of creating a democracy-at-the-base, was undermined by "urban political agitation" that was encouraged by the Americans and "wholly unconnected with the pacification effort per se."[130] "The fact was that the Buddhist crisis in 1963 crystallized urban opposition to Diem and Nhu and ultimately brought them down, bringing down also the Strategic Hamlet. The Strategic Hamlet," therefore, "was primarily a casualty and not a cause of the fall of the House of Ngo."[131]

NOTES

This essay condenses and develops ideas presented in my book *The Unimagined Community: Imperialism and Culture in South Vietnam* (Manchester, UK: Manchester University Press, 2020).

1. Gabriel Kolko, *Anatomy of a War* (New York: Pantheon Books, 1985), 84.

2. Kolko, *Anatomy of a War,* 208.

3. Kolko, *Anatomy of a War,* 519.

4. Philip Catton, *Diem's Final Failure: Prelude to America's War in Vietnam* (Lawrence: University Press of Kansas, 2002), 14.

5. Catton, *Diem's Final Failure,* 35, 90.

6. Edward Miller, *Misalliance: Ngo Dinh Diem, the United States, and the Fate of South Vietnam* (Cambridge, MA: Harvard University Press, 2013), 42–47.

7. Quoted in Zeev Sternhell, *Neither Right Nor Left: Fascist Ideology in France* (Princeton, NJ: Princeton University Press, 1983), 281.

8. Edmond Hameau, "La propriété littéraire: les droits d'auteur," *Esprit: revue internationale,* April 1934, 161.

9. Miller, *Misalliance,* 138.

10. Meeting Minutes #36, Inter-Ministry Committee for Strategic Hamlets, February 1, 1963, Texas Tech University, Douglas Pike Collection, Other Manuscripts, Inter-Ministry Committee for Strategic Hamlets, Box 02, Folder 04, 1820204001, Virtual Vietnam Archive (VVA).

11. Meeting Minutes #20, Inter-Ministry Committee for Strategic Hamlets, September 7, 1962, Douglas Pike Collection, Other Manuscripts, Inter-Ministry Committee for Strategic Hamlets, Box 01, Folder 08, 1820108001, VVA.

12. Nguyễn Xuân Hoài, "Đảng Cần Lao Nhân Vị," Luutruvn.com, January 4, 2016, http://luutruvn.com/index.php/2016/04/01/dang-can-lao-nhan-vi/.

13. *President Ngo Dinh Diem on Democracy: Addresses Relative to the Constitution* (Saigon: Press Office, 1958), 15.

14. Emmanuel Mounier, *Œuvres,* vol. 1 (Paris: Éditions du Seuil, 1961), 623.

15. Marguerite Higgins, *Our Vietnam Nightmare* (New York: Harper and Row, 1965), 166.

16. Nguyễn Công Luận, *Nationalist in the Viet Nam Wars: Memoirs of a Victim Turned Soldier* (Bloomington: Indiana University Press, 2012), 219.

17. Francis Winters, *The Year of the Hare* (Athens: University of Georgia Press, 1997), 11–12.

18. The argument that personalism was a form of Marxist humanism may seem implausible given Mounier's Catholicism and his criticism of Soviet communism. As scholars have noted, however, the latter was marked by a conspicuous failure to unequivocally condemn the excesses of Stalinism. Moreover, Mounier attempted to reconcile his Christian theology with his rejection of capitalism. This may have been one significant difference between Mounier's personalism and Nhu's, which was perhaps less spiritual and more Marxist in its orientation than has been acknowledged in previous scholarship. As Nhu explained in an interview, "my Personalism . . . has no relationship to the Christian Personalism taught by the Catholic organizations in . . . Vietnam. . . . [T]he Personalism . . . I advocate is a militant democracy . . . [aimed at] modifying the superstructure of the present government" (*Press Interviews with President Ngo Dinh Diệm, Political Counselor Ngo Dinh Nhu* [Saigon: Republic of Vietnam, 1963], 68). This statement suggests the need to go beyond a monolithic view not only of the Republic of Vietnam but also of communism and Catholicism. For a discussion of Mounier's equivocal view of Soviet communism, see Tony Judt, *Past Imperfect: French Intellectuals, 1944–1956* (Berkeley: University of California Press, 1992), 155; Seth Armus, *French Anti-Americanism (1930–1948): Critical Moments in a Complex History* (Lanham, MD: Lexington Books, 2007), 81. For a discussion of the difference between Soviet communism and the personalist notion of a decentralized communitarian communism, see Duy Lap Nguyen, *Unimagined Community,* 72–73.

19. For the quote, see Ngô Đình Nhu, "Viet Nam, le cerveau de la famille," interview by Raoul Goulard, *Cinq colonnes à la une,* RTF Télévision (Saigon), October 3, 1963. For more on the elections of village councils, see Bert Fraleigh, "Counterinsurgency in Vietnam: The Real Story," in *Prelude to Tragedy: Vietnam, 1960–1965,* ed. Harvey Neese and John O'Donnell (Annapolis, MD: Naval Institute Press, 2001), 102.

20. Nguyễn Xuân Hoài, "Đảng Cần Lao Nhân Vị."

21. *President Ngo Dinh Diem on Democracy,* 15.

22. Adrian Jaffe and Milton C. Taylor, "A Crumbling Bastion," *New Republic,* June 19, 1961, 17.

23. Jaffe and Taylor, "A Crumbling Bastion," 17.

24. Catton, *Diem's Final Failure,* 25.

25. Jerome T. French, "Politics and National Development in Vietnam, 1954–1960," Pol. Sci. 287A, undated, John B. O'Donnell Collection, Folder 39, Box 01, 13510139001, VVA.

26. Robert Daniels, *Year of the Heroic Guerrilla: World Revolution and Counterrevolution in 1968* (Cambridge, MA: Harvard University Press, 1996), 21.

27. For example, see Catton, *Diem's Final Failure,* 210.

28. George Herring, *America's Longest War: The United States and Vietnam, 1950–1975,* 4th ed. (Boston, MA: McGraw-Hill, 2002), 59.

29. Neil Sheehan, *A Bright Shining Lie: John Paul Vann and America in Vietnam* (New York: Random House, 1989), 124.

30. Sheehan, *Bright Shining Lie,* 309–311.

31. For the quote, see Jaffe and Taylor, "A Crumbling Bastion," 17. For the claim that the program destabilized the political situation, see Seth Jacobs, *Cold War Mandarin: Ngo Dinh Diem and the Origins of America's War in Vietnam, 1950–1963* (Lanham, MD: Rowman & Littlefield, 2006), 185.

32. Quoted in John Donnell, "Politics in South Vietnam: Doctrines and Authority in Conflict" (PhD diss., University of California, Berkeley, 1964), 157.

33. *President Ngo Dinh Diem on Democracy,* 13.

34. Piero Gheddo, *Catholiques et bouddhistes au Vietnam* (Paris: Groupe des éditions Alsatia, 1970), 154.

35. Gheddo, *Catholiques et bouddhistes au Vietnam,* 154.

36. Tân Phong [Ngô Đình Nhu], "Ấp chiến lược: một thực hiện mới của chính phủ để diệt cộng và xây dựng nông thôn," *Quê hương* 37 (1962): 41–42.

37. Quoted in Jean Lacouture, *Le Vietnam entre deux paix* (Paris: Éditions du Seuil, 1965), 37.

38. Lucien Sève, "Les troisième voies," *La pensée,* July-August 1960, 44.

39. Emmanuel Mounier, *Le personnalisme* (Paris: Presses universitaires de France, 1959), 37.

40. Emmanuel Mounier, *De la propriété capitaliste à la propriété humaine* (Paris: Desclée de Brouwer, 1936), 27.

41. Mounier, *Le personnalisme,* 14.

42. Mounier, *Œuvres,* 1:271.

43. Mounier, *Le personnalisme,* 16.

44. Mounier, *Œuvres,* 1:271.

45. Hameau, "La propriété littéraire," 161.

46. Mounier, *Le personnalisme,* 115.

47. Emmanuel Mounier, *Révolution personnaliste et communautaire* (Paris: F. Aubier, 1935), 198.

48. Mounier, *Révolution personnaliste et communautaire,* 218.

49. Quoted in Thomas L. Ahern Jr., *CIA and the House of Ngo: Covert Action in South Vietnam, 1954–1963* (Washington, DC: Center for the Study of Intelligence, 2000), 157.

50. "Personalism–Vietnamese Specialists; Also Others Somewhat Relevant," undated, John Donnell Collection, Folder 14, Box 03, 0720314001, VVA. See also Bernard B. Fall, "Problems of Freedom in South Vietnam," *International Journal* 17, no. 4 (1962): 436–440.

51. Quoted in Bửu Lịch, "Les idéologies dans la République du Sud Vietnam 1954–1975" (PhD diss., Université de Paris VII, 1983–1984), 39.

52. *"Đảng cương Cần Lao Nhân Vị Cách Mạng Đảng"* (Principles of the Cần Lao Personalist Revolutionary Party), circa 1955, Folder 29361, Office of the Prime Minister Collection (Phông Phủ Thủ Tướng Việt Nam Cộng Hòa [PThTVNCH]), National Archives Center 2 (Trung Tâm Lưu Trữ Quốc Gia 2 [TTLTQG2]), Ho Chi Minh City.

53. Quoted in Donnell, "Politics in South Vietnam," 168.

54. On production, see *President Ngo Dinh Diem on Democracy,* 29. On democracy, see *Press Interviews,* 37.

55. Phạm Văn Lưu, *Chính quyền Ngô Dình Diệm, 1954–1963: chủ nghĩa và hành động* (Reservoir, Vic., AU: Centre for Vietnamese Studies Publications, 2017), 30–31.

56. Paper, The Political Factor in Pacification: A Vietnam Case Study [Draft], undated, Vincent Puritano Collection, Box 01, Folder 22, 21470122001, VVA.

57. *Press Interviews,* 69.

58. Meeting Minutes #36, Inter-Ministry Committee for Strategic Hamlets.

59. Phạm Văn Lưu, *Chính quyền Ngô Đình Diệm,* 30–31.

60. *Press Interviews,* 70–71.

61. *Press Interviews,* 22.

62. Mieczysław Maneli, *War of the Vanquished* (New York: Harper and Row, 1971), 145–146.

63. *Press Interviews,* 71.

64. Maneli, *War of the Vanquished,* 145–146.

65. Meeting Minutes #36, Inter-Ministry Committee for Strategic Hamlets, 14.

66. Gabriel Kolko, *Vietnam: Anatomy of a Peace* (New York: Routledge, 1997), 5.

67. Meeting Minutes #36, Inter-Ministry Committee for Strategic Hamlets, 14.

68. Maneli, *War of the Vanquished,* 145.

69. Meeting Minutes #36, Inter-Ministry Committee for Strategic Hamlets, 14.

70. Mounier, *Révolution personnaliste et communautaire,* 25.

71. Francis Fitzgerald, *Fire in the Lake: The Vietnamese and the Americans in Vietnam* (New York: Vintage Books, 1972).

72. Emmanuel Mounier, "Prague," *Esprit* 143, no. 3 (1948): 353–364, especially 364.

73. See Phạm Văn Lưu and Nguyễn Ngọc Tấn, *Đệ Nhất Cộng Hòa Việt Nam, 1954–1963: một cuộc cách mạng* (Melbourne, AU: Centre for Vietnamese Studies, 2005).

74. Nguyen Chi Thanh, *Who Will Win in South Viet Nam?* (Peking: Foreign Languages Press, 1963), 3.

75. US Department of State, *Foreign Relations of the United States, 1961–1963 [FRUS],* vol. 2, *Vietnam, 1962* (Washington: Government Printing Office, 1990), Document 323, "Memorandum of Conversation, Gia Long Palace, Saigon, December 1, 1962, 11:30 a.m."

76. For the quote, see *President Ngo Dinh Diem on Democracy,* 27. For more on colonial capitalism, see *Press Interviews,* 4.

77. William Duiker, *US Containment Policy and the Conflict in Indochina* (Stanford, CA: Stanford University Press, 1994), 19.

78. For the quote, see William Egan Colby, *Lost Victory: A Firsthand Account of America's Sixteen-Year Involvement in Vietnam* (Chicago: Contemporary Books, 1989), 28. On the Ngôs' views toward the elite, see also Nguyễn Văn Châu, *Con đường sống* (Saigon: Nhóm Văn Chiến, 1961), 7–31. For Diệm's failure to eliminate the middle class through land reform, see William Colby, "William E. Colby Oral History, Interview I," recorded interview by Ted Gininger, June 2, 1981, 13–14, Oral History Program, Lyndon Baines Johnson Library, University of Texas, Austin.

79. *President Ngo Dinh Diem on Democracy,* 24.

80. See *Land Reform in Free Vietnam* (Saigon: Review Horizons, 1956).

81. See Miller, *Misalliance,* 160.

82. Colby, *Lost Victories,* 32. See also "FOI Declassified Document, NSC Memo on US Objectives in Vietnam War July 1963," July 1, 1963, Douglas Pike Collection, Unit 02—Military Operations, Box 03, Folder 02, 2130302004, VVA.

83. Leo Cherne, "Vietnam's Internal Problems—Vietnam's Economy," 1956, Douglas Pike Collection, Unit 06—Democratic Republic of Vietnam, Box 19, Folder 01, 2321901005, VVA.

84. "The Economic Renovation of the Republic of Vietnam," 1959, Douglas Pike Collection, Unit 06—Democratic Republic of Vietnam, Box 19, Folder 05, 2321905001, VVA.

85. Vũ Quốc Thúc, "National Planning in Vietnam," *Asian Survey* 1, no. 7 (September 1961): 3–9, especially 7–8.

86. *New York Times*, "Ky Says US Economic Aid Has Failed," July 5, 1970.

87. George McT. Kahin, *Intervention: How America Became Involved in Vietnam* (New York: Anchor Books, 1987), 86.

88. "Economic and Social Development," undated, Wesley R. Fishel Papers (UA 17.95), Box 1192, Folder 35, UA17-95_000362, Michigan State University Archives and Historical Collection.

89. Catton, *Diem's Final Failure*, 31.

90. "Article on the Much Debated Interview of Counsellor Ngo Dinh Nhu from the *Times of Viet Nam*," June 7, 1958, Douglas Pike Collection, Other Manuscripts, American Friends of Vietnam, Box 01, Folder 19, 1780119019, VVA.

91. Minh Võ, *Ngô Đình Diệm và Chính Nghĩa Dân Tộc* (Hồng Đức, 2008), 131.

92. US Department of State, *FRUS, 1958–1960*, vol. 1, *Vietnam* (Washington: Government Printing Office, 1986), Document 85, "Despatch from the Chargé in Vietnam (Elting) to the Department of State, Saigon, July 30, 1959."

93. Stanley Millet, "Under Diem—The Image Sharpens," July 1965, Douglas Pike Collection, Unit 08—Biography, Box 09, Folder 26, 2360926080, VVA.

94. "Despatch from the Chargé in Vietnam (Elting) to the Department of State, Saigon, July 30, 1959."

95. US Department of State, *FRUS, 1961–1963*, vol. 1, "Memorandum of Conversation, Gia Long Palace."

96. US Department of State, *FRUS, 1961–1963*, vol. 3, *Vietnam, January-August 1963* (Washington: Government Printing Office, 1991), Document 226, "Memorandum of Conversation, Saigon, July 17, 1963."

97. US Department of State, *FRUS, 1961–1963*, vol. 2, *Vietnam, 1962* (Washington: Government Printing Office, 1990), Document 127, "Airgram from the Embassy in Vietnam to the Department of State, Saigon, March 23, 1962."

98. "Diệm's War or Ours?" *Eyewitness*, CBS, December 29, 1961.

99. Interview, Mr. Bert Fraleigh, 34–35, February 3, 1967, Rufus Phillips Collection, Box 02, Folder 16, 23970216021, VVA.

100. US Department of State, *FRUS, 1961-1963*, vol. 2, "Airgram from the Embassy."

101. Discussion Paper, from Strategic Hamlets to Self Defense Village (translated from Vietnamese), undated, Vladimir Lehovich Collection, Box 02, Folder 05, 12050205002, VVA.

102. Robert Thompson, *Defeating Communist Insurgency* (Saint Petersburg, FL: Hailer Publishing, 2005), 59–60.

103. Thompson, *Defeating Communist Insurgency*, 163.

104. Meeting Minutes #2, Inter-Ministry Committee for Strategic Hamlets, February 23, 1962, Douglas Pike Collection, Other Manuscripts—Inter-Ministry Committee for Strategic Hamlets, Box 01, Folder 01, 1820101002, VVA.

105. "Tuyên ngôn Cần Lao Nhân Vị Cách Mạng Đảng," Folder 29361, PThTVNCH, TTLTQG2.

106. For the quote about the people's war, see Catton, *Diem's Final Failure*, 90. For the quote about ending capitalism, see Maneli, *War of the Vanquished*, 145–146.

107. Colby, *Lost Victories*, 32.

108. Philip Catton, "Parallel Agendas: The Ngo Dinh Diem Regime, the United States and the Strategic Hamlet Program, 1961–1963" (PhD diss., Ohio University, 1998), 220.

109. Meeting Minutes #36, Inter-Ministry Committee for Strategic Hamlets.

110. Maneli, *War of the Vanquished*, 145–146.

111. US Department of State, *FRUS, 1961–1963,* vol. 2, "Airgram from the Embassy."

112. US Department of State, *FRUS, 1961–1963,* vol. 3, *Vietnam, January–August 1963,* Document 192, "Telegram from the Embassy in Vietnam to the Department of State, Saigon, June 28, 1963."

113. Paper, The Political Factor in Pacification.

114. *Press Interviews,* 69.

115. On limiting central authority, see *Press Interviews,* 70–71. On bypassing the ministries, see Paper, The Political Factor in Pacification.

116. "Some General Operating Patterns of VC Political Cadres," June 1970, Douglas Pike Collection, Unit 05—National Liberation Front, Box 09, Folder 08, 2310908007, VVA. See also interview, Mr. Bert Fraleigh.

117. Report, A Report on Counter-Insurgency in Vietnam, July 20, 1962, Rufus Phillips Collection, Box 01, Folder 28, 23970128002, VVA.

118. Thompson, *Defeating Communist Insurgency,* 126.

119. Maneli, *War of the Vanquished,* 145.

120. Colby, "William E. Colby on Vietnam."

121. "Memorandum of Conversation, Gia Long Palace, Saigon, December 1, 1962, 11:30 a.m."

122. Colby, "William E. Colby on Vietnam."

123. Booklet, The Strategic Hamlet Program in Kien Hoa Province, South Vietnam, undated, Rufus Phillips Collection, Box 01, Folder 33, 23970133011, VVA.

124. Colby, "William E. Colby on Vietnam."

125. Gregory A. Olson, *Mansfield and Vietnam: A Study in Rhetorical Adaptation* (East Lansing: Michigan State University Press, 1995), 45.

126. Paper, The Political Factor in Pacification.

127. *Times of Vietnam,* July 7, 1960, 1.

128. Daniels, *Year of the Heroic Guerrilla,* 77.

129. US Department of State, *FRUS, 1961–1963,* vol. 2, *Vietnam, 1962,* Document 191, "Telegram From the Embassy in Vietnam to the Department of State, Saigon , October 9, 1963, 11 a.m."

130. Paper, The Political Factor in Pacification.

131. Paper, The Political Factor in Pacification.

CHAPTER SEVEN

"They Eat the Flesh of Children"

Migration, Resettlement, and Sectionalism in South Vietnam, 1954–1957

Jason A. Picard

"They eat the flesh of children!" The rumor gripped southern Vietnam in late March 1955. Migrants arriving from North Vietnam were abducting southern children and using their flesh to make northern delicacies such as beef noodle soup (*phở*), pressed meat (*chả lụa*), and spring rolls (*nem*).[1] The story paralyzed Saigon and the surrounding provinces—an area then home to 25 to 30 percent of South Vietnam's population and sheltering the majority of these Northern migrants, known as *Bắc di cư*. Newspapers printed sensational headlines, schools and markets emptied, and Southerners refused to venture out of their homes.

By all accounts, the gruesome claims proved baseless. Still, the consequences forced the city's mayor, Trần Văn Hương, to respond in a public address. The rumors were the product of a "sophisticated hoax" by communist agents seeking to sow Southern "hatred and fear of the *Bắc di cư* and a climate of sectional discord and division," he claimed.[2] As evidence, the government in Saigon pointed to numerous articles published in *The People* (*Nhân dân*), the official daily newspaper of the communist party in North Vietnam, that blamed the alleged abductions on the desperate conditions facing Northern migrants in the South.[3]

Yet dismissing the affair as simply the result of communist machinations neglects a fundamental question. Why did so many Southerners believe the rumor? The simple answer behind Southerners' susceptibility to such claims is sectionalism. But then how do we explain this sectionalism? What accounts for its presence?

Scholarship about the Vietnam War has conventionally diagnosed this hostility and distrust toward the Northern migrants as the consequence of two interrelated factors: religion and favoritism. Essentially, the argument goes, although most Southerners were Buddhists, the vast majority of Northern migrants were,

143

like Ngô Đình Diệm, Catholics. This religious bond led Diệm to fete the evacuees with favor and privilege and organize them into unassimilated villages concentrated around the Church.[4]

Many contemporary scholars continue to adopt the idea that sectional conflict was a by-product of privilege and religion. Mark Bradley explains that refugees "were well provided for by Diệm and often allowed to settle on land already occupied by non-Catholic Southerners," thus igniting sectional animosity.[5] Seth Jacobs agrees: "Diệm's pro-Catholic bias disposed him favorably toward . . . the refugees from the North."[6] In addition, despite trying to cast the experiences of the Vietnamese in a more complex light, Jessica Chapman writes that Diệm's "blatant favoritism" toward Catholic refugees spurred sectional distrust.[7]

Speculation about government favoritism undoubtedly stirred Southern antipathy, as the migration became one of the most pressing and contentious issues confronting the regime in South Vietnam. Nevertheless, presuming this animosity to be merely the product of religion or perceived preferential treatment both glosses over the history of sectionalism in Vietnam and the profound impact of the migration on Southern society and politics after 1954.[8] In this chapter, I examine how these elements coalesced to transform sectional hostility into a force antithetical to the vision that Ngô Đình Diệm set out for the Republic of Vietnam.

A word of explanation: I define sectionalism as a fidelity to one's place of origin based on its social and cultural characteristics and a belief that one's interests resembles the interests of people who share the same origin. Northern migrants continued to identify with their native region and those from the same place even decades after the migration, and migrants and the existing inhabitants in South Vietnam perceived each other as being culturally distinct. Moreover, the two groups understood themselves as having competing interests and at times clashed violently over access to economic resources. Thus my understanding of sectionalism emphasizes interests and interaction between different groups as much as geographical origin. How does this differ from regionalism and communalism? I view regionalism as more overtly political, and Northern migrants did not demand an autonomous zone or a separate state. Communalism is typically associated with distinctions like language or ethnicity, and despite Khmer and highlander separatist movements in South Vietnam, Northerners and Southerners still saw themselves as Vietnamese.

Although sectional hostility was widespread between the Northern migrants and the existing inhabitants, perceptions of their affiliation and identities varied. The two sides often defined themselves as belonging to one of the three geographical regions of Vietnam—north, central, or south—and pointed to the other side as belonging to a different region. Meanwhile, the government and the media emphasized the contrasting experiences of the population in North and

South Vietnam, that is, the two zones of partitioned Vietnam. In many cases, historical actors used the terms "north" (*bắc*) and "south" (*nam*) without clarifying whether they were referring to the tripartite division of the country or the partition, but what is clear is that both migrants and long-time residents understood each other as belonging to profoundly different groups. Now let us turn to the event that triggered the crisis, the migration.

THE "GREAT MIGRATION"

On July 21, 1954, the Geneva Conference on the Indochina peninsula came to an end. Among the stipulations of the conference agreements were the temporary partition of Vietnam and a national plebiscite to be held in two years to reunite the two zones under a single government. In addition, and most significant in relation to this chapter, the accords provided for three hundred days of free passage between the zones that began with the conclusion of the conference.

During the ensuing evacuation, more than 860,000 North Vietnamese fled to the South, the majority of whom were Catholic.[9] Because the arrivals made up nearly 8 percent of the entire Southern population, the Diệm government faced a displaced persons' crisis of dramatic proportions. Considering the size and scope, I would argue, one cannot properly understand Vietnam during the post-1954 period without apprehending the impact of the migration.

On the one hand, it handed the Southern government an international public relations victory. With both the Democratic Republic of Vietnam in Hanoi and the Republic of Vietnam (RVN) in Saigon claiming to be the rightful representative of Vietnamese aspirations, the latter and its backers portrayed the flight of hundreds of thousands from the North as a referendum of sorts, a "voting with the feet" in support of the Southern regime.[10] The government alternately dubbed the passage the Historic Migration (Cuộc Di Cư Lịch Sử) or Great Migration (Cuộc Di Cư Vĩ Đại).[11]

On the other hand, however, the migration produced a host of complications for the South. As one American journalist posited in the June 1955 issue of *National Geographic:*

> Suppose half a million Maine farmers and town dwellers were suddenly uprooted, moved a thousand miles south by ship, and resettled in North Carolina. Imagine the countless problems such an upheaval in human geography would involve, and you have some idea of the gigantic task of transplanting [hundreds of thousands of] men, women, and children from [the North to the South].[12]

To complicate this depiction, South Vietnam of 1954–1955 could not have been more different from the United States. A newly minted, temporary authority overseeing half of a country, the RVN was coping with a nation just recently emerged from war and colonialism. The situation appeared so hopeless that the *New York Times Magazine* ran an article titled "Saigon in the Shadow of Doom."[13]

A BRIEF HISTORY OF SECTIONALISM PRIOR TO 1954

Although ethnic Vietnamese might trace their historical origins to the North, regional and sectional distinctions had already long been a part of Vietnamese society by the time that Northern evacuees arrived in the South in 1954. Since at least the sixteenth century, Vietnamese expansion southward had occurred in a series of migrations and annexations known today collectively as *Nam Tiến*.[14] Over the centuries, this would produce numerous social and cultural variations as migrants and their descendants adapted to local customs and practices. In the seventeenth century, a Vietnamese breakaway kingdom called Đàng Trong emerged on the central coast and gradually expanded into what is now the southern third of the country. Li Tana argues that the kingdom developed its own culture, one distinct from the existing Vietnamese polity in the North. The culture of Đàng Trong developed different culinary and linguistic characteristics, followed new customs on land use, and exhibited a more open approach to trade and the presence of outsiders compared to its Northern counterpart.[15] Although Nguyễn Phúc Ánh's ascension as Emperor Gia Long united the two kingdoms in 1802, French colonialism and the creation of French Indochina halted Vietnamese political unification. By 1883, the French had divided the country into three administrative regions: Tonkin or Bắc Kỳ (north), Annam or Trung Kỳ (center), and Cochinchina or Nam Kỳ (south).

Exacerbating these historical realities, French authorities encouraged sectional separation and identity.[16] In the early twentieth century, officials recruited men from Tonkin to work on rubber plantations in Cochinchina. By 1930, Pierre Gourou estimated that ninety thousand people had emigrated for this and other work programs.[17] The French, however, did not integrate migrants into local communities. On the contrary, officials established separate *tonkinois* communities for recruits from Tonkin, who for the most part were either young single men or men who left families behind in Tonkin.[18] In the late 1930s, such men had gained reputations as "dangerous lechers," in part due to a series of abductions and rapes of local women along the Đồng Nai River by "roving bands of Bắc Kỳ men." By this time, the term Bắc Kỳ had become a popular Cochinchinese expression of derision and suspicion for northerners. In Tây Ninh, Mỹ Tho, and Cần Thơ, parents scolding children for being "naughty" might threaten that, if they did not behave, the "Bắc Kỳ will abduct you."[19]

Compounding this were Southern assumptions about the extreme poverty in Northern Vietnam, a view only enhanced by the great famine of 1944–1945, which caused the deaths of more than a million people and entrenched the belief that Northerners were willing to eat human flesh. French colonial rule ended in 1954, but sectional stereotypes and distrust persisted.[20] The exodus and the RVN's efforts to deal with it revived the legacy of prejudice.

RVN MANAGEMENT OF THE MIGRATION

The RVN launched the General Commission for Migrants and Refugees (GCMR), or Phủ Tổng Ủy Di Cư và Ty Nạn, on September 17, 1954. The new cabinet-level agency was tasked with rehabilitating the refugees. Rehabilitation occurred in three phases: reception, relocation, and localization. Ideally, the reception stage provided Northern migrants temporary shelter, food, and living allowance while they awaited permanent resettlement. It was supposed to conclude a few months after the end of the three-hundred-day period of free passage. The second phase, relocation, was intended to settle migrants in areas appropriate to their occupations. Thus, farmers would be resettled in locations with land suitable to agriculture and fisherfolk near water. During this stage, new villages were to be erected. This included the construction of homes, wells, schools, churches, and pagodas by and for the new inhabitants.[21] By the final stage, localization, these new communities would be incorporated into local society, and government assistance would cease. The entire process would allow Bắc di cư to achieve individual self-sufficiency and collective integration.

The United States provided enormous assistance totaling $83 million, and Northern clergy provided both spiritual and administrative leadership in many of the communities subsequently established.[22] In May 1957, just two years after the conclusion of the free-passage period, resettlement was being hailed as a remarkable success as the RVN prepared to end its assistance to Bắc di cư.[23] Well over five hundred thousand migrants were now living in 319 resettlement sites across the South, most notably in the Mekong Delta, the Central Highlands, and Biên Hòa province. In addition, hundreds of thousands had settled in cities and towns across the South.

By international measures, the RVN's handling of the crisis was a remarkable success. So what was the problem? In the sections that follow, we explore several interconnected issues that paved the way for confrontation between Southerners and migrants: the chaotic conditions for migrants, Southern hardship, and the government's efforts to combat it all.

PERCEPTION AND CHAOS

The rehabilitation process was haphazard and did not keep up with the countless problems that arose. On September 21, 1954, thousands of recently arrived migrants housed at the reception centers across Saigon demonstrated. The protests turned violent as five hundred *Bắc di cư* clashed with Saigon police. By the end of the day, the police had slain five protesters and arrested fifty more.[24] Investigations into the cause of the riots revealed that since the end of August no migrant in any of the reception centers had received the full stipend promised. By September 13, 40 percent of the centers were not receiving any assistance at all. As a result, migrants were "selling the few belongings they had in exchange for food."[25]

The protests and the underlying situation behind them should not come as a surprise. The GCMR had come into existence only four days before the strikes. In the two months prior, no single organization or government agency oversaw the effort to welcome and shelter migrants. Instead, the RVN had relied on a ragtag collection of organizations and underfunded ministries that had little coordination or even contact between them.[26] As a result, the GCMR was two months behind in confronting the resettlement challenge, a fact that loomed large throughout its thirty-nine-month existence.[27]

Indeed, fourteen months after the first migrants began to arrive in the South, the GCMR's general director admitted that large numbers of *Bắc di cư* remained in Saigon and that many were resorting to "panhandling" (*hành khất*) and sleeping on the city's streets.[28] In central Saigon, migrants lay cloth or traditional Vietnamese rice mats, called *chiếu,* in front of shops, establishing makeshift homes. *New York Times* reporter Robert Alden described one girl sweeping the sidewalk just as she might tidy up her family's home.[29] Illustrating the turmoil outside Saigon's Notre Dame Cathedral, one Vietnamese journalist described finding a middle-age woman sleeping with all of her belongings next to her. This amounted to some cloth and "a red can containing a bit of rice."[30]

The First Indochina War and the subsequent flight South had left *Bắc di cư* ravaged by malnutrition and illness. Every shipload of *Bắc di cư* brought with it various illnesses. Malaria, dysentery, pneumonia, chickenpox, and smallpox left migrants in and around Saigon "devastated."[31] In February 1955 in a single camp, smallpox caused the death of twenty people and the hospitalization of two hundred more.[32]

Yet one would be mistaken to imagine that the newcomers' struggles aroused the sympathy of their Southern compatriots. A combination of historical sectional conflict, refugee struggles during rehabilitation, and Southerners' own hardship during the First Indochina War fanned ill will between the two groups.

SOUTHERN HARDSHIP

Although the First Indochina War may not have had the devastating impact on Vietnam's South that it did on Vietnam's North, nonetheless, the war badly disrupted the Southern economy. The 1954 and 1955 harvests of major crops such as rice and sugarcane were lower than those of the years before World War II.[33] Gerald Hickey writes that "There was widespread damage to systems of communication, and vast areas of paddy fields [were] abandoned by peasants who fled to the urban areas."[34] As a result, in the spring of 1955, hundreds of thousands of farmers from the Mekong Delta remained displaced.[35] Many eked out an existence in Saigon or other large towns, living in makeshift shelters and shanties, a problem nearly as grave as that of the arriving migrants.[36]

The end of French colonial rule also created an uncertain business climate affecting Southern labor. French companies responded by reining in Vietnamese employees' wages and scaling back operations.[37] In December 1954, employees at the Bến Củi rubber plantation went on strike in response to both wage reduction plans and poor working conditions.[38] The strike led to a general work stoppage by more than ten thousand workers across the city in support of the rubber company employees.[39] Three months later, a thousand Vietnamese employees walked out of the Bastos cigarette factory in Saigon, claiming that the company forced them to work long hours with no additional pay.[40] Coupling the tenuous economic situation with the presence of so many new arrivals, one report estimated that more than seven hundred thousand people in the Saigon capital region faced unemployment by late 1955, a crisis many Southerners blamed on the *Bắc di cư.*[41]

Meanwhile, the northernmost portion of South Vietnam, a region already known for its poor agriculture, confronted perhaps the greatest challenges. The war and a succession of terrible harvest seasons placed hundreds of thousands of Southerners in Quảng Trị, Quảng Nam, Phú Yên, Quảng Ngãi, and Bình Định provinces on the edge of famine; a million more were only slightly better off.[42] However, given the migration crisis, government ministries tasked with assisting victims of the famine saw much of their budgets redirected to migration issues. In 1955, for instance, the budget of the Ministry of Social Action and Health was cut from 50 million piasters ($1.43 million) to 7.2 million (about $205,000). Unable to cope with the famine, the ministry projected that by that summer between thirty to fifty thousand civilians in Quảng Ngãi and Bình Định alone would perish.[43] Although none of these crises was attributable to the migration, that the government provided migrants assistance even as many Southerners struggled only aggravated sectional friction.

The hostility sparked by the demands of the migration was felt even inside the government. In August of 1954, the RVN urged Southern officials to give a portion of their salary to help migrant civil servants build homes. The pressure to participate was, in the words of one official, "immense."[44] Concurrently, the government furnished Northern migrant civil servants with two-month advances on salaries, a special lunar new year bonus, and a portion of any back pay owed them.[45] Southern bureaucrats felt slighted. In an expression of resentment, several ministries led by Southerners refused to employ supposedly qualified *Bắc di cư.* In a memorandum sent to all RVN offices, Minister of the Interior Nguyễn Ngọc Thơ warned that any delay or refusal to fulfill Prime Minister Ngô Đình Diệm's promise to employ *Bắc di cư* would have serious repercussions.[46]

Bishop Phạm Ngọc Chi, head of the Catholic arm for resettlement, feared that relocated migrants would be perceived as both handmaidens of antagonistic government policy as well as the regime's favored group and that this would fuel sectional conflict. As a result, in May 1955, the bishop floated a scheme to reorganize and expand the GCMR into one General Commission for War Victim Relief (Phủ Tổng Ủy Cứu Trợ Nạn Nhân Chiến Tranh). The new agency would consist of two committees, one responsible for *Bắc di cư* and the other for Southern evacuees.[47] The idea gained support from several high-ranking officials in the RVN and several Vietnamese newspapers.[48] Diệm and the GCMR, however, had other plans.

Rather than expanding assistance to include Southerners as well as Northern migrants, the government chose to launch campaigns that emphasized self-sufficiency and strengthened ties between Southerners and *Bắc di cư.* Unfortunately, these only strained relations further and provoked violent conflict.

THE NORTH-SOUTH COMPASSION CAMPAIGN

Introducing the North-South Compassion Campaign (Thông Cảm Nam Bắc) in the spring of 1955, the RVN aimed to create "an environment of understanding among people of different regions."[49] The GCMR dispatched speakers to educate communities about cultural differences. Teams of Northern refugees visited Southern villages to discuss their lives, customs, and reasons for fleeing the North, and groups of Southerners met with *Bắc di cư* communities to explain their culture and the expectations they had for the new arrivals.[50]

Literature, movies, newspapers, and folk songs about the migration emphasized the supposed root causes of the exodus. If Southerners could learn of the struggles that their Northern compatriots had suffered, the logic went, then they could not help but feel compassion. Produced in 1956, the film *We Want to Live* (*Chúng tôi muốn sống*) was set in North Vietnam between 1952 and 1954. The film's protagonist, Vinh, is a patriot who serves the Việt Minh during the First Indochina War. With the success of the communist revolution, however, Vinh's parents fall victim to a Land Reform struggle session and are sentenced to death and buried alive despite their innocence. The first major motion picture produced in the RVN, the film won high praise from the Saigon press for capturing the communists' "bloodthirsty" (*khát máu*) machinations.[51]

In its inaugural issue, the journal *Creativity* (*Sáng tạo*) published an article by the *Bắc di cư* writer Mai Thảo titled "Saigon, the Cultural Capital of Vietnam" ("Sài Gòn thủ đô văn hóa Việt Nam"). With the communist takeover in the North, Mai Thảo argued, Saigon had replaced Hanoi as the heart of Vietnamese "national life" (*sinh hoạt dân tộc*), and it was the *Bắc di cư* who had carried the torch of Vietnamese culture across the seventeenth parallel that it might "shine" in the South.[52]

But such propaganda ignored critical issues that inflamed sectional animosity on the part of Southerners. First, many Southerners had ties to the Việt Minh or the communist party. Tens of thousands of southern Việt Minh cadres and their dependents regrouped (*tập kết*) to the North following the Geneva Conference. Many others remained in the South, and for them as well as the family members of those who had regrouped, the anticommunist rhetoric was alienating. Their disaffection became compounded by fear when, on the first anniversary of the Geneva Accords, the regime announced the Communist Denunciation (Chiến Dịch Tố Cộng) campaign aimed at locating and destroying communist agents operating in the South. Second, at the same time, by memorializing the exodus from communism as embodying national sacrifice, the government cast Northern migrants as epitomizing the regime's ideal citizen.

Third, although demanding poor and dispossessed Southerners sympathized with the displaced Northerners, the RVN was *officially* bestowing vast amounts of aid on migrants during the resettlement stage. At the height of resettlement, 604,384 refugees had been "securely relocated" by the GCMR at hundreds of resettlement sites across the South in less than eighteen months.[53] By the autumn of 1956, according to official statistics, those living in GCMR resettlement areas had built 83,758 homes and a total of 6,669 wells had been excavated. Each family that completed a home received 3,000 piasters ($86) for their labor and expenses.[54]

It was immaterial that the government's statistics reflected neither the experiences of Northern refugees nor their ability to survive without assistance, as will be seen. In the eyes of Southerners, the official figures and the sight of strangers taking possession of land confirmed the perception of a regime playing favorites and intensified Southern resentment toward the new arrivals. It was under these conditions that migrants—the apparent face of the RVN's policy—arrived at permanent relocation sites.

LAND AND SECTIONAL HOSTILITY

Suddenly whole villages of Northern refugees appeared in places with little consideration given either to the sites' potential or the people who lived there. In Chợ Lớn province, for example, the GCMR unilaterally decided to transfer more than two thousand *Bắc di cư* to Cầu Xáng village without consulting provincial authorities. The province chief, Võ Văn Ngọ, was furious.[55] The commission had assured officials that resettlement would be based on each province's capacity and, as Ngọ stressed, the province was already stretched well beyond that point.

The government had asked the country to sympathize and had insisted that "everyone needed to sacrifice."[56] The Northern migrants were making the life-altering decision to flee South, and the government had an obligation to provide for these arrivals, repeated Nguyễn Ngọc Thơ in November 1954.[57] But to Ngọ, the government had missed the point. Whatever hardships migrants faced, their arrival was also upsetting local inhabitants, according to the province chief. In the case of Cầu Xáng, the reason for the land's supposed availability was that its inhabitants had been forced to evacuate in the 1940s due to the chaos of the First Indochina War. In the intervening years, the land remained empty. The evacuees, however, now wanted to "return" (*hồi cư*). If the government insisted on allowing *Bắc di cư* to occupy this land, the province chief warned, conflict would be unavoidable because Southern families' "livelihoods" (*bát cơm*) were at stake.[58]

In the Central Highlands, disputes arose between *Bắc di cư* and non-ethnic Vietnamese over land in Đồng Nai Thượng province. The new arrivals began using uncultivated lands near their village settlement. Claiming the land as their own, local inhabitants belonging to the Rhade ethnic group demanded that the migrants stop. Demonstrating little concern for the customs of highland ethnic minorities, RVN officials described ethnic highlanders' approach to land claims this way: "the practice of the savage [*dân mọi*] is basically, if they can see it with their eyes, the land belongs to them."[59]

In the case of the indigenous, non-ethnic Vietnamese population—such as the Rhade, Jarai, and K'ho—Diệm hoped to assimilate them "into the Vietnamese cultural sphere."[60] Ultimately, officials believed, this would bring economic development to the highlands and modernity to its people.[61] "Within two or more years," one province chief eagerly explained, "we hope to bring all highlanders in a single city . . . and in another generation, their tribal customs will be just a memory."[62] The resettlement of evacuees seemed a practical instrument to achieve these ends. In the process, Diệm imagined the Central Highlands becoming a key engine of agricultural development in Vietnam, referring to it as "the California of Vietnam."[63]

Preparing for the arrival of several thousand migrants in 1954 and 1955, Cần Thơ officials ordered local inhabitants to stop using certain "deserted lands." Inhabitants protested claiming that the RVN was "confiscating" their property. The Cần Thơ province chief claimed that he explained to the protesters that the land in question belonged to the state and that therefore they had no right to it. Local inhabitants were understandably furious. The people of the region, they argued, had long claimed these lands.

Riots erupted. Soldiers were called in to put down the uprising, leaving ten people dead and seventeen injured.[64] Two weeks later, the tragedy still fresh in the minds of local inhabitants, *Bắc di cư* began to arrive in Cần Thơ. The problem in cases such as Đồng Nai Thượng and Cần Thơ was that Southern land use practices were not consistent with government plans, and the RVN desperately needed to relocate the Northerners. It is little wonder that Northern migrants were becoming the personification of a hated policy.

SELF-RELIANCE: REIFYING SECTIONALISM

In part because of the deepening anger toward *Bắc di cư,* the GCMR announced the Self-Reliance Campaign (Tự Lực Mưu Sinh) on July 21, 1955, as part of the first anniversary commemorating the signing of the Geneva Accords.[65] The campaign aimed both to stimulate production at resettlement sites and to "eliminate" migrant dependency on government aid.[66] The campaign also furnished the regime an opportunity to test its personalist (*nhân vị*) ideology.

The initiative demanded that *Bắc di cư* look to community-based institutions to resolve challenges. By encouraging the independent spirit of the migrant, officials argued, the campaign would allow the RVN to preserve its resources in the struggle against communism.[67] President Diệm himself repeatedly reminded *Bắc di cư* of their obligation to the nation and of the need to rely on their own communities for assistance.[68]

Authorities also hoped the campaign would compel migrants to cooperate with their Southern neighbors. Resettlement villages and centers would no longer be "distinct and isolated" areas but instead integrated and contributing members of their new communities. Ultimately, practicing self-reliance would help all Vietnamese form a united "citizens bloc" (*khối công dân*) that was blind to sectionalism.[69]

Was the government's hope in this campaign genuine or merely an effort to wash its hands of responsibility? The answer is unclear, but either way, the expectation that the initiative could somehow foster warm relations and cooperation between refugees and Southerners ignored the critical problems underlining state-directed resettlement. First, migrants were not settled among Southerners in existing villages. Instead, they were being transplanted to 319 corporate resettlement sites established solely for them. Second, the government's reliance on the Catholic clergy to resolve the GCMR's manpower shortage meant that the main community-based institution that Northern migrants turned to was the Church. As a result, clergy provided leadership in these new villages. Third, in the eyes of local inhabitants, the government had taken supposedly deserted land from Southerners and presented it to the new arrivals. These factors coalesced to render the incorporation of Northern migrants into

Southern society nearly impossible. Rather than promoting cooperation, the Self-Reliance Campaign functioned to deepen rifts and left migrants no choice but to struggle on their own.

Local conditions and poor management compounded the problem. In the Mekong Delta, the soil in places chosen for resettlement tended to suffer from high concentrations of alum (*nước phèn*), making rice difficult to cultivate and the water undrinkable.[70] In numerous places in the delta, land had been left uncultivated during the First Indochina War and was now overgrown. According to estimates by officials, it would take five years to create conditions for "stable" agriculture.[71] In mid-September 1955, the residents of Dốc Mơ (Gia Kiệm, Biên Hòa province) filed a grievance with the GCMR. They had built 869 homes for which each family should have collected 3,000 piasters but received none. In addition, 935 *Bắc di cư* of Dốc Mơ had received no living stipend, and another thousand had been given just a portion of the promised funds.[72]

Consequently, migrants had to rely on themselves to resolve the many challenges they faced. For instance, in Biên Hòa and Tây Ninh, living near forests and having few alternatives, parishes organized families into wood collection teams and established a lumber factory.[73] In Bà Rịa, the poor soil content forced parishes under the direction of Father Trần Đình Cảnh to capture tigers roaming the forests around their new home. Despite the risks, the reward of 20,000 piasters per animal was too attractive. The migrants in this community had no training, but as one in the flock noted, "What choice do we have? We must risk our lives to save our lives."[74]

The government was not unaware of the problems. In an effort to dissuade the GCMR from resettling migrants in areas around Ban Mê Thuột, the Ministry of Agriculture's director on farming warned in late February 1956, "Do not resettle people there, it will be a disaster."[75] The GCMR had claimed that the tens of thousands of hectares selected could support two rice crops each year. However, the farming chief explained that even under the best of circumstances the region could only sustain one crop. A subsequent soil survey revealed, in fact, that it "could not even support life." The GCMR ignored this counsel.[76] Exasperated, the director of farming bemoaned how the GCMR seemed to have just one standard for selecting land, "its availability."[77]

The GCMR did not dispute the farming chief's appraisal. Having had to tackle immense overcrowding, an internal report conceded, the GCMR had hurriedly designated resettlement sites with little consideration given to the possibility of success.[78] Such an indiscriminate approach "cast a dark shadow" over the entire program, according to the refugee chief of the United States Operations Mission, the wing of the American embassy that handled nonmilitary aid.[79]

Required to navigate resettlement and basic survival on their own in less than hospitable places, migrants reproduced many of their Northern regional and religious institutions, further straining relations with local inhabitants in the process and ensuring that they would lead largely segregated lives. In the section that follows, I explore the case of Cái Sắn in the lower Mekong Delta, the government's so-called model resettlement center, and how migrant relocation devolved into resentment and violence.

LAND POLICIES AND GROWING RESENTMENT IN THE LOWER MEKONG DELTA

Tucked in the lower Mekong Delta is a region called Cái Sắn, divided administratively between the provinces of Kiên Giang and An Giang and the city of Cần Thơ. A response to the shortcomings and pitfalls of previous resettlement in the South, Cái Sắn was supposed to eventually house more than a hundred thousand Northern evacuees and serve as a model for future land reform in South Vietnam, including subsequent projects like New Lands (Dinh Điền), Agrovilles (Khu Trù Mật), and Strategic Hamlets (Ấp Chiến Lược). Unfortunately, the story of Cái Sắn also exposes many of the obstacles confronted elsewhere in the South.

The economy of the lower Mekong Delta was shaped by the dynamics of local agriculture, security, the tropical environment, and a demographic pattern that distinguished it from the eastern Red River Delta, where most Northern migrants originated. In North Vietnam, peasants generally farmed two or three rice harvests annually. In the lower Mekong Delta, farmers cultivated only one annual harvest of a distinct type of rice, known as floating rice (cây lúa nổi).[80] Peasants also supplemented their income through two methods of fishing.[81] First, many had fishing holes for year-round use, in which they raised aquaculture. In times of war and disorder, these ponds became particularly important to locals, supplementing income and diet. For instance, a secret government document admitted that the "insecurity" (tình thế bất an) caused by the First Indochina War complicated rice cultivation and rendered fishing "the chief source of income" (huê lợi chánh) for local inhabitants.[82]

Second, the monsoons submerged the lower Mekong in two to three meters of water between August and December, and poor farmers and tenants from surrounding areas descended on the flooded lands to go fishing. Local inhabitants tolerated this seasonal influx of "floating people" because local population pressures were relatively low.

As local residents discovered, however, the government employed a narrow definition for land use. The RVN viewed land as unused if it was left uncultivated for just a year. Fishing ponds did not meet government criteria for cultivation and thus were subject to expropriation. In late 1955 and early 1956, these same lands were cordoned off without any explanation. When the inhabitants tried to enter, the police informed them that the area was off limits (bị cấm không được vào).[83]

As a result, at least a thousand families lost these ponds during the first four months of 1956. Local inhabitants pleaded with officials to recognize their claims to the fishing holes. They explained that the region's normally low rice yields, the result of poor soil quality (*đất xấu*), had been worsened by the "wartime instability" of the past ten years. For these reasons, they had embraced the local environment and dug fishing holes.[84]

A Saigon daily pointed out that, in light of the poor soil composition, improved rice production in the lower Mekong Delta required major expenditures to construct necessary dyke or canal systems.[85] The local population did not have the financial resources to tackle such an enormous undertaking. And now that "they were losing an essential source of their income," what would they do?[86] Over the coming weeks and months, the land would become occupied by the *Bắc di cư*.

LOCAL INHABITANTS AND THE ARRIVAL OF THE BẮC DI CƯ

On January 28, 1956, the first 602 migrants arrived in Cái Sắn.[87] Over the next five months, their population would balloon to 42,427.[88] The numbers and speed of resettlement were remarkable, but they also reveal an existing disparity between this region and the land the *Bắc di cư* left behind.

Whereas the lower Mekong Delta's population averaged 63 people per square kilometer, that of the Red River Delta averaged 430.[89] This discrepancy helps illuminate regional variations in how land was used. In the lower Mekong Delta, a sparse population and a relatively gentle climate factored significantly in the rise of open, linear villages set along canals and roads. Conversely, in the Red River Delta, a large population, more severe flooding, and land shortages encouraged the corporate village structure commonly found there. Faced with a harsher environment, northerners had relied more on village institutions, particularly the parish church or communal house (*đình*), than their Southern counterparts did.[90]

Having already lost land, the inhabitants of the region feared being overwhelmed by the influx of *Bắc di cư*. By the summer of 1956, Northern settlers outnumbered their local counterparts nearly 3.5 to 1, and the Cái Sắn population had more than quadrupled.[91] With the establishment of Cái Sắn and the arrival of the *Bắc di cư* to cultivate the land, an adviser to Diệm later admitted, many challenges arose for the local peoples as they suffered the loss of "certain rights they had enjoyed for a long time."[92] Local inhabitants suffered government land seizure and then watched helplessly as it was granted to newcomers.

Compounding the Southerners' sense of alienation, the government's plans for migrant resettlement included the excavation of seventeen canals, each about eleven kilometers in length. The canals were to become key transportation conduits for inhabitants and important means for cleansing the soil of salt and alum. Dozens of *Bắc di cư* villages were established along the canals, all but three led by parish priests. The government outfitted each *Bắc di cư* family with three hectares of land for cultivation. Each canal community was supposed to have a clinic, an elementary school, and a church. For local inhabitants, their way of life was being transformed by the presence of the new arrivals with the apparent help of the government.

The first indication of sectional trouble dated from mid-1956. On June 16, long-time residents confronted a *Bắc di cư* funeral procession in the vicinity of Canal 4. The encounter escalated into a fistfight when the mourners refused to leave after local residents accused them of trespassing on their lands. The following day, a meeting was held that included the Tân Hiệp District Chief, Father Vũ Ngọc Bân (a spiritual leader of the Northern migrant community), and a man named Kiệt, one of the aggrieved local parties. Kiệt explained, "I do not want to interfere with funerals of Northern migrants. But I expect that those wanting to traverse lands that I have tirelessly [*khó nhọc*] worked will seek my permission."[93] In defense, Father Bân adamantly defended the right of the newcomers to organize funerals on the land. "If locals interfere again," observed Bân, "confrontations will be unavoidable." He was especially concerned about the prospect of violence breaking out when he planned to be away during an upcoming visit to Saigon: "I am very worried that during my absence there will be no one able to prevent blood from being spilled [*đổ máu*]."[94] Officials interpreted this comment as a threat. The minister of land reform criticized the priest for trying to sow "North-South division and condoning violence to achieve *Bắc di cư* demands."[95] Father Bân may have angered authorities with his warning, but his statement had the desired effect: the RVN prevailed on the local residents to move elsewhere in Cái Sắn with the promise of land and cash. The precedent reinforced the impression of *Bắc di cư* privilege and indicated that the government could be pressured by the threat of violence.

Following the resolution to the Canal 4 conflict, other Northern migrant communities requested the expulsion of native residents in response to similar clashes. In May 1957, Father Triết of nearby Canal 3 demanded that all canal lands be turned over to the *Bắc di cư*. The request was made following a confrontation between a local family using land along the canal and several newcomers working nearby.[96] The newcomers hurled stones, insults, and threats at the local family.[97] Moving the local residents, the priest maintained, would prevent future violence. This time, however, authorities resisted the pressure. Instead, officials argued that the local inhabitants had been exploiting the land well before the *Bắc di cư* arrived and, therefore, had the right to continue to use it. The decision did nothing to resolve the underlying issues.

A year after the establishment of the Cái Sắn resettlement center, conflicts over land and fishing holes remained "an everyday feature" of sectional relations.[98] Three confrontations during a single week in late 1956 give a sense of the situation's seriousness. In the first clash, a local Southern family entered Canal 2 by boat to gather fish at a pond they had claimed prior to the arrival of Northern settlers. As they emptied their fishing traps, a group of migrants appeared and demanded that they leave the area. Other native residents joined the confrontation. A brawl followed, during which *Bắc di cư* participants attempted to seize control of the boat and the fish in it. During the fight, a migrant detonated a grenade in the boat, destroying it and more than a hundred kilograms of fish. A classified government file revealed that a few days later, a second altercation erupted when dozens of Northern migrants surrounded local "trespassers" and beat them "nearly to death" (*gần chết*) for intruding in "their" canal.[99] Finally that same week, a *Bắc di cư* murder victim was discovered lying in a "pool of blood" (*ao máu*) on land claimed by native inhabitants in Canal E.[100]

As conditions deteriorated, the RVN blamed subversive forces for the conflict. "Communist plots to divide Southerners and Northerners," warned an official, "must be monitored."[101] The Kiên Giang province chief expressed fear that communist elements might exploit current conditions to further stoke discord between the native and *Bắc di cư* communities.[102] Captured flyers certainly supported these allegations. On the eve of the Lunar New Year in 1957, the authorities discovered a cache of pamphlets with slogans such as "Mỹ-Diệm [US-Ngô Đình Diệm] activities serve only the interests of Northern migrants" and "The American puppets have stolen your land."[103]

Nevertheless, although the communists may have sought to fan hostility between local inhabitants and newcomers, *Bắc di cư* leaders, particularly clergy, in Cái Sắn exploited the situation. On the evening of April 5, 1957, the Canal D elementary school was the target of an apparent arson. Seventeen days later, vandals struck the parish again. They damaged the parish church and attempted to kill several residents of the resettlement site.[104] Father Nguyễn Đức Dọ, the canal's spiritual leader, fingered communists for the attack, but the Resettlement Committee blamed dissident Hòa Hảo bands. Panic swept the *Bắc di cư* communities. In the days that followed the second attack, migrant leadership organized rallies in Tân Hiệp and Rạch Giá. Thousands of Cái Sắn settlers traveled to the protests by boat. Assembling at the offices of the provincial and district authorities, they demanded that the government provide arms to *Bắc di cư* militias.[105]

A provincial inquiry, however, determined that Father Do was looking to militarize the new communities by preying on the anxieties of government officials about Hòa Hảo and communist threats. The probe revealed that in the three months before the attacks, Father Do had requested weapons "no less than half a dozen times."[106] The investigation concluded that Father Do and his supporters sought weapons to defend their lands against illegal entry by local Southerners, *not* against attacks by communist or Hòa Hảo forces. In his report to the interior minister, Province Chief Nhan Minh Trang of Kiên Giang ominously concluded, "Look at what the Northern migrants have done without arms [in Cái Sắn]. Once they have weapons in their hands, consider how these [sectional] confrontations might become bloodbaths [*án mạng đẫm máu*]."[107] This may have been an egregious attempt of manipulation, but the question of militarizing villages was neither a new idea nor unique to the lower Mekong Delta.

CONCLUSION

Conventional wisdom has held that Southern hostility toward *Bắc di cư* was due to favoritism and religion. As this chapter argues, although both were present, the roots of this animosity are not so simple. Sectionalism existed long before the arrival of the Northern migrants, and we must account for differences in culture, language, and agricultural practices and how they further upset relations. Seemingly lavish aid for migrants and the RVN's mismanagement of the resettlement inadvertently caused tensions between newcomers and natives. Moreover, the government's decision to settle migrants in separate villages under the direction of religious leaders made integration and cooperation unlikely.

Most importantly, this was a migration crisis equivalent to nearly 8 percent of the South's population. Even a society with strong political and civil institutions and a stable economy would have found providing basic assistance an immense challenge. But in a divided Vietnam, struggling to recover from the consequences of war and colonialism, this proved nearly impossible.

NOTES

1. The terms "North" and "South" (together with "Northern," "Northerners," "Southern," and "Southerners") in this chapter refer to people and things from the two regions of Vietnam north or south of the 17th parallel that divided Vietnam between 1954 and 1975.

2. "Đồng bào hãy bình tĩnh," *Tự do*, March 26, 1955; "Những tin đồn ghê gớm: 'giết trẻ nít lóc lấy thịt làm phở tái' chỉ là một thứ cạm bẫy âm mưu chia rẽ Bắc Nam một lần nữa," *Buổi sáng*, March 28, 1955.

3. "Những chuyện đau lòng ở miền Nam: Một số người di cư vì đói khổ đã ăn thịt con nhỏ," *Nhân dân*, April 2, 1955.

4. David Halberstam, *The Making of a Quagmire* (New York: Random House, 1965), 200–201; George McT. Kahin, *Intervention: How America Became Involved in Vietnam* (New York: Anchor Books, 1987), 84; Marilyn Young, *The Vietnam Wars, 1945–1990* (New York: Harper Perennial, 1991), 95; and Frances FitzGerald, *Fire in the Lake: The Vietnamese and the Americans in Vietnam* (New York: BackBay Books, 2002), 88.

5. Mark Bradley, *Vietnam at War* (New York: Oxford University Press, 2009), 85.

6. Seth Jacobs, *Cold War Mandarin: Ngo Dinh Diem and the Origins of America's War in Vietnam, 1950–1953* (Lanham, MD: Rowman & Littlefield, 2006), 67.

7. Jessica Chapman, *Cauldron of Resistance: Ngo Dinh Diem, the United States, and 1950s Southern Vietnam* (Ithaca, NY: Cornell University Press, 2013), 9.

8. For some exceptions to the conventional interpretation, see Peter Hansen, "The Virgin Heads South: Northern Catholic Refugees in South Vietnam, 1954–1964" (PhD diss., Melbourne College of Divinity, 2008); Phi Van Nguyen, "Les résidus de la guerre, la mobilisation des réfugiés du nord pour un Vietnam non-communiste (1954–1964)" (PhD diss., Université du Québec, Montreal, 2015); and Jason Picard, "Fragmented Loyalties: The Great Migration's Impact on South Vietnam" (PhD diss., University of California, Berkeley, 2014).

9. 217 VP/TU/M, July 15, 1955, File 4041, Office of the President Collection, First Republic (Phông Phủ Tổng Thống Đệ Nhất Cộng Hòa [PTTĐICH]), National Archives Center 2 (Trung Tâm Lưu Trữ Quốc Gia 2 [TTLTQG2]), Ho Chi Minh City. By November 1955, official RVN sources claim, the total number of refugees had reached 887,861.

10. John Ernst, *Forging a Fateful Alliance: Michigan State University and the Vietnam War* (East Lansing: Michigan State University, 1998), 22.

11. Phủ Tổng Ủy Di Cư và Tị Nạn, *Cuộc Di Cư Lịch Sử tại Việt Nam* (Saigon: Phủ Tổng Ủy Di Cư và Tị Nạn, 1957).

12. Gertrude Samuels, "Passage to Freedom in Viet Nam," *National Geographic,* June 1955, 858.

13. Peggy Durdin, "Saigon in the Shadow of Doom," *New York Times Magazine,* November 21, 1954.

14. For instance, see Phạm Quỳnh, "Cuộc Nam Tiến của dân Việt Nam," *Nam phong* 169 (February 1932): 154–156; Nguyễn Đăng Thục, "Nam Tiến Việt Nam," *Sử địa* 19–20 (July-December 1970): 25–43; Phù Lang Trương Bá Phát, "Lịch sử cuộc Nam Tiến của dân tộc VN," *Sử địa* 19–20 (July-December 1970): 45–137; Keith Taylor, "Nguyen Hoang and the Beginning of Vietnam's Southern Expansion," in *Southeast Asia in the Early Modern Era: Trade, Power and Belief,* ed. Anthony Reid (Ithaca, NY: Cornell University Press, 1993), 42–65; Li Tana, *Nguyen Cochinchina: Southern Vietnam in the Seventeenth and Eighteenth Centuries* (Ithaca, NY: Cornell University, Southeast Asian Program, 1998); Choi Byung Wook, *Southern Vietnam under the Reign of Minh Mang, 1820–1841: Central Policies and Local Response* (Ithaca, NY: Cornell University, Southeast Asia Program, 2004).

15. Li, *Nguyen Cochinchina,* 99.

16. David Biggs, *Quagmire: Nation-Building and Nature in the Mekong Delta* (Seattle: University of Washington, 2010), 130.

17. Pierre Gourou, *Les paysans du delta tonkinois: étude de géographie humaine* (The Hague: Mouton, 1965), 278.

18. The trope of men seeking employment in the south during the colonial era was a feature found in literature both before and after 1954. For instance, see Nam Cao, "Lão Hạc," in *Nửa đêm: tập truyện* (Hanoi: Công Lực, 1943); Mai Thảo, "Tháng giêng cỏ non," in *Tháng giêng cỏ non* (Saigon: Sáng Tạo, 1956), 11–23; and Duyên Anh, "Người quê hương," in *Văn học miền nam,* ed. Võ Phiến (California: Văn Nghệ, 1999), 671–687.

19. Nguyễn Vạn An, "Người Bắc vô Nam: có những anh chàng 'tích việt' Nam Tiến, tự xưng là con cụ tổng, cháu cụ tuần," *Tự do,* December 16, 1954.

20. Jeffrey Race, *War Comes to Long An: Revolutionary Conflict in a Vietnamese Province* (Berkeley: University of California Press, 2010), 6.

21. Phủ Tổng Ủy Di Cư và Tị Nạn, *Cuộc Di Cư Lịch Sử tại Việt Nam,* 115–209; and Ralph Smuckler, Walter Mode, and Frederic Wickert, "Research Report: Field Study of Refugee Commission," Michigan State University Group, September 1955, 1820201001, Vietnam Project, Texas Tech University, Vietnam Virtual Archive.

22. Phủ Tổng Ủy Di Cư và Tị Nạn, *Cuộc Di Cư Lịch Sử tại Việt Nam,* 148; "Mỹ chấm dứt viện trợ định cư," *Tự do,* February 20, 1957.

23. Bùi Văn Lương, "The Role of Friendly Nations," in *Viet-Nam: The First Five Years,* ed. Richard Lindholm (East Lansing: Michigan State University), 50; and Phủ Tổng Ủy Di Cư và Tị Nạn, *Cuộc Di Cư Lịch Sử tại Việt Nam,* 182.

24. Associated Press, "5 Refugees Slain in Saigon Clash," *New York Times,* September 22, 1955.

25. "Tình hình tổng quát các trạm chiêu đãi Saigon–Chợ Lớn," September 28, 1954, File 14614, Office of the Prime Minister Collection (Phông Phủ Thủ Tướng Việt Nam Cộng Hòa [PThTVNCH]), TTLTQG2.

26. 2768-HCSV, August 20, 1954, File N21–19, Government Delegate of Southern Vietnam Collection (Phông Tòa Đại Biểu Chính Phủ Nam Phần [TĐBCPNP]), TTLTQG2.

27. The GCMR officially ceased operations on December 31, 1957.

28. Memorandum from Bùi Văn Lương to Mayor of Saigon–Cholon, 6526 VP/TB, October 24, 1955, File 14769, PThTVNCH, TTLTQG2.

29. Robert Alden, "Refugees' Misery Evident in Saigon," *New York Times,* April 11, 1955.

30. Nguyễn Đình Tạo, "Tiếng nói của đồng bào di cư," *Thời luận,* March 30–31, 1955.

31. Nguyễn Đình Tạo, "Tiếng nói của đồng bào di cư."

32. "Sur une epidemie de variole," February 7, 1955, File 14656, PThTVNCH, TTLTQG2.

33. Bernard Fall, "South Viet-Nam's Internal Problems," *Pacific Affairs* 31, No. 3 (September 1958): 241–260, especially 247.

34. Gerald Hickey, *Free in the Forest: Ethnohistory of the Vietnamese Central Highlands, 1954–1976* (New Haven, CT: Yale University Press, 1982), 2.

35. Trần Ngọc Sơn, "Tìm hiểu để giải quyết thực trạng của nạn thất nghiệp," *Tiếng chuông,* April 12, 1955.

36. "Tỵ nạn và hồi cư," Lập trường column, *Tự do,* May 21, 1955.

37. "Đồng bào BV di cư không thay thế anh em đình công," *Tự do,* December 17, 1954.

38. "Tổng đình công," *Buổi sáng,* January 6, 1955.

39. "Trên 10,000 công nhơn thuộc ngành vận tải đình công cảnh cáo," *Tin mai,* November 30, 1954.

40. "Chủ hãng 'Bastos' ra lịnh đóng chặt cửa," *Tiếng chuông,* April 13, 1955.

41. "Ai gây nên nạn thất nghiệp ở miền Nam," *Thời luận,* January 18, 1956.

42. 1192 XH/HC/KT, March 26, 1955, File 29215, PThTVNCH, TTLTQG2.

43. 1192 XH/HC/KT, File 29215, PThTVNCH, TTLTQG2.

44. Nguyễn Ngọc Thơ, 22-BNV/CV/NNV, September 15, 1955, File 3945, PThTVNCH, TTLTQG2.

45. Ngô Đình Diệm, 66-CV, December 16, 1954, File 3945, PThTVNCH, TTLTQG2.

46. Nguyễn Ngọc Thơ, 19-BNV/CV/NNV, September 4, 1954, File C0–66, TĐBCPNP, TTLTQG2.

47. Bishop Phạm Ngọc Chi to Ngô Đình Diệm, 1099/CDC, May 8, 1955, File 14757, PThTVNCH, TTLTQG2.

48. "Lời hiệu triệu của Đức GM Phạm Ngọc Chi," *Tự do,* August 5, 1955.

49. Bùi Văn Lương, November 22, 1955, File 4042, PTTĐICH, TTLTQG2; "Thông cảm Nam Bắc," Lập trường column, *Tự do,* October 12, 1955.

50. "Tuyên truyền gây đoàn kết giữa đồng bào Nam Bắc định cư tại các làng định cư," March 4, 1955, File T4–2488, TĐBPCP, TTLTQG2; "Kế hoạch," October 23, 1954, File 14769, PThTVNCH, TTLTQG2.

51. "Điện ảnh Việt Nam đang vươn lên: phim Chúng tôi muốn sống đã đánh dấu thành công vẻ vang," *Thời luận,* October 29, 1956.

52. Mai Thảo, "Sài Gòn thủ đô văn hóa Việt Nam," *Sáng tạo* 1 (October 1956): 1–5, especially 2. For more on *Creativity,* see chapter 8 in this volume.

53. Report for March 1956, 588/TU/HC/M, April 19, 1956, File 4401, PTTĐICH, TTLTQG2.

54. Phủ Tổng Ủy Di Cư và Tị Nạn, *Cuộc Di Cư Lịch Sử tại Việt Nam,* 148.

55. 189-VP/HC, February 9, 1955, File 14758, PThTVNCH, TTLTQG2.

56. 25/TU/VP/TT, November 2, 1954, File 14758, PThTVNCH, TTLTQG2.

57. Nguyễn Ngọc Thơ, September 4, 1954, File C0–66, TĐBCPNP, TTLTQG2.

58. 189-VP/HC, February 9, 1955, File 14758, PThTVNCH, TTLTQG2.

59. 4453/TU/VP/M, July 26, 1955, PThTVNCH, TTLTQG2.

60. Hickey, *Free in the Forest*, 6.

61. Stan Tan, "'Swiddens, Resettlements, Sedentarizations, and Villages': State Formation among the Central Highlanders of Vietnam under the First Republic, 1955–1961," *Journal of Vietnamese Studies* 1, no. 1–2 (February/August 2006): 210–252.

62. John Montgomery, *Cases in Vietnamese Administration* (Saigon: National Institute of Administration and Michigan State University Vietnam Advisory Group, 1959), 165.

63. "Buôn Ma Thuột: Californie của Việt Nam," *Ngôn luận*, February 23, 1957.

64. "Vụ Đỗ Văn Bình bị bắn ở La Ghì," November 1954, File B7-21, TĐBCPNP, TTLTQG2.

65. The anniversary of the Geneva Accords was known in the south as the National Day of Shame or the National Day of Resentment (Ngày Quốc Hận).

66. 290/TU/VP/M (Secret), August 23, 1955, File 14744, PThTVNCH, TTLTQG2.

67. "Chiến Dịch Tự Lực Mưu Sinh," *Dân Việt*, July 28, 1955.

68. Press Office, *Major Policy Speeches by President Ngô Đình Diệm* (Saigon: Press Office of the Presidency of the RVN, 1956), 33–34.

69. Đề Quyên, "Phổ biến những luật lệ hiện hành tận mỗi trại định cư để sửa soạn cho việc địa phương hóa đồng bào tỵ nạn," *Dân Việt*, September 27, 1956.

70. 23/M/VP/HC, February 11, 1955, File 14758, PThTVNCH, TTLTQG2.

71. 189-VP/HC, February 9, 1955, File 14758, PThTVNCH, TTLTQG2.

72. "Xét đơn khiếu nại của trại Dốc Mơ," 5464/TU/VP, September 7, 1955, File 14768, PThTVNCH, TTLTQG2.

73. Nguyễn Đình Tạo, "Các trại định cư Biên Hòa mong muốn những gì?," *Thời luận*, April 13–14, 1955.

74. "4 mãnh hổ Bà Rịa bị hạ trong vòng nửa tháng," *Tự do*, February 15, 1957.

75. 260/CN, February 27, 1956, File 4483, PTTĐICH, TTLTQG2.

76. "Phủ Tổng Ủy Dinh Điền," 558/TUDĐ/DĐC, June 12, 1957, File 10848, PTTĐICH, TTLTQG2.

77. 260/CN, February 27, 1956, File 4483, PTTĐICH, TTLTQG2.

78. 5421 VP/TU, September 5, 1955, File 14769, PThTVNCH, TTLTQG2.

79. Alfred Cardinaux, "Commentary," in *Viet-Nam: The First Five Years*, ed. Richard Lindholm (East Lansing: Michigan State University, 1959), 89.

80. "Mách nghề," *Tự do*, February 10, 1957.

81. 32-VPĐB/M (Top Secret), January 14, 1957, File 10865, PTTĐICH, TTLTQG2.

82. 32-VPĐB/M (Top Secret), January 14, 1957, File 10865, PTTĐICH, TTLTQG2.

83. "Hệ thống hành chánh hỗn hợp, đìa cá tranh chấp," 118-VPDB/M, March 8, 1957, File D32–17, TĐBCPNP, TTLTQG2.

84. "Tình hình tại Cái Sắn," March 13, 1957, File N21–18, TĐBCPNP, TTLTQG2.

85. "Sáp nhập 16 kênh định cư tại Cái Sắn vào nền hành chính tỉnh," *Tự do*, September 28, 1957.

86. "Về việc xem xét sự thiệt hại đìa bào của dân địa phương," January 25–26, 1957, File N21–18, TĐBCPNP, TTLTQG2. A partial list from seven canals includes the names of 748 local families who lost ponds.

87. "600 đồng bào di cư tình nguyện định cư tại Cái Sắn," *Ngôn luận*, February 1, 1956.

88. "Hồ sơ về hoạt động tại khu định cư Cái Sắn năm 1956–1958," undated, File 11787, PTTĐICH, TTLTQG2; and Phủ Tổng Ủy Di Cư Tỵ Nạn, monthly report of activities, June 1956, File 4401, PTTĐICH, TTLTQG2.

89. A. Terry Rambo, *A Comparison of Peasant Social Systems of Northern and Southern Viet-Nam: A Study of Ecological Adaptation, Social Succession, and Cultural Evolution* (Carbondale: Southern Illinois University Center for Vietnamese Studies, 1973), 169; and "Hệ thống hành chánh hỗn hợp, đìa cá tranh chấp," 118-VPDB/M, March 8, 1957, File D32–17, TĐBCPNP, TTLTQG2. Cái Sắn's regional population was roughly 12,439 in 1955.

90. Gerald Hickey, "The Social Systems of Northern Vietnam" (PhD Diss., University of Chicago, 1958).

91. "Hệ thống hành chánh hỗn hợp đìa cá tranh chấp," March 8, 1957, File D32–17, PThTVNCH, TTLTQG2. According to government population figures, *Bắc di cư* numbered 42,550 and local inhabitants 12,439.

92. 999/BPTT/VP/M, May 8, 1957, File N21–18, TĐBCPNP, TTLTQG2.

93. 39-VP/M, June 17, 1956, File 14411, PTTĐICH, TTLTQG2.

94. 39-VP/M, June 17, 1956, File 14411, PTTĐICH, TTLTQG2.

95. "V/v tranh chấp giữa đồng bào di cư và địa phương," 1800/M/ĐTCC/VP, June 21, 1956, File 14411, PTTĐICH, TTLTQG2.

96. 1838-VP, May 3, 1957, File N21–9, PThTVNCH, TTLTQG2.

97. "V/v hội đồng hỗn hợp 2 xã, Tân Hiệp và Thạnh Đông," 567-M/BT.2, June 24, 1957, File N21-9, PThTVNCH, TTLTQG2.

98. 61-VPĐB/M, February 7, 1957, File N21-18, TĐBCPNP, TTLTQG2.

99. 61-VPĐB/M, February 7, 1957, File N21-18, TĐBCPNP, TTLTQG2.

100. Hiến Binh Quốc Gia, February 6, 1957, File N21-18, TĐBCPNP, TTLTQG2.

101. "Vấn đề Cái Sắn," 149/M/VPĐB, April 1, 1957, File N21-18, TĐBCPNP, TTLTQG2; and "V/v hội đồng hỗn hợp 2 xã, Tân Hiệp and Thạnh Đông," 567-M/BT.2, June 24, 1957, File N21–9, PThTVNCH, TTLTQG2.

102. Nhan Minh Trang, June 13, 1957, File N21-18, TĐBCPNP, TTLTQG2.

103. 61-VPĐB/M, February 7, 1957, File 10865, PTTĐICH, TTLTQG2.

104. "V/v xô xát giữa đồng bào định cư Kinh D Cái Sắn và Bảo an Sở máy cày," 12527 PCl/M, May 18, 1957, File 10869, PTTĐICH, TTLTQG2.

105. Minister of the Interior, 3076 BNV/NA/MP2, May 27, 1957, File 10869, PTTĐICH, TTLTQG2.

106. Minister of the Interior, 3076 BNV/NA/MP2, May 27, 1957, File 10869, PTTĐICH, TTLTQG2.

107. Nhan Minh Trang, June 13, 1957, File N21-18, TĐBCPNP, TTLTQG2.

CHAPTER EIGHT

Creating the National Library in Saigon

Colonial Legacies, Republican Visions, and Reading Publics, 1946–1958

Cindy Nguyen

This chapter examines the development of the National Library in Saigon from 1946 to 1958 (now the General Sciences Library at 69 Lý Tự Trọng). I argue that government officials and library administrators pursued two intersecting visions of the library as both a national and a public institution. Leaders conceived of it as the protector of national heritage that would assemble and preserve Vietnamese literature, reference works, and historical periodicals. Officials and administrators also envisioned it as a modern, public service of popular education for Saigon urbanites and students. The articulation of these twin functions contributed to the definition of republicanism as both governmental vision and quotidian practices. The institution brought to the surface a wide array of issues that were foundational to republicanism in the Republic of Vietnam (RVN) in the 1950s, including the value of public access and civil society, the intertwined processes of decolonization and nation-building, and governmental responsibility to a collective citizenry.

Through tracing the development of the National Library, I shed light on the role of public and cultural institutions in the early RVN. The first part examines the origins of the library from 1946 to 1954 and demonstrates that institutional decolonization was a drawn-out, nonlinear process in which Vietnamese library administrators transformed the colonial Cochinchina Library to serve the reading public. The second part focuses on the logistics of creating a national library system for the RVN from 1954 to 1958. In striving to serve both the Vietnamese nation and the public, the National Library confronted essential questions similar to those that challenged the postcolonial government at large: What is the modern nation of Vietnam? Who is the public and how should the state serve its citizens? The library was not just a symbol of the regime but an institutional articulation of the RVN's national vision and republican values.

The National Library was one of the most important cultural, educational, and governmental institutions of the Republic of Vietnam yet has been starkly absent from the scholarship. The limited literature provides narrow institutional histories of the libraries in Vietnam as either apolitical storehouses of colonial literature or as weapons of French and American intellectual hegemony. In both cases, the builders and users of libraries are simplified as passive, static subjects.[1] The existing literature positions libraries within a nationalist narrative of Vietnamese cultural heritage, from the inheritance of colonial institutions to the eventual independence from Western cultural imperialism and propaganda.[2] The teleology toward a unified communist Vietnam reifies a rigid division between colonialism and postcolonialism and ultimately elides the complex history of libraries in southern Vietnam from 1945 to 1975.

This chapter contributes a significant revision to the body of work on libraries by situating the National Library within the larger context of nation-building, decolonization, and the establishment of a republican regime. I argue that the premier library in the RVN was an integral element of Vietnamese nation-building rather than a tool of Western powers. I position my work within the Vietnam-centric turn toward local agency and draw on recent scholarship on the politics, discourse, and practices of nation-building in the RVN.[3] Specifically, my work builds on Nu-Anh Tran's dissertation "Contested Identities: Nationalism in the Republic of Vietnam (1954–1963)" and Matthew Masur's dissertation "Hearts and Minds: Cultural Nation-Building in South Vietnam, 1954–1963."[4] They find that the Saigon regime sought to exert authority over all of Vietnamese culture and, in doing so, asserted political legitimacy across the seventeenth parallel that divided North and South Vietnam. Tran also argues that the government tried to create a single national identity through the creation of cultural institutions and the standardization of the Vietnamese language. Extending these insights, I contend that the National Library was essential to this larger project in the RVN. Officials and administrators conceived of the library as the guardian of Vietnamese culture and sought to unite disparate collections from the colonial period into a centralized national institution.

Although the National Library traced its origins to French colonial libraries, the process of decolonization was never simple nor predetermined. The dismantling of colonial cultural institutions was gradual, and the transfer and regrouping of materials tentative and halting. Moreover, even as the government placed the library in service of nation-building, librarians continued to draw on French library sciences and looked to the French literary world as the cultural standard. A close examination of the National Library also reveals new insight into republican institutions in the RVN. Everyday library users were active agents who facilitated their own individual learning and use of urban public space. They challenged reading room rules and participated within civic discourse by publicly demanding increased access, improved facilities, and Vietnamese-language materials. Thus the institutionalization of republicanism was not a simple top-down process led exclusively by library administrators and government officials. Library users contributed to the development of republicanism in their engagement with public institutions. This chapter demonstrates how colonial legacies, republican visions of nation and public, and changing urban reading publics defined the role of the National Library.

COLONIAL LEGACIES, LANGUAGE POLICY, AND THE DIVISION OF THE HANOI COLONIAL COLLECTIONS, 1946–1954

From the earliest days of French colonialism in Vietnam, colonial officials understood that to build a library was to build the state. The Cochinchina Library (Bibliothèque de Cochinchine, Thơ Viện Nam Kỳ) was first founded in 1865 as an administrative library and information archive for the colonial government, and library users consisted mainly of French and Vietnamese officials. In 1919, it became a public branch of an Indochina-wide network of libraries and archives. Libraries legitimized the authority of the colonial state throughout the Indochinese territories as both a symbol of modernity and control of print circulation. At the same time, library users shaped the everyday function of the library as a space of intellectual nourishment and self-directed education. The Cochinchina Library was housed in the cramped government secretariat building at 34 Lagrandière (later 34 Gia Long, now 34 Lý Tự Trọng.) together with the central archives of Cochinchina. A popular lending section provided novels to Saigon urbanites, and several book wagons brought thousands of pedagogical texts and novels in French and the romanized Vietnamese script (quốc ngữ) to readers in the Cochinchinese provinces. By 1938, the Reading Room held a collection of more than thirty-six thousand volumes and welcomed more than 133 readers each day despite offering only forty-four seats.[5] The Lending Section recorded a total of thirty-one thousand borrowers and fifty-five thousand book loans that same year. In 1939, the Cochinchina Library designated a small corner of the library as a Children's Reading Room for young patrons to read books on-site.

Gradual Decolonization, 1946–1954

The decolonization of the Cochinchina Library was a gradual process that reflected the slow progress of decolonization in southern Vietnam. In the fall of

1945, Allied forces arrived in southern Vietnam to disarm the Japanese. The Allies attacked the fledgling Democratic Republic of Vietnam (DRV) and assisted French troops in retaking the former colony of Cochinchina. Fighting engulfed the region even before the formal outbreak of the First Indochina War at the end of the following year. For the next decade, Saigon and southern Vietnam emerged as the locus of successive attempts to create an autonomous Vietnamese government, and the shifting status, leadership, and priorities of the old Cochinchina Library mirrored the tentative and halting character of decolonization in the southern third of the country.

In June 1946, a few months after the departure of the Allied forces, the French high commissioner and a handful of Vietnamese politicians established the Provisional Government of the Republic of Cochinchina, a supposedly semiautonomous state in southern Vietnam separate from the DRV. The High Commission signaled Vietnamese semi-autonomy by transferring the Cochinchina Library to the provisional Vietnamese government at the end of the month. The library appears to be one of the first institutions to be transferred and thus was an important symbol of the eventual decolonization of all cultural institutions. Placed within the Service of Education for Southern Vietnam, it was renamed the National Library of Southern Vietnam (Thơ Viện Quốc Gia Nam Việt).[6] Even with the renaming, Vietnamese readers often referred to the library by its various names, including the old colonial name of the Cochinchina Library (Bibliothèque de Cochinchine, Thơ Viện Nam Kỳ), colloquial names such as the Saigon Library (Thơ Viện Saigon), and the new administrative name of the Library of Southern Region or the Library of Southern Vietnam (Thư Viện Nam Phần, Thư Viện Nam Phần Việt Nam). Library administrators and other government bodies often referred to the institution as the National Library since 1946, and it was officially renamed the National Library (Thư Viện Quốc Gia) in 1957. To avoid confusion, I refer to the institution as the National Library for the period from 1946 to 1957 even when the name and status of the library were both in flux. The National Library carried out four primary services: acquisitions, legal deposit, Reading Room, and Lending Section.

Subsequent negotiations between the French High Commission and Vietnamese politicians resulted in the establishment of a Provisional Central Government of Vietnam in 1948. This government incorporated all three regions of the country, including the short-lived Republic of Cochinchina. In 1949, after another round of negotiations, the Provisional Central Government reconstituted as the nominally independent State of Vietnam (SVN). The SVN was part of the Indochinese Federation along with Laos and Cambodia, and the federation belonged to the French Union, which included other former French colonies. Saigon was the capital of the various national states and the subsidiary southern regional government throughout the latter half of the 1940s. Reflecting these larger changes, the decolonization of the National Library occurred gradually through three interlocking processes: the designation of the institution as the premier library of an ascending national capital, the management of the library by the first Vietnamese director, and the expansion of the library's Asian-language materials.

Đoàn Quan Tấn became the first Vietnamese director of the National Library in February 1948 following the death of French director Rémi Bourgeois. Tấn was active in cultural affairs and Saigon scholarly life. He had been the chairman of the Study Encouragement Society (Hội Khuyến Học) in 1940, a mutual aid society focused on education, the improvement of the Vietnamese language, and the study of literature, fine arts, and national history. From 1950 to 1952, Tấn was the chairman of the France-Vietnam People's Academy Association and the Indochina Archaeology Association; from 1953, he served as the assistant chairman of the French Literary Alliance Association.

In an interview with Radio Saigon in May 1949, Director of the National Library Đoàn Quan Tấn highlighted the mission of the National Library as a public institution.[7] This interview sheds light on the popular use of the libraries even during the politically uncertain transition between 1945 and 1949. Tấn explained that the Reading Room was open all day on Mondays to Saturdays and on Sunday mornings and was "heavily frequented by the Saigonese public such as high school and university students." The room served an average of eighty readers daily, approximately half of whom were Europeans. Tấn was also proud of the collections and explained that his staff was acquiring new library materials to better serve Vietnamese readers and to encourage greater understanding between Vietnamese and French readers. By 1949, the library held fifty-seven thousand volumes on the humanities, arts, philosophy, religion, and geography; the most popular works among readers were texts about history, the sciences, and law. Because most works were in French, library administrators sought to add more Vietnamese translations of French books on popular science and technology. Administrators also encouraged translation of Vietnamese works into French and recognized translation as an act of political exchange so "that the effort of mutual understanding was not one-sided." For Đoàn Quan Tấn and other library administrators, it was not enough that the library itself had come under the purview of a Vietnamese government; they believed that even the collection had to undergo a process of decolonization to encourage parity between Vietnamese and French library users.

Between 1949 and 1954, Tấn prioritized the building of the collections in two ways: completion of missing Vietnamese-language serials and creation of a comprehensive collection of Vietnamese, Chinese, and English works. Tấn justified the importance of building the Vietnamese collections because Vietnamese

had been designated as the official language of archives and governmental operations in the southern regional government. Furthermore, another library report
argued that building a Chinese-language collection could also help the advancement of literacy in *quốc ngữ*. In 1951, the Chinese collection emerged from the
collaborative efforts of the Chamber of Commerce of Cholon Overseas Chinese
director Viên Thâu Thạch and chairman Phù Lâm Anh. A committee of ethnic
Chinese-Vietnamese scholars, journalists, and bookstore owners personally
donated books from their private libraries or even ventured to Hong Kong to
purchase books. Through these private donations, the Chinese-language section
of the National Library came to contain 3,563 chronicles, historical encyclopedia, and valuable works on Buddhist philosophy and education.[8] The English-
language collection grew out of book donations from international offices such
as the American and British information services, United Nations Education,
Scientific, and Cultural Organization (UNESCO), and the German, British,
Dutch, and Indian consulates.[9]

The National Library slowly increased and diversified its collections
through purchases, gifts, and mandatory legal deposit of copies of new publications. By 1954, the collection had increased by fifteen thousand works, bringing the total to 79,081 books (6 percent in Vietnamese, 5 percent in Chinese,
and 88 percent in French).[10] Yet a closer analysis of the periodicals in the
Reading Room reveals an increasing trend to publish periodicals in Vietnamese
rather than in French (see figure 8.1).

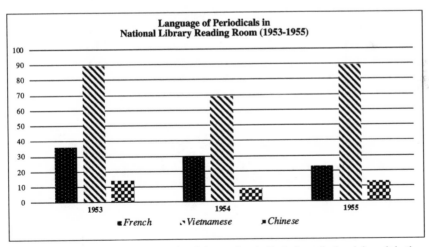

Figure 8.1.   Comparative language breakdown of periodicals from the legal deposit in the
Reading Room of the National Library, 1953–1955. Lê Ngọc Trụ, "Tổ chức Thơ Viện Quốc
Gia—phần thứ nhất," c. 1954; and "Le développement des bibliothèques au Viet-nam de 1953
à 1957," c. 1957, TVQGNV, TTLTQG2, Folder 102.

Growing Popularity as a Public Library for Vietnamese Readers, 1953–1955

Whereas a substantial number of library users had been European in the late 1940s, the composition shifted to overwhelmingly favor Vietnamese users in the early 1950s (see table 8.1). During the same time, the number of total readers steadily increased. In 1953, the monthly average was 1,630, of whom almost 95 percent were Vietnamese. In 1954, the monthly average increased to 2,056, of whom 97 percent were Vietnamese.[11] During this period, the Reading Room offered only forty-four seats, constraining the maximum capacity for reader consultation. Students made up the majority of Vietnamese readers and enjoyed growing clout due to their numbers. In 1954, university students formally requested the administration to shift the opening hours to later in the evening in order to accommodate readers who were busy during the day with school or work. Library administrators honored the students' request and extended opening hours to nine in the morning until nine at night on Mondays through Saturdays as well as Sunday mornings. Because the Reading Room usually received few readers during lunchtime hours, it now closed for a three-hour break at noon.[12] These adjustments point to the influence of readers to shape library operations.

Ever since the French colonial period, the Lending Section had been more popular than the Reading Room. In March 1944, the Lending Section relocated from Catinat Street to Saigon's city hall for safekeeping and temporarily closed in 1945 during the August Revolution and subsequent transfer of authority. In 1951, it moved to the Indochinese Circle Association building on 14 Lê Văn Duyệt (formerly 14 Thủ Tướng Thinh, later 194 D Pasteur) in order to accommodate more visitors. In 1954, it welcomed 2,100 readers each month, of whom more than 75 percent were Vietnamese.[13] Fourteen percent were students who

Table 8.1.   Statistics of Readers Visiting National Library Reading Room, 1953–1955

	1953	1954	1955
Total readers by year	20,915	26,174	31,997
Daily average of readers	80	92	110
Total number of books in collection	77,289	79,081	80,396

Source: Authors' tabulation based on "La Bibliothèque nationale du Sud-Vietnam," May 1956, Folder 102, TVQGNV, TTLTQG2.
Note: Note the gradual increase in daily average of readers visiting the library.

often borrowed textbooks. Readers frequently checked out materials from the valuable collection totaling ten thousand works, including literature, scientific texts, textbooks, and novels.

End of the First Indochina War and the Transfer of the Hanoi General Library to Saigon, 1954–1955

During the First Indochina War, decolonization entailed the breakup of French Indochina as a single entity. Accordingly, the Indochina-wide Directorate of Archives and Libraries and the former colonial collections in Hanoi, Saigon, Phnom Penh, Huế, and Vientiane were slowly divided between France, the State of Vietnam, Laos, and Cambodia.[14] The Geneva Accords that partitioned Vietnam at the end of the war also marked the formal division of the General Library and Central Archives in Hanoi, the former capital of French Indochina. Between 1954 and 1955, a quarter of the collection of the Hanoi General Library, materials from the University of Hanoi and the Central Archives, and sixteen library and archives personnel were transferred to Saigon. A newspaper article from 1956 noted that at the time of the relocation, the Hanoi library was "considered the largest and most valuable library in Vietnam and judged by other countries as the second greatest in the Far East."[15] The remaining collections and personnel of the General Library (now renamed the Central Library of Hanoi, or Thư Viện Trung Ương Hà Nội) continued to operate in Hanoi, the capital of the Democratic Republic of Vietnam.

Between May 11 and May 26, 1955, soldiers of the State of Vietnam transported boxes of documents, books, and newspapers from the Hanoi General Library, Central Archives, and University of Hanoi to Saigon. The transferred materials included more than seventeen thousand books, half of the serials from the colonial period, the archives of the Kinh Lược viceroy located in northern Vietnam (thirty-eight boxes), and thirty-five thousand legal deposit items, which combined to total more than seven hundred boxes.[16] Administrators claimed that most of the transferred collections were duplicate copies or from the Indochina legal deposit collected up to June 1954. According to a report from 1955 by the archivist-librarian Nguyễn Hùng Cường, who was transferred to Saigon from the General Library, the move signaled the "transformation of the General Library into a completely Vietnamese (library)."[17] For Cường, the physical movement of the Hanoi collections southward suggested the official separation of the General Library from its Hanoi and French colonial lineage and the library's rebirth as a Vietnamese national institution based in Saigon.

CREATING A NATIONAL LIBRARY: ORGANIZATION AND VISIONS, 1954–1958

As early as 1949, the State of Vietnam proposed the development of a new national library on Boulevard Norodom (later Thống Nhất Street, today Lê Duẩn Street) to address the overcrowded facilities inherited from the French colonial government.[18] This proposal made clear that the SVN intended to make libraries part of the government's effort at cultural nation-building. The new buildings would serve as the cultural capital for the entire country and a grand integration of the colonial and postcolonial library collections. The director of the library, Đoàn Quan Tấn, argued that the Norodom project would "equip Saigon—the capital of South Vietnam and a university city—with a museum-library worthy of it."[19] The original vision included a cultural center with an archives repository, a two-part library with a central room for study and reference and a lending section intended for youth, and a historical museum of Indochina. The museum would be the most important part of the cultural center and devoted to the work of France in the Far East. That the museum should focus on France and Indochina rather than Vietnam made clear that decolonization was still incomplete and called attention to the ambiguity of the SVN as a national government within the French Union.

With the official end of French claims to authority in Indochina in 1954, the postcolonial state made new plans for a national library of a fully independent Vietnam. The Norodom project rooted in French colonial cultural preservation evolved into a Vietnamese project of decolonization, nation-building, and republican aspirations. In 1955, government officials replaced the Norodom project with an ambitious proposal for a "National Library and Cultural Center" (Thư Viện Quốc Gia và Trung Tâm Văn Hoá) with a 150-seat reading room, an eight-story storage building large enough for at least three-hundred thousand volumes, a cultural center with two lecture rooms, and a stage auditorium that could seat up to a thousand attendees.[20] Furthermore, the grounds of this new complex would include the new National Administration Institute, and the Faculty of Humanities and the Faculty of Law in the University of Saigon. President Ngô Đình Diệm proposed constructing the building on the site of the former Saigon Maison Centrale prison (Tù Khám Lớn) at 69 Gia Long Street (now 69 Lý Tự Trọng) and, on July 3, 1956, inaugurated the building of the National Library and Cultural Center project.

Officials used the project to showcase the RVN as the guardian of Vietnamese culture and the legitimate government to preserve and represent Vietnamese culture and history domestically and globally. At the inaugural ceremony in 1956, President Diệm declared that the new building preserved Vietnamese cultural heritage and symbolized national progress and modernization. Drawing attention to the international significance of the project, Diệm argued that "our country stands as a trailblazer in Southeast Asia—we remember the lessons gifted to us from our ancestors. In addition, our national spirit must evolve in concert with that of the modern peoples of the free world."[21]

At the bricklaying ceremony marking the beginning of construction in 1968, Secretary of State in Charge of Cultural Affairs Mai Thọ Truyền delivered a speech emphasizing the legacy of the colonial prison and the significance of the library for national culture:

> Those tiles and stones of the former prison left on the ground bear witness to the noble sacrifices of those fighting for the nation's freedom and its culture. The ghosts of these heroes, if any of them are still haunting this site, certainly would be satisfied with our present enterprise which aims at protecting and developing our national culture.[22]

He continued to describe his dream of the new national library as a "meeting center for Eastern and Western cultures as well as a source of information and communication for mankind." The new National Library would be centrally located in Saigon—at the "heart of the capital and near buildings that represent the power of the nation, such as the Independence Palace, Gia Long Palace, and the Court of Justice."[23] However, due to economic difficulties and political instability, plans to build a centralized institution fragmented into separate building projects in different parts of the city. Construction of a new building for the National Library officially began in 1968 at 69 Gia Long Street, and the location was not opened until December 23, 1971.[24]

National Ambitions and Colonial Legacies

On June 26, 1954, Phan Vô Ky, the assistant director of the Service of Library and Archives of Southern Vietnam, summarized library services from the time of French handover in 1946 to the time of writing.[25] Ky noted that the National Library of Southern Vietnam continued to carry out its essential services even with a severe deficit in personnel and budget. Three library personnel had been conscripted for the war, and the budget was inadequate for the size of the library and demands from readers. Ky argued that the library must advance into a fully functional institution that was worthy of the capital of an independent Vietnam:

> With the complete independence of our motherland and the designation of Saigon as the national capital, the National Library is far too small to provide services for the Saigon population of over two million. The library is too crowded, unable to store books and documents shipped to the library. With only forty-six chairs in the Reading Room, some readers come to the library but end up leaving due to lack of seating. The estimated annual budget of the library is not enough to

purchase books or several copies of certain books in order to let readers check out the books to read at home. The hope is that the National Library will be able to expand and provide the same level of conveniences and services as other large libraries of civilized and modern countries. The National Library must become a space worthy to collect the spiritual artifacts of a people with four thousand years of civilization.[26]

For Kỵ, the National Library carried two primary tasks: the preservation of Vietnamese cultural heritage and a public service to the growing population of Saigon. Although he used a vague benchmark of "civilized and modern countries" to evaluate the capabilities of the library, it is significant that he depicted the library as both an everyday institution serving the public and a symbol of nationhood.

In the nine-page plan titled "Organization of the National Library" ("Tổ chức Thơ Viện Quốc Gia"), Lê Ngọc Trụ outlined the importance of library collections and methodic organization.[27] The self-taught linguist Lê Ngọc Trụ (1909–1979) worked in the National Library in Saigon from 1948 to 1961 as deputy secretary and then as director of the collections department from 1961 to 1964. Like other administrators, Trụ was an intellectual in his own right outside his work for the library. Trụ self-studied Vietnamese linguistics, published in the newspapers Đông Dương (1939–1941), Đọc (1939), Nghệ thuật (1941), and Bút mới (1941), and was an active member of the Study Encouragement Society of Southern Vietnam (Hội Khuyến Học Nam Kỳ). In 1954, Trụ became the director of the Institute of History and later worked as a linguistics professor at the University of Arts and University of Pedagogy in Saigon. He declared that the National Library must not be merely a "storage space of books" but must also be systematically organized for ease of reader access, research, and use.[28] "Books and newspapers are the foundation of the library," Trụ proclaimed. "We cannot call our library a proper institute with such a large number of books in the library organized without a rational order; with the increasing number of print media published each day, we cannot blindly purchase texts for the library without selective intention." Trụ believed that the first stage of library organization required reassessing the collections (thâu thập sách báo) and that the later stages included organization (sắp đặt) and preservation of materials (gìn giữ sách báo).

He described in fine-grained detail the National Library collections, focusing especially on accumulating books "of value." Trụ measured the value of books based on the scope and depth of their content, their rarity, and their publication date. Because the budget for book acquisitions and storage space was limited, Trụ explained, the library director must be deliberate in book acquisitions. Trụ requested that the director first prioritize fundamental books (căn bản), which included Larousse encyclopedias, dictionaries, bibliographies, and other classic French reference works on geography, history, and biography.

After establishing this collection, the library director must follow the contemporary news on popular books to determine future acquisitions. Trụ specified that the measurement of "international cultural acclaim" could be based on the following designations: book prizes, such as the Nobel, Goncourt, Feminia, and Ville de Paris; books that were translated into French; new research on society, economics, religion, art, architecture, medicine, and science; and books about Vietnam, the French Union, and Southeast Asia. Trụ advised the library director to read the National Bibliography of France each month and follow the major cultural and literary review magazines in France such as *Revue des deux mondes, Revue de Paris, Mercure de France, Esprit, Europe, Études,* and *Nouvelles littéraires* to guide library purchases. Trụ's statement reveals the meticulous logic of library collections policy and assessment of "cultural value." He outlined a hierarchy of books based on notions of "value" deeply rooted in French library sciences (*bibliothéconomie*) and in French literary benchmarks. The reliance on French literary reviews, the French national bibliography, and direct purchase from French booksellers was a legacy of the pervasive French colonial print economy and libraries in Indochina. As a consequence of this colonial carryover, French colonial ideas of cultural value permeated Trụ's standards for library acquisitions and organization of the National Library in Saigon. Thus the premier library of the RVN reflected an amalgamation of colonial and postcolonial ideas, simultaneously a legacy of the French past and a concerted effort to build a national future.

The Public Library Mission:
"To Inform, to Educate, and to Entertain"

Vietnamese administrators sought to define the National Library as a public library in addition to a national institution. A lengthy report titled "La Bibliothèque Nationale du Sud-Vietnam," written in 1956 by a library administrator, ambitiously declared the institution to be "a library of information and general culture. With a collection of selectively chosen books and intended for the public, the library has a three-part goal like all public libraries: to inform, to educate, and to entertain."[29] The public function of the National Library made it distinctly modern and distinguished it, according to the report, from previous libraries that had existed in Vietnam. The author briefly summarized the history of libraries prior to French colonialism and noted that private libraries and the royal court maintained literary works and documents written in classical Chinese during the Lý and Trần dynasties (eleventh to fourteenth centuries). Later, the French colonial government established the library and archives in Cochinchina for documentation purposes, the report added. In highlighting the differences between the National Library and its predecessors, the author made a temporal distinction between private or administrative libraries of the past and the national public library of the future.

In the rest of the report, the author examined the meaning, role, and function of the public library after the transfer of the library service in 1946. The author defined a public library based on its responsibility to serve its reading publics. For the library to accomplish this mission, it first needed to understand its readers and their preferred reading matter. The National Library conducted a study on this question and found that the composition and interests of library users had changed significantly in recent years. The report summarized the conclusions of the study:

> The loyal clientele of the library consists of university students. The most requested books are for textbooks [on subjects] such as history, geography, law, and science. Novels, in particular French novels, are less and less in demand. Foreign readers search history books or books on customs and morals of Vietnam. Administrators request texts such as the *Journal officiel de l'Indochine* or administrative bulletins of different regions of Vietnam.[30]

Although administrators and foreign readers still relied on the library, university students now made up the majority of users. This shift in clientele reflected the expansion of higher education in the RVN due to the relocation of the University of Hanoi and the most prestigious high schools in Hanoi to Saigon. Further, the overall increase of library users mirrored the rising Vietnamese-language literacy rates and rapidly increasing population of Saigon.

The library administrator argued that acquisitions of new books and periodicals should align with the needs of its changing readers as well as the three-part mission of a public library to inform, educate, and entertain. The author elaborated on the importance of selective acquisitions based on reader behavior:

> In other words, acquisitions must respond to the public's demand for information and above all operate as a public service to enable the public to do their work through access to documentation. The new acquisitions must also help students who are preparing for their exams or their research in a specific field. Lastly, the new acquisitions must provide good reading matter for the other frequent patrons of the library: novels of undisputed literary and moral value and good works of scientific popularization. In all ways possible, the library is enriched with good works in its collections. The library strives to complete its existing collections. It also creates new major collections of general culture and information, not just specialty works of this or that scientific branch.

The purposeful acquisition of varied reading matter suggests that administrators framed the library as a public resource and supplementary education for the increasingly diverse reading publics, including Vietnamese students, administrators, foreign researchers, and general readers.

The General Library at Pétrus Ký and Serving Cholon Readers, 1955–1958

While awaiting the construction of the National Library and Cultural Center, the materials from Hanoi remained in a storage facility in Khánh Hội near the Saigon River because the colonial library building at 34 Gia Long was not large enough to receive the seven hundred boxes. In 1955, the abandoned refectory hall of the Pétrus Ký School on Nancy Street (today Nguyễn Văn Cừ Street) was designated as a temporary library for the transferred collection. The temporary library was often referred to as the General Library (Tổng Thơ Viện) or the National Library at Pétrus Ký. The General Library was placed under the management of the University of Saigon (Viện Đại Học Sài Gòn).

According to a report from 1956 written for the Ministry of National Education, the General Library at Pétrus Ký began operations in January of that year. The report described the important new location of the library:

> A beautiful room, but abandoned and unused for sometime now, has been well-arranged for storing the boxes carried away during the evacuation of the library [from Hanoi]. Well-ventilated, surrounded by a vast field, the library offers a quiet retreat for workers and ordinary readers. The installation of this library in Saigon—the university and administrative capital of Vietnam—meets the needs of a cultured population and a Vietnamese elite.[31]

The report noted, however, that the General Library at Pétrus Ký was located too far from the urban center of Saigon. If relocated, the "numerous [members of the] Saigon intellectual class who have a great taste for reading" could enjoy better access to the important resources at the General Library.

Not until 1957 did the library obtain an approved budget to purchase essential supplies and officially open to the public. The report commended the "dedication and hard work of Nguyễn Hùng Cường (the head manager of the storage depot) who emphasized the importance of technical standards, books, and furniture." Under Cường's management, twenty-five thousand items of the transferred collection were finally incorporated into the Pétrus Ký location and accessible to the public. Cường reported regretfully that only a seventh of the boxed-up books had been opened, cataloged, and put in circulation by June 1957. Many of the commonly used reference books were in poor condition, Cường observed, and needed to be rebound. Further, the library had only a limited number of tables and chairs, for a maximum of forty readers.[32]

Decree 544/GD/CL, dated June 20, 1957, officially placed the General Library under the direct administration of the RVN Ministry of National Education. The General Library merged with the existing National Library of Southern Vietnam on Gia Long Street to form a centralized and similarly named National Library system that would function as the model for other libraries in the country.[33] The National Library system was integrated into the new Central Library and Archives of Vietnam (Thơ Viện và Văn Khố Trung Ương Việt Nam), which controlled all libraries, archives, and the national legal deposit.[34] During this time, the National Library system comprised three locations scattered across Saigon: the reading and consultation library at 34 Gia Long still known as the National Library (formerly the Cochinchina Library), the General Library located at Pétrus Ký School (transferred materials from Hanoi), and the temporarily closed Lending Section and Children's Reading Room at 194D Pasteur.

Discussions regarding the physical merger of the three-part National Library continued throughout 1957. A report by a librarian-archivist at the General Library reveals the complex challenges of merging the libraries to form a centralized institution.[35] The author argued that transferring the entirety of the General Library at Pétrus Ký would be expensive and impossible, given that the current location on Gia Long Street would not be able to receive the large collection from Pétrus Ký. Furthermore, the building at Pétrus Ký stood on a unique concrete and metal foundation higher than the ground floor, which was ideal for the storage of materials and protection from humidity and termites. For these logistical reasons, the report proposed that the libraries at the Pétrus Ký School and on Gia Long Street continue to operate separately until the future National Library and Cultural Center could readily receive the entirety of the combined collections.

The librarian-archivists at Pétrus Ký library argued that their current location served the large intellectual community of Cholon:

After evaluating the Pétrus Ký library, we recognize that this library has already been organized with the most appropriate and advanced methods. The number of library readers has been increasing each day—intellectuals of the large and crowded Cholon region (and the neighboring universities such as the Faculty of Sciences [in the University of Saigon], Pétrus Ký School, Chu Văn An School, and the Military University) often visit the library. The library has a great number of valuable reading matter that benefit readers when they are looking for specific information or reading books and newspapers to entertain their spirits. The Pétrus Ký library has forty seats for readers. Thus, in the meantime while we await the construction of the new National Library and Cultural Center, we propose to use the Pétrus Ký library to serve Cholon intellectuals and, more generally, all those who are thirsty for knowledge.

By 1958, the Pétrus Ký library received an estimated number of 2,148 readers in April and 2,780 in June, averaging 109 readers each day.[36] It received new books in Vietnamese, French, and English donated from other departments, associations, and research institutes. For example, the US Information Service donated Ketchum Richard's "What Is Communism," "Việt Mỹ" (pamphlets from the Office of the Vietnam-American Association), and UNESCO's *Des bibliothèques publiques pour l'Asie,* and *Bulletin of the National Academy of Library Administration* (*Tập san Học Viện Quốc Gia Hành Chánh Thư Viện*).

The Disorganized National Library on Gia Long Street and the Demand for Lending Services, 1957–1958

From 1946 to 1958, the National Library system existed in a transitional three-part organization and struggled to serve the increasing population of Saigon-Cholon readers. The National Library at 34 Gia Long Street inherited the collections from the old Cohinchina Library, including Indochinese and French historical periodicals such as the *Revue indochinoise, Bulletin de l'Ecole Française d'Extrême-Orient,* and *Bulletin des amis du Vieux Hué.* This initial collection, however, did not include popular Vietnamese-language periodicals such as *Nam phong, Tri tân,* and *Đông Dương tạp chí,* and the serials it did include were often incomplete.[37] The National Library at Gia Long Street continued earlier efforts to expand its collection and actively requested books and serials on contemporary politics, science, libraries, and economics from France, new books from America, and other contemporary international works. Additionally, many libraries and institutions from across the world such as UNESCO, the French national bibliography, and the Michigan State University Vietnam Advisory Group donated many works to the National Library.[38]

Attempts to build the library collection through legal deposit encountered severe limitations. Standardized requirements for legal deposit of new publications had not yet been implemented since 1944. Phan Vô Ky, who replaced Đoàn Quan Tấn as the director of the library in July 1957, sent regular demands to newspapers, publishers, and institutions to figure out incomplete publication information. Correspondence documents point to how Ky individually tracked down publishers to determine where their works were officially printed and whether they had been filed into legal deposit.[39] By 1957, of a total of 1,946 legal deposits, 1,562 were nonperiodical Vietnamese works; only 132 were French works.[40] Additionally, in 1957 the number of legal deposits in other languages as well as bilingual or trilingual works was substantial: English (98), Vietnamese-English (80), Vietnamese-French (26), Vietnamese-Chinese (32), English-Chinese (4), and Vietnamese-French-English (2). Periodical legal deposits were mainly Vietnamese (833), though some were in other languages: French (60),

English (39), Vietnamese-English (49), Vietnamese-French (13), and Vietnamese-Chinese (12). The number of legal deposits in various languages points to the extensive multilingual publishing industry and reading publics of Saigon-Cholon in the 1950s. Further, many works in the library were Vietnamese translations from French translations of books in other languages, such as Margaret Mitchell's *Gone with the Wind* or Carlo Lorenzini's Italian-language *Pinocchio.*[41]

In general, the Reading Room at 34 Gia Long Street continued to apply the rules from the colonial period. To access the collections, readers consulted the catalog and could request up to two books at a time, whereupon library staff pulled the books from the nearby storage area. Reports boasted that the staff could retrieve the books within an impressive five minutes because the books were methodically organized by size and topic. Reference books, dictionaries, encyclopedia, directories, manuals, and more than fifty journals in French, Vietnamese, and English were openly accessible on the shelves for free perusal.[42]

In actuality, internal letters, library reports, and complaints from readers reveal a different reality. Regular reports and exchanges from 1957 to 1958 make clear that the everyday state of library affairs in the new republic was poor, frantic, and disorganized. The Service of Library and Archives of South Vietnam were severely understaffed at all levels—from high-level management to typists and guards. In 1956 and 1957, working with the National University and the Ministry of National Education, the Service of Library and Archives organized a course to train almost a hundred civil servants in administrative organization, archiving official documents, and library management. Yet even with this newly trained cohort, the libraries and archives still did not have enough personnel. In the letter on March 8, 1957, Phan Vô Ky requested that the Ministry of National Education provide another typist to help the National Library at 34 Gia Long.[43] Ky lamented that the current typist was too tired from his military duties to stay awake and complete his work and that the second typist was preoccupied with fulfilling his obligations at the Ministry of Interior. Everyday infractions such as stolen trash cans and disruptive library patrons demonstrated how the library lacked guards and monitors for the Reading Room. On March 4, 1957, a library administrator even deplored the poor state of the building, reporting that pieces of the ceiling fell off during reading hours and nearly hit readers.[44]

Several readers publicly complained about the library's limited services and space. Despite claims that the Lending Section on Pasteur Street would soon reopen, it remained closed to the public and the building was occupied by governmental offices. In 1956, the newspaper *Dân chủ* published a letter from "a few soldiers and civil servants" urging the Ministry of National Education to find a location where it could reopen the Lending Section.[45] The Lending Section remained closed. In April 26, 1957, Đoàn Quan Tấn from the National Library on

Gia Long street issued a similar request to the ministry and submitted a copy of the article from *Dân chủ* as evidence of popular demand.

Requests for reopening the Lending Section continued throughout the year, including specific demands for a large building, adequate staff, more books, additional furniture, and the transfer of the existing collections out of storage. On April 1958, the Lending Section reopened together with the Children's Reading Room and was renamed the Lending Library and Children's Reading Room (Thư Viện Cho Mượn và Phòng Đọc Thiếu Nhi). It reportedly boasted 13,700 books and a daily average of 115 readers.

Hierarchies of Readers and Library Surveillance

The limited space and resources of the National Library at 34 Gia Long meant that it did not meet the needs of the reading public; administrators developed policies to restrict access, enforce regulations, and favor certain readers while shutting others out. The growth of the population in Saigon led to increased demand; the library reported a daily average of two hundred users in the late 1950s, double that during the colonial period. In particular, the expanding number of schools in Saigon produced an ever-growing population of students, who transformed the National Library into a space for studying and socializing. Students were the most ardent and eager readers, actively using the library to access expensive textbooks and reference matter and to supplement classroom materials with valuable periodicals, novels, and translated texts.

Yet the Gia Long Reading Room only had forty-eight seats, and Saigon readers competed to secure a spot. In a letter to the police, the library director Phan Vô Kỳ explained that the problem was especially acute during the summer holiday, when earnest students aggressively fought over the limited seats:

> During the summer months, university students clamber in front of the library doors before the morning and noon opening hours. When the library reopens, students rush and flood the central staircase—yelling and pushing each other, necessitating the military police to come to keep them quiet. Because of this commotion, female students hesitate to be part of the scramble and instead retreat home.[46]

Kỳ scolded the students for their behavior and reminded them that order and propriety had to be maintained because the library was located next to the Ministry of the Economy where the president worked. These warnings proved ineffective. Frustrated, Kỳ pleaded with the local police to send security back up during the opening hours and the early afternoon.

Students not only competed against each other for space but also crowded out other library users that administrators favored. In a letter to the Ministry of

National Education in summer 1957, Phan Vô Ky proposed adding more tables and chairs to the Reading Room and opening a researcher's room with twelve seats. The addition would bring the total number of seats to ninety. Additionally, the creation of a researcher's room would separate those he considered more serious readers from the rowdy students in the main room. Ky also suggested a series of changes to take place after the annual closure of the library from July 15 to August 15.[47] He wanted to create a system of daily reading cards to monitor and limit access based on the number of available seats. Each week, the library would issue 480 access cards, color-coded by day and session (morning or afternoon session). Each day, eight seats would be reserved for infrequent but important readers such as professors and administrators. Ky developed this system to restore order to the Reading Room and "to prevent groups of university students from turning the Reading Room into a study room for themselves." He also wanted "to allow those who wish to consult library materials to not have to push and shove and to guarantee a proper seat for readers . . . and for the library to be able to monitor greedy readers and thieves."[48]

Clearly, administrators envisioned greater surveillance and discipline of readers. The National Library at Gia Long created new regulations to take place after the annual closure that year. On entering the library, readers now had to provide their card so that the library could collect reader usage statistics. On exiting the Reading Room, all belongings and bags had to be inspected to detect any stolen materials.[49] Further, the regulations included a clause that emphasized the communal and public use of the library: "For the benefit of the collective, the library requests that readers protect the books and newspapers by not writing on them, folding the pages, or overextending the binding." Readers must also return reference books where they belong "to convenience and not disadvantage other readers." For the first time, the rules also included a clause that permitted the library to refuse entrance to any reader who "dressed inappropriately or behaved impolitely." Library users who failed to conform to standards of dress and behavior set by the administrators could be denied access altogether. Library administrators called for a "complete education" for readers, issuing detailed regulations on reader behavior and proper care of library materials.[50] These extensive rules defined proper reader comportment, cultural norms, and the proper use of a modern public library.

The separation of readers into different categories sheds light on the underlying hierarchy of library readers. The complaint of library administrators at 34 Gia Long in the 1950s about the lack of decorum and the crowding out of more serious readers was similar to the discourse on the Hanoi Central Library in the 1920s and 1930s.[51] The distinction between leisure and serious readers and the decision to prioritize the latter reflected a continual debate over the mission of the libraries in Vietnam. Was the National Library a public educational resource for all readers, whether they were students, researchers, or government officials? Should the space be used for study by Vietnamese university students or as a research institution for officials and professors? What should the public read and how should they behave? These questions were central to the visions, development, and organization of the National Library in the RVN.

CONCLUSION

This chapter examines the slow and fragmented development of the National Library in Saigon from 1946 to 1958. I show how the inheritance of the colonial institutions intersected with decolonization, nation-building, and modernization efforts. In this transitional period, the mission of the library was brought into question. As in the colonial period, the library held tremendous symbolic value of modernity, legitimacy, and state capacity. French colonial practices of library science continued to inform acquisitions and overall library functions. Further, the National Library of the RVN sought to redefine the library as a public, educational resource for its citizens and use the cultural institution to enhance the regime's position in the contest against the Democratic Republic of Vietnam for national legitimacy.

Administrators of the National Library envisioned a new social, political, and educational mission of the library as both a national and a public institution. They discussed how to transform the largely French-language collections to meet the needs of urban Vietnamese readers. Administrators justified the importance of the library using republican values of state responsibility to provide public services and educational resources to its citizens. The pursuit of a public and national library intersected with the larger decolonizing and nation-building project to create a culturally coherent national identity, a republican government serving a loyal citizenry, and an engaged civil society based in the self-anointed capital of Saigon.

NOTES

1. For example, see the retrospective history of the library produced by the staff of the National Library of Vietnam every five years: Lê Văn Viết, Nguyễn Hữu Viêm, and Phạm Thế Khang, *Thư Viện Quốc Gia Việt Nam—90 năm xây dựng và phát triển* (Hanoi: Thư Viện Quốc Gia, 2007); and *Thư Viện Quốc Gia Việt Nam: 85 năm xây dựng và trưởng thành, 1917–2002* (Hanoi: Thư Viện Quốc Gia, 2002).

2. The nationalist narrative of cultural imperialism is most apparent in studies of library development in the RVN, where libraries are framed as part of American cultural imperialism and propaganda. For a schematic comparison of socialist libraries in the Democratic Republic of Vietnam and supposedly imperialist libraries in the RVN during the Vietnam War, see Phạm Tân Hạ, "Hoạt động thư viện ở thành phố Sài Gòn thời kỳ 1954–1975" (PhD diss., Trường Đại Học Khoa học Xã hội và Nhân Văn, Ho Chi Minh City, 2005).

3. This chapter builds on the important scholarship on the RVN state and society by Nu-Anh Tran, Van Nguyen-Marshall, Christopher Goscha, Brett Reilly, Edward Miller, Matthew Masur, and Thaveeporn Vasavakul. I especially thank Nu-Anh Tran for sharing her research material and insights to frame my project.

4. Matthew Masur, "Hearts and Minds: Cultural Nation-Building in South Vietnam, 1954–1963" (PhD diss., Ohio State University, 2004); Masur, "Exhibiting Signs of Resistance: South Vietnam's Struggle for Legitimacy, 1954–1960," *Diplomatic History* 33, no. 2 (April 2009): 293–313; and Nu-Anh Tran, "Contested Identities: Nationalism in the Republic of Vietnam (1954–1963)" (PhD diss., University of California, Berkeley, 2013).

5. Rémi Bourgeois, *Rapport sur la direction des archives et des bibliothèques (1938–1939)* (Hanoi: Imprimerie Le Van Tan, 1939).

6. Đoàn Quan Tấn's response to interview questions from *Ngôn Luận* newspaper, March 26, 1955, Folder 2, National Library of Southern Vietnam Collection (Phông Thư Viện Quốc Gia Nam Việt [TVQGNV]), National Archives Center 2 (Trung Tâm Lưu Trữ Quốc Gia 2 [TTLTQG2]), Ho Chi Minh City.

7. Đoàn Quan Tấn's response to interview questions from Radio Saigon, May 1949, Folder 2, TVQGNV, TTLTQG2.

8. Đoàn Quan Tấn's response to interview questions from *Ngôn Luận* newspaper, March 26, 1955, Folder 2, TVQGNV, TTLTQG2.

9. Lê Ngọc Trụ, "Tổ chức Thơ Viện Quốc Gia," c. 1954, Folder 102, TVQGNV, TTLTQG2.

10. "La Bibliothèque nationale du Sud-Vietnam" c. 1956, Folder 102, TVQGNV, TTLTQG2.

11. "La Bibliothèque nationale du Sud-Vietnam" c. 1956; "Le développement des bibliothèques au Viet-nam de 1953 à 1957," c. 1957, Folder 102, TVQGNV, TTLTQG2.

12. "La Bibliothèque nationale du Sud-Vietnam" c. 1956, folder 102, TVQGNV, TTLTQG2.

13. Report from Phan Vô Ky to attaché of French information in Southern Vietnam, January 23, 1953, Folder 102, TVQGNV, TTLTQG2.

14. Conventions, 1949–1953, Folder 2041-05, Direction des Archives et des Bibliothèques (DABI), National Archives Center 1 (Trung Tâm Lưu Trữ Quốc Gia 1 [TTLTQG1]), Hanoi; and Conventions and Statutes, 1953, Folder 60-205, Haut Commissariat de France pour l'Indochine (HCI), Archives Nationale d'Outre-Mer (ANOM), Aix-en-Provence.

15. "La Bibliothèque générale nationale du Viet-Nam est la seconde bibliothèque de l'Extrême-Orient," *Mouvement de la Révolution Nationale* 232 (April 18, 1956), Folder 48, Archives Privées Papiers Boudet (PB), ANOM.

16. Information on the transfer of collections is compiled from the following sources: Internal reports and inventory lists, 1954–1958, Folder 11, Service of the National Archive Collection (Phông Nha Văn Khố Quốc Gia [NVKQG]), TTLTQG2; and Internal reports, 1957–1958, Folder 12, NVKQG, TTLTQG2.

17. Report by Nguyễn Hùng Cường, January 12, 1955, Folder 11, NVKQG, TTLTQG2.

18. Đoàn Quan Tấn's response to interview questions from Radio Saigon, May 1949, Folder 2, TVQGNV, TTLTQG2.

19. Đoàn Quan Tấn's response to interview questions from Radio Saigon, May 1949, Folder 2, TVQGNV, TTLTQG2.

20. Report, March 18, 1955, Folder 2, TVQGNV, TTLTQG2.

21. Ngô Đình Diệm's speech at the inaugural ceremony published in *Việt Nam Thông Tấn Xã*, 1949 (July 3, 1956, afternoon edition), Folder 18141, Office of the President Collection, First Republic (Phông Phủ Tổng Thống Đệ Nhất Cộng Hòa [PTTĐICH]), TTLTQG2.

22. Speech by Mai Thọ Truyền delivered at the bricklaying ceremony for the National Library, December 28, 1968, found in "Hồ sơ v/v xây cất Thơ Viện Quốc Gia tại 69 Gia Long, Sài Gòn năm 1960–1971, Tập 2: Lễ đặt Viên đá đầu Tiên," Folder 383, TVQGNV, TTLTQG2.

23. Speech by Mai Thọ Truyền, 1968, Folder 383, TVQGNV, TTLTQG2.

24. Internal reports, architectural plans, and proposals, Folders 389 and 382, NVKQG, TTLTQG2.

25. Phan Vô Kỳ, "Hoạt động của Thơ Viên Quốc Gia từ khi giao lại cho chánh phủ Việt Nam đến ngày nay," June 26, 1954, Folder 102, TVQGNV, TTLTQG2.

26. Phan Vô Kỳ, "Hoạt động của Thơ Viên Quốc Gia từ khi giao lại cho chánh phủ Việt Nam đến ngày nay," June 26, 1954, Folder 102, TVQGNV, TTLTQG2.

27. Lê Ngọc Trụ, "Tổ chức Thơ Viện Quốc Gia," c. 1954, Folder 102, TVQGNV, TTLTQG2.

28. Lê Ngọc Trụ, "Tổ chức Thơ Viện Quốc Gia," c. 1954, Folder 102, TVQGNV, TTLTQG2.

29. "La Bibliothèque nationale du Sud-Vietnam," May 1956, Folder 102, TVQGNV, TTLTQG2.

30. "La Bibliothèque nationale du Sud-Vietnam," May 1956, Folder 102, TVQGNV, TTLTQG2.

31. "Situation générale, rapport 1956," Folder 11, NVKQG, TTLTQG2.

32. Nguyễn Hùng Cường, "Tờ tường trình về Tổng Thư Viện Quốc Gia," July 18, 1957, Folder 11, NVKQG, TTLTQG2.

33. Nguyễn Hùng Cường, "Tờ tường trình về Tổng Thư Viện Quốc Gia," July 18, 1957, Folder 11, NVKQG, TTLTQG2.

34. "Phúc trình tổng quát, " c. 1957, Folder 102, TVQGNV, TTLTQG2.

35. Nguyễn Hùng Cường, Trịnh Huy Đào, and Nguyễn Văn Tấn, internal report, December 19, 1957, Folder 11, NVKQG, TTLTQG2.

36. "Báo cáo hoạt động và thành tích của Tổng Thơ Viện Quốc Gia Năm, 1954–1958," Folder 11, NVKQG, TTLTQG2.

37. "La Bibliothèque nationale du Sud-Vietnam," May 1956, Folder 11, TVQGNV, TTLTQG2.

38. Correspondence and inventory lists, 1957, Folder 7, NVKQG, TTLTQG2.

39. Correspondence from Phan Vô Kỳ, 1957, Folder 7, NVKQG, TTLTQG2.

40. Statistics of legal deposits and purchases of periodicals at 34 Gia Long, 1957, Folder 10, NVKQG, TTLTQG2.

41. Survey on the state of translation in Vietnam, July 17, 1957, Folder 7, NVKQG, TTLTQG2.

42. "La Bibliothèque nationale du Sud-Vietnam," May 1956, Folder 102, TVQGNV, TTLTQG2.

43. Phan Vô Kỳ to Minister of National Education, March 8, 1957, Folder 7, NVKQG, TTLTQG2.

44. Internal reports, 1957, Folder 7, NVKQG, TTLTQG2.

45. Phan Vô Kỳ to Ministry of National Education, August 2, 1957, Folder 7, NVKQG, TTLTQG2; and "Xin mở thơ viện cho mượn sách đọc," Tiếng dân kêu column, Dân chủ, March 21, 1957.

46. Phan Vô Kỳ to the District 1 Police, Saigon, June 13, 1957, Folder 7, NVKQG, TTLTQG2.

47. Phan Vô Kỳ to Ministry of National Education, June 28, 1957, Folder 7, NVKQG, TTLTQG2.

48. Phan Vô Kỳ to Ministry of National Education, June 28, 1957, Folder 7, NVKQG, TTLTQG2.

49. Library regulations, August 14, 1957, Folder 7, NVKQG, TTLTQG2.

50. Đoàn Quan Tân's response to Radio Saigon questionnaire, May 1949, Folder 2, TVQGNV, TTLTQG2.

51. Cindy Nguyen, "Reading Rules: The Symbolic and Social Spaces of Reading in the Hà Nội Central Library, 1919–1941," Journal of Vietnamese Studies 15, no. 3 (August 2020): 1–35, esp. 17–18.

CHAPTER NINE

Striving for the Quintessence

Building a New Identity of National Literature Based on Creative Freedom

Hoàng Phong Tuấn and Nguyễn Thị Minh

> Open the free window
> Leaving stuffy and closed space
> Smashing chains and walls
> Winning a fragrant drop of passion
> And dreaming as a poet
>
> —Trần Thanh Hiệp

To answer the question whether the art and literature of the Republic of Vietnam (1955–1975) was a branching or a new construction in the process of Vietnamese cultural history, we need to examine not only their inheritance from and differences with the preceding period, but also the construction of their identity through their self-recognition as a national culture in general and a national literature in particular. Research on identity images of this period builds on the world historical views of postcolonial space and the context of the Cold War.[1] Such an approach ignores the imagination and efforts to create a new identity for the national literature by writers and advocates of art and literature who were insiders and found themselves playing a role in building a new culture.

To fill the gap of research on this topic, this chapter analyzes the process of identity construction through the discourse and works of writers and editors in three prominent magazines, *Culture Today* (*Văn hóa ngày nay*), *Encyclopedia* (*Bách khoa*), and *Creativity* (*Sáng tạo*), during the early years of the First Republic from 1956 to 1960. Our theoretical stance assumes that discourses in the arts, the media, and literature play a role in identity construction.[2] In this case, writers and editors of that period attempted through their works to construct the idea of a liberal environment and creative freedom as the identity of a new national literature and culture. In later years, doubts about this identity emerged as a result of different perspectives and attitudes toward that identity constructed earlier.

Our explorations into the views of those who advocated and built the new culture reveal a process of identity construction largely disconnected from the world historical perspective of the Cold War and the postcolonial context. To them, what the new culture and new society would look like in their imagination was more important than what social and political ideologies they followed or were opposed to. Such an ideological stand, if any, was secondary, or, to put it another way, a result of the earlier imagination.

How editors and writers of three magazines constructed their new identity centered on the concept of creative freedom, which allowed them not only to appreciate their role in Vietnamese history in contrast with their counterparts in North Vietnam, but also to contribute to building a new cultural space for the nation-in-forming in South Vietnam. The concept also promoted literary innovations, encouraged a diversity of perspectives, and produced a new history of national literature. Challenges to the new identity arose in later years but it was reaffirmed rather than abandoned.

"FREEDOM" AS A DISCOURSE AND NARRATIVE OF IDENTITY

Each new phase of cultural history often begins with the first generation positioning their role in history with a new perspective, searching for their image while creating a new communal identity. An important part of a community's identity are the characteristics of the cultural life that individuals imagine about their community.[3] A correlation is evident between the newly formed community and the individuals playing their role in its formation: they take on the role of identity constructors, protecting those characteristics and forming the future perspective for their community. Thus identity is the result of the correlation between the individuals' imagination of the community's characteristics and of themselves as members who make contributions to the construction of those characteristics.

The implementation of the Geneva Accords in 1954, on the one hand, led to the temporary separation of the country and, on the other, made it possible for people in the two parts of Vietnam to choose a new living space where their expectations and longing for a new life would become reality. But what that reality would be almost entirely depended on the efforts of the individuals and the collective who had taken their place in it. From this aspect, having the same vision and a common imagination of an identity are clearly indispensable.

From social and political perspectives, the reason many Northern Vietnamese migrated to the South was their fear of living under tight government control and their dislike of many economic policies in the North, which made their dream and hope of a liberal cultural space become even stronger. For Southerners, the right to establish a cultural space out of the French colonial rule was a dream and hope from the beginning of the century—a common dream for all Vietnamese—and the basis and motivation for the search and imagination of identity. The questions of "who am I?" and "which community do I belong to?" required a new interpretation of identity of the new cultural space, or the answer to the question "what is this community?" This question in various forms had appeared before and reemerged after the Republic of Vietnam (RVN) was established.[4]

It is precisely at this point that we can see the challenges for people when they searched for that identity: the members of this historical space knew that they, on the one hand, were born and belonged to a cultural world that had originated in North Vietnam and, on the other, were now living in a new cultural and historical context and had to place themselves in a different position from their compatriots across the seventeenth parallel. In this search, the past and the present created a dilemma for their choices. This dilemma was that their imagination about themselves and the culture they were building had to be culturally distinct and authentic at the same time. These two characteristics, though, had a contradictory element: although that culture had its roots in the North, it now had to distinguish from and prove itself to be more original than those roots. In this case, envisioning the liberal environment became the fulcrum for defining the distinctness and authenticity of the new historical period and thereby providing a solution to the contradiction. The new culture was distinctive because it gave people an absolute freedom, therefore, in their mind and their will, it was authentic. Freedom was thereby an identity that afforded all their demands.[5]

The idea of freedom was thus determined as the starting point of a new culture by the first generation of writers and artists of the new country. This idea was developed by those who founded and contributed to the literary and cultural magazines published in the First Republic, including the three that are the focus of this chapter. *Sáng tạo* was a monthly magazine managed by Mai Thảo that left imprints and achievements in literary innovations. The original series included thirty-one issues published between October 1956 and September 1959, when the magazine was suspended. The new series restarted in July 1960 and continued until September 1961, totaling seven issues. *Văn hóa ngày nay* was famous for inheriting and recreating the literary and cultural quintessence of the prewar period despite its brief existence. Managed by Nhất Linh, the magazine published eleven weekly issues starting in mid-June 1958. The bimonthly *Bách khoa*, which was founded by Huỳnh Văn Lang and managed by Lê Ngộ Châu, enjoyed a long life, from January 1957 to April 1975, totaling 426 issues. These three magazines in different ways played a crucial role in constructing the identity of the new literature.

Many contributors to the three magazines were émigré artists from North Vietnam. They carried with them a deep frustration and trauma for having earlier been denied the freedom to raise their voices in their writing and reflections on the nature of art. In their memory, the cultural space under the Democratic Republic of Vietnam (DRV) did not accept creative freedom. By contrast, the new social and cultural space in the South gave them new hopes and realities that facilitated the desire for freedom in creativity. There could be a new land where they could be free to create a new literature "built up according to our aesthetic appeal," in the words of Mai Thảo, in contrast to the unidirectional concept of art in the North that prompted writers like him to leave. Therefore, for these writers more than those who were not émigré, the idea of creative freedom both expressed their aspiration and interpreted their choice to migrate, and, above all, was an imagination of the identity of the new national culture. Thus creative freedom as identity was the way they situated themselves vis-à-vis the new culture they could contribute to building.

In the interpretation of these self-proclaimed builders of the new culture, a certain ideological correspondence apparently existed between the writers' and artists' imagination of freedom as identity and personalism as a political doctrine applied in the cultural realm by the Ngô Đình Diệm government. The liberal environment was a condition for carrying out the policy of developing personalism. But the model of personalism placed individuals within their relation to society, meaning that the freedom the personalist individual enjoyed was only a conditional one.[6] For this reason, it did not meet the expectations for the builders of the new culture, in which people expected to find true, unconditional freedom. The writers we examine seemed to have felt this incongruity. Therefore, despite official attempts to associate the new cultural phase with personalism, writers and advocates of art and literature in this period were more attracted to creative freedom as the identity of the new culture.[7]

The introductory essays published in the first issue of all three magazines did not mention the concept of personalism as something at which literature should aim. Instead, they emphasized the opening to freedom of thought and theories. *Văn hóa ngày nay* claimed that the magazine aimed to introduce and collect past and present works.[8] In contrast, *Bách khoa* emphasized its openness to different perspectives rather than limiting itself to any one in particular.[9] The editors did not use the concept of personalism but rather that of "compassion" or "compassion for people" (*lòng nhân*) and defined this aspect as

> not to sacrifice human dignity for any rhetorical fallacies and not to make undue sacrifices for any narrow collectives, for any distant and uncertain futures, for the achievement of unlimited freedom in the manner of 'a tiger in a goat barn,' or for small and short-term benefits to the extent of neglecting the ultimate meaning of humanity.

Although the concept of compassion here might be interpreted as resonating with the doctrine of personalism, it was placed in opposition to the notions of any "narrow collective" and any "distant and uncertain future," and thus asserted a different vision of freedom in the desires of its authors. It might be argued that, by not directly evoking the concept of personalism, editors of the magazine wanted to appeal to people of various perspectives. But this choice can also be seen as an expression of their desire for an unconditional freedom.[10]

The imagination of creative freedom as the identity of a new culture by the writers and editors of the three magazines was connected to the emergence of Saigon as a new cultural capital. Mai Thảo, a writer and one of the founding members of *Sáng tạo,* wrote an open and constructive essay in the first issue to express his and his group's vision in which Saigon was imagined as "the new cultural capital" of Vietnam.[11] The article offered a new interpretation of Saigon's position, through which the city appeared as the focal point of a new free space and an elite cultural place around which all regions around the country converged.

> No longer a limb, Saigon is a heart. The great events in the history of the country from the past has shifted their center of national activities. The growing Saigon, replacing a faded Hanoi, has naturally turned into a bastion gathering all constructive goodwill and every effort to contribute to existing cultural activities in every field and every aspect. . . . Cultural materials are still scattered around, but the form of a cultural castle can be seen. This castle will be built in Saigon [as the] center. It will be beautiful [and] quintessential [*tinh túy*] because it is built up according to our aesthetic appeal. It will be healthy and robust because it is rooted in the health and robustness of a free and democratic life and people.[12]

Mai Thảo built an image of Saigon as a central position in opposition to Hanoi: "Saigon [as the] center," "Saigon has been a heart," "Saigon is growing," and "a faded Hanoi." Here spatial images were given historical and political significance. The new space provided an image of leaving the old world and building a new one with new rules, where people lived as they wished "to build up according to [their] aesthetic appeal." Democratic freedom here was emphasized as the identity of the new cultural space. In this article, and in some of Mai Thảo's later ones, we can see a desire to build a new culture rather than an anticommunist spirit of the group of émigré writers to which he belonged. Any reference to the cultural policy of the Northern communist society was only to affirm their own identity, which was not positioned on the premises of anticommunism, anticolonialism, and antifeudalism as Nu-Anh Tran analyzes for many political groups at the time.[13]

Quách Thoại (1930–1957), a young poet who died at twenty-seven, was as excited and hopeful of a new future of free life as Mai Thảo was. He composed many poems on the first issue of *Sáng tạo* on this topic, including "Green" ("Xanh"), "Democratic Flag" ("Cờ dân chủ"), and "Spring Night Sleep" ("Giấc ngủ đêm xuân"). In these poems, contrasting images of dawn and night ("Cờ dân chủ") and darkness and light ("Giấc ngủ đêm xuân") gave a sense of space and time in the past as something fading away and today as a new hope. In "Cờ dân chủ," joy and hope for a new period of history were expressed through strong adjectives and adverbs such as "radiant" (*rạng rỡ*) and "proudly" (*nghênh ngang*): "I joyfully look up, today is an ideal day / Green season, green love / Glowing dawn radiates the rays of heaven / Night died with the past / I walk in the sunshine of future / Big streets laugh, avenues sing proudly" ("Ta ngưỡng vọng hôm nay trời lí tưởng / Ngát mùa xanh, xanh thắm của yêu thương / Rực bình minh rạng rỡ ánh thiên đường / Đêm gục chết theo với thời quá khứ / Ta bước tới nắng tương lai đầy ứ / Phố lớn cười đại lộ hát nghênh ngang").[14]

Nguyễn Sỹ Tế was an émigré writer and a founding member of *Sáng tạo*. In the article titled "1802," he recounted the history of national expansion southward since the fifteenth century that culminated in the inauguration of the Nguyễn dynasty and the establishment of a new capital in Huế by Gia Long. He asserted that 1802 not only marked a historical transformation but also opened a new period in which a new national literature, for the first time, expanded evenly and rapidly transformed in all three regions, becoming mass-oriented (*đại chúng hoá*) in the old North, stately (*tôn nghiêm*) in the central region where the new capital was located, and promising in the South. He concluded by declaring that "the third capital [i.e., Saigon] has been established and grown up. How young and strong a capital it is! We have the right to believe that as the youngest brother, with the energy contributed by the great migration [from the North], it will make its [two] older brothers proud."

The works by writers such as Mai Thảo, Quách Thoại, and Nguyễn Sỹ Tế expressed strong hopes and beliefs as they situated themselves in a new historical period. From a comparative point of view, the discourse on a changing center and the construction of a new cultural space with the identity of freedom was in fact not new but had appeared in 1945 and 1946, when Việt Minh writers envisioned Hanoi as the capital of freedom.[15] However, the idea of freedom there was built on Marxist-Leninist conception of class struggle and national liberation, whereby the mission was first to liberate the people and then to liberate the working class from oppression. It was a condition for freedom. Nguyễn Đình Thi and Hồng Lĩnh were perhaps the two authors who stood out in building a discourse and narrative about the new historical period, in effect extending communist leaders Hồ Chí Minh and Trường Chinh's conceptions of revolution. For example, Nguyễn Đình Thi relied on Marxist-Leninism to reinterpret the ideas of "the independence of man, the independence of thought, and the freedom of the individual" in Western liberal thought. According to him, "the individualism that imperialist powers used to poison us cannot be deeply rooted in Vietnamese soil. . . . We [as individuals] can neither live nor exist outside the nation and the masses. It is thanks to [living within the nation and the masses] that we could surpass the old and worn-out bourgeois humans and to become the humans of the future."[16] Given such a premise, the historical mission of culture and art envisioned by the communists was to serve the anti-French resistance for national independence and the liberation of the working class. The concept and imagination of such freedom differed from those of the first generation of Republican writers and artists in the RVN. For this generation, freedom was the very nature of human beings, and people should build a cultural space consistent with that nature. The mission of culture and art for their generation was to build a new cultural space to promote human values. In contrast, the social environment in the North under a proletarian revolution made people lose their freedom.

The imagination of identity in this direction was reflected in the concept of freedom as a condition for creativity. In the imagination of writers and artists of this period, only freedom could bring the best conditions for them to reveal their true talents.[17] Nguyễn Thành Vinh, a literary critic, argued that artists must be completely free to escape from the historical time and space of their age to create works having eternal value. On that basis, he criticized the policies and orientations in the resistance period under Việt Minh leadership to make literature and art serve the political needs of the time, resulting in "the soul of [all] artists cast in the same mold," and "art becoming mere boring propaganda, not enough to arouse in the hearts of readers rich feelings."[18] Nguyễn Thành Vinh's article reinforced the orientations of the magazine published by Nhất Linh, a famous writer and politician before 1945 and the managing editor of *Văn hóa ngày nay*. In the opening essay of *Văn hóa ngày nay*'s first issue, titled "*Văn hóa ngày nay* and Vietnamese Culture," he wrote, "Pure art must reach the quintessence, and especially must not allow temporary and local tastes to make art a thing that is only valid for a while or in a particular place."[19] Thus, freedom as conceived here was not only a condition for the artist to compose but also an essential aspect of creative activity; freedom was the erasure of all boundaries for the work to reach the quintessence. Therefore, it was only the circumstances of this new era that could allow creative activity to be what it really was.

The concept of freedom of expression was also reflected in the narratives about writers and artists. In Mai Thảo's short story "The fingers endowed by God" ("Những ngón tay bắt được của giời"), the narrator recalled the story about a painter named Tường.[20] Tường was a painter who had once left the city for the jungle to follow the communist-led resistance but cherished the concept of creative freedom by which "the artist as an individual must be completely free to pursue pure and original art." He was accused and punished only because he insisted on following his own creative path. But he found freedom to develop his talent in the "cultural capital of today." At the end of the story, Tưởng and the narrator shared their beliefs about a future culture that "we see in the cooling night of the city [in] the impression of an artistic horizon under construction." The narrative about the artist's life that circled around a turning point when he arrived in the new cultural space demonstrated that freedom allowed him to express himself freely, and only in this way could art become what it really was.

Mai Thảo's perspective can be compared with the narrative about the role of artists and writers in North Vietnam at the time. An example is the short story "The Eyes" ("Đôi mắt"), published in 1948 by Nam Cao, a writer and soldier in the resistance. This story showed that writing revolutionary literature could bring inspiration and a new outlook to the writer's life.[21] The work depicted the difference between the outlook and attitude of a writer named Hoàng, who was indifferent to the resistance and despised the people involved in it, and of another writer called Độ, who was excited to join, eat, and stay with the farmers involved in the resistance and found new themes and subjects for his stories that came from life. From Độ's perspective, works by writers like Hoàng who did not join the revolution were one-sided and disconnected from the reality of people's lives. The plot did not mention creative freedom or the necessary role of the liberal environment for creativity but presupposed that serving the revolution was a meaningful purpose of literature.

The discourses and narratives in *Sáng tạo, Bách khoa,* and *Văn hóa ngày nay* argued that the liberal environment of the new period was an essential condition for creativity, and that creative freedom was a necessary condition for valuable works to be created. Such narratives and discourses helped shape the identity of the new culture and the characteristics of a new literature. For émigré writers, and to some extent other writers who lived in the South but always looked back to the origins of the country in the North, that identity also helped them have a strong mind when they needed to escape the Northern homeland where they had once belonged.

INNOVATION AND DIVERSITY: A PERSPECTIVE ON LITERARY HISTORY

The conception of freedom and the imagination of creative freedom as the identity of a new literature allowed writers and editors of these magazines to have a different vision of literary history and culture than their counterparts in North Vietnam. It first built for them a fulcrum for repositioning literary values and, second, helped them visualize the past and envision the future of literature. In other words, they could build themselves a vision and from there an imagination of how a new literature would form and develop.

It was based on that vision and imagination that Nhất Linh, the leader of Self-Reliant Literary Group (Tự Lực Văn Đoàn) before 1945, declared that the magazine he founded, *Văn hóa ngày nay,* published "works of anytime from anywhere" based solely on their artistic value.[22] *Văn hóa ngày nay* often selected literary themes that gathered excellent works from the previous period. For example, the fifth issue of the magazine published on the occasion of the Mid-Autumn Festival had the theme of the moon in poetry and published earlier poems on the subject by Tản Đà, Xuân Diệu, and Vũ Hoàng Chương.[23] Some poems by Xuân Diệu and Vũ Hoàng Chương in this issue belonged to the New Poetry movement (Thơ Mới), an innovative movement of writing poetry in the early twentieth century in Vietnam. The selection of these poems showed that the conception of literary history Nhất Linh had in mind connected the new period with the literary achievements of the past. This view excluded the revolutionary literature associated with the previous resistance period (1946–1954) and the present (1958) in the North in which the Thơ mới movement was deemed to be the literature of the bourgeoisie, counterrevolutionary, traitorous, and without any value. At the same time, Nhất Linh's view inherited the pre-1946 conception of literary history as the evolution of works with high artistic value. As Nguyễn Thành Vinh elaborated, "The genuine artists must keep improving their own art. They should not follow the tastes of the times or limit themselves to certain models . . . Even if literary values could not avoid being temporarily constrained [by non-artistic things], they need to [eventually] transcend those things."[24]

The idea that literature evolved thanks to the innovation of artistic techniques on the basis of creative freedom was most manifest in writers who founded or contributed to *Sáng tạo.* The writers and editors of this magazine both expressed their conception and imagination about the development of literature and practiced it in their work. They conceived that the nature of art was diverse and progressive, and thus every artist needed to make the effort to follow their own path to reach true value. In this case, the history of art was the history of free creation and constant innovation. Mai Thảo discussed this idea in an important article on the magazine's one-year anniversary that likened writers to the athletes who climbed to the peak of the mountain of art from different sides.[25]

Thinking about innovations in literary history, Mai Thảo (representing the strategy of *Sáng tạo*) and Nguyễn Thành Vinh (representing the strategy of *Văn hoá ngày nay*) both argued that the free nature of art was also reflected in sublation: the path of art had always to confront and displace the old, even sublating itself when it was just born.[26] The history of art and literature considered from that perspective would require writers and artists to be able to envision and pursue its inevitable and continuous path to innovation. The constant process of innovation and sublation was both free and necessary.[27] Such visualized artistic perspective expressed a strong inspiration drawn from the new cultural space and from the aspiration of this generation to contribute to its construction "[following] their own aesthetic appeal."[28]

In another aspect of perspectives on literary history, Mai Thảo and the editors of literary magazines in this period argued that continuous innovation in literary history required the presence of different voices and a variety of experiments by writers and artists. In response to many readers' concerns that works published in *Sáng tạo* tended to be scattered, "lacking focus," "containing clashing viewpoints," and "contradictions," Mai Thảo argued that it was "absurd" to build a house of art on the same materials because art required constant revolutionary progress and therefore diversity.[29] He concluded this idea with an impressive image typical of his writing style: "It is only the unchanging minds and sick souls that deny that diversity and mistake it as chaos and disordered."[30] Thus, for them, diversity was an expression of creative freedom and a condition for the constant evolution of art history in its purest aspect: each different voice, by sublating each other, would cause art to make progress constantly. Such a perspective was one of the important contributions by writers and editors of this period in shaping the identity of the new literature.

However, each magazine had its own particular interpretation of what diversity meant. Explaining the characteristic of the *Văn hóa ngày nay* he had founded, Nhất Linh borrowed two verses on orchids to illustrate his vision: "Distilling the purest of dew and wind / Not only manifold differences in colors and nuances but also in fragrances" (*Kết tụ tinh anh của gió sương / Muôn màu muôn vẻ lại muôn hương*).[31] He also emphasized the magazine's policy to support "the manifold differences in colors and nuances." Here the image of the literary space that the magazine created in the minds of its readers suggested a diverse and differentiated scene. The variety that Nhất Linh had in mind was among "the purest," and because of that was perhaps somewhat limited and excluded what was not the purest in his view.[32]

Another interpretation of diversity is in the opening editorial of *Bách khoa*, when the managing editor called for a variety of views and voices that did not have to come "from the same religion," "from the same political views," or "from a single cohesive organization."[33] In this magazine, in addition to works showing the author's critical attitude toward the regime and society in North Vietnam, the magazine also published those recounting memories and expressing nostalgia toward the Việt Minh army by its former soldiers.[34] The conception of diversity here was more open, accepting new voices, however few.

The attitude of respecting and facilitating creative freedom of those who contributed to these magazines opened up an early stage of literature that was diverse, innovative, and exploratory. Poets and writers with different, even opposing styles, were numerous and some would become major literary figures of the later period. *Sáng tạo* had Trần Thanh Hiệp and Thanh Tâm Tuyền and their powerful innovative poems as well as Quách Thoại and his poems full of revolutionary inspirations. The absurd and surreal stories by Thạch Chương found their place next to Duy Thanh's realistic ones. *Văn hoá ngày nay* published works that continued prewar literature by Nhất Linh and Đỗ Đức Thu as well as renovation efforts by Bình Nguyên Lộc, Duy Lam, and Đặng Phi Bằng. *Bách khoa* contributed to literature with realistic works by Vũ Hạnh and Võ Phiến but also introduced new voices with a lyrical tone and the ideas of existentialism in the works of writers such as Hoàng Ngọc Tuấn, Nguyễn Thị Hoàng, and Nhã Ca.

In general, the literary magazines in the early years of the First Republic facilitated the development of diverse literary trends and styles. Their most important contribution was that they built an identity and thereby brought a historical perspective to the new literature. However, over time, doubts and criticisms emerged about their writing practices and literary innovations as well as about their argument that the liberal environment of the new era was a condition for works of high value.

CHALLENGES AND AFFIRMATIONS: IDENTITY CONFRONTING REALITY

From the last years of the First Republic to the beginning of the Second (1967–1975), these writers and editors did not envision or expect the oppressive political and social context that prevailed. Simultaneously, criticism emerged that literature and art had not fulfilled the task of building a new culture. This perception is evident in remarks and comments on the first issue of the magazine *Voice* (*Tiếng nói*). In the editorial that inaugurated the magazine in 1966, the managing editor—in the belief that the role of literature was to express the mind and consciousness of its time and to protect and promote that role—evaluated art and literature over the years. Art and literature, he argued, had been "helpless" until then in their mission, had failed to protect their values, had made no significant progress, and had not contributed to the zeitgeist (*ý thức sinh hoạt tinh thần*) of the age: "Therefore, in every recent [political] event, we could hear the voices and feel the power of Buddhists monks, Catholic priests, students, small traders, but we have not heard any voice nor felt the power of a writer or artist."[35] In terms of advances in art, some critics criticized the innovations made in an effort to build a new culture. They were considered to be "immoral, corrupt, unethical, rootless, foreign, and revolting art."[36] Another opinion mocked those innovations as obscure and opaque.[37] Still another considered the very free space at the beginning of the new age to be nothing but an empty space in which each person could no longer see or be seen by their predecessors; for that reason, they had no basis on which to develop and position themselves. The liberal space and environment in this view was no longer a condition for development; on the contrary, it destroyed development.[38]

On the one hand, these comments and others like them stemmed from premises other than the ones of early writers and editors. For the latter, art must rise above and not depend on the actual conditions of life; therefore, the demand for art to join social groups to fight against the autocratic rule of the Ngô Đình Diệm government was beyond its mission. On the other hand, the criticism also showed that the idea of those who advocated innovation and sublation in order to reach the highest value and essence of art was simply an ideal path. For art and literature to be influential, writers and editors had to meet the spiritual needs of readers and viewers; thus readers' and viewers' expectations and doubts about the relevance of the new literature in the political and social context of the 1960s was understandable.

Such critical judgments perhaps made Mai Thảo and those of like mind realize that their earlier imagination of a liberal art going beyond the constraints of reality needed some adjustments. In an article published in late 1965, Mai Thảo recalled the twenty-year history of Vietnam's path to independence. This path, he said, was covered in so much "blood, sweat, and tears." Art and literature, he concluded, must "enter into the reality of war" to show people the extraordinary and brave journey of the country.[39] Thus, in response to the demands of the reading public, the identity and perspective of the new literature had been adjusted from the original imaginations. Literature and art could not rely on innovation and avoid reality; instead, it needed to pay attention to reality and to the aspirations of people who were suffering daily because of the war.

However, for those writers, the identity of the new literature remained the freedom to write and make art in a social context that respected human freedom, at least at its core. In late 1960, faced with the charges that the *Sáng tạo* group's literary innovations were "immoral, alien, rootless, reactionary," Mai Thảo still expressed his confidence in the value and prospects of a literature built on the identity of creative freedom. Living in a liberal democracy embodied the brave choice of this generation, he argued: they should only "smile" in response to those accusations.[40] Five years later, a group of writers, some of whom had participated in the earlier *Sáng tạo* magazine, affirmed the notion: "Art is a free forum. Freedom is the first and eternal criterion of art."[41] To them, only a collective effort on the basis of freedom could help art overcome the dismal reality. In the imagination of these writers, the free identity of the new cultural space would of course create unwanted voices and criticism, but its value remained strong. At the same time, that criticism represented a great challenge, one that true art was obliged to face and overcome to prove its worth.

CONCLUSION

This chapter analyzes the contributions of three magazines to the literature of the First Republic, whereby they built up their identity and projected the vision of a new literary history while facilitating the diverse forms and creative innovations of literature. It points out various responses to that identity in later years, suggesting that the writers and editors of those magazines still believed in the value of the identity they had imagined and constructed. It also compares the thought and beliefs of their counterparts in the DRV to demonstrate differences in orientation between the two groups despite their shared paradigm of nation-building and identity construction in the prewar period.

From these findings, the chapter suggests an internal point of view from the perspective of the first generation of cultural builders of the RVN. The policy of the state and the regime could have been formulated from the point of view of decolonialization and the Cold War, in the context of the struggle against colonialism, feudalism, and communism. However, the writers and editors of the three magazines, who found themselves playing a role in building a new culture, were primarily concerned with imagining a new identity and a perspective of its future so that it could unite them as a community and help them create culture together. For them, this society was not a continuation but an entirely new beginning.

NOTES

We thank and are grateful to Tuong Vu for his valuable encouragement and suggestions as well as Nguyễn Mạnh Tiến (Institute of Literature) and Trần Hoài Thu (https://tranhoaithu42.com) for the valuable information they kindly provided us.

Epigraph. Trần Thanh Hiệp, "Passionate Journeys Each Season" ("Say những chuyến mùa đi"), *Sáng tạo* 2 (1956): 21–22.

1. Nu-Anh Tran, "Contested Identities: Nationalism in the Republic of Vietnam (1954–1963)" (PhD diss., University of California, Berkeley, 2013).

2. On the creation of a national literature and community identity, see the comparative analysis in Fredrik Engelstad, "National Literature, Collective Identity and Political Power," *Comparative Social Research* 21 (2001): 111–145. On constructing the national identity, see also Ruth Wodak, Rudolf de Cillia, Martin Reisigl, and Karin Liebhart, *The Discursive Construction of National Identity,* 2nd ed., trans. Angelika Hirsch, Richard Mitten, and J. W. Unger (Edinburgh: Edinburgh University Press, 2009).

3. Wodak et al., *Discursive Construction of National Identity,* 26.

4. From a social inclusion perspective, cultural differences and regional conflicts remained during the early resettlement period. See chapter 7, this volume.

5. See also the discussion in chapter 5, this volume.

6. The conditional character of freedom, including artistic freedom, was discussed at the National Cultural Congress, convened by the government from January 7 through January 16, 1957. During the conference, the Catholic priest and professor of philosophy Bửu Dưỡng argued that it was "necessary to adhere to personalist principles, to respect the conditions of freedom and independence of others and later to apply those principles to all the realms [of human activities] from family to society, from the national to international politics, from culture to the economy." See *Đại Hội Văn Hoá Toàn Quốc 1957* (Saigon: Xã Hội Ấn Quán, 1957), 50, http://ndclnh-mytho-usa.org /KhoSachCu/Dai%20Hoi%20Van%20Hoa%20Toan%20Quoc_.pdf (accessed April 21, 2022). When a member of the audience questioned the possibility of freedom to practice personalist principles in society, Bửu Dưỡng argued that one still could practice personalism while seeking to change

society. To him, living according to personalist principles involved having a responsibility to change society by first acting and spreading personalist beliefs at home (*Đại Hội Văn Hoá Toàn Quốc 1957*, 51). An idea of freedom within the scope of personalism as explained here was envisioned as a conditional freedom, implicitly expressed in the concept of responsibility, which is in fact a responsibility to society. The idea of conditional freedom was also evident in the Congress summary report:

> The purpose of all national activities is the full development in harmony and freedom of the individuals within all their social relationships . . . Within our own selves, the right to freedom of thought is unconditional freedom. [Yet,] when expressing our ideas, we must put our [national] Culture above [all], and it is the social responsibility of practitioners in the cultural realm that set conditions for the use of freedom of expressing and transmitting our thoughts. In terms of artistic pursuits, we cannot accept placing culture under [political] command. However, the country has the responsibility to support our people in the cultural realm because the purpose [*cứu cánh*] of our nation is to serve the people and culture is a form of human activity. (*Đại Hội Văn Hoá Toàn Quốc 1957*, 381–382)

7. See the speech by Professor Bửu Dưỡng and a summary of the address by presidential adviser Ngô Đình Nhu at the National Cultural Congress (*Đại Hội Văn Hoá Toàn Quốc 1957*, 41–50, 196–200).

8. "Văn hóa ngày nay với văn hóa Việt Nam," *Văn hóa ngày nay* 1 (June 17, 1958): 17–20.

9. Bách khoa, "Thay lời phi lộ," *Bách khoa* 1 (January 15, 1957): 1–2.

10. Nguyễn Vy Khanh claims that "it is well-known that *Bách Khoa* was founded to implement the policy to promote personalism" by the regime. However, our analysis agrees more with Võ Phiến's opinion (as quoted by Nguyễn Vy Khanh) that this magazine "broadly accommodated many [political] perspectives." See Nguyễn Vy Khanh, "Tạp chí Bách khoa và văn học miền nam," NamKyLucTinh.com, 2–3, http://www.namkyluctinh.com/a-tgtpham/nvkhanh/nvkhanh-bachkhoa.pdf (accessed August 15, 2019).

11. Mai Thảo, "Sài Gòn, thủ đô văn hoá Việt Nam," *Sáng tạo* 1 (1956): 1–4.

12. Mai Thảo, "Sài Gòn, thủ đô văn hoá Việt Nam," 1, 4.

13. Nu Anh Tran, "Contested Identities."

14. Quách Thoại, "Cờ dân chủ," *Sáng tạo* 3 (1956): 15–16.

15. For example, in the first article of a special issue of *Pioneer* (*Tiên phong*), an artistic and literary magazine of the National Salvation Culture Association published in Hanoi in the mid-1940s, the editorial board wrote,

> In the excited air of liberation, *Tiên phong* got out of clandestine operation, being intoxicated with independence and freedom, and constructing a flag of a 'new culture.' Being immersed in the common struggle of the nation, *Tiên phong* tries to walk on the open road in front of us, with the belief that our policy and our views would contribute to the construction of a new Vietnam. ("Huy động lực lượng văn hoá," special issue, *Tiên phong* 15–17 [August 19, 1946]: 3)

16. Nguyễn Đình Thi, "Xây dựng con người," special issue, *Tiên phong* 15–17 (August 19, 1946): 96.

17. In fact, *Sáng tạo* published a joint statement signed by eight contributing writers that explicitly stated that freedom was a condition for creativity. Doãn Quốc Sỹ, Duy Thanh, Mai Thảo, Mặc Đỗ, Nguyễn Sỹ Tế, Thanh Tâm Tuyền, Trần Thanh Hiệp, and Vũ Khắc Khoan expressed a shared commitment to "take advantage of the basic conditions of freedom and independence that are essential for the existence and development of thought, literature and art." See Doãn Quốc Sỹ et al., "Bản lên tiếng chung của tám tác giả Việt Nam," *Sáng tạo* 12 (September 1957): 1.

18. Nguyễn Thành Vinh, "Văn chương phải có giá trị vượt thời gian và không gian," *Văn hóa ngày nay* 1 (June 17, 1958): 22–25.

19. Văn hóa ngày nay, "Văn hóa ngày nay với văn hóa Việt Nam," *Văn hóa ngày nay* 1 (June 17, 1958): 17–20.

20. Mai Thảo, "Những ngón tay bắt được của giời," *Sáng tạo* 3 (December 1956): 7–14.

21. Nam Cao, "Đôi mắt," *Văn nghệ* (Việt Bắc zone) 2 (April 1948): 27–39.

22. This phrase was the subtitle of *Văn hóa ngày nay*. For more on the Self-Reliant Literary Group, see chapter 3, this volume.

23. "Trăng trong thơ," *Văn hóa ngày nay* 5, Mid-Autumn Festival special issue (1958): 148–149.

24. Nguyễn Thành Vinh, "Văn chương phải có giá trị vượt thời gian và không," *Văn hóa ngày nay* 1 (June 17, 1958): 22–25.

25. Mai Thảo described writers as climbers and the summit of the mountain as art: "A very sunny and very high mountain, the art is standing on the top, and the climbers to do the right thing to get to that beautiful peak must go on separate paths. Four mountain directions figure for the perfection, therefore, art denies the unidirectional regulation. There is not only one road, no monopoly of climbers." See Mai Thảo, "Một vài ý nghĩ gởi bạn đọc," *Sáng tạo* 13 (October 1957): 1–8. Trương Vũ asserts a friction between two opposing literary movements between *Sáng tạo* and *Văn hóa ngày nay*. We find that both magazines had much in common in their concepts of creative freedom, innovation, and value, but that the writers behind *Sáng tạo*, especially Mai Thảo, more forcefully aimed to look toward the new and displace the old. To create new things, according to Mai Thảo, there was no need to inherit the old. See Trương Vũ, "Vị trí của *Sáng tạo* trong sự phát triển văn học miền Nam sau năm 1954" (paper presented at the Hội Thảo về 20 Năm Văn Học Miền Nam, 1954–1975, Westminster, California, December 2014), http://www.tienve.org/home/activities/viewTopics.do?action=viewArtwork&artworkId=18389 (accessed April 21, 2022).

26. Mai Thảo, "Một vài ý nghĩ gởi bạn đọc"; and Nguyễn Thành Vinh, "Văn chương phải có giá trị vượt thời gian và không gian," *Văn hóa ngày nay* 1 (June 17, 1958): 22–25.

27. Several years later, Mai Thảo clarified this idea: "The new trends are the inevitable outcome of the dialectical process of artistic development in modern Vietnamese art. . . . They involve and contain the true voice and aspiration of a new generation of Vietnam, a generation that is aware of the evolution of history and art and is aware of its role to history and to art." See Mai Thảo, "Con đường trở thành và tiến tới của nghệ thuật hôm nay," *Sáng tạo*, n.s., 6 (December 1960-January 1961): 1–15.

28. Mai Thảo, "Sài Gòn, thủ đô văn hoá Việt Nam," 1, 4.

29. Mai Thảo, "Một vài ý nghĩ gởi bạn đọc."

30. Mai Thảo, "Một vài ý nghĩ gởi bạn đọc."

31. Nhất Linh explained these two verses as follows:

Văn hóa ngày nay not only uses these two verses to illustrate the painting on the cover, but also borrows these two verses to demonstrate its nature with an ambition to gather the essence of not only our country, but also other countries . . . The two verses also praise the principle of *Văn hóa ngày nay* that culture "must be manifold differences in color and nuance." ("Thơ vịnh lan," *Văn hóa ngày nay* 1 [June 17, 1958]: 21)

32. Văn Hóa Ngày Nay, "Văn hóa ngày nay với văn hóa Việt Nam."

33. Bách khoa, "Thay lời phi lộ."

34. *Bách khoa* was remarkably open to the voices and memories of those who sided with Việt Minh. For example, the magazine published a poem by Phan Lạc Tuyên that invoked the communist-led resistance. The poet recalled his time in the Việt Minh's Northwest military campaign of 1952–1953, dedicated the verses to his former comrades, and described the soldiers' arduous march through rugged mountains: "Remember the campaign in the old days / The road to the Northwest through sky-high mountains, / In Sơn La mountains followed mountains / Water bottle, rice tube, gun behind one's back / Than-Uyên's wind blew dust and stone / The fire lit up the nighttime forest, invoking memories" (*Nhớ về chiến dịch ngày nào / Đường lên Tây Bắc núi cao biếc trời / Sơn La dằng dặc núi điệp trùng; / Nước bầu cơm ống súng đeo lưng / Than-Uyên gió cuốn mù bụi đá / Lửa*

sáng rừng đêm gợi nhớ nhung). Phan Lạc Tuyên, "Đường lên Tây Bắc," *Bách khoa* 18 (October 1, 1957): 52.

35. Ban Chủ Biên, "Tiến tới vận động một nền văn học thật lực," *Tiếng nói* 1 (April 1966): 3–6.

36. Cited by Mai Thảo in his "Con đường trở thành và tiến tới của nghệ thuật hôm nay."

37. For example, the writer Thế Uyên suggested that the incomprehensible literary style of *Sáng tạo* enabled the magazine to evade censors and expressed frustration with the lack of freedom under the harsh censorship policy of regime. He recalled in the mid-1960s,

> Writing love stories was not easy because the government instructed censors that only certain kinds of love would be permitted to appear. There was a period of time I felt like whenever I described kisses, that passage would be censored, so I just wrote something like "he started-to-bend-down or she-started-looking-up" and then I stopped. . . . One time I became so irritated and told Duy Lam, "Well, perhaps we should try to imitate the obscure and opaque [*tối tăm*] style of *Sáng tạo* or just quit writing altogether. Imitating *Sáng tạo*'s writing was not easy because its style would require writing [in such a way that] readers could not understand—perhaps censors themselves did not understand either, so that's perhaps why it was relatively easy for the *Sáng tạo* group to publish under the old era?" (Thế Uyên, "Mười năm văn hóa kiểm duyệt Miền Nam," *Văn học* 40 [June 1965]: 14–18)

38. Indeed, the editors of *Voice* characterized the cultural space of the early RVN as empty rather than free:

> We entered an empty house, an abandoned garden, an uninhabited universe, there was really no one in front of us. Each of us picked up a stick and waved and danced up. We praised and criticized each other. For a while, we also disparaged our predecessors. No one responded— how excited! But once the excitement had faded, the subjective curtain fell to show the empty house [and] the deserted garden. (Ban Chủ Biên, "Tiến tới vận động một nền văn học thật lực")

39. Mai Thảo, "Văn học nghệ thuật trong chiến tranh hiện tại và hòa bình tương lai," *Nghệ thuật* 1 (October 1965): 5.

40. Mai Thảo described the possible responses of artists: "So, assume that the artists who are called vandals and rebels here, I say 'assume,' are concerned about the screaming denunciations and calls for punishment by the government, the artists can just evoke some minimal democratic principles, some minimal liberal rights, [and] a minimally democratic government, to smile [in response]." See Mai Thảo, "Con đường trở thành và tiến tới của nghệ thuật hôm nay." Mai Thảo's views on freedom are reminiscent of Northern poet Trần Dần, who insisted on the value of constant innovation as the nature of creative freedom. Living in different circumstances, the two writers pursued different methods. Trần Dần expressed his beliefs by quietly writing and Mai Thảo spoke out to protect and contribute to literary activities, but they both had a passionate and intense will for making true art.

41. "Ý nghĩa một cuộc họp mặt," *Nghệ thuật* 1 (October 1965): 4.

CHAPTER TEN

When State Propaganda Becomes Social Knowledge

Y Thien Nguyen

Save for its reference to the Republican administration and Ngô Đình Diệm, the following description penned in 1956 could very well have been written about the 1975 Fall of Saigon:

> And on this last attempt which was their 6th, they were finally fortunate enough to escape the fangs of the Việt Cộng to arrive at the shore of Freedom . . . [T]hey prepared fishing nets, faked a fishing expedition, but had to proceed in the dead of night. At communist police stations on the way, they had to keep women and children underneath the deck of the boat and had to cover the mouths of children to prevent them from coughing or crying as to avoid the suspecting eyes of the communist police. For some 7 to 8 days . . . the adults endured starvation and thirst to save rice and water for the children because, in fear of the communist police, they dared not bring with them much provisions. Floating on the vast ocean, placing their fate upon the winds and waves of the endless ocean. All they had was their belief, a firm belief in the protection of the Omnipotent and a hope; a hope yearning for a life of freedom and warmth under the safeguard protection of the Republican government led by President Ngô.[1]

One would need to look no further than Ham Tran's acclaimed 2007 film *Journey from the Fall.* The 1956 passage appears to articulate a scene-by-scene narration of passengers' experiences on the rickety fishing boat of Đại Nghĩa, from hiding below a deck and fleeing in the dead of night to the broader experiences of fear and desperation. The description—excerpted from a propaganda document of the Communist Denunciation Campaign (CDTC; Chiến Dịch Tố Cộng) waged under the regime of Ngô Đình Diệm—highlights themes all too familiar in Vietnamese American politics: freedom, flight, communist repression,

202

and sacrifice. These are the cornerstone of how Vietnamese Americans articulate rationale for, as one Vietnamese film reviewer puts it, "why are we here? Why were we forced to leave our homeland and chose some strange, faraway land to start our lives anew?"[2] In other words, it places the contemporary Vietnamese American experience within a historical narration of significance and meaning.

How is it that a story produced in the Republic of Vietnam (RVN) in 1956 can so closely resemble a Vietnamese American film released in 2007 about events in 1975? Despite commonalities in the migrations following the Geneva Accords and after the Fall of Saigon, the similarities in how these two events were depicted cannot be reduced to something innate in the events. Vietnamese America in 2007 and South Vietnam in 1956 were worlds apart, separated by regime changes, political turmoil, fragmentation, warfare, and, ultimately, forced migration. Indeed, the similarities between these two markers are less an obvious consequence of being refugees in flight of communism than they are the survival and perpetuation of a political narrative that dates to the formation of the First Republic (1955–1963) and continues to influence Vietnamese America today. This perpetuation is a political achievement of nation-building efforts on the part of the South Vietnamese republic in the context of war. This perpetuation makes Vietnamese America a political legacy of the ideological work designed to form not only an anticommunist Vietnamese nation, but also an anticommunist citizenry whose political loyalty will remain to that of the Republic, its flag, and its ideals.

The phenomenon of continuity between Republican Vietnam and Vietnamese America is an absent theme in both the Vietnamese American and the Vietnam War scholarship. That on Vietnamese America has largely emphasized "memories of war" and the trauma of the refugee journey as the root of Vietnamese American anticommunism. Despite a preoccupation with the Vietnamese past, the omission when it comes to the history of the anticommunist RVN is notable.[3] A reliance on memories rather than historical documentation has prevented empirical exploration into the ways in which the South Vietnamese republic bears—politically, symbolically, institutionally—on the Vietnamese diaspora. This inability of the Vietnamese American scholarship to actually interrogate the structural legacies of the southern Republic is in part the fault of the historiography on the Vietnam War. For much of the period after the war, the American scholarship emphasized the communists' conduct of war and American involvement in the conflict rather than the anticommunist republic that lost that war. Indeed, Republican Vietnam is all but absent.[4] Because such a documented history did not exist, the scholarship relied primarily on memories, oral histories, and the documentation trauma to provide insight to the relationship that Vietnamese Americans have to their past.

Yet another reason for such a historical omission of the RVN is perhaps possible. The 1956 description, as mentioned in passing, came from a piece of state propaganda crafted during a state campaign designed to legitimize a newly founded republic and to craft an anticommunist political culture in South Vietnam. The similarities between a piece of propaganda in 1956 and a contemporary film lauded as an articulation of silenced truth highlight a contradiction in the story that Vietnamese Americans tell themselves and others. The Vietnamese American story finds its moral reasoning in that of "refugee victimhood." This, in part, is a consequence of the way Vietnamese refugees were depicted as passive, desperate, and in need of American benevolence following the war and was a way Vietnamese Americans acquired state resources and legitimized their presence in the American fold.[5] Yet that "refugeeism"—one that is markedly anticommunist—resembles a Vietnamese state-enforced narrative that predates the war.[6] Indeed, it is as if Vietnamese American identity—the answers to that question of "why are we here?"—is but a mere consequence of state propaganda.

Historical continuity, in a sense, poses a contradiction to the constitution of Vietnamese American identity. On the one hand, Vietnamese Americans often trace their family histories to the South Vietnamese past. Their fathers, uncles, and grandfathers were once military officers of the Army of the Republic of Vietnam or had served in the Republican administration. Many families had lived through the destruction and death of war, are related to men who endured reeducation camps, and had left behind their homeland in hopes of a better life. On the other hand, Vietnamese American politics can be traced to the ideological work of the South Vietnamese republican state. Vietnamese Americans reuse the flag of the RVN, sing the Republican anthem at social and cultural ceremonies, deploy anticommunist terminologies that originated from the war, and publish oeuvres of pamphlets, books, and memoirs reminiscing on the anticommunist struggle, commemorating their fallen, and glorifying the Republican nation.

As Maurice Halbwachs argues, past events and experiences provide a collective framework through which the present is made intelligible.[7] However, how we engage the past is influenced by routine and patterns that have been externally imposed by states, institutions, or other sources of power.[8] Lived experiences are interpreted through these readily available and shared interpretative frameworks, allowing people to collectively make sense of their past.[9] This theoretical perspective in no way diminishes the real and lived experiences of Vietnamese refugees or the war experiences of the South Vietnamese people. Nor does it claim that Vietnamese American anticommunism is simply derivative of state messaging. Instead, it problematizes the interpretations attached to shared past events and centers on an important historical process in the making of anticommunist beliefs and politics. By critically examining the shared discourse through which lived experiences are interpreted rather than assuming interpretations are somehow innate to these experienced events themselves, scholars can be attentive to how embedded ideas, practices, and values are socially constructed and transformed, linking unquestioned beliefs in the present to their origins in the past.

This chapter is concerned with the historical continuity of anticommunism as an ideology. It attempts to articulate the process through which this historical continuity was possible by locating the mechanisms that ensured perpetuation, consistency, and routine. This historical continuity, as argued here, is not an automatic product of history. It is instead an achievement of purposeful human activities to create an ideologically unified nation that could combat the threat of Vietnamese communism. I use the Political Study Program (Chương Trình Học Tập Chính Trị)—an unstudied political education initiative that endured throughout the Republican era—to explore the ways in which anticommunist narratives were articulated and perpetuated. I hope to effectively demonstrate how the South Vietnamese anticommunist discourse was constructed, disseminated, used, and reused by the Republican state and to provide context for the knowledge and narratives that Vietnamese refugees carried with them as they arrived on American shores.

IDEOLOGY AND CONTINUITY

The Republican revival in Vietnam studies has been fruitful in articulating and documenting the political and social dynamics in the South during the war. What Nu-Anh Tran refers to as the "new Vietnam War scholarship" is taken as a challenge to the communist-centric literature that prioritizes documents from American, North Vietnamese, or the National Liberation Front (NLF) sources to craft the history of the Vietnam War.[10] Using documents from the Republic of Vietnam, this emerging scholarship attempts to recraft the republic as a politically autonomous, historical agent that played a major role in nation-building in South Vietnam.[11] Bringing the republic back has generated refreshing new scholarship that highlights the agency, relationships, programs, and ideals of the southern Republic.[12] Although many of these works focus on the Republican state itself, recent dissertations have also engaged the social universe of the Republican era, demonstrating the complexities and vibrancy of cultural politics of the South.[13] These trends indicate that the scholarship has begun moving beyond the military fronts of the war and into the "imagined community" being built behind them.

Despite these advances, the historiographic privileging of the First Republic over any other period of the Republican era prevents a satisfactory appraisal of continuity and change.[14] Although the Diệm administration was consequential in establishing the political and ideological foundations of the Republic, the period that followed is significant in transforming, contesting, and redefining values once laid out under Diệm. Indeed, the scholarship has yet to identify the mechanisms that could adequately explain how ideological narratives and state programs that originated in the First Republic could manifest after its demise. Although the recent trends in Vietnam War studies hearken to the Republic, its empirical coverage has been largely that of those first nine years rather than the twenty years of the Republican era as a whole.

When we seriously acknowledge that the republic extended beyond the death of Ngô Đình Diệm, immediately apparent is the historical consistency and hegemonization of what this chapter refers to as "Republican anticommunism," that is, the distinct form of anticommunism that developed in South Vietnam under the influence of the RVN. For much of the literature on the Vietnam War, anticommunism in South Vietnam is often depicted as an imitation or a reflection of American foreign policy. However, anticommunism as it existed in South Vietnam drew on stories, anecdotes, historical events, and ideological positions that did not necessarily reflect that of American Cold War concerns.[15] The anticommunism in question was one that was indigenously derived and entailed concepts, beliefs, and narratives unique to the Vietnamese experience.[16] A historically contextual and dynamic ideology, Republican anticommunism emerged organically out of the real activities of the people in South Vietnam and gained its emotional and affective appeal from how it relates to South Vietnamese conditions.[17] Indeed, for Republican anticommunism, it is the Vietnamese experience—not the experiences of other "peoples"—that are prioritized and mobilized. It was this anticommunism that was perpetuated and articulated in the Republican South, and it is this anticommunism that the scholarship must attend to in order to comprehensively understand the Republican era and the historical legacies it left behind. For this chapter, the constancy and persistence of Republican anticommunism as a hegemonic ideology is what requires explanation. As a consistent and hegemonic ideology, Republican anticommunism cannot be taken as a given of the Republican era. Instead, like all ideologies, it must be viewed as a product of ideological work by Vietnamese actors in South Vietnam.[18]

To explore the process through which Republican anticommunism was discursively articulated, disseminated, and perpetuated, as mentioned, I rely on an unstudied political education program enacted by the Republican state upon its civil servants and soldiers. Innocuously titled the Political Study Program (PSP), this initiative adopted a pedagogical format entailing regular study sessions, organized presentations, ideologically focused study materials, and group discussion. Study sessions regularly entailed a presider who served as both a discussion moderator and organizer, a presenter who orally summarized the study document, and a secretary who recorded the study session.

Examining the PSP is beneficial for several empirical reasons. First, the PSP was one of the few state projects implemented during the formation of the First Republic that survived to the end of the Second (1967–1975), providing a relatively complete chronology to trace the activities of the state's ideological work.

Second, the practice of political study was a routinized aspect of administrative life. Third, although the PSP was a regular practice within the administration, its designs were also enacted outside the state and it can function as a proxy to examine broader discourse generated in the media and through state propaganda. Last, although designed to be implemented nationwide, the PSP was most effectively implemented among members of the RVN administration and military—men and women who operated as the agents of the state.

This last point provides both empirical and theoretical contributions to the study of Republican anticommunism. First, the vast majority of works on the RVN focus on the high politics of the state and largely ignore the internal, quotidian dimensions of administrative work under the republic. To properly comprehend the effects of the Republican state, we must look to the state agents who carried out policies and programs. Without them, there would have been no Communist Denunciation Campaign, no Strategic Hamlet initiative, no Open Arms Program, or any of the other policies that made their way into the historical record.

Second, because the PSP can potentially shed light on the ideological work of civil servants and soldiers of the Republican state, examination of this program is essential for understanding the political and ideological knowledge that would eventually migrate to what is now Vietnamese America. Indeed, former state agents would later become political leaders and community organizers who wielded the power to influence the political and ideological direction of the Vietnamese American community.[19] The PSP thus sheds light on not only the ideological work of the Republican state during the Republican era, but also the legacy of that ideological work in Vietnamese America and how Republican anticommunism survived beyond the collapse of the RVN.

WHAT IS POLITICAL STUDY?

One of the few state projects that was implemented during the formation of the First Republic and actually survived to the end of the Second, the PSP was a mechanism of indoctrination and political warfare that aided the crafting, dissemination, and perpetuation of Republican political discourse. Initiated as a core aspect of the Communist Denunciation Campaign in 1955, the philosophy behind the PSP was that, through standardized study materials, organized presentations, and controlled discussions, political loyalty could be cultivated for the regime while ensuring that those attending these classes would "absorb" (*thấm nhuần*) the ideals of nationalism, anticommunism, and modernity. Indeed, it was not enough for students to simply know the materials presented; they were to integrate the lessons taught into everyday conduct and into the way they viewed the world, Vietnam, and their personal and leadership role in the development of the Vietnamese nation.

Original Concept of Political Study

Political study was conceived as part of a philosophy that sought to change the human condition. This change entailed not only the social and economic circumstances in which people lived, but also the way they thought, behaved, and acted. The idea behind these often two hour-long, weekly seminars were not only to convey ideology to participants, but also to ensure that the ideas presented permeated their minds and behavior. Such a pedagogical conception came about in tandem with the personalism of the Cần Lao Party (Personalist Labor Revolutionary Party). A philosophy premised on the holistic liberation of the totality of human existence, personalists advocated for a "personalist revolution" that would create a new society through the transformation of not only economic and political structures but also the remolding of individual thought, behavior, and spirit.[20]

For the Cần Lao Party, the starting point was the cadre. As early as January 1955, the party instituted a class called "study and discussion" (*học tập thảo luận*), during which party members would first learn, then ask, and finally enact.[21] These classes entailed presentational sessions when talks were given on ideological and political topics, and cadres were expected to integrate what was taught into their political, social, and everyday life. Outside these general conferences, local chapters that had the responsibility of "education and cultivation" were to provide cadres assignments that would aid in the practical application of the personalist ideal and ensure regular study, criticism, and self-criticism so that the cadre could develop morally and ideologically into a model representative of the party.[22]

During the Republican era, both state campaigns like the CDTC and initiatives like the PSP were modeled on the organizational and mobilizing structure of the Cần Lao Party. Although the First Republic collapsed in 1963, later revitalization of political study built on earlier models and adopted not only the organizational framework but also the philosophy behind the program. For much of its history, the PSP was structured in accordance to existing administrative divisions, the head of each ministry or department being responsible for political study activities within their jurisdiction. Like the training operations conducted in the Cần Lao Party, the PSP implemented regular sessions of ideological training, structured sessions in a presentation-discussion format, disseminated ideas from the top through a tightly monitored apparatus, and sought the transformation of an individual's mind and subsequently actions.

Institutional History of the PSP

Historically, structural changes to the PSP often reflected key administrative transitions within the Republican state. For the most part, political study activities were led by a central directing body that usually included the representatives from the Information Ministry, the Education Ministry, the Interior Ministry, and the Office of the President or the Prime Minister. Major changes within the governmental body, at times, shifted the composition of the central directing body but primary responsibility for organizing, implementing, and overseeing political study ultimately fell on the Ministry of Information or an administrative organ with comparable function. This central directing body had the responsibility of assigning and disseminating study materials and appraising the progress of political study from submitted reports (see table 10.1).

Although major administrative changes often brought with them different ideological emphases, values of nationalism and anticommunism were readily apparent in PSP materials regardless of which administration was in power. For the first three years of the First Republic, political study was under the supervision of the Ministry of Information headed by Trần Chánh Thành, who directed the CDTC. During this period, political study was largely a vehicle for proselytizing of Republican anticommunism, was dominated by ideologically trained and properly vetted CDTC cadres, and emphasized three themes: the condemnation of the Geneva Accords, anti-neutralism and the necessity of "resolute thoughts," and making known "communist atrocities."[23]

Table 10.1.   Administrative Changes to the Political Study Program

Phase	Time Span	Body Established for Oversight of PSP	Ideological Focus	Primary Directing Organ	Primary Official(s) Responsible	Administration
...ublic	August 1955– August 1958	Central Directive Committee for the Communist Denunciation Campaign (Ủy Ban Lãnh Đạo Chiến Dịch Tố Cộng)	Communist denunciation	Ministry of Information	Minister of Information Trần Chánh Thành	Prime Minister Ngô Đình Diệm (later president)
	August 1958– December 1960	Central Directive Committee for Political Study (Ủy Ban Hướng Dẫn Học Tập Trung Ương)	National development and international recognition	Ministry of Information	Minister of Information Trần Chánh Thành	President Ngô Đình Diệm

Table 10.1. (continued)

Phase	Time Span	Body Established for Oversight of PSP	Ideological Focus	Primary Directing Organ	Primary Official(s) Responsible	Administra
	January 1961– November 1963	Central Directive Committee for Political Study (Ủy Ban Hướng Dẫn Học Tập Trung Ương)	Personalism and South Vietnamese development	Directorate General of Information under the Ministry of Civic Action (Giám Đốc Thông Tin, Bộ Công Dân Vụ)	Ngô Đình Nhu (political adviser to the president), Director of Civic Action Ngô Trọng Hiếu, Director General of Information Phan Văn Tạo	President Ngô Diệm
Interregnum	June 1965– November 1967	Central Directive Council for Study Materials (Hội Đồng Hướng Dẫn Tài Liệu)	Democratic development and justification for military rule	Ministry of Psychological Warfare; Ministry of Information and Open Arms (Bộ Thông Tin Chiêu Hồi)	Minister of Psychological Warfare Đinh Trịnh Chính; Minister of Information and Open Arms Nguyễn Bảo Trị	Prime Minister Nguyễn Cao Kỳ
Second Republic	April 1968– May 1969	Central Directive Council for Study Materials (Hội Đồng Hướng Dẫn Tài Liệu)	President's position on peace and negotiations	Directorate General of Information; Ministry of Information	Director General of Information Nguyễn Ngọc Linh; Minister of Information Trần Văn Ân; Minister of Information Tôn Thất Thiện; Minister of Information Nguyễn Ngọc Ân	Prime Minister Trần Văn Hương

Table 10.1. (continued)

Phase	Time Span	Body Established for Oversight of PSP	Ideological Focus	Primary Directing Organ	Primary Official(s) Responsible	Administration
	May 1969–October 1969	Central Directive Committee for Political Study (Ủy Ban Chi Đạo Học Tập Trung Ương)	Peace, Paris Conference, and general mobilization for war effort	Ministry of Information	Minister of Information Nguyễn Ngọc Ân	Prime Minister Trần Văn Hương
	October 1969–December 1972	Committee for Political Encouragement (Ủy Ban Động Viên Chính Trị); Central Committee for General Information (Ủy Ban Thông Tin Đại Chúng, Trung Ương)	Peace, Paris Conference, and general mobilization for war effort	Central Council for Pacification and Development, Office of the Prime Minister (Hội Đồng Bình Định và Phát Triển Trung Ương, Phủ Thủ Tướng)	Minister of Information Ngô Khắc Tịnh; Minister of Information Trưởng Bửu Điện	Prime Minister Trần Thiện Khiêm
	January 1973–January 1975	Directorate General of Civic Mobilization (Phủ Tổng Ủy Dân Vận)	Paris Peace Accords	Directorate General of Civic Mobilization, Office of the President (Phủ Tổng Ủy Dân Vận, Phủ Tổng Thống)	Director of Civic Mobilization Hoàng Đức Nhã; Acting Minister of Information and Civic Mobilization Hồ Văn Châm	Prime Minister Trần Thiện Khiêm

Source: Author's tabulation.

The second period began in 1958, during which the PSP underwent a major structural reconfiguration in response to changing political imperatives to progressively move away from mere "communist denunciation" and toward national development and international recognition.[24] Leadership and oversight of the PSP moved from the Ministry of Information to the Office of the President, and local PSP activities were no longer led by CDTC cadres but headed instead by the highest-ranking individual in each organ. A tiered system was instituted in which rank 1 cadres were selected among state agents to draft study materials, attend specialized training, and serve as presenters and organizers for the lower-tier rank 2 cadres.[25] The last period of the PSP under the First Republic lasted from the beginning of 1961 until its collapse in 1963 and was marked by the dominating presence of personalism, emphasis on national development, and the Strategic Hamlet and the Open Arms Programs. As the main orchestrator of these two state initiatives, Ngô Đình Nhu took a leading role in PSP operations, the training of cadres, and the development of study materials.[26] Toward the end of the regime, the PSP was deployed to defend the regime's response to the Buddhist crisis of 1963.[27]

After the collapse of the First Republic, regular and systematic political study ceased for some twenty-odd months as the RVN experienced a period of political upsurge and social activism. In June 1965, when the military once again seized national power, the PSP was reestablished alongside various other initiatives of the Nguyễn Cao Kỳ administration to stabilize South Vietnamese society, revamp the war effort, exert state control, and eliminate all forms of social and political ills.[28] Refashioned as the Discussion Movement, the revived PSP was used to reinforce the political legitimacy of the National Leadership Council (Ủy Ban Lãnh Đạo Quốc Gia), refashion the military as champions of revolution and democracy, mobilize an increasingly apathetic population for anticommunist activities and war, and construct a modicum of national solidarity to stave off political unrest.[29] Like the PSP of the First Republic, the new Discussion Movement was a tool for indoctrination and propaganda.[30] Although the structural and theoretical components of the Discussion Movement differed very little from the PSP, the lack of cadre selection and training was notable, and individual organs were given greater autonomy on topics of study and scheduling.[31]

During the Second Republic, political study no longer emphasized the legitimacy of military rule but focused instead primarily on the position of the South Vietnamese republic in the Paris peace talks. Most important was the prospect of peace and the transfer of military duties to the RVN's military. The Nguyễn Văn Thiệu administration pushed themes of "self-reliance" and "self-sufficiency," attempting to convert the loss of American support for the war into an opportunity for South Vietnamese economic and political "self-determination" and progress.[32] This message sought to combat the daunting challenges brought about by the inevitability of American departure, assuage wavering public confidence, and rhetorically deflect calls for a new government in which the NLF would have a formal role.[33]

Catalyzed by the Tết Offensive, the ideological reach of the PSP greatly expanded under the Second Republic.[34] To push for an intensified ideological effort that could foment anticommunist solidarity around the Thiệu administration,[35] the Ministry of Information holistically reconfigured the PSP from February 1969 to April 1970. During this period, the program underwent different iterations, although each emphasized the regime's position at the Paris conference and is best understood as a step in a process that increasingly standardized study materials and sessions, centralized control over the political activities of individual administrative organs, and attempted to dispense the state ideological contents on a mass scale.[36] Structurally modeled on previous formats, the new PSP stressed the "regular, obvious, and necessary" nature of political study, increased programmatic coordination between various ministries, emphasized the selection and training of cadres, and implemented measures to ensure that state messages would systematically reach the broader population.[37]

The last phase of the PSP paralleled efforts by the Thiệu administration to establish the official narrative on the significance of the Paris Peace Accords and was largely an extension of the General Information Program. The PSP nevertheless did undergo a substantial structural change. In early January 1973, Thiệu disbanded the Ministry of Information and established instead a new General Directorate of Civic Mobilization. Widely interpreted as a move to shore up support for Thiệu in a potential contest for power following the accords, the new office was subsumed under the Office of the Presidency and headed by Hoàng Đức Nhã, Thiệu's thirty-year-old cousin, and appropriated the responsibilities of not only the Ministry of Information but also that of the presidential press secretary and several duties once delegated to the Department of Political Warfare.[38]

Structural changes did little to alter the actual operations of political study. Study materials continued to be sent out every month, regular cadre training conferences were held, and the ideological content of the period largely reflected the established anticommunist position on peace, though materials now framed the Paris Peace Accords as a political victory for the RVN, condemned communist violation of the ceasefire, and justified the administration's decision to sign the agreement.[39] However, as the South Vietnamese republic entered 1974, the administration became quickly embroiled in scandals and controversy resulting in national political turmoil and instability.[40] By the time North Vietnam launched its final offensive in January 1975, Saigon was on the verge of internal collapse.[41]

The gradual disintegration of the Republican state, strangely, registered very loosely with the PSP. Indeed, although the regime faced unending protests in its final year, study sessions continued to primarily emphasize the communist violations of the Paris Peace Accords rather than engage in direct defense of the regime. As communist forces took Phước Long province in January 1975, political study proceeded as usual in reviewing the previous two years after the Paris Peace Accords, condemning communism, and continuing to call for belief in the ultimate victory of the republic and its ideals.[42]

The seemingly anticlimactic end to the PSP highlights the embeddedness and quotidian nature of political study by the end of the RVN. Indeed, even as the nation was imploding within itself, political study seemed oddly divorced from national realities as sessions proceeded unhindered.[43] This odd removal from reality was in fact an achievement of the PSP—an achievement of routine and normalization. The practice of political study had become so regular and expected within the administration that even the prospect of internal collapse did not hamper its activities. The next section turns to how this routinization was achieved and segues into how the continuity of political study as practice allows for a continuity of South Vietnamese anticommunist ideas.

CONTINUITY OF PRACTICE

Since its early days, the Communist Denunciation Campaign emphasized the regularity of sessions and importance to which participants needed to grant political study, responding to the lackadaisical nature in which it was originally received. When Trần Chánh Thành initiated the PSP in August 1955, he requested that all state organs send capable representatives to nationwide training sessions on CDTC ideological topics. It was expected that those trained would return to their respective organs and begin regular study sessions. Despite the information minister's request for leaders and capable individuals, the few selected to attend the training courses were lower-level aides.[44] Dissatisfied, Trần Chánh Thành requested that Diệm formally demand that CDTC activities and political study be "consolidated" with "capable and responsible" individuals. For the minister of information, the study of CDTC materials needed to be taken as "a paramount activity." He lamented that "these organs have not yet recognized the importance of the CDTC."[45] The president responded as requested.[46]

Throughout the First Republic, frustration inherent to implementing a well-attended, regularized program of political study was evident. A memo from 1955, for example, bemoaned that state employees eschewed study sessions and instead "got together to converse outside [in] the alley."[47] Not only did participants skip study sessions, when they did attend, some had not read their materials beforehand and others did not even take notes.[48] Directives emphasized that participants must pay attention during sessions, engage materials with dedication, and not "view political study as a pastime." Participants used study sessions to "criticize individuals on issues that have no relation to Communist Denunciation."[49] Some viewed direct participation as a form of "punishment," hesitant and unwilling to approach the podium to speak.[50]

Attempts to rectify these issues began with the reconfiguration of the PSP in 1958. Guidelines emphasized the cultivation of a dedicated cohort of presenters who were eventually expected to devise ways to make sessions more "enthusiastic" by using "the black board, maps, pictures, statistics, concrete examples, realistic stories, the experience of different nations, etc." Understanding a successful session relied on "the ingenuity of the presenters," and guidelines dictated that organs must be carefully select presenters who had "cultural aptitude and know how to enthusiastically converse."[51] Other suggestions included organizing "cultural activities" during heated moments integrating occupation-related topics to be used alternatively with politics-related materials, and including talks on nonpolitical topics to liven up the quotidian drab of indoctrination.[52] Later PSP directives also explicated that absences were to be recorded and, as a rule, that the only valid excuses for absence were community service or hospitalization.[53]

Problems of regularity and participation would continue into later iterations of the PSP. Following the initiation of the Discussion Movement, for example, Minister of Psychological Warfare Đinh Trịnh Chính lauded the success of the project and suggested that formal guidelines be established.[54] This, however, masked the litany of concerns that administrative personnel had expressed over military rule, national austerity, cessation of civil liberties, and the halt in democratic progress that came with the rise to power of the National Leadership Council.[55] These discontents would manifest in slacking PSP participation during the Struggle Movement in 1966, reports noting poor performance in sessions. Đinh Trịnh Chính described reports that were submitted as "extremely meager" and requested that Kỳ take measures to rectify the issue.[56]

Although regularity was found wanting during the Interregnum (1963–1967), proper implementation of political study was emphasized during the Second Republic as the administration of Trần Thiện Khiêm channeled tremendous resources toward training cadres in methods of presentation and propaganda. In 1970, an extensive training program was implemented for leaders of study sessions. Covering four months, this training regimen entailed the participation of more than a thousand governmental personnel.[57] Training sessions dove not simply into ideological materials, but also into the history of political study practices, informational technology, methods of public speaking, rumor spreading, and even how to draft a news report.[58] As political study underwent reconfiguration and the General Information Program prepared for nationwide expansion, these skills were deemed necessary for the administrative men and women who would all be transformed into "information cadres" of the state.[59] In doing so, the Republican administration sought not only to ingrain a sense of importance for political study activities but also to provide knowledge of the various strategies that could enhance participation and enthusiasm.

Throughout the Republican era, the PSP was modified through various initiatives, tactics, suggestions, encouragement, and directives to combat the problems of participation and enthusiasm inherent in the practice. Although these issues were never completely resolved, the historical record indicates tremendous effort by different Republican administrations to ensure that political study was regular and routine in all state activities. The PSP, after all, was viewed as a vehicle through which capable and inspired cadres could be forged. This ideal motivated constant and unrelenting efforts by successive regimes to control the internal working of the practice. Moreover, the history of the PSP highlights the reuse of specific strategies such as routine reporting, attendance monitoring, and cadre training to resolve long-standing issues. This state effort helps explain the durability of the PSP despite numerous regime changes and frequent turmoil.

CONTINUITY OF IDEAS

The embeddedness of political study in the Republican administration was an achievement of real human effort to transform the practice into something institutionally routine. This routinization not only ensured that political study persisted as a practice, but also aided the normalization of ideological content read, discussed, and articulated in sessions. Themes, rationales, caricatures, and lessons related to the Geneva Accords of 1954 developed during the First Republic would make their way into the study documents of the Second. If the PSP of the First Republic was crucial to disseminating how the Geneva Accords were interpreted in the RVN, the PSP during the Second Republic reused the themes of communist violations and atrocities to frame the Paris Peace Accords of 1973. This reuse allowed the lessons taught in one period of the republic to apply to developments temporally removed from the events that originally inspired them. Given the strictures of the PSP, it was mandatory for state agents to internalize these lessons; repetition of these ideas over twenty-odd years transformed what was once a novel state narrative into presupposed truths habitually used to interpret new events and historical developments.

Narrative of the Geneva Accords

At its inception, the narrative on the Geneva Accords was politically intertwined with "communist denunciation" and Diệm's political legitimacy in his contest against Bảo Đại to become chief of state.[60] Diệm first came out against the accords four days before the first anniversary of the close of the Geneva Conference of 1954. Although the ceasefire had been signed a year before by the French and the Democratic Republic of Vietnam (DRV), Bảo Đại's State of Vietnam vehemently opposed both the process and the terms. The accords divided Vietnam into two temporary regroupment zones, established procedures for the regrouping of political and military forces, and scheduled nationwide elections for the reunification of Vietnam in July 1956.[61]

Then serving as prime minister of the State of Vietnam, Diệm's position on the Geneva Accords was adamant. As Diệm argued, although the State of Vietnam was committed to peace and national reunification, it rejected the proposal laid out in the accords because the independence and reunification of the country must be "in freedom, rather than in slavery." The communists were unlikely to satisfy the requirement of free and fair elections, Diệm asserted; he insisted that the communists demonstrate that they placed the "good of the nation" over that of communism. The foundations of independence and reunification must come through democracy and not through communist authoritarianism and terrorism. For Diệm, it was within the legal and political rights of the State of Vietnam to reject the accords. Also, because the State of Vietnam did not sign, his government was "not bound in any way by these agreements, signed against the will of the people."[62]

When the PSP was officially initiated as part of the CDTC in August 1955, Diệm's position on the accords became the ideological cornerstone for study documents. Among those assigned at that first conference for political study was the "Origins and Consequences of the Geneva Signing." The document recapped communist atrocities during the First Indochina War and explained that experiences during that war had demonstrated that the communists were deceivers "who wore the cloak of nationalism" and who hid their communist nature to exploit Vietnamese nationalism. Lackeys of international communism, the Vietnamese communists aimed to use the Geneva Accords to divide Vietnam into two countries and to "offer" the North to the Soviet Union and China.[63]

The depiction of Vietnamese communists as deceitful national sellouts who did the bidding of the "red imperialists" was a staple caricature during the First Republic. Another original CDTC study document depicted this betrayal as a "scheme" orchestrated by the Vietnamese communists in collaboration with the French colonialists. As argued, the betrayal rightfully provoked outrage and condemnation because the communist-induced war had subjected the "entirety of the Vietnamese people . . . [to] countless suffering." Emotionally laden, the narrative of the Geneva Accords bounded the communists—the deceivers—to a betrayal of Vietnamese nationalist yearnings and depicted them as perpetrators of the vivid horrors of war. The piece further details the deceptive nature of the communists' proposal of "normal relations" between the DRV and the State of

Vietnam, an innocuous sounding concept that would in actuality allow the communists to "infiltrate [and] dominate the country of Vietnam . . . through propaganda." The phrase was intended to "seduce" civilians and was part and parcel of the communists' promotion of peace as means to wage war. That is, if they could not fight militarily, the communists would engage psychologically and politically to "colonize" the South.[64]

During the approximate two-year span of the CDTC, the Geneva narrative was widely disseminated through study sessions, propaganda, cultural productions, and books. Indeed, by 1957, the minister of information confidently declared that the study of the topic had been completed in "virtually every locality."[65] As the CDTC ended, modifications were introduced to the narrative. The first major development came in 1957 as the RVN prepared for the third anniversary of the Geneva Accords. Although much of the content of study documents was similar, emphasis was laid on the issue of freedom to demarcate difference between the Republican South and the communist North. Indeed, as Trần Chánh Thành argued in a PSP directive from 1957, the failure of unification was not due to any actions of the republic; blame should instead be placed on the communists who failed to establish adequate conditions for free and fair elections. For the information minster, this was a fact, documented in a litany of evidence publicized through the CDTC that detailed the repressive authoritarianism experienced in the North.[66]

The contrast between the supposedly free South and the repressive North was an elaboration of the position the Republic had established in 1955. It built on demands made by the Saigon-based government, namely, the cessation of monitoring and the institution of democratic practices. In 1955, the position of the Republic had been that any elections for reunification had to be held "in conditions that are completely free" and demanded that the North provide evidence that they placed the "good of the nation above benefits for communism."[67] In 1957, those prerequisites were defined as "freedom of movement, freedom of organization, freedom of press, and freedom of occupation." The prerequisites of free and fair elections for reunification evolved into a broader strategy to pressure the Northern government to adhere to democratic practices. Believing that it was its duty to vocalize the suppressed voices of the North Vietnamese population, the Republican government mobilized for a "struggle to demand freedom and democratization of the North"—a staple political mantra for the years to come.[68]

The next year, 1958, also saw the beginning of the trend of castigating the DRV as military aggressors and violators of the Geneva Accords. Alongside its emphasis on democracy and freedom, the 1958 Declaration by the RVN pointed to increasing military build-up in the North as an indication that the communists were preparing for war.[69] This point did not come into full focus until January

1959, when the PSP was used to defend the South Vietnamese republic against a response by Prime Minister Phạm Văn Đồng of the DRV, who relayed denunciations against the RVN on Northern airwaves.[70] As argued in study materials, the allegation by Phạm Văn Đồng that the "South is preparing for war" was a propagandistic statement that disguised the mandatory military service and martial law of the North. A PSP session observed that the 150,000 troops of the RVN's military fell far short of the 350,000-strong North Vietnamese army. Using these statistics as evidence, study materials argued that the DRV should demilitarize to match the existing troop count of the RVN. The North, furthermore, refused to release its military numbers and national security expenditures to mask the fact that "when the Việt Cộng [Vietnamese communists] propose to lessen troop count, they are increasing it."[71]

Building on claims of Northern military aggression, the PSP turned to the issue of alleged communist violation to reinforce the Republican stance. As the White Papers released in July 1959 argued, "The Việt Cộng signed the Geneva Accords then, precisely the Việt Cộng, violated the agreements they had signed." The RVN, on the other hand, "did not sign the Geneva Accord . . . [but,] because we desire peace," had worked to implement the agreement. Elaborating on the White Papers, study materials of the PSP detailed a litany of alleged violations committed by the communists, particularly the expansion of the North Vietnamese military, importation of arms, and refusal to exchange all prisoners of war. Further, communist forces were left in the South to continue "war and terrorism against the people" while the DRV infiltrated additional forces to destabilize the RVN. Indeed, the White Papers depicted the continued narration of the communists "beating the drums while stealing"—that is, the communists called for peace while preparing for war.[72] Deception and treason remained fundamental aspects of the caricature but was extended to demonstrate aggression and violation against not just the Vietnamese people but also an international agreement.

The new themes of military aggression and violation of the accords became staple aspects of the Geneva narrative for the remainder of the First Republic. In study materials, the Geneva Accords were a turning point after which communist infiltrators began mobilizing armed insurgent activities. The accords thus historically signified not only the painful division of Vietnam as a country but also the starting point of subsequent suffering and atrocities.[73] The documentation of violations and atrocities allowed for South Vietnamese anticommunists to stifle the rhetoric of peace or neutrality—such as the call for peaceful coexistence or normal relations—as deceptive ideas propagated by international communism as part of its "schemes" to "colonize" or militarily infiltrate the RVN.[74] In 1961, one study session presented the question "How does the Việt Cộng hope to invade the South?" during discussion. The answer reflected the accepted narrative of the time: "The Việt Cộng utilizes the Geneva Accords. . . . They grasp onto that fallacious dream of [reunification] elections to infiltrate the South."[75]

Despite the death of Diệm in 1963, the Geneva narrative established under his rule continued into the Interregnum. Indeed, one of the lasting accomplishments of the administration of Nguyễn Khánh was the establishment of the National Day of Resentment (Ngày Quốc Hận). Beginning on July 20, 1964, the National Day of Resentment would become an annual commemorative occasion, marking the close of the Geneva Conference of 1954 and the signing of the Geneva Accords. Largely state orchestrated, the week leading up to the commemoration of "ten years of communist atrocities" involved state-funded public events stoking resentment toward the Geneva Accords.[76] Although the focus of these commemorations was directed at "communist atrocities," events proselytized the ideological rationale for a Northward March (Bắc Tiến)—a relatively vague political term that came to mean bringing the war to the North.[77] Seizing this ideological novelty, the Khánh administration used the Northward March to unify the discordant political components within the republic around an anticommunist drive centered on grievances about alleged communist atrocities and the possibility of military retribution.[78] Similar messages were deployed as part of the Discussion Movement to promote Kỳ's so-called National Front to Liberate the North.[79]

Under the Second Republic, the Geneva narrative took on novel dimensions applied to frame the peace negotiations under way in Paris. Because the process was wrought with controversy, the Thiệu administration sought to carefully toe the line between efforts to intensify war mobilization while participating in the ongoing peace talks. One of its core tactics, in light of the contradictions evident in the regime's diplomatic policies, was to return to certain aspects of the original Geneva narrative. Unlike in the early days of the CDTC, however, formal provisions within the Geneva Accords were initially embraced rather than rejected by the Thiệu administration. This aided the regime in justifying domestic policies and specific positions taken in peace negotiations.[80]

The position of the Thiệu administration on peace was consistently articulated through study sessions. Fundamentally, peace can be accomplished only if communists "withdraw all their troops from South Vietnam." As argued, the prospect of such peace was slim given the well-known duplicity of communist actions, and any promise of peace "is but a quackery for their war of annexation." The RVN would participate in the negotiations, but it had to remain vigilant.[81] The republic had to build up military and political potential because, "knowing the communists," peace could only be accomplished through the military defeat of the enemy. Given this premise, study documents provided rationale for the universal draft as well as renewed efforts to revamp the state's informational infrastructure.[82] Through the Geneva narrative, the Thiệu administration justified its opposition to any form of coalition government with the communist enemy, attacked neutralists as communist sympathizers, claimed military successes, and asserted its political autonomy in the negotiation process.[83] For the remainder of the RVN's existence, study documents continued the mantra that communists were military aggressors and the South Vietnamese republic was the victim of war, called for the mobilization of national reserves for the war, pointed to communist atrocities, and promised ultimate victory.[84]

Despite efforts by the Republican state to control the discussion on peace, critiques of alleged contradictions between the established Geneva narrative and Republican involvement in peace talks were widely evident, some arising within study sessions. Drawing on established precepts of communist duplicity and aggression, participants questioned the possibility of NLF involvement in elections through Thiệu's six-point peace plan, hearkened to the idea of the Northward March to urge immediate military action, and problematized the administration's position on the Geneva Accords that "we did not accept and did not sign." Unanswered in study sessions, these questions were sent to the Ministry of Information, which defended government policies by arguing that the RVN should engage with ongoing talks strategically, regurgitating the Republican mantra of peace, and presenting the Geneva Accords as the "best means" to conclude the war.[85]

As Washington and Hanoi neared a deal at the end of 1972, political study materials quickly reversed the Republican stance on negotiations and instead emphasized communist duplicity and the inevitability of communist violations of any signed treaties. Indeed, once signed, the Paris Peace Accords would be framed in accordance to the familiar rhetoric that had informed Republican policies for almost two decades. Thiệu's speech in October 1972 pointed to the history of communist duplicity, attacked the proposition of a coalition government in South Vietnam, emphasized the inevitability of treaty violation, and argued that caution that must be taken when a ceasefire was enacted. In his speech, Thiệu argued that a ceasefire must be seen not as a victory of the communists but instead as a victory of the RVN, which had militarily forced the communists to sue for peace. Thiệu hearkened back to the "situation in 1954 . . . [which demonstrated] the deceptive and cunning activities of the communists" and pushed for measures that could "immediately squeeze to death" all communist schemes. To "firmly deal" with the communists, the president called for a nationwide anticommunist effort to combat the communists' alleged propaganda of divisiveness, terrorism and coercion, and attempt to infiltrate the administration.[86]

Latching onto the political message of Thiệu's speech, the study sessions on the ceasefire reinforced themes of communist duplicity and the necessity of vigilance. A nationwide campaign, the effort entailed highly structured mass gatherings of state agents, soldiers, and the populace.[87] Intended to prevent the possibility of a communist offensive during the ceasefire, state directives laid out evacuation plans for rural communities, counterpropaganda strategies, and communist denunciation rallies in which "those with loved ones who were killed by communists" would speak out. General Information cadres were sent to various political and religious organizations to propagate for the regime, hosting daily and uniformed sessions with anticommunist slogans displayed and the Republican flag erected.[88]

Once the Paris Peace Accords was signed, another campaign was waged under Hoàng Đức Nhã to recapture the peace narrative by depicting the RVN as the victor in the peace deal. As argued, the agreement was an achievement of the Republican military, "which had defeated the communist invaders and forced them to sign."[89] However, study documents quickly returned to the issue of communist violations as sporadic fighting once again erupted. Once glorified as a Republican success, the accords quickly became a symbol of communist duplicity and aggression in violating ceasefire provisions. Subsequent study materials examined communist negotiations and strategies of deception, reemphasized the communist's intent to "colonize" South Vietnam and the RVN's good will in properly implementing provisions, described measures undertaken by communist forces to obstruct international monitoring during the ceasefire, attacked the Provisional Government of South Vietnam as an illegitimate entity that had no bargaining power, and listed various cases of guerrilla violence and troop movement that violated the accords.[90] As was consistent throughout the Republic, the PSP continued to denounce alleged communist schemes to "intentionally destroy the Paris Accords," violate its measures, and threaten to peace until the very last of study sessions.[91]

CONCLUSION

The Vietnamese American community came about through the mass migration of South Vietnamese bodies following the collapse of the RVN in 1975. These Vietnamese refugees were not blank slates on which the values and beliefs of the host country could be written; they came instead with their own set of historically derived knowledge. Vietnamese refugees carried with them state-derived, anticommunist knowledge about their nation, about their war, and about the peace that should have come. This knowledge, instead of vanishing into the historical abyss, was reframed and reused as Vietnamese Americans created their communities.

An extended historical exploration of anticommunism as it exists in Vietnamese America goes beyond the confines of this chapter. Suffice it to say, however, anticommunist narratives, symbols, and rhetoric derived from the war persisted and continue to persist in Vietnamese American politics.[92] Take, for example, Vietnamese American depictions of the Geneva Accords during the Phục Quốc Movement (Homeland Restoration Movement) of the 1980s.[93] Led by Hoàng Cơ Minh, the National United Front for the Liberation of Vietnam (NUFLV; Mặt Trận Quốc Gia Thống Nhất Giải Phóng Việt Nam) sought to mobilize support by deploying familiar themes drawn from the ingrained narrative on the Geneva Accords to situate the contemporary plight that Vietnamese refugees experienced. In a propaganda pamphlet from 1982, photographs of death and destruction caused during and after the war were evocatively used to conjure an image of perpetual communist brutality. In one photograph depicting communist tanks, the caption reads, "Immediately after signing the Geneva Accords, the Northern Communists trampled them underfoot, invaded and occupied the South with weapons and the full support of Russia." Beside it was an image of a rickety craft floating above the seas under the caption, "In 1954 . . . more than 800,000 people had to flee to the South by every means." Similar images and messages were depicted of the postwar era, conjoining themes of communist brutality and migratory flight.[94] It was by appealing to familiar anticommunist themes that the NUFLV received the outpouring of support it did. In contemporary Vietnamese American politics, alleged communist atrocities—both personal and national—were mobilized to provide moral and ideological justifications to contest the passage of Bill AB22 in California, which would allow state employees to be members of a communist party, or to push for a "no-communist zone" in Westminster and Garden Grove, California.[95]

That Vietnamese America looks as anticommunist as it does today is a legacy of the active and regular ideological work of the Republican state. Far from an accident of history, Republican anticommunism was the product of purposeful and meaningful human activities. Yet anticommunism has transformed into something more than just propaganda. It is a mode of meaning-making embedded into how Vietnamese Americans understand themselves, their community, and their past.[96] The anticommunist frameworks that were novel at their point of inception in 1955 are now readily drawn-on, presumed discourses used to not only politically mobilize against contemporary human rights violations in Vietnam but also push for legal measures to protect Vietnamese America from communist infiltration. Anticommunism is part and parcel of how Vietnamese American narrate and retell the stories of their lives and their experiences in the war.

Vietnamese Americans are thus historically constituted subjects—a historical constitution that does not exist without the South Vietnamese republic—and the study of the republic allows historical contextualization for the issues, politics, and norms that prevail in a present-day community. It permits the history of the RVN to take on dimensions that are not geographically or temporally contained. Instead, as scholars, we can begin to talk about the contemporary legacies and relevance of a political entity that has ceased to formally exist some four decades ago and spatially removed half a world away. Our discussion can begin to shed light on the ways in which knowledge, ideas, institutions, norms, values, and beliefs that belonged to a lost era can somehow survive. The legacies of the South Vietnamese republic are yet to be fully explored. As scholars on the era, perhaps it is time that we do so.

NOTES

1. "Đồng bào Bắc Việt vẫn tiếp tục thoát ly vùng Việt Cộng, vào Nam tìm tự do," circa 1956, Folder 52, General Commission for Migrants and Refugees Collection (Phông Phủ Tổng Ủy Di Cư và Tỵ Nạn [PTUDCTN]), National Archives Center 2 (Trung Tâm Lưu Trữ Quốc Gia 2 [TTLTQG2]), Ho Chi Minh City.

2. Thanh Nguyên, "Sáu năm cho một cuốn phim Vượt Sóng—Journey from the Fall (Kỳ 2)," *Người Việt Daily News,* March 20, 2007, https://web.archive.org/web/20070328173936/http://www .nguoi-viet.com/absolutenm/anmviewer.asp?a=57305&z=124 (accessed April 21, 2022).

3. For example, see C. N. Le, "Better Dead Than Red: Anti-communist Politics among Vietnamese Americans," in *Anti-communist Minorities in the U.S.: Political Activism of Ethnic Refugees,* ed. Ieva Zake (New York: Palgrave Macmillan, 2009), 189–210; Karin Aguilar-San Juan, *Little Saigons: Staying Vietnamese in America* (Minneapolis: University of Minnesota Press, 2009); Thuy Thanh Vo-Dang, "Anticommunism as Cultural Praxis: South Vietnam, War, and Refugee Memories in the Vietnamese American Community" (PhD diss., University of California, San Diego, 2008); Yen Le Espiritu, *Body Counts: The Vietnam War and Militarized Refuge(es)* (Oakland: University of California Press, 2014); and Viet Thanh Nguyen, *Nothing Ever Dies: Vietnam and the Memory of War* (Cambridge, MA: Harvard University Press, 2016).

4. William Duiker, *The Communist Road to Power in Vietnam* (Boulder, CO: Westview Press, 1981); Marilyn Young, *The Vietnam Wars: 1945–1990* (New York: Harper Perennial, 1991); Mark Lawrence, *The Vietnam War: A Concise International History* (New York: Oxford University Press, 2008); and Fredrik Logevall, *Embers of War: The Fall of an Empire and the Making of America's Vietnam* (New York: Random House, 2012).

5. Espiritu, *Body Counts,* 1–23.

6. For a definition of refugeeism, see James Morrissey, "Migration, Resettlement, and Refugeeism: Issues in Medical Anthropology," *Medical Anthropology Quarterly* 15, no. 1 (1983): 3, 11–14. For use of the concept in Asian American studies, see Trịnh T. Minh-Hà, *Elsewhere, Within Here: Immigration, Refugeeism and the Boundary Event* (New York: Routledge, 2010). Anticommunism was "enforced" in the sense that laws, constitutions, and state-directed programs in the RVN explicitly made it criminal to be a communist or be affiliated with communist guerrillas. Anticommunism—as the political ideology guiding state action—was enforced through the state's military, legal, and political apparatus. For examples of anticommunist legal measures under the First Republic, see Ordinance 47 of 1956, Law 10/59, and Law 91 ("Tòa án quân sự đặc biệt đã thành lập," *Saigon mới,* June 1, 1959; Mike Gravel, ed., "Origins of the Insurgency in South Vietnam, 1954–1960," chapter 5 in *Pentagon Papers: The Defense Department History of United States Descision Making on Vietnam,* vol. 1 [Boston, MA: Beacon Press, 1971], 242–269; and "Quốc hội đã chập thuận dự luật 91: Lập tòa án đặc biệt," *Saigon mới,* April 30, 1959). Law 093-SK/CT passed under Nguyễn Khánh placed heavy penalties on communists and communist sympathizers ("Lần đầu tiên, chính phủ chống cộng miền Nam VN," *Tự do,* February 18, 1964). The constitutions of both the First and Second Republics (Articles 7 and 4, respectively) made explicit that all

communist-related activities were illegal. For the constitutions, see "Nguyên văn bản Hiến pháp Cộng Hòa VN đã được Tổng Thống sửa đổi và Quốc hội chấp thuận," *Saigon mới,* October 26, 1956; "Hiến pháp Việt Nam Cộng Hòa," May 24, 1967, Folder 29738, Office of the Prime Minister Collection (Phông Phủ Thủ Tướng Việt Nam Cộng Hòa [PThTVNCH]), TTLTQG2.

7. Maurice Halbwachs, *On Collective Memory* (Chicago: University of Chicago Press, 1992).

8. Eric Hobsbawm, "Introduction: Inventing Traditions," in *The Invention of Tradition,* ed. Eric Hobsbawn and Terrence Ranger (New York: Cambridge University Press, 1983), 1–14.

9. Jeffrey Alexander, "Toward a Theory of Cultural Trauma," in *Cultural Trauma and Collective Identity,* ed. Jeffrey Alexander et al. (Oakland: University of California Press, 2004), 8; and Y Thien Nguyen, "(Re)Making the South Vietnamese Past in America," *Journal of Asian American Studies,* 21, no. 1 (2018): 65–103.

10. Nu-Anh Tran, "Contested Identities: Nationalism in the Republic of Vietnam (1954–1963)" (PhD diss., University of California, Berkeley, 2013), 3–12.

11. Edward Miller, *Misalliance: Ngô Đình Diệm, the United States, and the Fate of South Vietnam* (Cambridge, MA: Harvard University Press, 2013); Philip Catton, *Diem's Final Failure* (Lawrence: University Press of Kansas, 2002); Matthew Masur, "Hearts and Minds: Cultural Nation-Building in South Vietnam, 1954–1963" (PhD diss., Ohio State University, 2004); and Geoffrey C. Stewart, *Vietnam's Lost Revolution: Ngô Đình Diệm's Failure to Build an Independent Nation, 1955–1963* (New York: Cambridge University Press, 2017).

12. For example, see Jessica Chapman, "Debating the Will of Heaven: South Vietnamese Politics and Nationalism in the International Perspective, 1954–1956" (PhD diss., University of California, Santa Barbara, 2006); David Biggs, "Americans in An Giang: Nation Building and the Particularities of Place in the Mekong Delta, 1966–1973," *Journal of Vietnamese Studies* 4, no. 3 (2009): 139–172; and Miller, *Misalliance.*

13. Tuan Hoang, "Ideology in Urban South Vietnam, 1950–1975" (PhD diss., University of Notre Dame, 2013); Huong Thi Diu Nguyen, "Eve of Destruction: A Social History of Vietnam's Royal City, 1957–1967" (PhD diss., University of Washington, 2017); and Mei Feng Mok, "Negotiating Community and Nation in Cho Lon: Nation-Building, Community-Building and Transnationalism in Everyday Life during the Republic of Vietnam, 1955–1975 (PhD diss., University of Washington, 2016).

14. Most books that grant the Republican government or South Vietnamese society a degree of agency have focused on the First Republic. The period of the Interregnum and the Second Republic remains greatly underexplored, and only a handful of scholars have sought to address some of the dimensions of domestic politics and society in the post-Diệm period. More recent general surveys of Vietnamese history do not examine the ideological, social, political, and institutional dimensions of the RVN in enough depth to consider the question of continuity and change that concern this chapter. For studies that privilege the First Republic, see Miller, *Misalliance*; Catton, *Diem's Final Failure*; and Stewart, *Vietnam's Lost Revolution.* For studies that examine the Interregnum and the Second Republic, see Olga Dror, *Making Two Vietnams: War and Youth Identities, 1965–1975* (Cambridge: Cambridge University Press, 2018), Van Nguyen-Marshall, "Student Activism in Time of War: Youth in the Republic of Vietnam, 1960s-1970s," *Journal of Vietnamese Studies* 10, no. 2 (2015): 43–81; and Sean Fear, "The Rise and Fall of the Second Republic: Domestic Politics and Civil Society in US-South Vietnamese Relations, 1967–1971" (PhD diss., Cornell University, 2016). For general surveys, see Christopher Goscha, *Vietnam: A New History* (New York: Basic Books, 2016); and Keith Taylor, *A History of the Vietnamese* (New York: Cambridge University Press, 2013).

15. Miller, *Misalliance,* 13–18.

16. See Tran, "Contested Identities," 3–9; and Olga Dror, "Raising Vietnamese: War and Youth in the South in the Early 1970s," *Journal of Southeast Asian Studies* 44, no. 1 (2013): 74–99. Vietnamese anticommunism has been defined as an "alternative nationalism" (Vo-Dang, "Anticommunism as Cultural Praxis," 10) or one of "two competing models for building a modern

nation" (Neil Jameson, *Understanding Vietnam* [Berkeley: University of California Press, 1993], 176).

17. Y Nguyen, "(Re)Making the South Vietnamese Past."

18. By "hegemonic," I mean the pervasive and dominating presence of an ideology that is reinforced and supported through power. These dominating ideas are engaged in a "process of continuous creation" and are shaped by the historical engagement of human actors (Walter Adamson, *Hegemony and Revolution: A Study of Antonio Gramsci's Political and Cultural Theory* [Oakland: University of California Press, 1980], 174). Although hegemonic ideas function to politically legitimize those in power, they also function as a broad interpretive "grid" or "cultural script" for people to frame and articulate their reality (Karen Fields and Barbara Fields, *Racecraft: The Soul of Inequality in American Life* [New York: Verso, 2012], 134; and Jose Itzigsohn and Matthias vom Hau, "Unfinished Imagined Communities: States, Social Movements, and Nationalism in Latin America," *Theory and Society* 35 [2006]: 193–212). "Hegemonic," in this sense, does not suggest an exclusivity in ideas, but instead the prevalence and dominance of a set of beliefs within a society. For relationship between routinization and ideology, see Eric Hobsbawn, "Introduction: Inventing Traditions," in *The Invention of Tradition,* ed. Eric Hobsbawm and Terrence Ranger (New York: Cambridge University Press, 1983); and Hobsbawn, "Mass-Producing Traditions: Europe, 1870–1914," in *The Invention of Tradition,* 263–307.

19. Y Nguyen, "(Re)Making the South Vietnamese Past."

20. "*Đảng cương Cần Lao Nhân Vị Cách Mạng Đảng,*" circa 1955, Folder 29361, PThTVNCH, TTLTQG2.

21. "Đề án kế hoạch công tác toàn bộ của Ban chấp hành Kỳ bộ Bắc Việt ngày 28-1-1955," January 28, 1955, Folder 29361, PThTVNCH, TTLTQG2.

22. "Đề án kế hoạch công tác toàn bộ của Ban chấp hành Kỳ bộ Bắc Việt ngày 28-1-1955"; "Dự án tổ chức cán bộ," circa 1955, Folder 29361, PThTVNCH, TTLTQG2.

23. Trần Chánh Thành to Prime Minister, August 4, 1955, and Trần Chánh Thành to Prime Minister, 1578/BTT/VP, August 13, 1955, in Folder 14734, PThTVNCH, TTLTQG2.

24. For Diệm's emphasis on development, see "Lễ Quốc Khánh, ngày 26–10–58 Hiệu triệu của Tổng Thống," *Saigon mới,* October 27, 1958.

25. "Chương trình học tập," August 18, 1958, Folder 20030, Office of the President Collection, First Republic (Phông Phủ Tổng Thống Đệ Nhất Cộng Hòa [PTTĐICH]), TTLTQG2.

26. Tracing the flow of memos and directives points to leadership by Diệm's political adviser Ngô Đình Nhu and the Special Commissariat for Civic Action. See Folder 20530, PTTĐICH, TTLTQG2. For study materials on the Strategic Hamlets and Strategic Areas (Khu Chiến Lược), see *Chiến Sĩ,* 84–93 (1962). The periodical regularly reported on the political study of governmental organs. On the connection between personalism (*nhân vị*) and human rights (*nhân quyền*), see "Kỷ niệm Tuyên ngôn quốc tế nhân quyền 10–12–1962," January 2, 1963, Folder 3463, General Department of Customs Collection (Phông Tổng Quan Thuế [TQT]), TTLTQG2. For study material on the Open Arms Program, see Minister of Health to Political Study Leaders, September 5, 1963, Folder 3031, Ministry of Health Collection (Phông Bộ Y Tế [BYT]), TTLTQG2.

27. Correspondence from the director of Tax Administration to Political Study Leaders, 4020-QT/HDHT, June 6, 1963; "Chương trình học tập đề tài: 'Bản Hiệu triệu của Tổng Thống Ngày 18/7/1963,'" July 31, 1963; director of Tax Administration to Political Study Leaders on the study of the government statement delivered August 21, August 29, 1963; "Thông cáo số 3," June 26, 1963; "Thông cáo số 4 của Phong Trào Thanh Niên Cộng Hòa," July 1, 1963; "Vấn đề tôn trọng nhân quyền," 153-CDV/TT/KHCT, September 16, 1963, Folder 3463, TQT, TTLTQG2.

28. For austerity measures and restriction of civil liberties with the inauguration of the Kỳ administration, see "Ky New Saigon Premier," *New York Times,* June 19, 1965; "Saigon Official Calls for 'War Government,'" *Los Angeles Times,* June 14, 1965. For the correction of social ills, see "Saigon Bars Dating with Americans," *Los Angeles Times,* July 25, 1965. On firing squads to

execute criminals, communists and war profiteers, see "Saigon Sets Up Firing Squad Posts in Crackdown," *Atlanta Constitution,* June 17, 1965.

29. "War Apathy Seen in South Viet Nam," *Boston Globe,* July 19, 1965.

30. Nguyễn Cao Kỳ to various ministries, 44-UBHP/CT, July 3, 1965, Folder 3726, TQT, TTLTQG2.

31. Nguyễn Cao Kỳ to various ministries, 69/UBHP/CT, October 11, 1965, Folder 3726, TQT, TTLTQG2.

32. Study materials: "Làm thế nào để tự quản," August 17, 1970; "Làm thế nào để tự túc," August 20, 1970; "làm thế nào để tự phòng," August 21, 1970; "Tại sao ta phải tự chế và làm thế nào để tự chế," September 21, 1970, Folder 30450, PThTVNCH, TTLTQG2; "Làm thế nào để tự lực cánh sinh," cited in PSP Report for October 1969, November 17, 1969, Folder 30271, PThTVNCH, TTLTQG2.

33. Study materials: "Tại sao chưa có hòa bình?" March 2, 1968, Folder 29918, PThTVNCH, TTLTQG2; "Không liên hiệp với cộng sản," July 16, 1969, Folder 299, Office of National Archives Collection (Phông Nha Văn Khố Quốc Gia [NVKQG]), TTLTQG2; "Tại sao chúng ta chủ trương 4 không?" August 18, 1971, Folder 3031, BYT, TTLTQG2.

34. Director of Psychological Warfare in 2nd Tactical Zone to Provincial Heads, September 26, 1968, Folder 29918, PThTVNCH, TTLTQG2.

35. Trần Văn Ân to Information Subsidiaries, April 15, 1968, Folder 29916, PThTVNCH, TTLTQG2.

36. See "Biên bản phiên họp Ủy Ban Điều Hợp Tâm Lý Chiến Trung Ương ngày 27-2-1969 tại Bộ Thông Tin," March 3, 1969, Folder 30273, PThTVNCH, TTLTQG2. For similar outlines established for the General Information Program, see "Thông tư Thủ Tướng Chánh Phủ v/v thực thi chương trình Thông Tin Đại Chúng," circa 1970, Folder 30445, PThTVNCH, TTLTQG2.

37. For the quote, see "Thông tư Thủ Tướng Chánh Phủ v/v tổ chức 'Phong Trào Học Tập Toàn Quốc,'" May 16, 1969, Folder 30273, PThTVNCH, TTLTQG2. For the coordination between ministries, training of cadres, and implementation, see Nguyễn Ngọc An to various ministries, July 31, 1969, Folder 30273, PThTVNCH, TTLTQG2; Ngô Khắc Tinh to information subsidiaries, April 9, 1970, Folder 30445, PThTVNCH, TTLTQG2; Trần Thiện Khiêm to various ministers, August 15, 1970, Folder 30445, PThTVNCH, TTLTQG2; General Office of the Prime Minister to affiliated organs, October 2, 1970, Folder 30445, PThTVNCH, TTLTQG2; "Kế hoạch tổ chức các buổi nói chuyện của các đảng phái chánh trị và tôn giáo với đoàn ngũ NDTV trên toàn quốc," circa 1972, Folder 30922, PThTVNCH, TTLTQG2; and "Chiến dịch Hậu Phương Yểm Trợ Tiền Tuyến" May 5, 1972, Folder 30922, PThTVNCH, TTLTQG2.

38. "Thieu Picks Cousin for Key Position," *Los Angeles Times,* January 11, 1973; and "Saigon's New Chief Spokesman," *New York Times,* January 11, 1973.

39. "Những bài học hòa đàm với Cộng Sản," October 22, 1973, Folder 31568, PThTVNCH, TTLTQG2; and "Những nỗ lực vô vọng trên mặt trận ngoại giao của CSBV trong tháng 11.1973," December 4, 1973, Folder 7757, Office of the President Collection, Second Republic (Phông Phủ Tổng Thống Đệ Nhị Cộng Hòa [PTTĐIICH]), TTLTQG2.

40. "Backers Ram Through Amendment: Thieu Made Eligible to Run for Third Term," *Los Angeles Times,* January 20, 1974; and "Most of Cabinet in Saigon Resigns," *New York Times,* February 17, 1974,

41. "All Guns, No Butter Make Saigon Desperate Town," *The Sun,* May 8, 1974; "Mood in Saigon Is That 'With Thieu There Is No Hope,'" *The Sun,* November 3, 1974; "Saigon Arrests Put at 17 in a Crackdown on Press," *New York Times,* February 5, 1975; and "Protest by Senators, Monks," *Washington Post,* April 1, 1975.

42. "Tổng kết hai năm ký kết Hiệp Định Ba Lê (27.1.1973–27.1.1975)," January 22, 1975, Folder 31568, PThTVNCH, TTLTQG2.

43. Report by Mayor of Saigon to Minister of the Interior, 1045/KH, December 18, 1974, Folder 31331, PThTVNCH, TTLTQG2.

44. Trần Chánh Thành to Office of the Prime Minister, 1468-BTT/VP, August 4, 1955; and Trần Chánh Thành to Office of the Prime Minister, 1477-BTT/VP, August 4, 1955, Folder 14734, PThTVNCH.

45. Trần Chánh Thành to Office of the Prime Minister, August 23, 1955, Folder 14734, PThTVNCH.

46. Ngô Đình Diệm to various ministries, August 25, 1955, Folder 14734, PThTVNCH.

47. General Office of the Prime Minister, to affiliated organs, August 30, 1955, Folder 14734, PThTVNCH.

48. "Báo cáo tổng kết của ban Chỉ Đạo Chiến Dịch Tố Cộng tại Phủ Tổng Thống," September 27, 1955, Folder 14734, PThTVNCH.

49. Trần Chánh Thành to CDTC branches, circa 1957, Folder 4922, PTTĐICH, TTLTQG2; and "Học tập chính trị," November 12, 1955, Folder 52, PTUDCTN, TTLTQG2.

50. Letter of critique and suggestions by participants sent to the Chairman of Representative Assembly of the South, November 21, 1955, Folder F 6-57/2425, Government Delegate of Southern Vietnam Collection (Phông Tòa Đại Biểu Chính Phủ Nam Phần [TĐBCPNP]), TTLTQG2.

51. "Chương trình học tập," August 18, 1958, Folder 3031, BYT, TTLTQG2.

52. "Học tập chinh trị," November 12, 1955, Folder 52, PTUDCTN, TTLTQG2; and Ngô Đình Diệm to various ministers, 15-TT/TN, October 14, 1956, Folder 53, PTUDCTN, TTLTQG2. For an example of including nonpolitical topics, see the decision of the Ministry of the Economy to invite an editor of a journal to discuss contemporary trends in theater arts in November 1958. See "Chương trình học tập chung cho cấp I và II tuần lễ từ 24 đến 30/11/58," November 18, 1958, Folder 20030, PTTĐICH, TTLTQG2.

53. "Chương trình học tập," August 18, 1958, Folder 3031, BYT, TTLTQG2.

54. Đinh Trịnh Chính to Nguyễn Cao Kỳ, September 22, 1965, Folder 29589, PThTVNCH, TTLTQG2.

55. For a compilation of unanswered questions and complaints raised during study sessions associated with Kỳ's policies, see "Bản giải đáp thắc mắc về tài liệu hội thảo: 'Tình Hình và Nhiệm Vụ Trong Giai Đoạn Mới,'" September 29, 1965, Folder 29589, PThTVNCH, TTLTQG2.

56. Đinh Trịnh Chính to Nguyễn Cao Kỳ, April 7, 1966, Folder 29577, PThTVNCH, TTLTQG2.

57. "Bảng đối chiếu nhân số hội thảo viên do các Phủ, Bộ gởi tới tham dự 15 khóa hội thảo tổ chức tại Bộ Thông Tin," circa 1970, Folder 30445, PThTVNCH, TTLTQG2.

58. "Bài thuyết trình về công tác hội thảo cơ quan trong lãnh vực Thông Tin Đại Chúng," July 30, 1970; "Tổ chức và hướng dẫn các buổi học tập, hội thảo," circa 1970; "Kỹ thuật thông tin tuyên truyền," circa 1970; "Đề tài: tổ chức Meeting biểu tình và chống biểu tình," circa 1970; "Nghệ thuật nói trước quần chúng," circa 1970; "Công tác mạn đàm ri tai," circa 1970; "Cách làm và phổ biến tuyên truyền phẩm," circa 1970; and "Thực hiện một bản tin," circa 1970, Folder 30445, PThTVNCH, TTLTQG2.

59. "Thông tư Thủ Tướng Chánh Phủ v/v thực thi chương trình Thông Tin Đại Chúng," circa 1970; Ngô Khắc Tinh to Information Subsidiaries on expanding the General Information Program, September 4, 1970, Folder 30445, PThTVNCH, TTLTQG2.

60. For documents relating to the national campaign directed by Trần Chánh Thành to collect signatures in support of Diệm and his position on the Geneva Accords, see Folder 1125, TĐBCPNP, TTLTQG2. In October 1955, the education and information ministries hosted the National Conference on Education (Đại Hội Giáo Dục Toàn Quốc) to mobilize support from students, educators, and youth for Diệm as the chief of state. See Folder 15993, PTTĐICH, TTLTQG2.

61. Nothing was actually signed at the Geneva Conference, apart from the ceasefire agreement, signed by the DRV and French military commands. The Final Declaration remained unsigned by the various parties involved. See Robert Turner, "Myths of the Vietnam War: The Pentagon Papers Reconsidered," *Southeast Asian Perspectives* 7 (September 1972): 28–30; and Ralph Smith, *An International History of the Vietnam War: Revolution Versus Containment 1955–61* (New York: St. Martin's Press, 1983), 22–23.

Nguyen 229

62. Ngô Đình Diệm, "Lời tuyên bố truyền thanh của Thủ Tướng Chánh Phủ ngày 16-7-1955 về Hiệp Định Geneve và vấn đề thống nhất đất nước," in *Con đường chính nghĩa*, vol. 2 (Saigon: Sở Thông Tin Phủ Tổng Thống, 1956), 11–12.

63. "Nguyên nhân và kết quả của cuộc ký kết tại Geneve," August 16, 1955, Folder 29164, PThTVNCH, TTLTQG2.

64. "Những tội ác của Việt Cộng," August 16, 1955, Folder 29164, PThTVNCH, TTLTQG2.

65. Trần Chánh Thành to information subsidiaries on possible communist propaganda, July 1, 1957, Folder 2488, General Department of Customs of Vietnam Collection (Phông Tổng Nha Quan Thuế Việt Nam [TNQTVN]), TTLTQG2.

66. Trần Chánh Thành to information subsidiaries on possible communist propaganda, July 1, 1957.

67. Ngô Đình Diệm, "Lời tuyên bố truyền thanh của Thủ Tướng Chánh Phủ ngày 16-7-1955," 11–12.

68. Trần Chánh Thành to information subsidiaries on possible communist propaganda, July 1, 1957.

69. "Tuyên Cáo Của Chánh Phủ VN Cộng Hòa Về Thống Nhứt Lãnh Thổ," *Saigon mới,* April 26–28, 1958.

70. Trần Chánh Thành to various ministries, January 8, 1959, Folder 20192, PTTĐICH, TTLTQG2.

71. "Phản ứng của Việt Cộng đối với bản tuyên cáo 26-4-58 của chính phủ Việt Nam Cộng Hòa," January 8, 1959, Folder 20187, PTTĐICH, TTLTQG2.

72. "Bản tóm tắt: Quyển bạch thư do Việt Nam Cộng Hòa công bố tháng 7-1959," Folder 20187, PTTĐICH, TTLTQG2.

73. "Tại sao chống cộng," July 4, 1960, Folder 20354, PTTĐICH, TTLTQG2.

74. "Chiến thuật 'sống chung hòa bình' của Cộng Sản," September 24, 1960, Folder 20357, PTTĐICH, TTLTQG2.

75. "Biên bản buổi học tập chính trị ngày 26-7-1961 tại tổ học tập cảnh sát cuộc Quận Bảy về đề tài 'Thông Điệp của Tổng Thống Việt Nam Cộng Hòa Đọc ngày Lễ Song Thất 1961,'" July 26, 1961, Folder 20531, PTTĐICH, TTLTQG2.

76. "Cuộc thi sáng tác văn nghệ do Nha Vô Tuyến Việt Nam tổ chức ngày 20-7-1964," June 5, 1964; "Chương trình Lễ Quốc Hận 10 Năm Tội Ác Việt Cộng 20-7-1964," July 7, 1964, both in Folder 1773, Ministry of Public Works and Transportation Collection (Phông Bộ Công Chánh và Giao Thông [BCCGT]), TTLTQG2.

77. "Nguyên tắc 'đánh Bắc' đã được chấp thuận," *Tự do*, March 19, 1964; Thái Minh, "Bắc Tiến để thống nhất VN," *Tự do*, March 23, 1964.

78. "Thủ Tướng Nguyễn Khánh cho biết: có nên tấn công ra Bắc không," *Tự do*, March 7, 1964; "Ý Chí," *Tự do*, July 20, 1964; and "Đoàn quân Bắc Tiến SV tiếp tục ghi tên," *Tự do*, July 29, 1964.

79. "Toàn dân đoàn kết xây dựng miền Nam, giải phóng miền Bắc," July 20, 1965, Folder 3031, BYT, TTLTQG2.

80. "Thông điệp của Tổng Thống Việt Nam Cộng Hòa đọc trước phiên họp khoáng đại lưỡng Viện Quốc Hội ngày 10/4/1968," April 13, 1968, Folder 29916, PThTVNCH, TTLTQG2.

81. "Thông điệp của Tổng Thống Việt Nam Cộng Hòa đọc trước phiên họp khoáng đại của lưỡng Viện Quốc Hội ngày 2-11-68," November 3, 1968; and "Thông cáo của chánh phủ Việt Nam Cộng Hòa," November 1, 1968, Folder 29916, PThTVNCH, TTLTQG2.

82. "Thông điệp của Tổng Thống Việt Nam Cộng Hòa đọc trước phiên họp khoáng đại lưỡng Viện Quốc Hội ngày 10/4/1968."

83. "Không liên hiệp với Cộng sản," July 16, 1969, Folder 299, NVKQG, TTLTQG2; "Xuân Canh Tuất-Xuân Tất Thắng," January 27, 1970, Folder 30455, PThTVNCH, TTLTQG2; and "Bảng hướng dẫn khai thác thắng lợi chính trị của Việt Nam Cộng Hòa," November 15, 1968, Folder 29916, PThTVNCH, TTLTQG2.

84. "Cộng sản phá hoại hòa bình như thế nào," July 16,1970, Folder 32656, PThTVNCH, TTLTQG2; "Thừa thắng xông lên tiêu diệt hết bọn Cộng Sản bán nước," June 29, 1970, Folder 7747, PTTĐIICH, TTLTQG2; "Thế tất thắng của Việt Nam Cộng Hòa," August 3, 1970, Folder 32656,

PThTVNCH, TTLTQG2; "Cộng Sản phản bội dân chúng như thế nào?" November 20, 1970, Folder 32656, PThTVNCH, TTLTQG2; "Hiện tình đất nước trước cuộc xâm lăng trắng trợn của Cộng Sản Bắc Việt," May 29, 1972, Folder 30922, PThTVNCH, TTLTQG2; and "Trận chiến quyết định," July 21, 1972, Folder 30922, PThTVNCH, TTLTQG2.

85. For the question raised regarding Thiệu's peace initiative, see Nguyễn Ngọc An to Provincial Chief of Phú Yên, September 2, 1969, Folder 30273, PThTVNCH, TTLTQG2. For questions on the Northward March, see "Báo cáo hàng tháng về công tác học tập (tháng 11 năm 1969)," November 3, 1969, Folder 30271, PThTVNCH, TTLTQG2. For the contradiction between policy and the Geneva narrative, see "Giải đáp các thắc mắc về hòa bình—ngừng bắn," January 5, 1973, Folder 31120, PThTVNCH, TTLTQG2.

86. "Bài nói chuyện của Tổng Thống Việt Nam Cộng Hòa với đồng bào các giới trên hệ thống truyền thanh và truyền hình ngày 24-10-1972," October 26, 1972, Folder 30917, PThTVNCH, TTLTQG2.

87. For telegrams on mass study sessions relating to the Paris Peace Accords sent from Kiến Tường and Phú Bổn, see Folder 18110, PThTVNCH, TTLTQG2.

88. For the attempt to prevent a communist offensive, see Trần Thiện Khiêm to various ministries, November 2, 1972, Folder 18110, PThTVNCH, TTLTQG2; "Nhiệm vụ và công tác của CB/PTNT khi có ngưng bắn," November 4, 1972, Folder 30922, PThTVNCH, TTLTQG2. For counter-propaganda, see Trương Bửu Điện to various ministries, December 14, 1972; and "Nhiệm vụ và công tác của CB/PTNT khi có ngưng bắn," November 4, 1972, Folder 30922, PThTVNCH, TTLTQG2.

89. Telegram from Provincial Chief of Đà Nẵng to National Assembly, Judiciary, and Prime Minister, February 12, 1973, Folder 18110, PThTVNCH, TTLTQG2. The telegram was sent in the context of a nationwide initiative by the General Directorate of Civic Mobilization titled "Week for the Study of the Paris Accords," intended to "prepare for political warfare, mobilization of the people to oppose communism." See Submission of Report from General Directorate of Civic Mobilization to Prime Minister, February 13, 1973, Folder 18110, PThTVNCH, TTLTQG2.

90. "Những bài học hòa đàm với Cộng Sản," October 22, 1973; "Nhận định của phái đoàn VNCH tham dự Hội Nghị La Celle Saint Cloud về đề nghị 6 Điểm ngày 22.03.74 của phía Cộng Sản," March 28, 1974; "Vấn đề tổ chức tự xưng là chánh phủ Cách Mạng Lâm Thời," March 1974; "Bản tin Hiệp Định Ba Lê," September 10, 1974, Folder 31568; and "Cộng Sản phá hoại và chối bỏ Hiệp Định Ba Lê," November 2, 1974, Folder 31568, PThTVNCH, TTLTQG2.

91. "Tổng kết hai năm ký kết Hiệp Định Ba Lê (27.1.1973–27.1.1975)," January 22, 1975, Folder 31568, PThTVNCH, TTLTQG2.

92. For extended discussion of how the anticommunism of the RVN was remade overseas, see Y Thien Nguyen, "When State Propaganda Becomes Social Knowledge" (PhD diss, Northwestern University, 2021), 397–457.

93. Y Nguyen, "(Re)Making the South Vietnamese Past."

94. National United Front for the Liberation of Vietnam, *Vietnamese People's Fight for Survival / Chúng tôi muốn sống* (Redwood City: General Directorate/Overseas, 1982).

95. Ngo Giao, "Cư dân Little Saigon 'dứt khoát không mở đường cho Cộng Sản,'" *Người Việt Daily News*, May 10, 2017; "Welcome to Our Cities, Unless You're Communist," *Los Angeles Times*, April 28, 2004; and "The Region; Garden Grove OKs Measure Opposing Visits by Vietnamese Communists," *Los Angeles Times*, May 12, 2004.

96. Vo-Dang, "Anticommunism as Cultural Praxis."

Bibliography

ARCHIVES AND RESEARCH LIBRARIES

United States

John F. Kennedy Presidential Library, Boston, MA
    Arthur Schlesinger Private Papers
    White House Central Subject Files
Lyndon Baines Johnson Presidential Library, Austin, TX
Michigan State University Archives, East Lansing, MI
    Wesley R. Fishel Papers
National Archives and Records Administration, College Park, MD
    Record Group 59, Central Decimal Files
Vietnam Virtual Archive, Texas Tech University, Lubbock, TX

Vietnam

National Archives Center 1 (Trung Tâm Lưu Trữ Quốc Gia 1), Hanoi
    Direction des Archives et des Bibliothèques
National Archives Center 2 (Trung Tâm Lưu Trữ Quốc Gia 2), Ho Chi Minh City
    General Commission for Migrants and Refugees Collection (Phông Phủ Tổng Ủy Di Cư và Tỵ Nạn)
    General Department of Customs Collection (Phông Tổng Quan Thuế)
    General Department of Customs of Vietnam Collection (Phông Tổng Nha Quan Thuế Việt Nam)
    Government Delegate of Southern Vietnam Collection (Phông Tòa Đại Biểu Chính Phủ Nam Phần)
    Ministry of Health Collection (Phông Bộ Y Tế)
    Ministry of Public Works and Transportation Collection (Phông Bộ Công Chánh và Giao Thông)
    National Library of Vietnam Collection (Phông Thư Viện Quốc Gia Nam Việt)

Office of the President Collection, First Republic (Phông Phủ Tổng Thống Đệ Nhất Cộng Hòa)
Office of the President Collection, Second Republic (Phông Phủ Tổng Thống Đệ Nhị Cộng Hòa)
Office of the Prime Minister Collection (Phông Phủ Thủ Tướng Việt Nam Cộng Hòa)
Revolutionary Military Council Collection (Phông Hội Đồng Quân Nhân Cách Mạng)
Service of the National Archive Collection (Phông Nha Văn Khố Quốc Gia, sometimes Phông Nha Văn Khố và Thư Viện Quốc Gia)

France

Archives Nationale d'Outre-Mer, Aix-en-Provence
Archives Privées Papiers Boudet
Haut Commissariat de France pour l'Indochine

PERIODICALS

Atlanta Constitution
Bách khoa
Boston Globe
Buổi sáng
Cach mạng quốc gia
Dân chủ
Dân Việt
Đăng cổ tùng báo
Esprit
La pensée
Los Angeles Times
Lửa sống
Nam phong
National Geographic
New Republic
New York Times
New York Times Magazine
Ngày nay
Nghệ thuật
Nghiên cứu lịch sử (Hanoi)
Ngôn luận
Người Việt Daily News
Phong hóa
Quần chúng
Quê hương
Quốc gia
Saigon mới
Sáng tạo
Sử địa (Saigon)
The Sun
Thần chung
Thời đại

Thời luận
Tiên phong (Hanoi)
Tiếng chuông
Tiếng nói
Times of India
Tin mai
Tự do
Văn hóa ngày nay
Văn học (Saigon)
Văn nghệ (Việt Bắc zone)
Việt chính
Washington Post
Xã hội (Saigon)

TELEVISION AND INTERNET SOURCES

Đại Hội Văn Hoá Toàn Quốc 1957. Saigon: Xã Hội Ấn Quán, 1957. Available at Hội Ái Hữu Trường Trung Học Nguyễn Đình Chiểu—Lê Ngọc Hân, http://ndclnh-mytho-usa.org /KhoSachCu/Dai%20Hoi%20Van%20Hoa%20Toan%20Quoc_.pdf.
"Diệm's War or Ours?" *Eyewitness.* CBS. December 29, 1961.
Lê Thanh Cảnh. "Thử đi tìm một lập trường tranh đấu cho dân tộc Việt Nam." Pham Ton's Blog, June 2, 2012. https://phamquynh.wordpress.com/2012/05/31/roi-mai-tranh-truong-quoc-hoc/.
Ngô Đình Nhu. "Viet Nam, le cerveau de la famille." Interview by Raoul Goulard. *Cinq colonnes à la une.* RTF Télévision (Saigon). October 3, 1963.
Nguyễn Vy Khanh. "Tạp chí Bách khoa và văn học miền nam." NamKyLucTinh.com. Accessed August 15, 2019. http://www.namkyluctinh.com/a-tgtpham/nvkhanh/nvkhanh -bachkhoa.pdf.
Nguyễn Xuân Hoài. "Đảng Cần Lao Nhân Vị." Luutruvn.com, January 4, 2016. http://luutruvn .com/index.php/2016/04/01/dang-can-lao-nhan-vi/.
"Tiểu sử chí sĩ Nhị Lang (1923–2005)." Việt Nam Hải Ngoại Liên Minh Chống Cộng. Accessed July 18, 2017. http://www.vnfa.com/vietlien/. Site discontinued.
Trương Vũ. "Vị trí của *Sáng tạo* trong sự phát triển văn học miền Nam sau năm 1954." Paper presented at the Hội Thảo về 20 Năm Văn Học Miền Nam, 1954–1975, Westminster, California, December 2014. Accessed April 16, 2022. http://www.tienve.org/home/activities /viewTopics.do?action=viewArtwork&artworkId=18389.
Vũ Ngọc Khánh. "Bàn thêm về Trần Trọng Kim." *Văn Hóa Nghệ An* (website). November 26, 2009. Accessed April 5, 2011. http://vanhoanghean.com.vn/dat-va-nguoi-xu-nghe/nguoi -xu-nghe/1485-ban-them-v-trn-trng-kim.html. Site discontinued.
Vương Kim [Phan Bá Cầm]. *Đức Huỳnh Giáo Chủ.* N.p.: VP Phật Giáo Hòa Hảo, 1997. HoaHao. org. Accessed May 6, 2020. https://www.hoahao.org/p74a2133/2/duc-huynh-giao-chu.

BOOKS, ARTICLES, AND THESES

Adamson, Walter. *Hegemony and Revolution: A Study of Antonio Gramsci's Political and Cultural Theory.* Oakland: University of California Press, 1980.
Aguilar-San Juan, Karin. *Little Saigons: Staying Vietnamese in America.* Minneapolis: University of Minnesota Press, 2009.

Ahern, Thomas, Jr.. *CIA and the House of Ngo: Covert Action in South Vietnam, 1954–1963.* Washington, DC: Center for the Study of Intelligence, 2000.

Alexander, Jeffrey. "Toward a Theory of Cultural Trauma." In *Cultural Trauma and Collective Identity,* edited by Jeffrey Alexander, Ron Eyerman, Bernard Giesen, Neil Smelser, and Piotr Sztompka, 1–30. Oakland: University of California Press, 2004.

Allen, Richard. *Korea's Syngman Rhee: An Unauthorized Portrait.* Rutland, VT: Charles E. Tuttle Company, 1960.

Anderson, Benedict. *Imagined Communities: Reflections on the Origin and Spread of Nationalism.* London: Verso, 1991.

Anderson, David. *Trapped by Success: The Eisenhower Administration and Vietnam, 1953–61.* New York: Columbia University Press, 1991.

Armus, Seth. *French Anti-Americanism (1930–1948): Critical Moments in a Complex History.* Lanham, MD: Lexington Books, 2007.

Bảo Đại. *Le Dragon d'Annam.* Paris: Plon, 1980.

Bergère, Marie-Claire. *Sun Yat-sen.* Translated by Janet Lloyd. Stanford, CA: Stanford University Press, 1994.

Biggs, David. "Americans in An Giang: Nation Building and the Particularities of Place in the Mekong Delta, 1966–1973." *Journal of Vietnamese Studies* 4, no. 3 (2009): 139–172.

———. *Footprints of War.* Seattle: University of Washington Press, 2018.

———. *Quagmire: Nation-Building and Nature in the Mekong Delta.* Seattle: University of Washington Press, 2010.

Boudarel, Georges, and Nguyễn Văn Ký. *Hanoi: City of the Rising Dragon.* Lanham, MD: Rowman & Littlefield, 2002.

Bourgeois, Rémi. *Rapport sur la direction des archives et des bibliothèques (1938–1939).* Hanoi: Imprimerie Le Van Tan, 1939.

Bouscaren, Anthony. *The Last of the Mandarins: Diem of Vietnam.* Pittsburgh, PA: Duquesne University Press, 1965.

Bradley, Mark. *Vietnam at War.* New York: Oxford University Press, 2009.

Brigham, Robert. *ARVN: Life and Death in the South Vietnamese Army.* Lawrence: University Press of Kansas, 2006.

Britto, Karl. *Disorientation: France, Vietnam, and the Ambivalence of Interculturality.* Hong Kong: Hong Kong University Press, 2004.

Brocheux, Pierre. *The Mekong Delta: Ecology, Economy and Revolution, 1860–1960.* Madison: University of Wisconsin, Center for Southeast Asian Studies, 1995.

Bùi Kỷ and Trần Trọng Kim. *Truyện Kiều chú giải.* Hanoi: Vinh Hưng Long, 1925.

Bùi Văn Lương. "The Role of Friendly Nations." In *Viet-Nam: The First Five Years,* edited by Richard Lindholm, 48–53. East Lansing: Michigan State University, 1959.

Buttinger, Joseph. *Vietnam: A Dragon Embattled.* 2 vols. New York: Frederick A. Praeger, 1967.

Bửu Lịch. "Les idéologies dans la République du Sud Vietnam 1954–1975." PhD diss., Université de Paris VII, 1983–1984.

Cao Văn Luận. *Bên giòng lịch sử.* Saigon: Trí Dũng, 1972.

Capoccia, Giovanni. "Militant Democracy: The Institutional Bases of Democratic Self-Preservation." *Annual Review of Law and Social Science* 9 (November 2013): 207–226.

Cardinaux, Alfred. "Commentary." In *Viet-Nam: The First Five Years,* edited by Richard Lindholm, 87–92. East Lansing: Michigan State University, 1959.

Carter, James. *Inventing Vietnam: The United States and State Building, 1954–1968.* Cambridge: Cambridge University Press, 2008.

Catton, Philip. *Diem's Final Failure: Prelude to America's War in Vietnam.* Lawrence: University Press of Kansas, 2002.

———. "Parallel Agendas: The Ngo Dinh Diem Regime, the United States and the Strategic Hamlet Program, 1961–1963." PhD diss., Ohio University, 1998.

Chang, Sidney, and Leonard Gordon. *All Under Heaven: Sun Yat-sen and His Revolutionary Thought.* Stanford, CA: Hoover Institution Press, 1991.

Chánh nghĩa đã thắng. [Saigon?]: no publisher, [1955?].

Chapman, Jessica. *Cauldron of Resistance: Ngo Dinh Diem, the United States, and 1950s Southern Vietnam.* Ithaca, NY: Cornell University Press, 2013.

———. "Debating the Will of Heaven: South Vietnamese Politics and Nationalism in the International Perspective, 1954–1956." PhD diss., University of California, Santa Barbara, 2006.

Cherry, Haydon. Review of *Nothing Ever Dies: Vietnam and the Memory of War,* by Viet Thanh Nguyen. *Journal of Southeast Asian Studies* 49, no. 1 (February 2018): 177–179.

"Chương trình của Việt Nam Dân Chủ Xã Hội Đảng." In *Sấm giảng thi văn giáo lý toàn bộ,* by Huỳnh Phú Sổ, 441–442. Saigon: Ban Phổ Thông Giáo Lý Trung Ương, 1966.

Colby, William. *Lost Victory: A Firsthand Account of America's Sixteen-Year Involvement in Vietnam.* Chicago: Contemporary Books, 1989.

Conklin, Alice. *A Mission to Civilize: The Republican Idea of Empire in France and West Africa, 1895–1930.* Stanford, CA: Stanford University Press, 1997.

Cung Giũ Nguyên. *Volontés d'existence.* Saigon: France-Asie, 1954.

Dalloz, Jacques. "Les vietnamiens dans la franc-maçonnerie colonial." *Revue française d'histoire d'outre-mer* 85, no. 320 (1998): 103–118.

Daniels, Robert. *Year of the Heroic Guerrilla: World Revolution and Counterrevolution in 1968.* Cambridge, MA: Harvard University Press, 1996.

Đào Đăng Vỹ. *L'Annam qui nait.* Hue: Imprimerie du Mirador, 1938.

Daughton, J. P. *An Empire Divided: Religion, Republicanism, and the Making of French Colonialism, 1880–1914.* Oxford: Oxford University Press, 2006.

Deweer, Dries. "The Political Theory of Personalism." *International Journal of Philosophy and Theology* 74, no. 2 (2013): 108–126.

Đoàn Thêm. *Những ngày chưa quên.* Vol. 2. Saigon: Phạm Quang Khai, 1969.

Dommen, Arthur. *The Indochinese Experience of the French and the Americans: Nationalism and Communism in Cambodia, Laos, and Vietnam.* Bloomington: Indiana University Press, 2001.

Donnell, John. "National Renovation Campaigns in Vietnam." *Pacific Affairs* 32, no. 1 (March 1959): 73–88.

———. "Personalism in Vietnam." In *Problems of Freedom,* edited by Wesley Fishel, 29–58. New York: Free Press of Glencoe, 1961.

———. "Politics in South Vietnam: Doctrines of Authority in Conflict." PhD diss., University of California, Berkeley, 1964.

Dror, Olga. *Making Two Vietnams: War and Youth Identities, 1965–1975.* Cambridge: Cambridge University Press, 2018.

———. "Raising Vietnamese: War and Youth in the South in the Early 1970s." *Journal of Southeast Asian Studies* 44, no. 1 (2013): 74–99.

Duiker, William. *The Communist Road to Power in Vietnam.* Boulder, CO: Westview Press, 1981.

———. *The Communist Road to Power in Vietnam.* 2nd ed. Boulder, CO: Westview, 1996.

———. *The Rise of Nationalism in Vietnam, 1900–1941.* Ithaca, NY: Cornell University Press, 1976.

——. *US Containment Policy and the Conflict in Indochina.* Stanford, CA: Stanford University Press, 1994.

Duyên Anh. "Người quê hương." In *Văn học miền nam,* edited by Võ Phiến, 671–687. CA: Văn Nghệ, 1999.

Eagleton, Terry. "Nationalism: Irony and Commitment." In *Nationalism, Colonialism and Literature,* by Terry Eagleton, Frederic Jameson, and Edward W. Said, 23–43. Minneapolis: University of Minnesota Press, 1990.

Elkind, Jessica. *Aid under Fire: Nation Building and the Vietnam War.* Lexington: University of Kentucky Press, 2016.

Elliott, David. *The Vietnamese War: Revolution and Social Change in the Mekong Delta, 1930–1975.* Concise ed. Armonk, NY: M. E. Sharpe, 2007.

Engelstad, Fredrik. "National Literature, Collective Identity and Political Power." *Comparative Social Research* 21 (2003): 111–145.

Ernst, John. *Forging a Fateful Alliance: Michigan State University and the Vietnam War.* East Lansing: Michigan State University, 1998.

Espiritu, Yen Le. *Body Counts: The Vietnam War and Militarized Refuge(es).* Berkeley: University of California Press, 2014.

Fall, Bernard. "Problems of Freedom in South Vietnam." *International Journal* 17, no. 4 (1962): 436–440.

——. "South Viet-Nam's Internal Problems." *Pacific Affairs* 31, no. 3 (September 1958): 241–260.

——. *The Two Viet-Nams: A Political and Military Analysis.* 2nd rev. ed. New York: Frederick A. Praeger, 1967.

Fear, Sean. "The Ambitious Legacy of Ngô Đình Diệm in South Vietnam's Second Republic, 1967–1975." *Journal of Vietnamese Studies* 11, no. 1 (winter 2016): 1–75.

——. "The Rise and Fall of the Second Republic: Domestic Politics and Civil Society in US-South Vietnamese Relations, 1967–1971." PhD diss., Cornell University, 2016.

Fields, Karen, and Barbara Fields. *Racecraft: The Soul of Inequality in American Life.* New York: Verso, 2012.

Fitzgerald, Frances. *Fire in the Lake: The Vietnamese and the Americans in Vietnam.* New York: BackBay Books, 2002. First published 1972 by Vintage Books.

Fontaine, Ray. *The Dawn of Free Vietnam: A Biographical Sketch of Doctor Phan Quang Dan.* Brownsville, TX: Pan American Business Services, 1992.

Fraleigh, Bert. "Counterinsurgency in Vietnam: The Real Story." In *Prelude to Tragedy: Vietnam, 1960–1965,* edited by Harvey Neese and John O'Donnell, 86–128. Annapolis, MD: Naval Institute Press, 2001.

Frankum, Ronald, Jr. *Vietnam's Year of the Rat.* Jefferson, NC: McFarland, 2014.

Fukuzawa Yukichi. *Bunmeiron no gairyaku* (An outline of a theory of civilization). Tokyo: Iwanami shoten, 1931.

Fung Po-Wa. "Ryo Keicho to Nihon: Fukuzawa Yukichi no keimō shisō to no kanren o chūshin ni" (Liang Qichao and Japan: On the connection with the enlightenment thinking of Fukuzawa Yukichi). *Hikaku bungaku bunka ronshū, Tokyo daigaku hikaku bungaku bunka kenkyūkai* (Departmental Bulletin Paper, Society of Comparative Literature and Culture University of Tokyo) 14 (September 1997): 49–62.

Gantès, Gilles de. "Protectorate, Association, Reformism: The Roots of the Popular Front's Republican Policy in Indochina." In *French Colonial Empire and the Popular Front: Hope and Disillusion,* edited by Tony Chafur and Amanda Sackur, 109–131. New York: St. Martin's Press, 1999.

Gellner, Ernest. *Nations and Nationalism: New Perspectives on the Past.* Ithaca, NY: Cornell University Press, 1983.

Gheddo, Piero. *Catholiques et bouddhistes au Vietnam.* Paris: Groupe des éditions Alsatia, 1970.

Gibbs, Jason. "Songs of Sympathy in Time of War: Commercial Music in the Republic of Vietnam." In *Republican Vietnam, 1963-1975: War, Society, Diaspora,* edited by Trinh Luu and Tuong Vu (Honolulu: University of Hawai'i Press, forthcoming).

Gilman, Nils. *Mandarins of the Future: Modernization Theory in Cold War America.* Baltimore, MD: Johns Hopkins University Press, 2003.

Goodman, Allan. *Politics in War: The Bases of Political Community in South Vietnam.* Cambridge, MA: Harvard University Press, 1973.

Goscha, Christopher. "Aux origines du républicanisme vietnamien: Circulations mondiales et connexions coloniales." *Vingtième siècle* 131 (July-September 2016): 17–35.

———. *The Penguin History of Modern Vietnam.* London: Penguin Books, 2017.

———. *Vietnam: A New History.* New York: Basic Books, 2016.

Gourou, Pierre. *Les paysans du delta tonkinois: étude de géographie humaine.* The Hague: Mouton, 1965.

Gravel, Mike, ed. *Pentagon Papers: The Defense Department History of United States Descision Making on Vietnam.* Vol. 1. Boston, MA: Beacon Press, 1971.

Guillemot, François. "Penser le nationalisme révolutionnaire au Viêt Nam: identités politiques et itinéraires singuliers à la recherche d'une hypothétique 'troisième voie.'" *Moussons: recherches en sciences humaines sur l'Asie du Sud-Est* 13–14 (2009): 147–184.

Gustafsson, Mai Lan. "'Freedom. Money. Fun. Love': The Warlore of Vietnamese Bargirls." *Oral History Review* 38, no. 2 (2011): 308–330.

Hahn, Ki-shik. "Underlying Factors in Political Party Organization and Elections." In *Korean Politics in Transition,* edited by Edward Reynolds Wright, 85–104. Seattle: University of Washington Press, 1975.

Halberstam, David. *The Making of a Quagmire.* New York: Random House, 1965.

Halbwachs, Maurice. *On Collective Memory.* Chicago: University of Chicago Press, 1992.

Hansen, Peter. "Bắc Di Cư: Catholic Refugees from the North of Vietnam and Their Role in the Southern Republic, 1954–1959." *Journal of Vietnamese Studies* 4, no. 3 (Fall 2009): 173–211.

———. "The Virgin Heads South: Northern Catholic Refugees in South Vietnam, 1954–1964." PhD diss., Melbourne College of Divinity, 2009.

———. "The Virgin Heads South: Northern Catholic Refugees and their Clergy in South Vietnam, 1954–1964." In *Casting Faiths: Imperialism and the Transformation of Religion in East and Southeast Asia,* edited by Thomas Dubois, 129–151. New York: Palgrave, 2009.

Hazareesingh, Sudhir. *Political Traditions in Modern France.* Oxford: Oxford University Press, 1994.

Hazlett, Henry. "L'Annam vu par Trần Văn Tùng." Master's thesis, University of Washington, 1950.

Heath, Elizabeth. *Wine, Sugar, and the Making of Modern France: Global Economic Crisis and the Racialization of French Citizenship, 1870–1910.* Cambridge: Cambridge University Press, 2014.

Hémery, Daniel. "En Indochine française, reformisme colonial et nationalisme vietnamien au XXe siècle: La sarrautisme at ses avatars." *Études indochinoises* 3, no. 25 (1993): 109–135.

———. "L'Indochine, les droits humains, 1899–1954: Entre colonisateurs et colonisés, la Ligue des droits de l'homme." *Revue francaise d'histoire d'Outre-mers* 88, no. 330–331 (January 2001): 223–239.

Herbst, Susan. "Surveying and Influencing the Public: Polling in Politics and Industry." In *The Cambridge History of Science*. Vol. 7, *The Modern Social Sciences,* edited by Ted Porter and Dorothy Ross, 577–590. Cambridge: Cambridge University Press, 2003.

Herring, George. *America's Longest War: The United States and Vietnam, 1950–1975.* New York: Wiley, 1979.

———. *America's Longest War: The United States and Vietnam, 1950–1975.* 4th ed. Boston, MA: McGraw-Hill, 2002.

———. *America's Longest War: The United States and Vietnam, 1950–1975.* 5th ed. New York: McGraw-Hill, 2014.

Hickey, Gerald. *Free in the Forest: Ethnohistory of the Vietnamese Central Highlands, 1954–1976.* New Haven, CT: Yale University Press, 1982.

———. "The Social Systems of Northern Vietnam." PhD diss., University of Chicago, 1958.

Higgins, Marguerite. *Our Vietnam Nightmare.* New York: Harper and Row, 1965.

Hoàng Cao Khải. *Gương sử Nam* [*Yue shi jing*]. Hanoi: Defour et Ng.-Văn-Vĩnh, 1910.

———. *Việt sử yếu.* Translated by Lê Xuân Giáo. Saigon: Phủ Quốc Vụ Khanh Đặc Trách Văn Hóa, 1971.

Hoang, Kimberly Kay. *Dealing in Desire: Asian Ascendancy, Western Decline, and the Hidden Currencies of Global Sex Work.* Berkeley: University of California Press, 2015.

Hoang, Tuan. "The Early South Vietnamese Critique of Communism." In *Dynamics of the Cold War in Asia,* edited by Tuong Vu and Wasana Wongsurawat, 17–32. New York: Palgrave Macmillan, 2009.

———. "Ideology in Urban South Vietnam, 1950–1975." PhD diss., University of Notre Dame, 2013.

Hoàng Xuân Hãn, Đào Thái Tôn, and Nguyễn Tài Cẩn. *Nghiên cứu văn bản "Truyện Kiều" theo phương pháp Hoàng Xuân Hãn.* Hanoi: Đại Học Quốc Gia Hà Nội, 2016.

Hobsbawm, Eric, and Terrence Ranger, eds. *The Invention of Tradition.* New York: Cambridge University Press, 1983.

Holcombe, Alec. "The Role of the Communist Party in the Vietnamese Revolution: A Review of David Marr's *Vietnam: State, War and Revolution, 1945–1946.*" *Journal of Vietnamese Studies* 11, no. 3–4 (Summer-Fall 2016): 298–364.

Honey, P. J. "The Problem of Democracy in Vietnam." *World Today* 16, no. 2 (February 1960): 71–79.

Huỳnh Kim Khánh. *Vietnamese Communism, 1925–1945.* Ithaca, NY: Cornell University Press, 1982.

Huỳnh Văn Lang. *Ký ức Huỳnh Văn Lang.* Vol. 2, *Thời kỳ Việt Nam độc lập.* Privately published, 2012.

Itzigsohn, Jose, and Matthias vom Hau. "Unfinished Imagined Communities: States, Social Movements, and Nationalism in Latin America." *Theory and Society* 35 (2006): 193–212.

Jacobs, Seth. *America's Miracle Man in Vietnam: Ngo Dinh Diem, Religion, Race, and the US Intervention in Southeast Asia, 1950–1957.* Durham, NC: Duke University Press, 2005.

———. *Cold War Mandarin: Ngo Dinh Diem and the Origins of America's War in Vietnam, 1950-1963.* Lanham, MD: Rowman & Littlefield, 2006.

Jamieson, Neil. *Understanding Vietnam.* Berkeley: University of California Press, 1993.

Jennings, Eric. *Vichy in the Tropics: Pétain's National Revolution in Madagascar, Guadeloupe, and Indochina, 1940–1944.* Stanford, CA: Stanford University Press, 2001.

Judt, Tony. *Past Imperfect: French Intellectuals, 1944–1956.* Berkeley: University of California Press, 1992.

Kahin, George. *Intervention: How America Became Involved in Vietnam.* New York: Anchor Books, 1987.

Kahin, George, and John Lewis. *The United States in Vietnam.* New York: Dial Press, 1967.

Karnow, Stanley. *Vietnam: A History.* New York: Penguin Books, 1997.

Kim, Charles. *Youth for Nation: Culture and Protest in Cold War South Korea.* Honolulu: University of Hawai'i Press, 2017.

Kim, In Soo. *Protestants and the Formation of Modern Korean Nationalism, 1885–1920.* New York: Peter Lang, 1996.

Kolko, Gabriel. *Anatomy of a War: Vietnam, the United States, and the Modern Historical Experience.* New York: Pantheon Books, 1985.

———. *Vietnam: Anatomy of a Peace.* New York: Routledge, 1997.

Lacouture, Jean. *Le Vietnam entre deux paix.* Paris: Éditions du Seuil, 1965.

Land Reform in Free Vietnam. Saigon: Review Horizons, 1956.

Langlois, Walter. *André Malraux: The Indochina Adventure.* New York: Frederick A. Praeger, 1966.

Lansdale, Edward. *In the Midst of War.* New York: Fordham University Press, 1991.

Larcher-Goscha, Agathe. "Bùi Quang Chiêu in Calcutta (1928): The Broken Mirror of Vietnamese and Indian Nationalism." *Journal of Vietnamese Studies* 9, no. 4 (Fall 2014): 67–114.

———. "La légitimation française en Indochine: Mythes et réalités de la 'collaboration franco-vietnamienne' et du réformisme colonial, 1905–1945." PhD diss., Université de Paris VII, 2000.

Lawrence, Mark. *The Vietnam War: A Concise International History.* New York: Oxford University Press, 2008.

Le, C. N. "Better Dead Than Red: Anti-communist Politics among Vietnamese Americans." In *Anti-communist Minorities in the U.S.: Political Activism of Ethnic Refugees,* edited by Ieva Zake, 189–210. New York: Palgrave Macmillan, 2009.

LeClerc, Jean. *De l'évolution et du développement des institutions annamites et cambodgiennes sous l'influence française.* Rennes: Edoneur et Ruesch, 1923.

Lê Thanh. *Phỏng vấn các nhà văn.* Hanoi: Đời Mới, 1943.

Lê Thanh Cảnh. "Thử đi tìm một lập trường tranh đấu cho dân tộc Việt nam." Vol. 3 of *Phan Châu Trinh toàn tập,* edited by Chương Thâu et al., 125–131. Đà Nẵng: Nhà Xuất Bản Đà Nẵng, 2005.

Lê Văn Viết, Nguyễn Hữu Viêm, and Phạm Thế Khang. *Thư Viện Quốc Gia Việt Nam—90 năm xây dựng và phát triển.* Hanoi: Thư Viện Quốc Gia, 2007.

Lew, Young Ick. *The Making of the First Korean President: Syngman Rhee's Quest for Independence 1875–1948.* Honolulu: University of Hawai'i Press, 2014.

Li, Kevin. "Partisan to Sovereign: The Making of the Bình Xuyên in Southern Vietnam, 1945–1948." *Journal of Vietnamese Studies* 11, no. 3–4 (Summer-Fall 2016): 140–187.

Li, Tana. *Nguyen Cochinchina: Southern Vietnam in the Seventeenth and Eighteenth Centuries.* Ithaca, NY: Cornell University, Southeast Asian Program, 1998.

Logevall, Fredrik. *Embers of War: The Fall of an Empire and the Making of America's Vietnam.* New York: Random House, 2012.

Luu, Trinh. "Vietism: Carl Jung and the New Vietnamese." In *Republican Vietnam, 1963-1975: War, Society, Diaspora,* edited by Trinh Luu and Tuong Vu (Honolulu: University of Hawai'i Press, forthcoming).

Mai Thảo. "Tháng giêng cỏ non." In *Tháng giêng cỏ non,* 11–23. Saigon: Sáng Tạo, 1956.

Maneli, Mieczysław. *War of the Vanquished.* New York: Harper and Row, 1971.

Marr, David. *Vietnamese Anticolonialism, 1885–1925.* Berkeley: University of California Press, 1971.

———. *Vietnamese Tradition on Trial, 1920–1945.* Berkeley: University of California Press, 1981.

Masur, Matthew. "Exhibiting Signs of Resistance: South Vietnam's Struggle for Legitimacy, 1954–1960." *Diplomatic History* 33, no. 2 (April 2009): 293–313.

———. "Hearts and Minds: Cultural Nation-Building in South Vietnam, 1954–1963." PhD diss., Ohio State University, 2004.

Miller, Edward. *Misalliance: Ngo Dinh Diem, the United States, and the Fate of South Vietnam.* Cambridge, MA: Harvard University Press, 2013.

———. "War Stories: The Taylor-Buzzanco Debate and How We Think about the Vietnam War." *Journal of Vietnamese Studies* 1, no. 1–2 (February/August 2006): 465–466.

Minh Võ. *Ngô Đình Diệm và chính nghĩa dân tộc.* Hồng Đức, 2008.

Mok, Mei Feng. "Negotiating Community and Nation in Cho Lon: Nation-Building, Community-Building and Transnationalism in Everyday Life during the Republic of Vietnam, 1955–1975." PhD diss., University of Washington, 2016.

Montgomery, John. *Cases in Vietnamese Administration.* Saigon: National Institute of Administration and Michigan State University Vietnam Advisory Group, 1959.

Moon, Nick. *Opinion Polls: History, Theory and Practice.* Manchester, UK: Manchester University Press, 1999.

Morrissey, James. "Migration, Resettlement, and Refugeeism: Issues in Medical Anthropology." *Medical Anthropology Quarterly* 15, no. 1 (1983): 3, 11–14.

Mounier, Emmanuel. *De la propriété capitaliste à la propriété humaine.* Paris: Desclée de Brouwer, 1936.

———. *Œuvres.* Vol. 1. Paris: Éditions du Seuil, 1961.

———. *Le personnalisme.* Paris: Presses universitaires de France, 1959.

———. *A Personalist Manifesto.* Translated by St. John's Abbey. New York: Longmans, Green, 1938.

———. "Prague." *Esprit* 143, no. 3 (1948): 353–364.

———. *Révolution personnaliste et communautaire.* Paris: F. Aubier, 1935.

Moyar, Mark. *Triumph Forsaken: The Vietnam War, 1954–1965.* Cambridge: Cambridge University Press, 2006.

Nam Cao. "Lão Hạc." In *Tuyển tập Nam Cao.* Hanoi: Công Lực, 1943.

National United Front for the Liberation of Vietnam. *Vietnamese People's Fight for Survival / Chúng tôi muốn sống.* Redwood City, CA: General Directorate Overseas, 1982.

Ngô Đình Diệm. *Con đường chính nghĩa.* 8 vols. Saigon: Sở Báo Chí Thông Tin, Phủ Thủ Tướng, 1955–1962.

Ngô Gia Văn Phái. *Hoàng Lê nhất thống chí.* Translated by Nguyễn Đức Vân and Kiều Thu Hoạch. Hanoi: Văn Học, 2004.

Nguyen Chi Thanh. *Who Will Win in South Viet Nam?* Peking: Foreign Languages Press, 1963.

Nguyen, Cindy. "Reading Rules: The Symbolic and Social Spaces of Reading in the Hà Nội Central Library, 1919–1941." *Journal of Vietnamese Studies* 15, no. 3 (August 2020): 1–35.

Nguyễn Công Luận. *Nationalist in the Viet Nam Wars: Memoirs of a Victim Turned Soldier.* Bloomington: Indiana University Press, 2012.

Nguyen, Duy Lap. *The Unimagined Community: Imperialism and Culture in South Vietnam.* Manchester, UK: Manchester University Press, 2020.

Nguyen, Huong Thi Diu. "Eve of Destruction: A Social History of Vietnam's Royal City, 1957–1967." PhD diss., University of Washington, 2017.

Nguyen, Lien-Hang. "Cold War Contradictions: Towards an International History of the Second Indochina War, 1969–1973." In *Making Sense of the Vietnam War: Local, National and Transnational Perspectives,* edited by Mark Bradley and Marilyn B. Young, 219–250. Oxford: Oxford University Press, 2008.

Nguyễn Long Thành Nam. *Phật Giáo Hòa Hảo trong dòng lịch sử dân tộc.* Santa Fe Springs, CA: Đuốc Từ Bi, 1991.

Nguyen, Martina Thucnhi. *On Our Own Strength: The Self-Reliant Literary Group and Cosmopolitan Nationalism in Late Colonial Vietnam.* Honolulu: University of Hawai'i Press, 2021.

Nguyen, Nathalie Huynh Chau. *South Vietnamese Soldiers: Memories of the Vietnam War and After.* Santa Barbara, CA: Praeger, 2016.

Nguyen, Phi Van. "Fighting the First Indochina War Again?: Catholic Refugees in South Vietnam, 1954–59." *Sojourn* 31, no. 1 (March 2016): 207–246.

———. "Les résidus de la guerre, la mobilisation des réfugiés du nord pour un Vietnam non-communiste (1954–1964)." PhD diss., Université du Québec, Montreal, 2015.

Nguyễn Thái. *Is South Vietnam Viable?* Manila: Carmelo and Bauermann, 1962.

Nguyễn Thái Bình. *The Problem and a Solution.* Paris: Viet-Nam Democratic Party, 1962.

Nguyễn Tuấn Cường. "The Promotion of Confucianism in South Vietnam (1955–1975) and the Role of Nguyễn Đăng Thục as a New Confucian Scholar." *Journal of Vietnamese Studies* 10, no. 4 (Fall 2015): 30–81.

Nguyễn Tường Thiết. "Chuyến tàu trong đêm." In *Nhất Linh, người nghệ sĩ, người chiến sĩ,* by Nhất Linh et al., 307–326. Westminster, CA: Thế Kỷ, 2004.

Nguyễn Văn Châu. *Con đường sống.* Saigon: Nhóm Văn Chiến, 1961.

Nguyen, Viet Thanh. *Nothing Ever Dies: Vietnam and the Memory of War.* Cambridge, MA: Harvard University Press, 2016.

———. *The Sympathizer.* New York: Grove Press, 2015.

Nguyen, Y Thien. "(Re)Making the South Vietnamese Past in America." *Journal of Asian American Studies,* 21, no. 1 (2018): 65–103.

———. "When State Propaganda Becomes Social Knowledge." PhD diss., Northwestern University, 2021.

Nguyen-Marshall, Van. Review of *Vietnam's Lost Revolution,* by Geoffrey Stewart. *H-Diplo Roundtable Review* 19, no. 45 (July 23, 2018): 14–15.

———. "Student Activism in Time of War: Youth in the Republic of Vietnam, 1960s-1970s." *Journal of Vietnamese Studies* 10, no. 2 (2015): 43–81.

———. "Tools of Empire? Vietnamese Catholics in South Vietnam." *Journal of the Canadian Historical Association* 20, no. 2 (2009): 138–159.

Nguyễn-Võ Thu Hương. "Life after Material Death in South Vietnamese and Diasporic Works of Fiction." *Journal of Vietnamese Studies* 3, no. 1 (Winter 2008): 1–35.

Nhã Ca. *Mourning Headband for Hue.* Translated by Olga Dror. Bloomington: University of Indiana Press, 2014.

Nhị Lang. *Phong trào kháng chiến Trình Minh Thế.* Boulder, CO: Lion Press, 1985.

Olson, Gregory. *Mansfield and Vietnam: A Study in Rhetorical Adaptation.* East Lansing: Michigan State University Press, 1995.

Osborne, Milton. *The French Presence in Cochinchina and Cambodia: Rule and Response, 1859–1905.* Ithaca, NY: Cornell University Press, 1969.

Ota, Norio. "*Wakon-Yosai* and Globalization." In *Japan in the Age of Globalization,* edited by Carin Holroyd and Ken Coates, 148–157. London: Routledge, 2012.

Pak, Chi-Young. *Political Opposition in Korea, 1945–1960.* Seoul: Seoul National University Press, 1980.

Peycam, Philippe. *Birth of Vietnamese Political Journalism: Saigon, 1916–1930.* New York: Columbia University Press, 2012.

————. "Intellectuals and Political Commitment in Vietnam: The Emergence of a Public Sphere in Colonial Vietnam, 1916–1928." PhD. diss., School of Oriental and African Studies, 1999.

Phạm Quỳnh. *Quelques conférences à Paris.* Hanoi: Imprimerie de Le Van Phuc, 1923.

Phạm Tân Hạ. "Hoạt động thư viện ở thành phố Sài Gòn thời kỳ 1954–1975." PhD diss., Trường Đại Học Khoa học Xã hội và Nhân Văn, Ho Chi Minh City, 2005.

Phạm Thế Ngũ. *Việt Nam văn học sử giản ước tân biên.* Vol 3. Saigon: Quốc Học Tùng Thư, 1965.

Phạm Tú Châu. *Hoàng Lê nhất thống chí: văn bản tác giả và nhân vật.* Hanoi: Khoa Học Xã Hội, 1997.

Phạm Văn Liễu. *Trả ta sông núi.* Vol. 1. Houston: Văn Hóa, 2002.

Phạm Văn Lưu. *Chính quyền Ngô Dình Diệm, 1954–1963: chủ nghĩa và hành động.* Reservoir, Vic., AU: Centre for Vietnamese Studies Publications, 2017.

Phạm Văn Lưu, and Nguyễn Ngọc Tấn. *Đệ Nhất Cộng Hòa Việt Nam 1954–1963: một cuộc cách mạng.* Melbourne, AU: Centre for Vietnamese Studies, 2005.

Phan Bội Châu. *Việt Nam quốc sử khảo.* Translated by Chương Thâu. Hanoi: Nhà Xuất Bản Giáo Dục, 1962.

————. *Việt Nam vong quốc sử.* In *Phan Bội Châu—tác phẩm chọn lọc,* edited by Trần Hải Yến, 115–134. Hanoi: Nhà Xuất Bản Giáo Dục, 2009.

Phan Châu Trinh. *Phan Châu Trinh toàn tập.* Vol. 2. Đà Nẵng: Nhà Xuất Bản Đà Nẵng, 2005.

Phan Quang Đán. *Volonté vietnamienne.*[Geneva?]: Thiêt Thuc, 1951.

————. *Volonté vietnamienne.* 2nd ed. Geneva: Imprimeries Populaires, 1955.

Phủ Tổng Ủy Di Cư và Tị Nạn. *Cuộc Di Cư Lịch Sử tại Việt Nam.* Saigon: Phủ Tổng Ủy Di Cư và Tị Nạn, 1957.

Picard, Jason. "'Fertile Lands Await': The Promise and Pitfalls of Directed Resettlement, 1954–1958." *Journal of Vietnamese Studies* 11, no. 3–4 (Summer-Fall 2016): 58–102.

————. "Fragmented Loyalties: The Great Migration's Impact on South Vietnam, 1954–1963." PhD diss., University of California, Berkeley, 2014.

————. "'Renegades': The Story of South Vietnam's First National Opposition Newspaper, 1955–1958." *Journal of Vietnamese Studies* 10, no. 4 (Fall 2015): 1–29.

Prados, John. *Vietnam: History of an Unwinnable War.* Lawrence: University Press of Kansas, 2009.

President Ngo Dinh Diem on Democracy: Addresses Relative to the Constitution. Saigon: Press Office, 1958.

Press Interviews with President Ngo Dinh Diệm, Political Counselor Ngo Dinh Nhu. Saigon: Republic of Vietnam, 1963.

Press Office. *Major Policy Speeches by President Ngô Đình Diệm.* Saigon: Press Office of the Presidency of the Republic of Vietnam, 1956.

Race, Jeffrey. *War Comes to Long An: Revolutionary Conflict in a Vietnamese Province.* Berkeley: University of California Press, 1972.

————. *War Comes to Long An: Revolutionary Conflict in a Vietnamese Province,* updated and expanded. Berkeley: University of California Press, 2010.

Rambo, A. Terry. *A Comparison of Peasant Social Systems of Northern and Southern Viet-Nam: A Study of Ecological Adaptation, Social Succession, and Cultural Evolution.* Carbondale: Southern Illinois University Center for Vietnamese Studies, 1973.

Reilly, Brett. "The Origins of the Vietnamese Civil War and the State of Vietnam." PhD diss., University of Wisconsin, Madison, 2018.

————. "The Sovereign States of Vietnam, 1945–1955." *Journal of Vietnamese Studies* 11, no. 3–4 (Summer-Fall 2016): 103–139.

Robinson, Michael. *Cultural Nationalism in Colonial Korea, 1920–1925.* Seattle: University of Washington Press, 1988.

Rubinger, Richard. "Education: From One Room to One System." In *Japan in Transition: From Tokugawa to Meiji,* edited by Marius Jansen and Gilbert Rozman, 195–230. Princeton, NJ: Princeton University Press, 1986.

Savani, A. M. *Notes sur le Caodaisme.* Saigon: self-published, 1954.

Scigliano, Robert. *South Vietnam: Nation Under Stress.* Boston, MA: Houghton Mifflin, 1963.

Shafer, John. *Võ Phiến and the Sadness of Exile.* Dekalb: Northern Illinois University Center for Southeast Asian Studies, 2006.

Shaw, Geoffrey. *The Lost Mandate of Heaven: The American Betrayal of Ngo Dinh Diem, President of Vietnam.* San Francisco, CA: Ignatius Press, 2015.

Sheehan, Neil. *A Bright Shining Lie: John Paul Vann and America in Vietnam.* New York: Random House, 1988.

Shiraishi Masaya. *Betonamu minzoku undō to Nihon, Ajia: Fan Boi Chū no kakumei shisō to taigai ninshiki* (The Vietnamese national movement, Japan, and Asia: The revolutionary thought of Phan Bội Châu and his perceptions of the outside world). Tokyo: Gannando shoten, 1993.

Smith, Ralph B. *An International History of the Vietnam War: Revolution Versus Containment 1955–61.* New York: St. Martin's Press, 1983.

Spencer, Herbert. "Progress: Its Law and Causes." *Westminster Review* 67 (April 1857): 445–485.

Sternhell, Zeev. *Neither Right Nor Left: Fascist Ideology in France.* Princeton, NJ: Princeton University Press, 1983.

Stewart, Geoffrey. *Vietnam's Lost Revolution: Ngô Đình Diệm's Failure to Build an Independent Nation, 1955–1963.* Cambridge: Cambridge University Press, 2017.

Tai, Hue-Tam Ho. *Radicalism and the Origins of the Vietnamese Revolution.* Cambridge, MA: Harvard University Press, 1992.

Tan, Mitchell. "Spiritual Fraternities: The Transnational Networks of Ngô Đình Diệm's Personalist Revolution and the Republic of Vietnam, 1955–1963." *Journal of Vietnamese Studies* 14, no. 2 (Spring 2019): 1–67.

Tan, Stan. "The Struggle to Control Land Grabbing: State Formation on the Central Highlands Frontier under the First Republic of Vietnam (1954–1963)." In *On the Borders of State Power in the Greater Mekong Region,* edited by Martin Gainsborough, 35–50. London: Routledge, 2008.

————. "'Swiddens, Resettlements, Sedentarizations, and Villages': State Formation among the Central Highlanders of Vietnam under the First Republic, 1955–1961." *Journal of Vietnamese Studies* 1, no. 1–2 (February/August 2006): 210–252.

Taylor, Keith. *A History of the Vietnamese.* New York: Cambridge University Press, 2013.

————. "Nguyen Hoang and the Beginning of Vietnam's Southern Expansion." In *Southeast Asia in the Early Modern Era: Trade, Power and Belief,* edited by Anthony Reid, 42–65. Ithaca, NY: Cornell University Press, 1993.

————. "Robert Buzzanco's 'Fear and (Self) Loathing in Lubbock.'" *Journal of Vietnamese Studies* 1, no. 1–2 (February/August 2006): 436–452.

————, ed. *Voices from the Second Republic of South Vietnam, 1967–1975.* Ithaca, NY: Cornell University Southeast Asia Program, 2014.

Thanh Lãng. *Mười ba năm tranh luận văn học.* Vol. 2. Hanoi: Văn Học, 1995.

Thayer, Carlyle. *War by Other Means: National Liberation and Revolution in Viet-Nam, 1954–1960.* Sydney, AU: Allen and Unwin, 1989.

Thiếu Sơn. "Lối văn phê bình nhơn vật, IV. Ông Trần Trọng Kim." *Phụ nữ tân văn* 97 (August 27, 1931): 13–14. Reprinted in Thiếu Sơn, *Phê bình và cảo luận*, 34–35. Hanoi: Nam Ký, 1933.

Thomas, Martin. "Albert Sarraut, French Colonial Development and the Communist Threat," *Journal of Modern History* 77, no. 4 (2005): 917–955.

———. *The French Empire Between the Wars: Imperialism, Politics and Society.* Manchester, UK: Manchester University Press, 2005.

Thompson, Robert. *Defeating Communist Insurgency.* Saint Petersburg, FL: Hailer Publishing, 2005.

Thư Viện Quốc Gia Việt Nam: 85 năm xây dựng và trưởng thành, 1917–2002. Hanoi: Thư Viện Quốc Gia, 2002.

Tôn Quang Phiệt. *Phan Bội Châu và Phan Chu Trinh.* Hanoi: Nhà Xuất Bản Ban Nghiên Cứu Văn Sử Địa, 1956.

Trần Huy Liệu. "Bóc trần quan điểm thực dân và phong kiến trong 'Việt Nam sử lược' của Trần Trọng Kim." *Văn sử địa* 6 (March-April 1955): 20–37.

———. *Lịch sử tám mươi năm chống Pháp.* Hanoi: Văn Sử Địa, 1957.

Trần Huy Liệu et al. *Tài liệu tham khảo lịch sử cách mạng cận đại Việt Nam.* 12 vols. Hanoi: Văn Sử Địa, 1957.

Tran, Nu-Anh. "Contested Identities: Nationalism in the Republic of Vietnam (1954–1963)." PhD diss., University of California, Berkeley, 2013.

———. *Disunion: Anticommunist Nationalism and the Making of the Republic of Vietnam.* Honolulu: University of Hawaiʻi Press, 2022.

———. "South Vietnamese Identity, American Intervention, and the Newspaper *Chính Luận* [Political Discussion], 1965–1969." *Journal of Vietnamese Studies* 1, no. 1–2 (February/August 2006): 169–209.

Trần Trọng Kim. *Nho giáo.* Hanoi: Trung Bắc Tân Văn, 1930.

———. *Phật giáo.* Hanoi: Lê Thăng, 1940.

———. *Phật giáo thuở xưa và Phật giáo ngày nay.* Saigon: Tân Việt. 1953.

———. *Phật lục.* Hanoi: Lê Thăng, 1940.

———. *Quốc văn giáo khoa thư.* 3 vols. Hanoi: Nha Học chính Đông Pháp, 1926.

———. *Việt Nam sử lược* [A Brief History of Vietnam]. 2 vols. Hanoi: Trung Bắc Tân Văn, 1920.

Trần Trọng Kim, Phạm Duy Khiêm, and Bùi Kỷ. *Văn phạm Việt Nam.* Hanoi: Lê Thăng, 1941.

Trần Văn Tùng. *Bach Yên ou fille au coeur fidèle.* Paris: J. Susse, 1946.

———. *The Fundamental Conditions for Victory.* No publisher, 1964.

———. *Le Viet-Nam au combat: nationalisme contre communisme.* Paris: Editions de la Belle Page, 1951.

———. *Le Viet-nam et sa civilisation.* Paris: Editions de la Belle Page, 1952.

———. *Le Viet-Nam face à son destin.* Paris: Editions de la Belle Page, 1950.

Trịnh T. Minh Hà. *Elsewhere, Within Here: Immigration, Refugeeism and the Boundary Event.* New York: Routledge, 2010.

Trương Bửu Lâm. *Colonialism Experienced: Vietnamese Writings on Colonialism, 1900–1931.* Ann Arbor: University of Michigan, 2000.

Turley, William. *The Second Indochina War: A Short Political and Military History, 1954–1975.* Boulder, CO: Westview Press, 1986.

Turner, Robert. "Myths of the Vietnam War: The Pentagon Papers Reconsidered." *Southeast Asian Perspectives* 7 (1972): 1–55.

US Department of State. *Foreign Relations of the United States, 1958–1960*. Vol. 1, *Vietnam*. Washington: Government Printing Office, 1986.

———. *Foreign Relations of the United States, 1961–1963*. Vol. 2, *Vietnam, 1962*. Washington: Government Printing Office, 1990.

———. *Foreign Relations of the United States, 1961–1963*. Vol. 3, *Vietnam, January-August 1963*. Washington: Government Printing Office, 1991.

Văn Tạo. "30 năm tạp chí Nghiên cứu lịch sử và sự cống hiến của nhà sử học Trần Huy Liệu." *Nghiên cứu Lịch sử* 3–4 (1989): 1–5.

———. "Khoa học lịch sử Việt Nam trong mấy chục năm qua." In *Sử học Việt Nam trên đường phát triển*, edited by Ủy Ban Khoa Học Xã Hội Việt Nam, Viện Sử Học, 9–35. Hanoi: Khoa Học Xã Hội, 1981.

Veith, George. *Black April: The Fall of South Vietnam, 1973–1975*. New York: Encounter Books, 2013.

Vĩnh Sính. "Chinese Characters as the Medium for Transmitting the Vocabulary of Modernization from Japan to Vietnam in the Early Twentieth Century." *Asian Pacific Quarterly* (October 1993): 1–16.

———. "Phan Bội Châu and Fukuzawa Yukichi: Perceptions of National Independence." In *Phan Bội Châu and the Đông-Du Movement*, edited by Vĩnh Sính, 101–149. Lạc Việt Series no. 8. New Haven, CT: Yale Center for International and Area Studies, Council on Southeast Asia Studies, 1988.

———. *Phan Châu Trinh and His Political Writings*. Ithaca, NY: Cornell University Southeast Asia Program, 2009.

Vo-Dang, Thuy Thanh. "Anticommunism as Cultural Praxis: South Vietnam, War, and Refugee Memories in the Vietnamese American Community." PhD diss., University of California, San Diego, 2008.

Vũ Ngự Chiêu. "The Other Side of the 1945 Vietnamese Revolution: The Empire of Viet-Nam (March-August 1945)." *Journal of Asian Studies* 45, no. 2 (February 1986): 293–328.

Vũ Quốc Thúc. "National Planning in Vietnam." *Asian Survey* 1, no. 7 (September 1961): 3–9.

Vu, Tuong. "Triumphs or Tragedies: A New Perspective on the Vietnamese Revolution." *Journal of Southeast Asian Studies* 45, no. 2 (2014): 236–257.

———. "Vietnamese Political Studies and Debates on Vietnamese Nationalism." *Journal of Vietnamese Studies* 2, no. 2 (2007): 175–230.

Vũ Ngọc Phan. *Nhà văn hiện đại*. Vol. 2. Saigon: Đại Nam, 1959.

Vũ Văn Thái. "Vietnamese Nationalism under Challenge." *Vietnam Perspectives* 2, no. 2 (1966): 3–12.

Vương Kim [Phan Bá Cầm]. *Lập trường Dân Xã Đảng*. [Saigon?]: Dân Xã Tùng Thư, 1971.

Warner, Dennis. *Last Confucian*. New York: Macmillan, 1963.

Wells, Kenneth. *New God, New Nation: Protestants and Self-Reconstruction Nationalism in Korea, 1896–1937*. Honolulu: University of Hawai'i Press, 1990.

Wiest, Andrew. *Vietnam's Forgotten Army: Heroism and Betrayal in the ARVN*. New York: New York University Press, 2008.

Wilder, Gary. *The French Imperial Nation-State: Negritude and Colonial Humanism Between the Two World Wars*. Chicago: University of Chicago Press, 2005.

Wilentz, Sean. Foreword to *The Politics of Hope and The Bitter Heritage: American Liberalism in the 1960s*, by Arthur Schlesinger, vii–xxxv. Princeton, NJ: Princeton University Press, 2007.

Winters, Francis. The *Year of the Hare*. Athens: University of Georgia Press, 1997.

Wodak, Ruth, Rudolf de Cillia, Martin Reisigl, and Karin Liebhart. *The Discursive Construction of National Identity*. 2nd ed. Translated by Angelika Hirsch, Richard Mitten, and J. W. Unger. Edinburgh: Edinburgh University Press, 2009.

Wolters, O. W. *History, Culture and Region in Southeast Asian Perspectives*. Rev. ed. Ithaca, NY: Cornell University Southeast Asia Program, 1999.

Woodside, Alexander. *Community and Revolution in Modern Vietnam*. Boston, MA: Houghton Mifflin, 1976.

Yi, Mahn-yol. "The Birth of the National Spirit of the Christians in the Late Choson Period." Translated by Ch'oe Un-a. In *Korea and Christianity*, edited by Chai-Shin Yu, 39–72. Seoul: Korean Scholar Press, 1996.

Young, Marilyn. *The Vietnam Wars, 1945–1990*. New York: Harper Perennial, 1991.

Zinoman, Peter. "'The Vietnam War' and the History of the Vietnam War." Review of *The Vietnam War*, directed by Ken Burns and Lynn Novick. *H-Diplo Roundtable Review* 21, no. 3 (September 13, 2019): 21–31.

———. *Vietnamese Colonial Republican: The Political Vision of Vũ Trọng Phụng*. Berkeley: University of California Press, 2014.

Contributors

Hoàng Phong Tuấn is lecturer in the Faculty of Linguistics and Literary Studies, Ho Chi Minh City University of Education. He is interested in the relationship between social institutions, on the one hand, and literature creation, literary reception, and mass culture, on the other. He is the author of *Literature, Reader, Institution* (2017) and has published various articles on the history of conventions and institutions of literary reception in Vietnam, the mass readers of Chinese romance novels on the internet, and mass media and rewriting war memories.

Cindy Nguyen is UC Chancellor's postdoctoral fellow in the Literature Department at the University of California, San Diego, and received her PhD in history from the University of California, Berkeley, in 2019. Her book manuscript, "Bibliotactics: Libraries, the Public, and Information Order in Vietnam, 1865–1958," examines the cultural and political history of libraries in Hanoi and Saigon from the French colonial period through to the decolonization of libraries.

Duy Lap Nguyen is associate professor in the Department of Modern and Classical Languages at the University of Houston. His research interests include critical theory and popular culture. He is the author of *The Unimagined Community: Imperialism and Culture in South Vietnam* (2019) and *A New Historical Materialism* (2022).

Nguyễn Lương Hải Khôi received his MA in literary theories from Ho Chi Minh City University of Education and his DPhil in Japanese aesthetics from Nihon University, Japan. He is the former head of the literary theory division at Ho Chi Minh City University of Education and a research fellow at Hiroshima University and Johns Hopkins University. He has translated into Vietnamese seven English and Japanese books about

Japanese thought and history and has published several articles about Japanese and Vietnamese aesthetic thought and literature. Currently, as managing editor of *US-Vietnam Review,* an online journal of the US-Vietnam Research Center at the University of Oregon, his research focuses on contemporary Vietnamese issues and the history of Vietnamese republicanism.

Martina Thucnhi Nguyen is associate professor in the department of history at Baruch College, City University of New York. A historian of modern Southeast Asia, her research focuses on colonialism, intellectual life, social and political reform, and gender in twentieth century Vietnam. Her first book, *On Our Own Strength: The Self-Reliant Literary Group (Tự Lực Văn Đoàn) and Cosmopolitan Nationalism in Late Colonial Vietnam,* was published in 2021 as part of Columbia University's Weatherhead East Asian Studies Institute book series. She is currently working on her second book, a gender history of how Vietnamese during the late colonial period actively constructed ideologies of sexual difference and wove these gendered categories into the fabric of Vietnamese national identity.

Nguyễn Thị Minh teaches in the Faculty of Linguistics and Literary Studies, Ho Chi Minh City University of Education. Her main research interests are comparative literature and film adaptation based on gender, subjectivity theory, and semiotics. She is a translator and cotranslator of many publications on philosophy, cultural studies, and social science as well as the cofounder of The Ladder—a Learning Space for Community, a space for those who love wisdom to share and make academic knowledge more available to everyone, especially Vietnamese youth.

Y Thien Nguyen is a research fellow at the US-Vietnam Research Center at the University of Oregon and received his PhD in sociology from Northwestern University in 2021. His research focuses on the political history of Republican Vietnam (1955–1975), the discursive development of South Vietnamese anticommunism, and the connectivity between Vietnamese America and Republican Vietnam. He is the author of "(Re)making the South Vietnamese Past in America," *Journal of Asian American Studies* 21 (2018): 65–103.

Jason Picard is founding assistant professor of Vietnamese History and Culture, Faculty of Arts and Sciences, VinUniversity. A historian of modern Southeast Asia, Jason earned his doctorate at the University of California, Berkeley. He has published in the *Journal of Vietnamese Studies* and is currently working on a manuscript about Vietnam's so-called Great Migration of 1954–1955.

Nu-Anh Tran is associate professor at the University of Connecticut with a joint appointment in the Department of History and the Asian and Asian American Studies Institute. Her research focuses on the Republic of Vietnam. Her first book, *Disunion: Anticommunist*

Nationalism and the Making of the Republic of Vietnam (2022), examines the relationship between Ngô Đình Diệm and the political opposition and is part of the Weatherhead East Asian Institute book series. Her work has also appeared in the *Journal of Vietnamese Studies* and *Diplomatic History.*

Tuong Vu is professor and department head of the political science department and director of the US-Vietnam Research Center at the University of Oregon. He is the author or coeditor of five books and numerous journal articles and book chapters. Among his recent books are *The Republic of Vietnam, 1955–1975: Vietnamese Perspectives on Nation-Building* (2020), coedited with Sean Fear, and *Vietnam's Communist Revolution: The Power and Limits of Ideology* (2017).

Yen Vu received her PhD in French studies from Cornell University in 2019. A postdoctoral fellow at Columbia University, she focuses on twentieth-century Vietnamese intellectual history and youth as well as the philosophical, linguistic, and political negotiation of ideas of freedom in cultural productions such as literature and theater. Her work has appeared in the *Journal of Southeast Asian Studies* as well as *Diaspora.*

Peter Zinoman is professor of history and Southeast Asian studies at the University of California, Berkeley. Founding editor of the *Journal of Vietnamese Studies,* he is the author of *The Colonial Bastille: A History of Imprisonment in Vietnam, 1862–1940* (2001) and *Vietnamese Colonial Republican: The Political Vision of Vu Trong Phung* (2014) as well as the editor and cotranslator of *Dumb Luck: A Novel by Vu Trong Phung.*

Index

Agrovilles (Khu Trù Mật) project, 155
Annamese monarchy, 1, 46, 73–76
anti-Chinese nationalism in Vietnam, 57
anticommunism: in Asia, 8; cultural expressions of, 150–151; in First Republic, 21; historical continuity of, 205–207; Ngô Đình Diệm and, 100–101; in Political Study Program, 216–222; Self-Reliant Literary Group and, 63; Trần Văn Tùng and, 88, 96–97; in Vietnamese American narratives, 203–205, 222–224; Vietnamese republicanism and, 10, 20
antiwar movement: impact on scholarship of, 32–34; North Vietnam communist government supported by, 3
Assembly of the French Union, 88
assimilation: Trần Văn Tùng on, 91; Vietnamese intellectuals' rejection of, 70–72
Association for Intellectual and Moral Advancement, 50
Association for the Restoration of Vietnam (ARV, Việt Nam Phục Quốc Hội), 104, 106, 108–109
Auriol, Vincent, 83
authoritarianism: under Ngô Đình Diệm, 20, 94, 107–109; in RVN, 5; Strategic Hamlet Campaign and, 121–122

Bắc di cư (North Vietnamese migrants): hostility and distrust of, 143–145; in Mekong Delta, 156–159; North-South Compassion Campaign and, 150–151; perception and chaos linked to, 147–148; sectional hostility toward, 151–153; Self-Reliance Campaign and, 153–155; South Vietnamese management of, 147–150
Bắc Kỳ. *See* Tonkin (North Vietnam)
Bảo Đại (Emperor), 10–12, 14, 17–18, 74, 83, 88, 101–106, 108–111, 216–217
Battle of Saigon (1955), 101, 104–105
Beau, Paul, 28, 31
Bình Nguyên Lộc, 196
Bình Xuyên group, 17, 101
Bourgeois, Rémi, 168
Bùi Kỷ, 50, 59n32
Bùi Quang Chiêu, 3, 9–10, 31
Bùi Văn Lương, 133–134
Bundy, McGeorge, 94–95
Burns, Ken, 32–33, 38
Bửu Dưỡng, 198n6

cadres: elite cadres, 103; North Vietnam regrouping of, 151; Political Study Program and, 208; propaganda training for, 215–216; in Strategic Hamlet campaign, 134–135
Cái Sắn resettlement dispute, 155–159
Cần Lao Party. *See* Revolutionary Personalist Labor Party (Cần Lao Nhân Vị Cách Mạng Đảng, or Cần Lao)

Studies of the Weatherhead East Asian Institute

Columbia University

Selected Titles

(Complete list at: https://weai.columbia.edu/content/publications/)

Recovering Histories: Life and Labor after Heroin in Reform-Era China, by Nicholas Bartlett. University of California Press, 2020.

A Third Way: The Origins of China's Current Economic Development Strategy, by Lawrence Chris Reardon. Harvard University Asia Center, 2020.

Disruptions of Daily Life: Japanese Literary Modernism in the World, by Arthur M. Mitchell. Cornell University Press, 2020.

Figures of the World: The Naturalist Novel and Transnational Form, by Christopher Laing Hill. Northwestern University Press, 2020.

Arbiters of Patriotism: Right-Wing Scholars in Imperial Japan, by John Person. University of Hawai'i Press, 2020.

The Chinese Revolution on the Tibetan Frontier, by Benno Weiner. Cornell University Press, 2020.

Making It Count: Statistics and Statecraft in the Early People's Republic of China, by Arunabh Ghosh. Princeton University Press, 2020.

Tea War: A History of Capitalism in China and India, by Andrew B. Liu. Yale University Press, 2020.

Revolution Goes East: Imperial Japan and Soviet Communism, by Tatiana Linkhoeva. Cornell University Press, 2020.

Vernacular Industrialism in China: Local Innovation and Translated Technologies in the Making of a Cosmetics Empire, 1900–1940, by Eugenia Lean. Columbia University Press, 2020.

Fighting for Virtue: Justice and Politics in Thailand, by Duncan McCargo. Cornell University Press, 2020.

Beyond the Steppe Frontier: A History of the Sino-Russian Border, by Sören Urbansky. Princeton University Press, 2020.

Pirates and Publishers: A Social History of Copyright in Modern China, by Fei-Hsien Wang. Princeton University Press, 2019.

The Typographic Imagination: Reading and Writing in Japan's Age of Modern Print Media, by Nathan Shockey. Columbia University Press, 2019.

Down and Out in Saigon: Stories of the Poor in a Colonial City, by Haydon Cherry. Yale University Press, 2019.

Beauty in the Age of Empire: Japan, Egypt, and the Global History of Aesthetic Education, by Raja Adal. Columbia University Press, 2019.

Mass Vaccination: Citizens' Bodies and State Power in Modern China, by Mary Augusta Brazelton. Cornell University Press, 2019.

Residual Futures: The Urban Ecologies of Literary and Visual Media of 1960s and 1970s Japan, by Franz Prichard. Columbia University Press, 2019.

The Making of Japanese Settler Colonialism: Malthusianism and Trans-Pacific Migration, 1868–1961, by Sidney Xu Lu. Cambridge University Press, 2019.

The Power of Print in Modern China: Intellectuals and Industrial Publishing from the end of Empire to Maoist State Socialism, by Robert Culp. Columbia University Press, 2019.

Beyond the Asylum: Mental Illness in French Colonial Vietnam, by Claire E. Edington. Cornell University Press, 2019.

Borderland Memories: Searching for Historical Identity in Post-Mao China, by Martin Fromm. Cambridge University Press, 2019.

Arc of Containment: Britain, the United States, and Anticommunism in Southeast Asia, by Wen-Qing Ngoei. Cornell University Press, 2019.

Sovereignty Experiments: Korean Migrants and the Building of Borders in Northeast Asia, 1860–1949, by Alyssa M. Park. Cornell University Press, 2019.

The Greater East Asia Co-Prosperity Sphere: When Total Empire Met Total War, by Jeremy A. Yellen. Cornell University Press, 2019.

Thought Crime: Ideology and State Power in Interwar Japan, by Max Ward. Duke University Press, 2019.

Statebuilding by Imposition: Resistance and Control in Colonial Taiwan and the Philippines, by Reo Matsuzaki. Cornell University Press, 2019.

Nation-Empire: Ideology and Rural Youth Mobilization in Japan and Its Colonies, by Sayaka Chatani. Cornell University Press, 2019.

Fixing Landscape: A Techno-Poetic History of China's Three Gorges, by Corey Byrnes. Columbia University Press, 2019.